To Augusta

Who made it all possible

— W.J.L.

CONTENTS

PART 6 OIL – THE YEARS AHEAD

PREFACE

Walter J. Levy, international oil consultant to governments and companies, has completed forty years of extraordinary thinking and writing about oil. Those four decades span the era in which the obtaining of oil first became of great commercial consequence and then the object of governments—a period in which the strategic dimensions of oil had become early apparent to only a comparative few who were closely involved in the terms on which it would be available. Today, the topic of oil pervades the interests of most states.

Those few—in international companies and in the highest reaches of government—who were fully aware of the growing importance of oil usually lacked the background to conceive how to deal with all its manifestations. It is exactly in these circumstances that Mr. Levy attracted notice. To a great extent, it is he who has defined the great issues of policy and of action revolving around access to oil. As the reader will discover, the intellectual ability of the author to look at the universe of oil has greatly informed public and private debates.

Born in Hamburg on March 21, 1911, Walter Levy was educated in Germany. He attended the universities of Heidelberg, Freiburg, Berlin, and Kiel, and received an LLD from Kiel in 1932. In 1933 he moved to London and continued his studies with special emphasis on the theory and application of statistics. As an assistant editor of the Petroleum Press Bureau, he began to deepen his knowledge of oil, which he then applied to the issues that would arise in wartime. As war came, Sir Mark Turner of the Ministry of Economic Warfare encouraged Mr. Levy to share his ideas, counseling on blockades and the vulnerabilities of the German petroleum industrial plant. In 1941 he came to the United States where his writing appeared in *World Petroleum* and *Fortune;* subsequently, Mr. Levy became part of the Office of Strategic Services (OSS) concentrating his already recognized analytical talents on the significance of critical aspects of petroleum logistics.

Toward the end of the war, Mr. Levy was asked to assist further in oil supply to liberated areas. Soon thereafter, as chief of the Petroleum Branch, Economic Cooperation Administration (the Marshall Plan), he

assisted in oil aspects of peace treaties and in the enormous task of helping assure petroleum supply to Europe in the postwar period of recovery
and reconstruction. Robert Marjolin, who was then secretary-general of
the Organization for European Economic Cooperation, credits him with
playing a "decisive role" in the success of the Marshall Plan.

In 1949 Mr. Levy formed his own consulting firm and was soon im-
mersed in the commercial interests of clients, among them the giants of
international oil and the larger concerns of governments. His experience
was applied to petroleum aspects of the Korean War (1950). He was
deeply involved in the critical U.S. attempts to cope with the Iranian oil
crisis of 1951 and the repercussions of Suez (1956).

The Iranian crisis summed up many of the issues certain to return and
to plague the relations between the oil producers and importers. Of that
key incident, Lieutenant General (USA, Ret'd.) Vernon A. Walters (now
ambassador at large) has written of Mr. Levy and the Harriman Mission
which attempted to mediate:

> On numerous occasions he explained the realities of the world oil pro-
> duction and distribution situation to the Iranian Premier, Oil Minister and
> other senior officials. He earned their respect and admiration despite the
> fact that they had not necessarily liked the realities which he was drawing to
> their attention.
>
> In addition, Walter's invariable, cheerful good humor during the months
> of extreme heat in Tehran in a threatening and sometimes dangerous situa-
> tion won for him the unstinting admiration of all members of Governor
> Harriman's party. His low key approach, his courtesy and obvious
> knowledge of the subject was of enormous assistance on this mission.

Moreover, the World Bank and the Indian government enlisted his aid
on the latter's oil policy. From the earliest years of the Organization of
Petroleum Exporting Countries (OPEC) — indeed, well before its found-
ing (1960) and thereafter — his counsel has been widely sought on the
ramifications of the extraordinary period of great change in the control
of oil. Among others, the governments and companies of Venezuela,
Canada, Indonesia, Malaysia, Thailand, Japan, the United Kingdom,
Germany, Spain, and Algeria have each sought his counsel on energy in
general and oil in particular; he has also had an extensive role in U.S. oil
affairs, governmental and private. The European Economic Community, the World Bank, and the United Nations have oil concerns in which
he has been active. Mr. Marjolin, mentioned earlier, went on to become
a vice president of the Common Market, and he writes of the help that he
obtained from Mr. Levy on perplexing oil questions, Mr. Levy being able
to be "a catalyst because of the confidence which he enjoyed."

For the United States, he has been a source of judgments about oil to presidents, and many of the papers selected for this volume are the outgrowth of memoranda provided secretaries of state and the White House. In fact, it might be hard to find a crisis affecting oil supply over the past forty years in which his talents were not engaged. No one would claim that his counsel has always been heeded; one can detect when this has occurred by noting the increasing frequency with which certain topics reappear: for example, the essential need for coordination among allies on oil.

What accounts for the insight and skills of an adviser who moves in the oil circle? Sir David Steel, chairman of British Petroleum, wrote of this when he commented that Mr. Levy's "very special contribution" is due to his "personal diplomatic gifts combined with a thoroughly realistic understanding of the oil business. He talked economics to the diplomats and diplomacy to the oil companies, gaining the confidence of both to a remarkable degree. For virtually an era I and many colleagues greatly valued his impartial advice offered from a position which his personal qualities and experience made unique."

Mr. John H. Loudon, who was chairman of the Committee of the Managing Directors of the Royal Dutch–Shell Group from 1952 to 1965 and an eminent leader of international oil, commented that Mr. Levy "frequently represented governments and was, therefore, on the other side of the fence. Before taking up such assignments he always informed my colleagues and me very fully in order that there might be no misunderstanding as to his position and endeavors. Acting for governments in negotiations with oil companies, he played a very important role as an expert adviser and catalyst, which frequently resulted in an agreement acceptable to both sides."

The role of a presidential emissary is particularly challenging. Abram Chayes has written to me of his 1963 experience with Mr. Levy on an Indonesia mission for President Kennedy, the purpose of which was

> to provide good offices for a negotiation between the major oil companies and the government of President Sukarno of Indonesia. We spent two weeks in intimate daily association on a matter of extreme delicacy. The Sukarno government had announced the forthcoming promulgation of regulations that would have amounted to expropriation of the western oil investments. Under the Hickenlooper Amendment, that would have required termination of U.S. aid to Indonesia. President [John F.] Kennedy was very anxious to avoid such a turn of events.
>
> He therefore suggested to President Sukarno that a presidential emissary might be able to provide good offices to bring the government and the companies to an agreement. Sukarno indicated his willingness to receive the

mission, and we finally caught up with him in Tokyo. Our chairman, the third member of the group, was Governor Wilson Wyatt of Kentucky.

Mr. Levy, of course, was the only member of the triumvirate with any experience in the oil business at all. His total grasp of the situation and his ability to educate us laymen were absolutely crucial to the success of the mission.

The outstanding impression I had, however, was not of his knowledge and keen intelligence, but his integrity and fairness. On several occasions in the course of the negotiations, there was danger that the Indonesians would be over-reached because of their failure to understand the significance of some of the issues in dispute. Mr. Levy understood that, as presidential emissaries, we could not be parties, even tacitly, to a grossly unfair bargain. On the other hand, we were not mediators and were not supposed to be taking sides in the proceedings. None the less, Mr. Levy, with great tact and skill, approached the company representatives and pointed out to them the problems involved. He persuaded them to recede from positions that I am confident would have been a source of friction and trouble over the future course of agreement.

Lord Rothschild, who was head of the "think tank" for then Prime Minister Edward Heath, reached a similar conclusion when he described Mr. Levy as "the greatest authority in the world on oil geopolitics, a subject which requires a deep knowledge of all aspects of the oil business together with macro-economics and finance. . . . It says much for his integrity that he has been able to achieve this without encountering any problems of conflicts of interest."

Such a person also has to possess the rare capacity for seeing further and more clearly and then writing lucidly on the complexities of oil.

Mr. Levy's career spans the great years of oil. In 1937-38, oil accounted for 22 percent of the world's energy, and coal stood for about 69 percent. Some four decades later, oil accounted for close to 50 percent of the world's energy, while coal represented 27 percent. The staggering volumes in oil represented by this energy revolution are hard to comprehend. Nearly forty years ago, about 5.6 million barrels a day were consumed worldwide; in 1980 the total was close to 57 million barrels daily. Moreover, the importance of sources of oil changed dramatically. Forty years ago, the Middle East was eclipsed by the production of North America; in 1980 Middle East (including Libya) production of nearly 20 million barrels a day was some 30 percent of world production, while North America (including Mexico) accounted for 20 percent. In terms of *international* oil—which is the principal subject of this collection—in 1980 oil from the Middle East accounted for nearly 66 percent of world production. The pervasive significance of the great increase in Middle East supply is now of central concern and dominates most of the articles presented.

My introduction to this book and to the parts and chapters are set in a sans serif italic type. Mr. Levy's chapters are set in a serif roman type.

Melvin A. Conant

ACKNOWLEDGMENTS

I was asked by Frederick Praeger to consider the publication of a representative selection of my reflections on oil during the last forty years. When my closest friend, Melvin A. Conant, added not only his voice but also offered his assistance for the undertaking I welcomed the opportunity. Melvin's role in the effort has been invaluable, and his collaboration in this work of friendship has been appreciated more than I can express.

I would like also to express my sincerest gratitude and thanks to Christa G. Conant who, with thoughtfulness and care, has prepared the index.

My thanks extend also to Theresa G. McConnell and Jacqueline C. Freeman who with patience typed successive drafts of the manuscript.

Walter J. Levy

INTRODUCTION

As the need has grown for a continuous and adequate oil supply at a price within an importer's capacity to pay through normal commercial exchanges, so has the involvement by governments that in the main could not leave the obtaining of oil to the commercial sector. As vital national interests were engaged, governments became increasingly involved in all aspects of supply. Today, there is scarcely one importing or producing country whose government does not intervene in oil; in fact, scarcely one barrel of oil moves internationally without an exporting government's involvement.

In many places, an additional cause for a government presence has been the historic and predominant role of U.S. and British companies in the production, transportation, refining, and marketing of oil, nationally and internationally. It has been widely believed by other states that these companies have been important to the pursuit by their home countries of overseas interests in times of war and of peace. This common concern helps account for that oversight of supply now practiced by so many governments, producers, and consumers of oil. It is to these complex factors that Mr. Levy repeatedly calls our attention.

In recent years, he has emphasized that the risks run in a continuing failure to link allies' needs and actions become vastly greater with the inevitable role of the Middle East as the principal supplier of the international barrel during the next several decades. In this troubled region, the interests of great, external powers, notably the United States and the Soviet Union, but Europe and Japan as well, all intersect. To the impact of these interests are added the strains arising from rivalries of peoples and of leadership within the region, and their traditional search for external patrons—all of which existed long before oil became so important. With oil, the stakes have assumed extreme importance.

With European and Japanese present dependence on Middle East oil (65–70 percent) so much more consequential than U.S. dependence (over 30 percent of imports), it is now elementary to observe that the latter considers it has a freedom to act in the region denied its allies. And the Soviet Union, perhaps unlikely to be a large importer of Middle East oil in this decade, is freest of all in defining its policies toward a neighboring region of immense geostrategic importance from which moves most of international oil supply. Indeed, war or peace in our time could well be determined by the skill and caution with which the interests and actions of states in this troubled region are pursued.

The fundamental circumstances that give oil its contemporary importance are thus both the sheer size of this daily global demand and the crucial fact that most of the industrial nations and an increasing number of developing states lack domestic reserves and are therefore dependent on imports, especially from the Middle East.

In more recent years, beginning with the 1970s, the cost of imported oil became a crucial factor for the first time as the oil-producing nations insisted upon very large and sudden increases in prices. Thus, access to someone else's oil and the means to pay for it are vital matters of present and future interest.

Considerations affecting allies may appear uppermost in most of these writings, but Mr. Levy also inquires into the internal circumstances of the oil-producing societies. The difficulties these oil-rich nations have in spending huge sums constructively have the attention of many observers, but Mr. Levy singles out for particular notice the extraordinary difficulties these societies face in attempting to create economies that can, in the years ahead, sustain the level of expectations built by the (largely) un-earned wealth suddenly theirs, through geologic "accident" and the requirements of the industrial world. As these oil-based societies move toward the time when reserves decrease to disturbing levels and alternatives to oil become more readily available, the sense of impending loss will surely multiply the tensions between these nations and the purchasers of their oil.

One of the other key themes in these pages—the continuing difficulty in arriving at a satisfactory process for relating the interests of private oil companies to those of governments—is a constant reminder of how their respective interests may diverge, especially with the change in their relationships to the governments of oil-producing countries to which Mr. Levy has referred. When international oil was so largely a commercial commodity, the possibility that important interests of companies could diverge from those of government seemed less consequential. Today, with oil's strategic dimensions, the possibility is nearly ever present. Yet, neither government (which has the responsibility of defining national interests and policies) nor companies (which need to know what these are) have yet been able to establish a meaningful relationship in which possible divergencies could be resolved. A system based on voluntary, infrequent, and sometimes superficial contacts does not suffice. Yet, as

Mr. Levy mentions, we have great difficulties in establishing an effective process. If such matters cannot be dealt with in periods of comparative freedom from strain, it is unlikely they will be resolved in a crisis atmosphere. Moreover, the U.S. history of government and oil interests as adversaries is in contrast to the relationship of key allied governments—the British, French, and Japanese—with their oil interests. The global interests and commitments of the United States and its crucial role in the Middle East will compel us to address these relationships sooner or later.

Despite all that has happened over the four decades covered by these articles and despite the magnitude of the interests involved in oil, it is worth noting how quickly American concerns can still vaporize when short-term phenomena such as more-than-adequate international supply, declining demand, and lower prices are interpreted by governments as well as the public as permanent. Even a brief inquiry into the range of causes that lie behind these phenomena should suffice to alert an intelligent citizen to the unpredictability of supply and to the variety of events that could suddenly complicate and make more difficult the obtaining of oil. The danger is, of course, that in relaxing one does not then pursue commitments previously agreed to that reduced vulnerability to oil producers' decisions and one thus ignores the very scope of "oil" as portrayed in these chapters.

Any reader of this volume will select other or additional themes; the singling out of these particular topics has been a highly subjective exercise. Nevertheless, in expecting we shall hear further on these matters from Mr. Levy, it is worth mentioning one characteristic of these papers that runs throughout the selection: the author is not a historian in the formalistic sense. Retrospection is not his forte. Looking into the future is clearly his interest and this accounts for our expectation of reading more articles by him in the years ahead.

Why should this volume appear now? And what of the selection? For these four decades, Mr. Levy has been an essayist, an interpreter of events, a counselor to governments and to companies. He saw early the extraordinarily difficult years ahead when the private corporate interest in oil would have to be considered in the light of the broader interests and responsibilities of government. How intelligently would each cope with the other? There is still no satisfactory answer to this—no process in law, not even effective consultation, at least for the United States. Mr. Levy will continue to be active on these matters and other concerns as they impinge upon oil and vice versa. During this period, oil has gone through startling transformations, many of these in the last decade. Hence, Mr. Frederick A. Praeger suggested it would be widely *appreciated if an effort were made to give perspective to those years and from it to gain a clearer appreciation of where we have been and may be going. What emerges from the reading is an awareness of how much the author anticipated and how consistent his analyses have been and of how his thoughts have led him not only to warn, but to prescribe.*

Although Mr. Levy's major work has been in counseling companies and governments, he has sought also to inform public debate and policy through his published writings. Necessarily, many of his analyses are proprietary to companies or private to governments. Those reproduced were chosen because they seemed to illuminate best both the key events affecting oil and the ways in which the author thought about them. Hence, the chapters reflect major stages in the principal history of oil from the beginning of World War II to 1981. The final selection leads the reader into the decade ahead.

On April 16, 1968, Secretary of State Dean Rusk presented Mr. Levy with a plaque of the Seal of the Department of State, inscribed: "To Walter J. Levy, in grateful appreciation of your invaluable contribution to the welfare of the United States." Mr. Rusk spoke these words:

> *In the pressure of rapidly changing events, we never seem to take the time to stop even for a moment to say "thank you" for a job well done. And in the nature of Federal Government activities, it is unfortunately all too seldom that we can single out the contribution of any individual. It gives me very great pleasure, therefore, that we should assemble here today to recognize the contribution to this Department and to the Nation of one man, and say thank you to him.*
>
> *Walter Levy has been providing his unique knowledge on world oil affairs to our Government for a very long time. During World War II he was the expert on any enemy petroleum operations. . . . Subsequently he was in charge of petroleum affairs for the Marshall Program and made important contributions to the success of that great effort. Over the years since then, the State Department has called upon him frequently for counsel, and he has met each request without hesitation and unstintingly. I recall his services on the occasion of the Iranian Crisis, in Indonesia, and on many many more occasions. . . . Let me therefore conclude briefly by saying again, thank you for your long, constructive, and often unremunerated services to the State Department and to the Country. . . .*

Mr. Levy replied:

> *I am very deeply moved by this occasion and your most gracious words. If I might, I should like only to take this occasion also to express a few of my deeply felt feelings. It is I who should be saying thank you for the oppor-*

tunities extended to me to serve in some small way the Nation that adopted me.

I came here as an alien during the trying days of war. I was welcomed, and I was given the opportunity to work for this Country without reservation or qualification and with regard only to the job that I might do. I owe a lasting debt of gratitude to the many people in Government who over the years have opened the doors of opportunity to me. . . . For my part, what has meant so much in my work and in my life has been the fact that I had these opportunities to serve. . . .

This exchange says much about the man, the respect in which he is held, and of his quality. It sums up why this friend wished to help prepare this volume.

Part 1
OIL AND WORLD WAR II

Introduction

Beginning in June 1941, when Nazi Germany had already conquered much of Europe, Walter Levy wrote trenchant analyses of the significance of oil in the war planning of Hitler and in the unexpected demands that the conquered lands would make on Germany for their own civil needs. These analyses appeared in the journal World Petroleum. They were important contributions by a person who had already made his mark in oil analysis with the Petroleum Press Service of London and in intelligence appraisals of the German refining and synthetic oil industry. He has been credited as having accurately assessed the vital importance and locations of that industry.

In those articles, the author discussed the extraordinary lengths to which the Germans and the Japanese had gone to deal with their parlous oil-supply situations. In each case, there was a major prewar effort to obtain substitutes for oil use in transport, to acquire additional refining capacity, to stock crude oil and oil products. Germany and Japan each realized its critical need to avoid a prolonged war in which existing oil vulnerabilities could only be exacerbated.

In that event, as was fully described (and anticipated) in these articles, the overwhelming need for more oil was a key factor in the decision to invade Romania and then Russia; a considered alternative was seizure of the oil of the Middle East. A large part of German strategic planning and operations was based on a desperate need for petroleum, as the British blockade of continental Europe halted oil flows that otherwise might have supplied Europe's war and civil needs from the Middle East and the Caribbean.

The counterpart to the German race eastward for the oil of Romania and of the Caucasus was the Japanese attack upon the crude-oil–producing regions of Southeast Asia. Obtaining these sources was made vital after the actions of the United States, Great Britain, and the Netherlands government-in-exile in the spring of 1941 effectively cut supply to Japan.

The ability of Germany and Japan to persevere long past the time by which each ought to have found it impossible to function, according to prewar estimates, was attributed by Mr. Levy to military strategies whose essence was the sharp and overwhelming "blitzkrieg" for which oil

requirements could be minimized, in contrast to prolonged engage-
ments. The lack of oil was acute in transport for both Germany and
Japan; the lack of lubricating oils was truly vital. Synthetic oils (from coal,
shale) could be and were developed; charcoal and gas-fired engines were
common; what could not be substituted for, except at an extraordinary
cost in time and effort, were the lubricating qualities of oil products.

In short, especially with United States aid to Britain in oil, tankers, and
convoy protection, the problem for the British was totally unlike that of
the Germans. The British could never be cut off from oil sources except
through a disruption of their logistics system; the Germans had logistic
demands, but their problem was inaccessible sources unless they expanded the war.

(One observation from these analyses seems pertinent today: Now that
nations are again seeking to determine those minimal levels of oil supply
that are their absolute need, the extent to which nations made do with
less in World War II is an instructive reminder of how much can be
achieved in a crisis.)

The strategic dimensions to oil were thus made clear.

The Paradox of Oil and War

Though it is difficult to talk about military setbacks in the war that Adolf Hitler has waged with such appalling success these last two years, there is no doubt that on one occasion the Führer and his generals and janizaries suffered a terrific defeat. It was not celebrated in the headlines and, indeed, was scarcely noticed outside the Nazi hierarchy. Nevertheless it occurred, and among the men responsible for the destiny of Greater Germany there must have been at least several who recognized it as a grave and possibly crucial event. The event was the incredible refusal of the British to make peace after the fall of France, after Dunkirk.

For upwards of twenty years the military and economic geniuses of the Reich had studied the history of the first World War in minute detail, and in planning for victory in World War II they had absorbed one fundamental lesson—that under no circumstances should Germany be forced into a long war. But after Dunkirk, and especially after failing to crush England in September 1940, Germany was in a long war.

It made little difference that in 1940–41 the Reich controlled the whole of Europe instead of the central portion of the Continent. The nations under German domination were not and never had been self-sufficient. Combining them and calling them the "New Order" did not make them any better off. Save for coal, iron ore, a few staple foodstuffs, and some other basic materials, Europe was dependent on the outer world for all the stuffs essential to a modern industrial society. This was a matter of geography and had nothing to do with politics. It would be the same whether Europe was a group of democracies or a single totalitarian unit. Hitler had made himself the master of Europe, but he had not yet won the war. If he expected his captives to produce for the benefit of Germany he had the heavy responsibility of keeping them supplied with all manner of goods in the face of a universal shortage. In a word it was no

Reprinted with permission from *Fortune,* September 1941, pp. 69 ff. © 1941 Time Inc. All rights reserved. This article (unsigned) was based mainly on the work of Mr. Levy and so acknowledged; it was preceded by an earlier exposition in *World Petroleum* dated June 22, 1941. — *Editor* longer Germany alone but the entire European Continent that required *Lebensraum*.

Europe and Oil

Of all the liabilities that Hitler acquired when he swallowed Europe at a gulp, by far the most serious was the problem of oil. It was the sine qua non of modern industry, modern warfare, modern transportation. It concerned an important part of agriculture, in so far as tractors and other power machinery had displaced the horse. It lighted the lamps in millions of homes, and provided the essential lubricants for the generators that provided electricity elsewhere. It was gasoline for automobiles and airplanes, kerosene for the tractors, Diesel oil for the tanks of the panzer divisions, and for the submarines raiding the Atlantic convoys. It was heavy fuel oil for battleships, merchantmen, and factories. It was, in short, the indispensable motive fuel of a modern state, and in addition it was the indispensable lubricant for all the moving parts of all machinery of such a state.

Europe never had produced enough oil for her own needs. In 1938, the last full year of peace, the total oil consumption of what is now [Adolf] Hitler's Europe amounted to between 200 and 210 million barrels. Total production from all sources (excluding the U.S.S.R.) was 75 million barrels, leaving a minimum of 125 million to be imported from overseas. As in other years the 1938 imports came chiefly from the world's two great reservoirs of natural crude oil—the Caribbean basin, extending roughly from the northern coast of South America to the central plains of the U.S., including most of the important U.S. fields; and the Near Eastern Mediterranean basin, including Iran, Iraq, Saudi Arabia, Egypt, and adjacent countries, and Rumania and part of southwestern U.S.S.R. as well. There are other large petroleum caches in the Dutch East Indies, in California, Canada, South America, and India. But in the Caribbean and Near East areas most of the world's proved reserves of an estimated 45 billion barrels are stored.

With the exception of the Russian fields, all major petroleum sources are controlled separately or jointly by the U.S., Great Britain, and the absentee government of the Netherlands. This control is exercised indirectly, via the great producing and refining companies—notably the Standard group, Royal Dutch–Shell, and the Anglo-Iranian. These companies together constitute a petroleum empire of worldwide dimensions. The money resources of this oil empire run into the billions. Its rulers are as powerful as the ministers of many sovereign states. It is as fluid as the stuff it deals in and is truly international. Thus the Shell Union Oil

Corp., a Royal Dutch–Shell affiliate, is one of the ranking producers in the U.S., while a jointly owned subsidiary of Standard of California and the Texas Company produces and refines oil on the island of Bahrein, a British protectorate in the Persian Gulf. In Iraq, production is controlled by British, Dutch, American (Standard and Socony), and French interests, except for 5 percent of the output, which is in the hands of an Armenian gentleman named Calouste Sartis Gulbenkian, known as the "mystery man of the Near East oil fields." In Sumatra and elsewhere in the Dutch East Indies, American companies operate along with Royal Dutch.

Although these groups governing the international empire of oil function nominally as private enterprise — at least in peacetime — the British Government has a controlling interest in Anglo-Iranian and also has a weighty influence in the affairs of Royal Dutch. The U.S. Government has no financial interest in Standard Oil or the other domestic producers, but the reader scarcely needs to be reminded that both production and exports are subject to state or federal regulation. In short, oil is not only a vital world commodity, but a powerful instrument of political and economic warfare which is principally available to the Anglo-Saxon democracies. As the world's great producers, refiners, and suppliers, they are in the driver's seat. At any time, and for any reason, they can cut off the flow of oil to any other nation or group of nations. And today, except for accidental trickles through the British blockade, they are not permitting a drop of crude to enter Germany's Europe. If occasional shipments are cleared from the U.S. for Spain or for Weygand's Africa, it is for reasons of high policy that have been earnestly deliberated in Whitehall and on Pennsylvania Avenue.

Admittedly, these are facts from the primer. By the end of World War I they were understood by all the countries of Europe, and after another dozen years, more or less, Europe began to make an effort to disprove them. Virtually every nation of any size or importance attempted to make itself less dependent on overseas imports of oil. The motive was to achieve "self-sufficiency," to fulfill the nationalist ambitions that swept the world after the rejection of the cooperative principles embodied in the League of Nations. In the case of Hitler's Germany — and later Mussolini's Italy — a primary aim was to gain control of oil sources, or create oil sources sufficient to carry on a war regardless of the imports or the lack of them.

Germany Tries to Close the Gap

Europe's only important producer outside the U.S.S.R. is Rumania, with a 1938 production of about 48,000,000 barrels. Less than 1,000,000 barrels were produced by Albania, now the only source of crude available to Italy, except for her own minute production. Poland just about covered her domestic consumption with domestic production of over 3,500,000 barrels, and Hungary has recently managed to strike a balance. In some parts of Europe there are small quantities of crude that can be obtained by assiduous drilling; and in addition oil can be extracted from beds of shale. However, in Germany and France these natural sources were entirely inadequate — even assuming the fullest possible development — and in Italy they were almost nonexistent.

The European campaign for self-sufficiency was therefore forced to depend mainly on a four-point program of starvation, storage, substitutes, and synthesis. Starvation meant the elimination of all nonessential consumption of oil. Storage meant the accumulation during prewar years of the largest possible stocks of petroleum products, mainly imported. Substitutes meant mixing alcohol and benzol with gasoline, and the introduction of compressed gases as motor fuel, or, more commonly, the use of so-called "gasogenes," wood- or charcoal-burning units that generated combustible gases. It also meant the substitution of castor oil, olive oil, and other vegetable products as lubricants wherever possible.

In general, the effort to substitute potato alcohol and other vegetable derivatives was impracticable on a large scale because the oil-poor European countries could not afford this diversion of their crops. In addition, industrial demand for alcohol had to be met. Far more important and significant was the development of the synthetic industry, which was sired by the Reich long before Hitler. This was based upon two major achievements of German chemistry and chemical engineering. One is the Bergius process (perfected by I.G. Farbenindustrie A.G.) of coal and lignite hydrogenation to yield motor fuel, heavy oil, and Diesel oil. The Fischer-Tropsch process produces lubricating oil, paraffin wax, and the hydrocarbon gases propane and butane, plus the Bergius products. More exactly, both the Bergius and Fischer-Tropsch processes convert coal or lignite into synthetic petroleum, which can then be refined and doctored to make products equivalent to crude-oil derivatives.

Since petroleum is a hydrocarbon, it can be synthesized in the laboratory from any source of carbon — including cornstalks — combined with hydrogen (which can be obtained from water) in the presence of a catalyst under proper conditions of temperature and pressure. But synthetic-oil production in volume depends upon coal and therefore is practical only in Germany, England, and some other countries with great coal reserves. France planned to build a synthetic industry before the war but abandoned the attempt because she was an importer of coal as well as petroleum and was as dependent on one as on the other. She finally reverted to the policy of constructing refineries and building up stocks.

She accumulated reserves, largely in the northern part of the country, which the Germans gleefully appropriated in 1940. Scandinavia and the Low Countries also followed this policy—and also lost their oil hoards to the Nazis.

But Germany pulled out all the stops in her endeavor to become independent in oil. The Hitler regime fostered a resurvey of possible national crude sources, based on the latest refinements of geophysics, then encouraged prospecting by private companies by offering to pay half the cost of all new drilling. The result was that crude production more than doubled between 1933 and 1938, and still was not at a peak because the Germans rightly considered that the best possible storage place for oil was in the underground pockets and therefore did not try to bring production to the maximum. However, the 1938 crude production of about four million barrels was less than eight percent of the year's consumption, after more than half a decade of energetic exploitation of all known sources.

Meantime, though Hitler laced the Reich with his splendid concrete *Autobahnen* and exhorted good Nazis to save toward their future *Volkswagen,* the majority of Germans moved about on foot and on bicycles, as soon as war became imminent. All consumption not essential to the creation and training of the machine of victory was stifled. Gasoline was mixed with alcohol and benzol, a byproduct of high-temperature carbonization, and liquid gas, byproduct of the synthetic industry, was to be the fuel for all trucks and busses over one and a half tons. All of this was subsidiary to the major effort of building the synthetic-oil industry. To encourage the desired expansion, the Reich made long-term contracts with the coal and chemical industries, providing for the purchase of synthetic output for many years to come at a price that guaranteed a profit sufficient to amortize the tremendous cost of constructing the needed plants. Where the plants should be built, what kind of oil they should produce, and in what amounts, the German mining companies were informed by the Wirtschaftsgruppe Kraftstoffindustrie, the Reich's central oil-planning and oil-control agency. By 1939 twenty-five synthetic plants were in full operation, with more under construction. In 1938 the German synthetic industry produced at least 10 million barrels of oil, or nearly a fifth of the nation's consumption, and production for 1941 is estimated at over 30 million barrels.

In this same year, 1938, Adolf Hitler told a Nazi Party Congress that already the German Reich was in a position to get along without imports from abroad. Yet in 1938 Germany imported some 41 million barrels of oil. Unquestionably, a large part of the imported oil was salted away in reserves. At the outbreak of war these were sometimes estimated as high as 50 million barrels. A more realistic figure would be two-thirds of that.

At any rate, while striving for self-sufficiency regardless of cost and effort, Germany had no objection to importing Anglo-American oil, which was much cheaper than the domestic product.

Oil for the Wehrmacht

What Hitler meant in 1938 was that Germany's reserves and Germany's expanding synthetic and crude production (plus imports that would still be available in wartime) would be sufficient for the blitzkrieg that his generals were then planning. They had studied the lessons of World War I more carefully than any Allied generals and they had overlooked nothing. They were mindful of Lord Curzon's remark that "the Allies floated to victory on a wave of oil," and they had also read Ludendorff's memoirs, wherein he states that lack of oil was one of the principal difficulties facing the German High Command.

By the end of World War I the Allied land armies and air fleets alone were consuming oil at the rate of 1,350,000 barrels per month, but this was nothing compared to what the experts thought would be needed in the war of the future, fought with tens of thousands of planes and huge mechanized forces. They estimated roughly that each belligerent would require at least two or three times its normal peacetime consumption. In other words, Britain might need over 200 million barrels annually, Germany more than 125 million barrels, and so on.

Such estimates, of course, started with the assumption that the new war would involve continuous fighting over a long period, and this assumption the Germans tried to circumvent. To procure sufficient oil for such a war was simply impossible, so the Nazis developed new weapons and new tactics. These have succeeded everywhere, and have operated with amazing economy. One of the great popular surprises of the war has been the relatively low oil consumption by the Wehrmacht. According to German claims and British estimates, the German Army and Luftwaffe used not more than 12 million barrels of gasoline, Diesel oil, and lubricants in actual fighting from the start of the Battle of Poland to the end of the Battle of France. This is about as much oil as the U.S. produces every three days. Furthermore, the stocks captured in France and the Low Countries probably were at least 20 million barrels, so the Nazis came out ahead of the game.

But even if these stocks had not existed, the oil produced within Greater Germany itself was sufficient to meet the needs of the army, German industry, and essential civilian demand for an indefinite time. It was not a comfortable supply, to be sure; it did not allow any prodigality; but it was enough for blitzkriegs that occurred at intervals during which stocks could be accumulated, and which then were over in a few weeks.

Furthermore, the sources of this oil were relatively secure, and production tended to increase despite the depredations of the R.A.F. The newer synthetic plants were in out-of-the-way places, and even if attacked were not very vulnerable targets, since vital parts were heavily protected.

Indeed, the problem of oil transportation was more troublesome than production. For example, the difficulty of replenishing gasoline dumps at scores of airfields used for the raids on Britain undoubtedly has had something to do with the fact that the Luftwaffe's assaults have tended to follow a distinct pattern of a series of prolonged mass attacks followed by several weeks of comparative inactivity. Marshal Göring certainly has had sufficient equipment and personnel available for continuous mass attacks, but it takes at least 100 gallons of gasoline to keep a Messerschmitt aloft for an hour, and supply and transportation difficulties probably checked the German air blitz.

No, the Germans would not run short of oil in any blitzkrieg of Hitler's making—only in a long war that kept the Luftwaffe in the air and the panzers rolling constantly for months. And it was precisely that kind of war that Hitler would avoid fighting.

The New Order Feels the Pinch

Blitzkrieg, after all, was merely the means toward the end of conquest. Adolf Hitler had organized the German Reich for the conquest of Europe; now he would organize Europe for the conquest of the world. His armies had shown great forbearance in sparing factories, railroads, and other industrial assets in enemy territory. As the chief landlord and stockholder in Europe, Germany would draw rich dividends from them for many years to come. Meantime, their maximum output was needed in an effort to counterbalance the growing U.S. war production.

But the higher the rate of production, the greater the need for oil. Hitler now possessed every drop of oil in Europe, and palpably it was not enough for the purposes of the New Order. Everywhere he had sliced consumption down to the bare bone, especially in the occupied countries. Here Germany tried to cut the oil ration by two-thirds to three-quarters, or down to the irreducible minimum below which local industry and agriculture no longer could function. Since she controlled all of Europe's sources, she likewise forced consumption reductions in the unoccupied Axis satellite countries simply by withholding supplies, and here again the forced savings amounted to perhaps three-fifths of the normal flow. Thus, after the conquest, France and the Low Countries probably were allowed, for all purposes, between 17 and 22 million barrels in place of their accustomed ration of nearly 70 million barrels, and similar cuts were effected throughout the rest of Europe.

Germany and Italy also throttled civilian consumption, but these savings were probably offset by military demand, and total consumption has not declined to any great extent. But the absolute minimum of total Italian consumption under wartime conditions is 20 million barrels. Prior to the war she built synthetic plants and refineries and boasted of soon achieving self-sufficiency, but she is a mendicant for coal as for so many other things. Albania, her only crude source, could produce two million barrels at the outside, actually was producing much less. Italy has an output of alcohol and other substitutes that may be equivalent to two million barrels of oil, but for the rest she is dependent on Germany. Her military feebleness in Africa was due to a considerable extent to her oil poverty, and today she adds little to Germany's strength save for her nuisance value in the Mediterranean. This dubious contribution is outweighed by her dependence on foreign oil and raw materials generally, and probably makes her a net liability for the Axis.

By the end of 1940 Germany had thus reduced oil consumption in Europe to the irreducible, yet was left with the prospect of something like a 15-million–barrel shortage in 1941. According to conservative estimates of several authorities, the rock bottom of 1941 consumption was 115 million barrels in Germany, Italy, and the occupied and satellite countries, assuming military and naval demand not exceeding that of 1940. Judged by the known output in these countries, German Europe's maximum production for 1941 could not exceed 100 million barrels. This includes Rumania's production which the Nazis hope will reach 45 million barrels this year, compared to about 43 million barrels in 1940. The Germans thought they could raise production by taking over the fields (largely controlled by Anglo-Dutch-American interests before the war), and this was one of the leading reasons for the bloodless invasion of Rumania in October, 1940. To make sure of routes, Germany later forced Bulgaria and Hungary into the Axis camp and overran Yugoslavia.

But even with German engineers in charge of the fields, there was a vast difference between crude underground in Rumania and refined oil products safely delivered to the right places in the Reich. Until Italy entered the war and the British fleet took over the Mediterranean, about 75 percent of Rumania's exports had gone out in tankers via Constantsa. With that traffic cut off, the only alternative was to send oil overland, by railroad tank car or—more important—by the Danube barge lines. However, both these facilities were insufficient. Railroads were mostly single-track; tank cars were scarce, and there was a shortage of barges on the Danube. That river ordinarily freezes for a month or two every winter; to the chagrin of the Nazis, it was frozen for more than three months during the winter of 1939-40, and Rumania was able to ship to

Germany an average of only 30,000 barrels a day instead of the 35,000 barrels that she had contracted to deliver throughout 1940. Since taking over Rumania the Nazis have concentrated on simultaneously boosting crude production and speeding up the transport system. They are supposed to have doubled the trackage across Hungary within recent months and are building pipe lines to shorten the barge haul on the Danube, using material extracted from lines under construction in occupied France and sent to Rumania. Since the fall of Crete, Germany has succeeded in shipping some oil out via the Dardanelles, but Rumanian production continues to decline.

Like Rumania, the Soviet Union was also a difficult and uncertain oil source. No amount of pressure apparently could force the Russians to increase deliveries, which came to six million barrels in 1940. Indeed, the U.S.S.R. to all intents and purposes had ceased being an oil-exporting nation. As explained in the article on "Soviet Industry" in *Fortune* for July [1941], the U.S.S.R.'s subsoil deposits might be astronomical, but the sluggish Russian production industry could barely manage to maintain the flow of crude at around 210 million barrels annually. All of this production was so desperately needed for domestic purposes that the Soviet Union had been forced to extend gasoline rationing in 1940 and was a customer of the U.S. petroleum industry to the tune of more than one million barrels last year. In short, the U.S.S.R. had no oil surplus. If she did export, it was out of political or economic necessity, for the purpose of obtaining vital goods in exchange, and there was no prospect of any generous surplus for years to come.

Theoretically, there was nothing to prevent the indefinite expansion of the synthetics industry, up to the point where most of Europe's oil would be obtained via the Bergius and Fischer-Tropsch processes. Actually any such expansion would require many years of plant construction and would be fearfully extravagant not only in capital investment but in subsequent costs. The main drawback to the synthetics industry is that a gallon of gasoline obtained from coal costs nearly three times as much as a gallon from crude.

But even if the Reich succeeded in meeting all gasoline needs with synthetics, it could never hope to do the same with lubricants. There is no chemical obstacle to this synthesis, but it entails a complicated series of processes beginning where the Fischer-Tropsch method leaves off. The cost is prohibitive, and the industry has not produced lubricants in commercial quantities. Today it would be quite impossible for Germany to produce either synthetically or from her available crude the eight million barrels of lubricants that will be Europe's minimum requirement this year, and there appears to be an increasingly severe shortage of quality lubricants suitable for use in internal-combustion engines and in transformers and high-speed machinery. Reports from England frequently mention analyses of crankcase drainings from downed German planes which indicate that the Luftwaffe is using inferior oil grades, or at any rate lacks supplies for changes at proper intervals.

Similarly, the German synthetics industry produces insufficient amounts of 100-octane gasoline, and the Luftwaffe flies mainly on 87- to 92-octane gas. The Messerschmitts equipped with direct-fuel-injection systems perform brilliantly with this product, but 100-octane spirit, produced mainly in the U.S., gives vastly better performance when used in the proper engines. New British and U.S. planes are designed to operate with this gasoline. Germany has neither the crude nor the synthetic resources for production of 100-octane fuel on any important scale.

Drang nach Osten

But the shortage in lubricants is merely a small reflection of the widening gap between minimum consumption and maximum production. In 1941 this could be made up by drawing on reserves, and perhaps the same could be done next year. But Hitler had now seized all of Europe's stocks and could expect to find no more. With deficiencies piling up and tending to increase year after year, the day inevitably would come when the machinery of the New Order would rattle and squeak and grind its way to destruction. By the spring of 1941 it was obvious that unless and until he secured a large source of oil, Hitler could not proceed to take over Europe and the world.

To say that oil was the only reason or even the leading reason for Germany's incredible decision to attack the U.S.S.R. probably would be exaggeration. Nevertheless, it is reasonable to suppose that Europe's growing thirst for oil provided a strong motive. A man who had dared as much as Adolf Hitler scarcely would let a paltry few million barrels of oil stand in the way of his destiny. And, indeed, two solutions were within the reach of his armies. One—the great fields of Iran and Iraq—lay southeastward, toward the Persian Gulf. The other, of course, was the Soviet Baku and Grozny fields on the Caspian Sea. Several factors combined to make the U.S.S.R. preferable to Iran and Iraq as an immediate target. First, while the Near East basin is probably destined to rival the U.S. as a crude producer, the Soviet Union's actual yield at present is larger. Second, it was extremely likely that the British would destroy their wells and refineries before letting them fall into German hands; at the very least, they would ruin the Iraq pipe lines to the Mediterranean. Third, even if the fields were taken intact, Germany would have to break Britain's hold on the Mediterranean in order to get the oil out. The only other approach would be by the Persian Gulf, over sea lanes ruled all the way around Africa and up to the Faeroe Islands by the British navy. Last, a German move on Iran and Iraq might well provoke a Russian attack from the north.

Thus, while the choice was a desperate one on both sides, the Russian side looked less desperate. Whether it actually proves to be in the end is anybody's guess. The experts forecast a Germany victory, but present indications are that it may cost Hitler far more than he anticipated. It is almost certain that the first four weeks of the Russian campaign have already cost him more in oil than the conquest of Europe. If the blitz technique fails against the Russians, Hitler will find himself fighting a war of position that will exhaust his reserves in no time, and it is significant that after the war had been in progress only a month the Italian Government issued a decree abolishing the last gasoline rations for private automobiles. German production facilities meantime will be under constant attack by the British and the Russians, and both they and Hitler know that to strike at German oil does not mean necessarily striking at refineries. The congestion and breakdown of German rail transportation during World War I was a prime reason for the building of the *Autobahnen* in preparation for World War II, but because of the oil shortage Germany has been forced to give up the motor-transport scheme and to pile as much traffic as possible onto the railroads and inland waterways. Thus damage to a railroad forces a diversion of traffic to the highways and increases oil consumption.

Of course, the prize—to say nothing of the internal necessity—makes the risk worth while. But it is far from certain that Hitler will immediately get the prize even though he achieves his first objective and wipes out the Red Army. For Stalin has instructed his cohorts to adopt a "scorched earth" policy, and perhaps the Russians will dynamite their oil fields and refineries while they burn their grain and smash their tractors. If they do, it will amount to national suicide. Thanks to the slaughter of 15 million horses in Russia in 1923 by peasants rebelling against the collectivization program, the Soviet eats and moves and lives by oil to an extent almost unheard of elsewhere. The direct and inevitable consequence of oil destruction will be famine.

But the Russians may figure that there will be famine in any case. For they have no reason to hope that Hitler will treat them more generously than he did his other enemies. Thus, if he decrees a mandatory 50 or 60 percent cut in Russian consumption in order to get more oil for himself while his technicians and workers try to raise output, the effect will be about the same as if the Russians wrecked the fields.

Even if the Nazis take the fields intact, it will be a long time before they can organize the 2,500-mile supply lines from the Caspian Sea to Central Europe. Indeed, it is doubtful whether any conceivable overland transport system will be adequate to carry oil in the quantity that Hitler needs. If he succeeds in the U.S.S.R., therefore, his next move may well be a southward thrust to capture Suez, seize Iran and Iraq, drive the British out of the eastern Mediterranean, and thereby open up the sea routes, the only convenient means of sending raw materials from southwestern U.S.S.R. to Europe.

Oil for Britain

Regardless of what takes place in the uncertain future, Germany's present oil squeeze must be a great comfort not only to the British nation as a whole, but especially to the British Ministry of Economic Warfare. It will be recalled that in the free-and-easy days before the Battle of France, many cocksure predictions were made to the effect that Germany's oil problem would cripple her war effort in short order. The revelation of the true state of affairs was painful to a degree, and the whole concept of economic warfare enforced by blockade fell into general disrepute. Now it would appear that this primary British weapon is not so puny as it seemed.

With free access to perhaps 85 percent of the world's crude-oil production, England's prewar preparations and present position differ radically from Germany's. She made almost no effort to achieve "self-sufficiency," which would have been impossible for her, but depended on her immemorial control of the sea to ensure imports. True, some exploratory drilling for crude went on for years in various parts of the island, but with negligible results. The only natural-petroleum source of consequence was in the Scottish shale-oil industry, which before the war produced about one million barrels a year, but at high cost. The British Government also encouraged the creation of a synthetics industry to take advantage of her coal, and Imperial Chemical Industries, Ltd. constructed a plant at Billingham that turned out some 1,200,000 barrels annually. Another plant, in a secret location and with unknown capacity, is said to have gone into operation recently.

However, Britain's home production met about 5 percent of consumption requirements, and she therefore had to count on imports and storage. Refining capacity in Britain was equal to about half the annual consumption, but the refineries were mostly located in the vulnerable areas close to the Channel, and it was decided to import mostly finished products. Today it is doubtful whether any crude to speak of is being imported. Thus far, stored-oil losses as a result of bombing have apparently been relatively low. The oil is kept in tanks surrounded by sandbag bulwarks, which stop shell splinters, and moats to catch any leakage. It takes a direct hit to cause any real damage. The British experience thus has been similar to that of Germany, where the synthetics industry has not yet been seriously impaired despite repeated attacks.

The extent of the stocks in England at the beginning of the war is a military secret, as are the figures on imports and wartime consumption. Though private automobile use has been severely restricted, England is heavily dependent on truck-and-bus transportation, and nonmilitary consumption probably has not been reduced to anything like the degree it was on the Continent. A reasonable estimate of the United Kingdom's total present consumption might be 100 million barrels a year, or almost as much as Germany's Europe. It is doubtful that refined products are reaching the British Isles in quantities sufficient to leave a balance over this demand. She is undoubtedly trying to speed up imports so as to accumulate a substantial stock pile against future emergencies.

Oil for England therefore is not a question of sources, which are more than ample, but of transportation, meaning the Battle of the Atlantic. Britain entered the war with a tanker fleet totaling 2,900,000 gross tons, plus another 350,000 tons owned by the dominions and colonies, and has since acquired most of the Norwegian and Dutch and part of the French, Belgian, and Danish tanker tonnage. All told, the combined fleets represented some six million tons, of which perhaps a million tons have been sunk by U-boats, the German Admiralty having announced its intention of concentrating on tankers. The loss greatly exceeds Britain's tanker-building capacity, and sinkings continued at this rate for long would produce an oil crisis in England. The tanker in wartime has its carrying capacity cut virtually in half, owing to the slow movement and longer routes of convoys, delays in port, and various other factors that reduce the number of voyages. In addition, much tonnage is constantly laid up for repairs.

Rations for the U.S.

To ease the strain on British transport facilities, the U.S. has withdrawn 50 privately owned tankers from their normal coast-wise runs and placed them in a sort of shuttle service, to move oil for England from the Caribbean and Gulf production and refining points up to North Atlantic ports. The British have requested still further tanker tonnage. Washington is inclined to meet the request, but some oilmen feel that the British are not making the most efficient use of what they have.

The 50 vessels already withdrawn or pledged represent about one-seventh of the U.S. tanker fleet, which is engaged chiefly in bringing oil from the Gulf to the Atlantic coast. Normally about 1,200,000 barrels per day of Gulf oil have arrived in the East by tanker, and the loss of 50 tankers means that this oil movement will be reduced by upwards of

200,000 barrels per day, on the average. The existing pipe lines from mid-continent to the eastern seaboard have a daily capacity of under 50,000 barrels.

It is this transportation bottleneck that may make for considerably higher oil prices on the Atlantic seaboard this autumn and may well lead to the "gasless Sundays" predicted by Mr. Ickes, or even to some form of rationing. The pinch will denote no shortage of U.S. oil. Current daily production of around 3,500,000 barrels can be raised an estimated 30 percent at any time, more than enough to cover the anticipated 10 percent over-all rise in domestic consumption, which will come about chiefly through "defense prosperity" rather than through defense preparation. Until the transfer of many more tankers seemed imminent, the industry hoped to avert "gasless Sundays" in the East (where some 40 percent of U.S. oil is consumed) by bringing as much oil as possible via inland waterways, the railroads, and other overland routes. The most effective solution (until more tankers leave the ways next year and thereafter) will be the building of a supplementary pipe-line network, to carry perhaps 250,000 barrels per day.

On [a] map of world oil will be seen the tanker routes from the U.S., the Dutch East Indies, and elsewhere to Japan. . . . Prior to the Japanese occupation of French Indo-China the tanker routes . . . were Japan's oil life lines. Her essential annual consumption ranges from 40 to 45 million barrels, yet she produced at the most 13 million barrels last year. In addition to a tiny domestic crude production, Japan obtains oil from Manchurian shale beds and from fields on Sakhalin Island, worked jointly by Japan and Soviet Russia. But her main source of domestic supply is the rapidly growing synthetics industry. Considering the size of her military establishment and the scale of her imperial ambitions, she is more vulnerable, perhaps, than any of the Axis members. Her stocks on hand are thought to be sufficient for about a year at the outside, but any threat to her continued supplies from overseas is a threat to her national existence.

To the bewilderment of many people in this country, the U.S. and Great Britain followed a policy of allowing oil exports to Japan in an effort to "appease" the Far Eastern wing of the Axis. Last year "appeasement" exports from the U.S. amounted to 24 million barrels, and from the Dutch East Indies Japan obtained another seven to nine million barrels. The theory behind the U.S. export policy was twofold: that to continue to supply oil might keep Japan out of mischief in the South Pacific, whereas to declare an embargo in accordance with popular sentiment would be likely to precipitate an immediate move toward Sumatra and Borneo. As President [Franklin D.] Roosevelt explained at the time of the thrust into Indo-China, in July: "One of our efforts from the very beginning was to prevent the spread of [the present war] in certain areas where it hadn't started. Therefore, there was . . . a method in letting this oil go to Japan, with the hope—and it has worked for two years—of keeping war out of the South Pacific for our own good, for the good of the defense of Great Britain, and the freedom of the seas."

The British for years followed a similar theory in regard to oil shipments to Italy. Like Japan, Italy was at the mercy of imports, which Britain permitted to go through in quantity, though it was plain that part of this oil was going to Germany, while the bulk was being stored up against the coming war. The British, still suffering a bad hangover from the debauch of appeasement, completely misjudged the potency of Italy's commitments to Germany and believed that Italy could be bribed with oil to stay out of the war. On the other hand, Italy became intoxicated by the blitzkrieg victories and obviously thought that the war would end after the collapse of France, whereupon the oil problem and all other problems would be solved automatically. Both sides were fooled. Britain strengthened the hand of her enemies, while Italy ended up being dependent not on Britain, with plenty of oil to spare, but on Germany, with none.

Japanese Strategy

In the month following the Japanese attack on Pearl Harbor, a more extensive reference to the oil factor in Japanese strategy appeared in World Petroleum. *It was by far the most revealing description that had appeared on this critical subject in the public press and was a fit companion to the earlier article in* Fortune.

The three Axis countries with whom the United States is now at war have for many years concentrated their energies to prepare themselves for this life and death struggle. One of the most difficult economic problems of their war planning has been the task of assuring sufficient quantities of oil in wartime. There is no doubt that the utmost attention has been paid to this program and that a common plan was formulated many years ago; as a matter of fact probably in 1934–35. It is perhaps worth mentioning that in the latter year a very high official of the Navy Department of the German War Ministry was sent to Japan to study the country's oil position in wartime, to advise the Nipponese Government on the Nazi plan for the solution of these problems and to prepare a report for the German Economic General Staff. His conclusions were published in 1936 and may be summarized as follows:

Japanese annual oil demand in wartime for civil and military purposes may be estimated (calculated in the form of crude oil) at 105,000,000 bbl. Of this quantity 56,000,000 bbl. would be required to produce gas oil and fuel oil for the Navy, assuming a tonnage of 1,100,000 – a figure which corresponds to the latest available estimate. An air fleet of 3,000 airplanes would require 8,000,000 to 9,000,000 bbl. of aviation gasoline, which would be produced from 21,000,000 bbl. of crude oil. The remaining 28,000,000 bbl. of crude would be used to supply the Army and to meet domestic demand. The report expressed not the slightest doubt that even with the most energetic efforts it would be impossible for Japan to produce this quantity of oil from domestic resources. A considerable balance would have to be covered by importation. As imports might be

Reprinted with permission from *World Petroleum,* January 1942, pp. 23–27.

cut off and as any war in which Japan would fight against the United States would be a long and costly war against an enemy possessing oil and oil-driven implements of war in abundance, Japan could not dare to depend on stocks alone. She would have to conquer first the foremost new sources of natural oil supplies. And here, according to the German expert, Japan is in a somewhat more favorable position than the Reich. The coastal and island territories in the Pacific contain most valuable oil fields, while the territories on the borders of the Atlantic Ocean in Europe lack natural petroleum resources.

These conclusions hold good even for today when the exaggerated estimates of oil requirements in wartime have been reduced after the actual experience of two years of war in Europe. To show the problem of achieving self-sufficiency in its true perspective a few data on Japanese oil requirements in the last few years will be given. Consumption, excluding Navy imports and the quantities which merchant ships bunkered abroad, amounted to about 24,000,000 bbl. in 1936. Only some 10 to 15 percent of this quantity was produced at home. The outbreak of the war with China led to a large increase in demand despite stringent economy in civilian consumption. Domestic requirements in Japan have always been relatively small. The country possesses only 210,000 motor vehicles as against 32 million units in the United States. Industrial requirements for heavy oils are also relatively unimportant, as the country, in view of its oil shortage, used coal instead of Diesel and fuel oil wherever possible. Principal consumer of motor fuel is the commercial road transport industry; heavy oils are used for the Navy and merchant marine. Lubricants are of course indispensable for industry and transport. In spite of all efforts to restrict consumption by the introduction of gasoline rationing in May 1938, the increase of motor fuel taxation to an excessive level, prohibiting the use of oil for heating and cooking purposes, and the compulsory use of substitutes, the field for possible savings without harming the country's war effort was very small indeed. On the contrary the extraordinary expansion in heavy industries, the development of vast territories in Manchuria and China which were largely dependent on road transport, led to an expansion of demand which, according to Japanese sources, has been appreciable. If we add to that the military and naval requirements for the war in China, which must also have been heavy, a consumption of between 35,000,000 and 40,000,000 bbl. in 1940—a figure frequently mentioned in American literature—seems certainly not exaggerated. The war with America will add considerably to requirements as long as the Japanese Navy, air force, and land army are operating over vast territories. At the same time the whole Yenbloc area including Thailand and Indo-China is cut off from its imported supplies and has to fall back on its domestic production, stocks and imports from

Japan. The crucial question is thus: how much is Japan able to produce at home, how big are her stocks, and how long will they be able to cover deficiencies, and finally, what strategy will Japan have to follow if she attempts to solve her wartime oil problem?

A review of Japan's oil policy immediately reveals striking similarities to the German pattern of war preparations with the one important difference that Germany did not count on overseas imports from neutral or conquered territories, while Japan definitely did. The practical consequence is that Germany did not strive to build up a big refining industry which would be able to treat crude oil from abroad nor did the Reich concentrate on the creation of a large and fast-moving tanker fleet. Japan, on the other hand, took all kinds of measures to establish a modern and efficient refining industry and to acquire a relatively large tanker fleet. As a matter of fact, Japan was one of the first countries to build tankers with the speed of 19 knots and over. The need for these vessels arose not only from the necessity to import oil from abroad but also from the problem of refueling the Navy outside home waters. In contrast to Germany the intention of the Japanese Naval Staff was obviously not to keep the fleet safely tucked away under the protection of Japanese ports.

The measures to increase the production of natural and synthetic oil in the country show a close resemblance to the German autarchy plan. Conditions for oil self-sufficiency were indeed somewhat similar. Domestic resources of natural crude oil in both countries are very limited while sufficient coal deposits are available for the creation of a large synthetic coal oil industry. A plan was formulated long before the whole economy of Japan could be put on a war footing by the National Mobilization Law of March 1938. Petroleum was one of the first raw materials for which a comprehensive war economy was introduced. The government set out systematically: (1) to control production, imports, refining, distribution and storage; (2) to encourage refining; (3) to intensify exploration and exploitation of natural resources; (4) to promote a synthetic oil industry; (5) to increase the use of substitutes; (6) to build up huge stocks; (7) to expand the tanker fleet; (8) to achieve a better utilization of available resources and a greater economy in consumption. The legal and economic instruments with which the government carried through its plans were first of all the Petroleum Industry Law of 1934. This law subjected production, imports, refining, and distribution to government control, entitled the government to fix maximum prices, and to prescribe quotas for imports and refining. Trade and industry had moreover to carry at all times a minimum of six months' stock. Foreign companies operating in Japan first refused to comply with the storage provision law, but in 1936 they came to an agreement with the government. Mitsubishi interests erected the necessary storage tanks for the foreign companies and leased the tanks to them, while the government promised to compensate them for any losses sustained through carrying out of the storage obligations. At the same time the Japanese tariff policy favored the importation of crude and heavy oil for further refining. Imports of finished products declined successively and the newly created Japanese refining industry supplied an ever-growing proportion of the market.

In June 1937 the government established a Fuel Bureau under the Ministry of Commerce and Industry to carry out the national fuel policy to encourage exploitation of all natural resources, to administer the petroleum industry laws, to help in the creation of a synthetic oil industry, and to promote a better utilization of oil products. In accordance with that plan the government created an alcohol monopoly and introduced the compulsory alcohol admixture bill. The production of alcohol became, as in Germany, a government monopoly. The rate of admixture was increased from 5 percent at that time to 20 percent in 1941. At the same session of the Diet the Synthetic Petroleum Production Law and the Imperial Fuel Development Company Law were passed (July–August 1937) and the Petroleum Resources Exploitation Law came into effect in March 1938. Licenses were issued for the erection of synthetic oil plants, subsidies were promised and exemptions from duty were granted for the imports of material for the next seven years. Plants were also free from local taxation. To safeguard the national character of the industry more than 50 percent of the capital had to remain in Japanese hands. In January 1938 the Imperial Fuel Industrial Co. was founded with a capital of 100,000,000 Yen ($23,500,000 at pre-war exchange rates), half of which was contributed by the government, and the right to issue debentures for another 300,000,000 Yen ($70,500,000). The chief object of this company was to provide capital for the synthetic oil industry. The government hoped with all these measures to carry through its Seven Year Plan which in 1936 had been formulated for Japan and Manchuria. It was planned to produce by 1943 17,650,000 bbl. of oil from domestic sources to meet at least half of the total demand. The capital necessary for this program was estimated at 770,000,000 Yen ($180,950,000), half of which would be provided by the Imperial Fuel Development Co. About 340,000,000 Yen ($79,900,000) were to be invested in hydrogenation, 150,000,000 Yen ($35,250,000) in synthetic processes, 120,000,000 Yen ($28,200,000) in low temperature distillation, and 130,000,000 Yen ($30,550,000) in the exploitation of coal mines. For the production of the 13,600,000 bbl. of coal oil it was estimated that 8,900,000 tons of coal would be needed for the processing and another 1,000,000 tons for the production of hydrogen. First experiments in the erection of coal oil plants were actually commenced in 1936 and three methods were to be used. First, direct liquefaction, developed by the Navy Fuel Depot together with the South Manchuria Railway Co. and the Chosen Nitrogen Fertilizer Co., or hydrogenation. It was hoped that these processes would yield gasoline with an octane rating of 70 to 80. Second, the Fischer-Tropsch process acquired by the Mitsui Mining Co., and third, low temperature distillation. The original program was frequently changed. First of all the plan was reduced from seven to five years so as to be ready for 1941. At the same time an increase by as much as 85 percent was decreed. This, however, proved impracticable, for according to all available information it was impossible even to fulfill the original plan figures.

Shortly after the announcement of the Seven Year Plan, war with China broke out, seriously deranging the schedule. The ambitious self-sufficiency program had, for some time at least, to be curtailed. It became increasingly difficult to follow the course of Japanese supplies and requirements. All information which might clarify the state of affairs in this important field was carefully suppressed by the authorities. Publication of detailed trade statistics for oil imports was stopped at the outbreak of hostilities, and no official figures on the success of the self-sufficiency program were any longer available. It is only known that as the war in China dragged on year after year, domestic consumption in Japan had to be severely and progressively restricted. Efforts were continued to enlarge crude oil production, to build new coal oil plants and to manufacture various substitute fuels. But by 1939 progress was still very slow indeed. The government itself stated that Japan's crude oil deposits were not entirely insignificant, that delays were experienced in the construction of the hydrogenation works, and that the first Fischer plant for the production of synthetic oil would start operations in the summer of 1939, while further plants were scheduled to start production in the early part of 1941. At the same time a new three-year plan was announced, according to which, by 1942, the production of gasoline from domestic crude oil was to be advanced by 30 percent and that of heavy oil by 40 percent. Synthetic motor fuel production was to be increased by 2,900 percent, synthetic heavy oils by 800 percent, and motor alcohol by 1,200 percent. But again, shortage of foreign currency and delays in the delivery of the necessary equipment from Germany, which was already involved in war against the western democracies, hindered progress. Another factor of primary importance was the difficulty of increasing coal production sufficiently, due to labor scarcity, lack of mining equipment, and transport problems. Alcohol production was hampered by irregular supplies of molasses and potatoes.

The finance for the ambitious plan was mainly provided by the Imperial Fuel Development Co., the various Mitsui, Mitsubishi, and No guchi interests and the Manchurian Government. According to these data there were to be some 22 plants in operation or under construction in 1940–41, with an estimated planned capacity of some 7,000,000–9,000,000 bbl. per annum. In the meantime it may be expected that new projects have been formulated. In some cases efforts probably have been made to increase the initial capacity of the plants. The Japanese laid out the whole synthetic oil program very carefully and spent many years in planning and experimenting, so that when the initial stage was over they would be able to erect a large industry within a comparatively short time. In many cases, however, probably for a majority of the plants, actual performance will have fallen far short of the program. The ever-growing scarcity of labor and materials and the economic upheaval caused by the European war and especially difficulties in obtaining supplies from Germany must have most seriously affected Japan's coal oil industry.

Great importance was also attached to shale oil production from the large fields in Manchuria. Reserves there are estimated at 5,000,000,000 tons with an average content of six percent of shale oil. It was first intended to increase producing capacity from 500,000 bbl. in 1935 to 2,500,000 bbl. by 1938. In March 1939, the South Manchurian Railway Co. decided to increase production to 3,500,000 bbl. by 1941 and to 7,000,000 bbl. by 1943 at an expenditure of 150,000,000 Yen ($35,250,000). It was considered to be more advantageous to produce oil from shale rather than from coal as the method had been tested, valuable coal was conserved and expenses were much lower. As a matter of fact there are many indications that the coal oil industry in Manchuria had to cope with many unexpected difficulties and the discrepancy between plan and accomplishment in this division was exceptionally large. As far as domestic crude oil production was concerned, not much hope was placed on a large expansion of output. To intensify exploitation, measures similar to those adopted in Germany were taken. The Petroleum Resources Exploitation Law formulated a five-year plan for an intensive search for crude oil. The government exercised supervision and control of drilling operations and could compel owners of concessions to cooperate among themselves. Subsidies for the drilling of new wells amounting to many millions of Yen were to be advanced in the form of loans repayable if and when the prospector struck oil.

Efforts to obtain control of foreign oil sources were made by systematic attempts to gain concessions in oil producing countries like Netherlands India, British Borneo, Mexico, Ecuador and even Rumania. A special company, the Pacific Petroleum Co., was formed in 1939 to acquire concession areas. The only important acquisition was the concession obtained in the Russian part of the Island of Sakhalin in 1925. There were many difficulties with the Soviets over the concession but it seems safe to say that without fighting it will be impossible to dislodge the Japanese from this area which supplies the Navy with part of its requirements. Production is in the hands of the North Sakhalin Petroleum Co., which received subsidies from the government. Formerly the Russians sold part of their Sakhalin output to the Japanese but these sales were stopped when the Soviet refinery at Khabarovsk on the Amur River was completed. Japan hoped to produce as much as 3,500,000 bbl. of oil by 1941 in Sakhalin, but actual output is just over half this figure. Though the reserves of this area would probably be sufficient to provide larger quantities of oil for Japan, transport of oil from Sakhalin constitutes a difficult problem; for nine months in the year shipping is hampered or prevented by ice so that huge storage installations for the production during this period have to be built and the whole output has to be shipped in the three or four ice-free months of the year.

The role of substitutes in Japanese oil economy has only lately become significant. The reasons are not only technical inferiority and higher costs compared with gasoline, but also difficulties in providing large quantities of substitute material. They can moreover not be used for military purposes because they would immediately give an initial advantage to the enemy who has abundant supplies of oil for his war machines. Their use is thus restricted to civilian purposes. Substitutes now in use are: (1) gas, generated from charcoal, firewood, coalite, acetylene, and (2) natural gas, petroleum gas, and methane gas from garbage, etc. Coalite, a semi-finished coke, is in great demand for the iron production so that supplies for motor car use are very small. Acetylene is also scarcely available as its raw material, carbide, is used for the manufacture of fertilizers. The use of natural gas and liquid gas is limited to the neighborhood of the producing centers unless the production of steel containers could be increased. But lack of steel makes that impossible. The only substitute fuel available in substantial quantities is charcoal and firewood. As early as 1933 the government encouraged its use, but the real impetus was given by the outbreak of the Chinese war. Until May 1938, when gasoline rationing was introduced, its use was only supplementary to the use of liquid fuel. It was gradually adopted in motor buses operating on fixed routes and the government paid nearly half of the conversion expenses. After the conclusion of the Tripartite Pact the use of substitute fuels became compulsory. But present supplies of charcoal are insufficient to satisfy the increased demand for industrial and mining uses and for burning in households. Production of charcoal even showed a decline, due to a shortage of labor. So firewood, which, from a technical point of view is inferior even to charcoal, must also be used. The Ministry of Agriculture and Forestry which was in charge of charcoal supplies spent some 100,000,000 Yen ($23,500,000) on its purchases in 1940 and planned to expend 205 million Yen ($48,175,000) in 1941–42. It is very doubtful, however, whether larger quantities could be put at the disposal of the transport industry. But the solution of the substitute fuel problem depends not only on the available supplies of generator fuel but perhaps to an even greater extent on the capacity to produce gas generators. A large increase in the output of generators would require great quantities of steel and occupy valuable plant space. In an economy like that of Japan where everything is scarce the use of productive capacity must be carefully balanced between deficiencies in the various branches of the economy. Finally, it should not be overlooked that little is known about the synthetic production of lubricants. This problem has certainly not been forgotten. Lubricants are most likely obtained from the Fischer-Tropsch process, and some quantities from the refining of domestic crude oil. Substitutes in the form of tar oil and animal and vegetable oil are also available. In the long run, however, the lack of high-grade American oils must detrimentally affect the machinery used in industry and transport.

As far as the expansion of refining capacity and the creation of a sufficient tanker fleet are concerned, results were not altogether unsatisfactory. According to latest available information, Japan possesses more than 30 refineries with an annual through-put capacity of 22,000,000 bbl. and a cracking capacity of 5,600,000 bbl. Some of her plants are able to produce aviation gasoline. The size of her tanker fleet increased between 1937 and 1939 from 223,000 tons to 440,000 tons and must be even larger now. This figure does also not include tankers belonging to the Navy. As stated in the Japanese Diet, a fleet of supertankers is an absolute prerequisite to the execution of Japan's oil policy. Under peacetime conditions her fleet would be able to carry between 40,000,000 and 50,000,000 bbl. of oil between Netherlands [Indies], British Borneo and Japan. But in war carrying capacity is very much reduced, probably by as much as one-half, not counting losses of tankers which will certainly occur on a growing scale.

Indigenous production constitutes only a small percentage of total requirements. The position in 1940 may be evaluated as follows: Though no official figures are available for the Japanese synthetic production during this year, a statement by the Director of the Fuel Office in the Japanese Ministry of Industry and Commerce early in 1941 is extremely interesting. He said that the government-owned company has so far invested some 150,000,000 Yen ($35,250,000), and private industry some 250,000,000 Yen ($58,750,000) in production of synthetic mineral oils. Investments in 1941 and 1942 will amount to a total of 500,000,000 Yen ($117,500,000) so that by 1942 the country will have spent some 130,000,000 Yen ($30,500,000) more for its oil program than originally intended. But due to the inflation of the Japanese currency and the large increase in costs, especially of imported machinery, actual production will fall appreciably below the planned figures. Supposing that all the plants for which money had been invested until 1940 were in full operation during this year, which certainly was not the case, the total production would not have exceeded 4,000,000 bbl. of synthetic oil, if one takes the British calculation for the cost of synthetic oil production as a basis. If the plants for which investments in 1941 and 1942 were planned, are in full production, Japanese synthetic oil output may reach 10,000,000 bbl. or so. Supplies from other domestic sources in 1940 amounted to approximately 2,600,000 bbl. of crude oil, some 2,000,000 bbl. from the Sakhalin concession, about 3,000,000 bbl. from the shale deposits in Manchuria, and some 500,000 bbl. of motor alcohol. At the very best Japan might have produced some 10,000,000–12,000,000 bbl. of domestic liquid fuel in 1940. The bulk of Japan's supplies therefore had to be covered by imports, mainly from the United States and to a smaller extent from Netherlands India. This is by no means surprising, considering that the original seven year plan, based on peacetime requirements, provided for large imports even in 1943. The development of American exports to Japan since 1936 [grew from 21,027,000 bbl. to 31,390,000 bbl. in 1938 and had declined to 22,833,000 bbl. in 1940]. In addition to American shipments another estimated 7,000,000 bbl. were sent in 1940 from Netherlands India and, according to an agreement with the Anglo-Iranian Oil Co., some further quantities, estimated at 1,000,000 bbl. from Iran. Further appreciable quantities were obtained from Borneo and other countries including Mexico which agreed in April 1940 to export 2,400,000 bbl. of oil to Japan within the next 18 months. In 1940 Japan and her possessions had thus about 46,000,000 to 48,000,000 bbl. of oil at their disposal, of which some 25 percent was produced at home. The rest came from American, Dutch and British sources. The danger in which Japanese oil supplies are in the present conflict with the Anglo-Saxon world is obvious.

Oil has for some time been a most important instrument of policy in relations between the United States and Japan. In July 1939, the American Government gave six months' notice of abrogation of the 1911 trade agreement with Japan. Since 1940 therefore America has been entitled to enforce discriminative measures against exports to Japan and imports from there. In 1940 exports of aviation gasoline, aviation lubricants, and machinery and patents for the manufacture of these products had been prohibited for every country outside the Western Hemisphere. Only the British Empire has received a general license for these kinds of exports. In the summer of 1941 a decree put the shipments of all oil products under export licensing regulations. Japan, it is true, received an export license, but in July 1941, when she occupied Indo-China the United States froze all Japanese assets. Licenses became necessary for every single transaction. Exports of low-grade aviation fuel and all crude oil suitable for its manufacture were also stopped. The reasons that impelled the United States to permit oil exports to Japan up to that time were effectively explained by President Roosevelt in July 1941. "There was a method in letting oil go to Japan with the hope—and it has worked for two years—of keeping war out of the southern Pacific for our own good, for the good of the defense of Great Britain, and the freedom of the seas." No wonder that Japan made continuous efforts to come to terms with Netherlands India for largely increased oil exports. In 1940 Netherlands India agreed to supply her with some 14,000,000 bbl. of oil per annum (but no aviation gasoline). In May 1941, this agreement was renewed, but towards the middle of June the general trade negotiations between the two countries were broken off. When America froze Japanese assets in July 1941, Netherlands India gave six months' notice of discontinuation of the oil agreement with Japan. Japan's contract with Iran was also cancelled by July 1941. Since that time the oil war has really started.

The oil economy of Japan was thus put on a total war footing even before the actual outbreak of war. Control had been established over production, imports, refining, transport, synthetic oil and marketing. This is, as the German naval expert whom we quoted at the beginning of this article, takes care to point out, a great advantage and even necessary in the case of Japan. But the most skillful and efficient organization cannot bridge the large gap between minimum requirements and actual production. It is true that Japan has accumulated large stocks over a number of years. The trade kept at least six months' supply, and much bigger reserves were carried by the Navy. Storage facilities have been constantly and systematically expanded. Figures for available storage even as early as 1933 mention a capacity of 15,000,000 bbl. It is known that further large tank installations have been built since then, especially in the years 1937–38. It is perhaps interesting to state in this connection that in 1935, the last year for which statistics for such a comparison are available, the export statistics of the United States, Netherlands India, and Russia show shipments to Japan, exceeding the quantity given in the Japanese import statistics by over 4,000,000 bbl. It can be assumed that this quantity was mainly for the Navy's account, and that part of it was refined in the Navy's own installations and stored in its tanks. This calculation does not take into account that in many cases export statistics of the oil producing countries do not show all the quantities destined for Japan. This applies especially to Netherlands India, where large cargos go first to trans-shipment points and are redirected from there to their ultimate destination. Quantities consigned to the great bunkering stations in the Far East may also later find their way to Japan or other countries. Japan is thus certainly prepared to live for a considerable time on her stocks, and will be able to satisfy the vastly increased requirements for naval, air and land warfare in the Far East. According to a recent statement by the President of the Japanese Planning Office, oil for the war machine is assured in the case of an embargo and private industry will also receive enough to satisfy its most essential requirements. But assurance of substantial stocks cannot mean adequate supplies for a protracted war.

The whole Japanese oil plan and as a matter of fact the whole Japanese war economy includes the gigantic gamble that Japan will be able within a comparatively short time to conquer new sources of supply. Netherlands India, British Borneo, and perhaps Burma are the obvious immediate objects of Japanese expansive aggression. The struggle for the control of various British and American naval and air bases is only the necessary preparation for the exploitation of the resources further south, of which Japan will be in dire need sooner or later. For Japan's problem consists not only in conquering new oil sources but also in establishing assured transport connections between Japan proper and Southeastern Asia. If Japan could succeed in destroying allied sea and air power in the Far East, she might, perhaps count on another attack in force on the Netherlands India, which would leave insufficient time for effective destruction of oil wells and refineries by the defenders. And it is by no means unlikely that Germany will try at the same time to gain control over the large oil resources in the Near and Middle East and will in case of success share the spoils with Japan.

Such a military strategy is one of the pillars of Japanese oil policy. Her tanker fleet would be ready to ship large quantities of oil to Japan and her refineries, which in the peace years have been carefully adapted to the treatment of the crude oil available in neighboring territories, [and thus] could refine oil even if the plants in the conquered countries should have been destroyed. At the time of writing, Japan has already occupied oilfields in British Borneo. The importance which she attaches to this conquest is shown by a speech of Premier [Hideki] Tojo before the House of Peers. He announced that though the British had destroyed 150 wells and other installations before withdrawing, some 70 wells could be brought into production again within one month. Japan, so he said, could count on some 5,400 bbl. daily from this source. The importance of such "local" supplies for Japan's military operations against the Allies is obvious.

But even if the worst comes to the worst, the economic advantages of Japan's military ventures may still be nullified by a successful naval and aerial strategy of the Allied forces. With determined aerial attacks on oil targets and a concentration of submarine warfare on the tanker fleet, conditions may change decisively. The experience of England with a tanker fleet manyfold that of Japan has shown that a concentration on tankers by the enemy may prove effective. Loss in carrying capacity through wartime conditions and sinking of tankers may still prove to be the Achilles heel of Japanese oil policy.

If Japan's expansion plans should fail, an immediate collapse through lack of oil alone can by no means be anticipated. It is true, the war might then enter another phase. Japan's military, air and navy operations would be hampered by lack of oil and her military power would lose much of its offensive strength. At the same time her industry would be affected by the lack of good lubricants and transport difficulties. But certain minimum quantities would always be available and it is interesting to note that the Japanese Navy is quite accustomed to the use of domestic tar oils, to the shale oil from Manchuria and to the fuel oil from Sakhalin, all sources relatively safe.

While the conquest of new oil supplies with assured transport connection might solve the Japanese oil problem if her tanker fleet and oil plants remain intact and thereby prolong the war, the failure to do so would weaken decisively the Japanese industrial and military structure and make final victory for her opponents much easier.

3

Axis Launches Desperate Offensive at Allied Oil Sources

In the third of the analyses selected, attention is given to the deepening oil plight facing the Axis powers. Germany's failure to reach the oil of the USSR was critical, for, without those sources, access to the oil of the Middle East was highly unlikely. Nevertheless, the effort to gain access to the Middle East would continue to be made, supported by the effort to interdict Allied oil supply.[1] On the Japanese front, the situation was reversed. Having obtained control over the producing areas of Southeast Asia, Japan's problem (and the Allies' challenge) was to defend long oil lanes against air and especially submarine attack. And finally, the author makes clear, the particular oil vulnerability of China would require exceptional efforts to provide even a minimal supply crucial to its air operations and transport. The magnitude of these challenges was set forth in the following paper.

As the pattern of the war unfolds more clearly it becomes increasingly evident that not only the Axis powers, but also the United Nations, are confronted with a formidable oil problem. While discussion heretofore has centered largely on a possible shortage in Axis countries, too little attention apparently has been devoted to their aggressive oil strategy which aims at depriving the Allies of oil superiority.

As the Axis powers set out on their path of conquest and tried to solve their immediate oil problem by occupation of nearby oil producing

Reprinted with permission from *World Petroleum*, April 1942, pp. 29–34.

1. Before the German push toward Stalingrad, when there was intense debate as to whether the Germans might make Leningrad or Moscow their objective—or move southward—Mr. Levy applied his techniques to studies of the German railroad tariff rates and discovered a new entry covering shipments from Baku. This piece of intelligence helped strengthen the argument that the German objective lay in the direction of the oil fields.   —*Editor*

countries such as Poland and Rumania, they deprived Allied and neutral states of a relatively small part of their former sources of supply. But Axis ambitions are not confined to assuring themselves of a safe and uninterrupted flow of oil for their own operations. They are also actively engaged in an offensive warfare against Allied oil supplies. This warfare plays an important role in their strategy and in their master plan for winning the war. Of the independent Allied nations, Great Britain, China, Australia, New Zealand, and the whole of Africa, except Egypt, are without any domestic oil worth mentioning. India and Burma cover only half of their peacetime demand, and with the exception of the small Sakhalin production, Russia's entire Far Eastern territory must be supplied from the Caucasus, the Urals, or by imports from the United States. In such a situation Axis strategy has followed an obvious course. If Hitler and his confederates could stop the regular flow of oil to the Allied nations they would be able not only to neutralize the potential superiority of their opponents in airplanes, tanks and other machines of war, but could dislocate their industrial and transport system from which tht future superiority most come. Since the entry of the United States into the war such a strategy must have appealed to the Axis leaders even more strongly. They might not be able to compete successfully with the American industrial machine once it was concentrated on war production. But if the war is being fought far outside the main petroleum producing areas, war machines are useless unless sufficient oil for continuous operation is available.

It is not only the interruption of sea communications between the various Allied possessions on which the Nazis and Japanese count. The distribution of oil resources over the world gives them, so they think, a chance to impede or even to stop the flow of oil from producing areas now under Allied control. This would, as they estimate, vastly increase the transport problem by compelling the Allies to ship oil to their possessions from distant producing centers. Until America's entry into the war in December 1941 the Allies obtained their oil from three main producing areas: First, the Western Hemisphere (especially the United States, Northern South America and the Dutch West Indies), with output of 1,761,756,000 bbl., and a refining capacity of 1,990,000,000 bbl., corresponding respectively to 78 percent and 73 percent of the world's total. Second, the Near and Middle East, including [Iran], Iraq, Egypt, Bahrein, Saudi Arabia, and the Russian Caucasus, with a production of 312,060,000 bbl., and a refining capacity of 360,000,000 bbl., corresponding respectively to 13 percent and 13 percent of the world's total. Third, the Far East, comprising the Dutch East Indies, British Borneo, India and Burma and the Russian part of Sakhalin, with an aggregate output of 82,326,000 bbl. and a refining capacity of 83,000,000 bbl., corresponding respectively to 4 percent and 3 percent of the world's totals. What remained in natural oil resources was the small production in Axis controlled countries, mainly Rumania, Germany, Poland, etc., with an output of 56,159,000 bbl., and a refining capacity of 210,000,000 bbl., corresponding respectively to 2 percent and 8 percent of the world's total. We may mention in passing that the large excess refining capacity of the Axis would enable it to treat crude oil from conquered oilfields even if the refineries in or near those fields had been destroyed. When the Allies change from a defensive to an offensive strategy, the Axis oilfields and oil installations, small as they are in world terms, will constitute one of the most important objectives for Allied attacks, the destruction of which may well nigh immobilize the enemy.

We may perhaps classify the first area, the Western Hemisphere, as a "safe" area which will always remain in Allied possession, though attacks by shelling from enemy vessels similar to that directed recently at the Aruba refinery and at California oil installations, by airplanes or by fifth column activity, must always be expected. The most daring and surprising means will doubtless be used to attempt the destruction of some key installations or interruption of operations. But the main efforts of the Axis to interfere with the oil supplies from the Western Hemisphere will be concentrated on the disruption of supply lines as exemplified by the sinking of more than a score of tankers off the East Coast of the United States. It is interesting to note that one of the foremost German oil experts, Dr. Ferdinand Friedensburg, mentioned in a recent book on *Oil in the World War,* that in the struggle of 1914 to 1918, the German General Staff devoted insufficient attention to Allied oil supplies. The Gulf of Mexico, he pointed out, would have been one of the most fruitful hunting grounds for submarines which were, however, concentrated on other sea lanes — a mistake which certainly would not be repeated. Since the outbreak of war many German high-command reports have mentioned specifically that tankers have been singled out for Nazi attack while press notices have announced an impending shortage of oil in Allied countries — interesting indications of German aspirations and hopes.

As far as the Far Eastern area is concerned, it was, of course, well known to the Allies that it would be difficult to defend in case of war with Japan, and it is not surprising that practically all of it has been lost in less than 3 months. This conquest by Japan represents the successful execution of a long cherished, well prepared plan, on which the whole future of Nipponese war economy was staked. What its loss means to the supplies of Allied territories in that part of the world will be discussed later on.

But the second area, the Near and Middle East, cannot also be qualified as a completely safe Allied possession. Here it is Germany that must be watched. Nazi intentions in regard to the oil of the Near and Middle East are well known, and expansion towards these regions is an old German dream unsuccessfully attempted in the war of 1914–18. The Libyan campaign with its changing fortunes, and the struggle in Southern Russia may be regarded as preliminaries to a final show-down. Aside from the effect which control of these areas might have on the oil situation of the Axis, it is worth considering the bearing which such an attempt, successful or not, may have on Allied oil supplies. It is to be hoped that Allied strategy in this area will not confine itself to emergency measures after the event, but will be directed to anticipating and forestalling the plans of the enemy. Even if the Axis fails to conquer these territories they may very well become a battle zone, and the oilfields and refining installations may have to be destroyed as a precautionary measure, transport may become impossible or other events may occur which would temporarily deprive the Allies of their use. It is worthy of note that the Nazis may first try to conquer or interrupt operations only in one or two of the oil producing countries of the Near and Middle East; but they will scarcely be able to utilize these conquests fully without assuring sea communications from the oilfields to Italy or Southern Europe. In the case of the Caucasus, this would mean control of the Black Sea, the Dardanelles, and the Eastern Mediterranean, while in the case of Persia they would have to be able to ship their oil via the Suez Canal and the Mediterranean. It is thus more than likely that the Nazis, once successful, will spread their attacks over a large part of the Near and Middle East including all the important oilfields.

Near and Middle East oilfields are the most suitable bases of supply for Allied possessions in Asia, Oceania, and East and South Africa. Of the producers in that part of the world, Iraq sent the bulk of its oil to European countries before the war, mainly to France, and a smaller part to England, Italy and Spain. Shortly after the outbreak of hostilities, however, the new refinery of Haifa started operations so that the Eastern Mediterranean area drew from then onwards a proportion of its oil from Iraq. Until 1939 [Iran] shipped over 50 percent of its export to England, Germany, and other European countries. With the beginning of the war, and especially after the entry of Italy into the fight, transport via the Suez Canal and through the Mediterranean became too dangerous, and the way around the Cape of Good Hope was too long to be practicable with the restricted transport capacity at hand. A reduction in output thus became necessary in the case of [Iran], as well as that of other producers, but as no official statistics are now published, exact data are not available. The only relevant point is that up to now as much oil as required was available in a geographical and strategically favorable position for the bases in Asia, Africa, and Oceania. Its importance for Allied

naval and merchant operations in these seas and for military requirements for the campaign in Libya and for the building up of an army
in the Near and Middle East can scarcely be exaggerated. The fact that
Britain occupied Iraq, Syria, and [Iran] (the latter in collaboration with
Russia), during the second half of 1941 is proof enough of the Allied
determination to maintain control over these territories. This Allied occupation put the oil production, which was mainly owned by British,
Dutch and American companies, in these countries under Allied supervi-
sion. All the necessary measures for defense against an Axis invasion
could then be taken. The final conquest of Eritrea and Abyssinia served
to protect the flank of this vital region and to deprive the Axis of bases
from which it might have been possible to launch attacks on the
transport routes and oil targets of the East. German attempts to conquer
Caucasian oil areas before winter set in were finally frustrated by the
unexpected Russian resistance.

Thus far it has been possible to keep the Near and Middle Eastern area
and its strategic approaches under Allied control. Even the fact that oil
from this area has been shut off almost completely from the United
Kingdom since the early stages of the war is without great strategic importance, for the Western Hemisphere is as convenient a source as [Iran]
or Iraq. Germany, it is true, had banked on the fact that Britain, compelled to buy her oil in America, would not possess sufficient foreign
resources to acquire petroleum stocks; but Lease-Lend shattered these
expectations. In the meantime Allied countries outside Europe and the
Western Hemisphere have continued to obtain most of their oil from the
Near and Middle East, with the exception of Oceania, which depended
largely on the Dutch East Indies, now lost, and India, which received a
large part of her requirements from Burma.

. . . Japan will not benefit immediately from its Eastern oil conquests
but may be able to replace the 20,000,000 to 30,000,000 bbl. previously
imported annually from the Western Hemisphere at some indefinite date
in the future, if allowed an opportunity to restore the East Indian fields
and provide sufficient transport capacity. The position of the Far
Eastern countries still in Allied possession is perhaps more difficult.
They imported in 1939 a total of 59,525,000 bbl. of which 21,619,000
bbl. came from the Near and Middle East, 28,836,000 bbl. from the Far
East, and 5,976,000 bbl. from the Western Hemisphere. While sufficient
oil is available in the Americas to replace the imports from the Far East,
and if need by those from the Near and Middle East, the loss of refining
capacity, especially for aviation gasoline in Netherlands India, is a
serious blow and difficulties may arise in replacing the output of other
products, as, for instance, that of [Iranian] fuel oil. More serious would
be the increased demand on tanker capacity if Oceania, India, or Africa

should have to depend completely on supplies from the East or West Coast of America, and if armies and navies in those areas had to depend on these same supplies. It would not be an easy task to maintain sea communications without proper bases and in waters infested by enemy raiders. The distance from the United States West Coast to Australia is 6,966 miles, compared with 3,800 miles from the Dutch East Indies, or 7,550 miles from [Iran]. It is worth mentioning that even last year the strained tanker position compelled Australia to import more oil from the Dutch East Indies, and less from [Iran].

It is this question of transport capacity and maintaining communications on which the oil problem, as practically all other supply problems, hinges. It is on interruption of communication that Germany bases her hopes for piecemeal invasion and conquest. Actually Axis attacks on tankers now must be looked upon as part and parcel of a comprehensive plan to dislocate Allied supply lines and even as preparation for land attacks on the oil centers of the Near and Middle East. Only if the Allies should be unable to replace the oil shipments from these countries could the Axis hope to benefit to the fullest extent from an eventual conquest of these territories. The Axis undoubtedly has learned a lesson from blunders it committed in the first phase of the war. At that time they might have been able to prevent so large a proportion of the then neutral tanker fleet from passing into the service of the British. In the meantime, they have learned that the clue to the Allied oil position is the question of sufficient transport capacity and maintenance of sea communications and they are fully aware of the effect which a conquest of Allied supply bases must ultimately have on the shipping position.

To prevent the United Nations' petroleum outlook from suffering critical deterioration it is evident that the oilfields of the Near and Middle East and of the Caucasus must be held at all costs. It would not be sufficient to destroy these fields, merely depriving the Axis of immediate use of this oil; continuous supply of petroleum products from the refineries at Abadan, Haifa and Bahrein is almost as essential to the Allies as it would be to the Axis. Their problem is thus to make good the actual loss of the Far East fields and to prepare for any emergency which might or might not arise in the Near and Middle East.

The country in the most difficult position is probably China. Less than 10,000 bbl. of gasoline a year are produced locally. After the loss of Rangoon the only remaining important line of supply is the North West Road, originating at Sergiobal on the branch of the trans-Siberian Railway and running some 2,000 miles through Sinkiang, Kansu, and Shansi to Chungking. A new highway from India's Assam province to Sikang is still under construction. Every drop of oil that can be spared in Russia or India and for which transport can be found presumably will be dispatched over these routes. The United Nations in the meantime can send oil to those two countries from which China may still be supplied. From a military viewpoint the vital importance to the United Nations of protecting the oil of the Caucasus and the Near East is evident from a glance at a map. Naval and land operations to reclaim the territory already lost and to attain final victory over the Axis powers must extend over a vast area and be maintained for an indefinite period of time. It will be far easier to fuel Allied ships from the Persian Gulf or the oil ports of the Eastern Mediterranean than from across two broad oceans. There is a great and obvious advantage in producing as much as possible of the aviation gasoline and other products required by planes and ships at Near East refineries instead of attempting to bring all of these essential war materials from the opposite side of the globe. Aside from the hazards of these long ocean voyages it is questionable whether transport capacity exists or can be provided quickly enough to sustain a prolonged offensive on the scale that obviously will be required.

In addition to protecting the all-important oil resources of the Near East which [the Allies] still hold and in addition to moving supplies to Britain, Russia and China in support of their war effort, large stocks need to be built up in selected and well-protected parts of Asia, Africa, and Oceania to compensate as well as possible for actual and threatened loss of supply sources and transport connections. Australia, New Zealand and South Africa received in 1939 over 18,000,000 bbl. from the now lost Dutch East Indies and British Borneo, while India's imports of over 5,000,000 bbl. from Burma are also interrupted by now. Another 15,700,000 bbl. went to these 4 countries from the Near and Middle East, while the Western Hemisphere participated in their supply with only 4,800,000 bbl. Domestic production of shale oil, motor alcohol and benzol in Australia is less than 500,000 bbl., or 3 percent of total imports, while India proper had an output of 2,270,000 bbl. in 1941. South Africa possesses some torbanite deposits though developed only on a small scale, while New Zealand is bare of any oil resources. The building up of large stocks in all of these countries is a precaution that cannot be neglected.

Allied resources should be still adequate to fulfill such a task if non-essential requirements were curtailed everywhere. This curtailment . . . is not necessary on account of lack of producing capacity. It is necessary in order to release sufficient tanker space for the transport of oil to the countries and bases in need. The reason for rationing in America is thus not the development of stocks on the Atlantic Coast or the Western Pacific area, but the level of reserves available in all the various United Nations. That the United States is aware of its responsibility toward the common cause is shown by the fact that rationing methods already have been instituted on the advice of the oil industry itself. Such a measure of strategic distribution of sufficient oil supplies over the various Allied nations should further be accompanied by an absolute cessation of all unessential uses of petroleum products in every country to which oil must be brought over perilous transport routes. The United States has a duty and a right to insist on such an economy.

Allied strategy to counter Axis efforts to disrupt the oil supplies of the United Nations is just emerging from a period of transition. In the first phase of the war, too much dependence was placed on an anticipated oil shortage in the Axis countries, while at the same time insufficient efforts were made to destroy their source of supply. Attacks on Axis oil sources will still form a part of the Allied campaign since they will be directed at one of the greatest weaknesses in Germany's and Italy's economic armament. But in this study we have been less concerned with this phase of economic warfare than with the necessary counter measures against Axis attacks on Allied oil supplies.

Successful defense of the oil-producing possessions of the United Nations is of first importance. Plans for the destruction of facilities in areas that cannot be defended have their place. But the purely negative measure of depriving the Axis of the potential benefits of its conquests is no longer sufficient. The United Nations must provide the replacement of lost raw material resources over increasingly dangerous and lengthening routes. In order to avoid possible shortages it is essential to accumulate large stocks at all strategic points within the theatre of future military operations. Other Allied countries can help by developing domestic resources wherever possible and restricting consumption to absolutely essentials. In the Western Hemisphere the oil industry is devoting its full energies to supplying the sinews of war for national and Allied needs, and Americans are prepared to undergo whatever restriction this program may involve, recognizing that the primary necessity is to maintain the supply of oil at all points it is needed for the utmost prosecution of the war.

Part 2

OIL AND POSTWAR RECOVERY

Introduction

The elements in the wartime oil situation and the requisite strategies to cope with shortages had thus been laid out, with explicit indications of the course which the Atlantic and Pacific campaigns would have to adopt to maximize pressures upon the Axis powers. In these accounts, the author was careful not to bestow upon oil a supreme importance. Outstanding military achievements and defeats, the vast increase in U.S. and Canadian war production, the gradual victory over German submarines, and the achievement of air superiority were all crucial factors in determining Allied strategy; so, too, were the extraordinary efforts of the Russian people to hold back German attack. In the Pacific the slow collapse of the Japanese island strategy, increasing attrition of Japan's tanker fleet, and the achievement, everywhere, of Allied air superiority were among the vital factors leading to victory.

But oil was an essential ingredient in all these events, as it indisputably was a key factor in the unfolding of strategies on both sides. World War II could have been lost for any of many reasons; deprivation of oil was surely one reason because its sheer availability to Allies was a prime reason for their victory. As in World War I, the Allies demonstrated again what their enemies already knew but could not deal with despite staggering efforts: Access to oil was instrumental to Allied victory. Another aspect which became especially significant in World War II was the growing interest in supply from the prolific fields of the Middle East—a harbinger, in effect, of the sudden and accelerating interest to burgeon over the next decades, dwarfing the strategic importance of all other oil-exporting regions. To this phenomenon, the author turned his attention next.

4

Middle Eastern Oil as an Objective of World Power

The U.S. National War College is the senior educational institution of the Department of Defense and, as such, invites leading authorities to discuss topics of high importance to the security of the United States.[1] The college welcomes diversity of views — and has long encouraged the broadening of the defense agenda to include discussion of new issues or trends that will be among the professional concerns of the armed forces in the years ahead. Consequently, the remarks of Walter Levy on the strategic consequences of Middle East oil were considered to be important indicators of the future, as indeed they proved to be. In this single paper, delivered January 22, 1947, are to be found the issues whose increasing complexity and importance have come to engage the many interests of virtually all nations.

At the time the lecture was delivered, the strains of World War II were far from eased. The economic plight of Europe and the requirements for its recovery were of deepening concern; moreover, it was now becoming clear to a broader group of Americans that the role of the Soviet Union in international affairs was certain to be a major, long-term challenge to the United States and its wartime allies. Some six months after the National War College lecture General George C. Marshall, then secretary of state in the administration of President Harry S Truman, enunciated what became famous as the Truman Doctrine — the first comprehensive call for support of states threatened by the actions of the USSR. The cold war was well underway. In 1947 the focus was largely on the threshold of the Near and Middle East, the border region between Iran and the USSR, on Greece, and on Turkey. The oil interests of the Allies, and of the Soviet Union, were defined in the lecture.

But in addition to those remarks, Mr. Levy opened a subject which had long been known privately to a few people in government and in the international oil industry. This was the sometimes close connections

---

Lecture given at the National War College, Washington, D.C., January 22, 1947.

1. The National War College and the Industrial College of the Armed Forces are now parts of the U.S. National Defense University.   — *Editor*

between oil companies and their host governments—especially in the case of Great Britain, France, and the United States—and the questions that were likely to arise as the importance of oil in the economies of states would impinge upon a broad array of national interests. Sometimes these interests would be linked closely to the interests of the oil industry, but they might not always be. Knowledge of these national interests and an awareness of the distinction between the public and private sectors was critical. Mr. Edward S. Mason, a leading U.S. Government adviser, noted that Mr. Levy was able to "present an objective view that not infrequently varied from the interested position of other experts." Still, in the lecture, the audience was told that we had "not yet succeeded in finding a completely satisfactory solution to the problem of controlling the complex relationship between private commercial activities [of the oil companies] and foreign political and economic policy." The ramifications of these relationships have shaped, in very large part, the history of international oil; the rise in influence over oil by governments in the producing and consuming countries was foreseen and particular attention was drawn to this phenomenon.

Why concentrate on the Middle East in the lecture? In 1947 it still was not apparent to many with policy responsibilities that the wartime importance of Middle East supply would be followed by an extraordinary expansion in the region's peacetime role in fueling industrial societies or that Western Hemisphere sources (the Caribbean region and the United States) and the USSR as principal suppliers of oil in world trade would be eclipsed by the vast and prolific fields of the Middle East. A profound transformation in the geopolitics of oil was already beginning.

I. The Statistical Position of Middle Eastern Oil

Middle Eastern oil has played an important role in the world oil picture since World War I when Iranian oil production was developed, mainly for the use of the British Navy. But only during the last fifteen years, following the development of Iraq oil, the discovery of oil in Saudi Arabia, Kuwait, Qatar, Bahrein, and other areas was it realized that the oil reserves of the Middle East are probably larger than those found hitherto anywhere else. The development of these resources poses difficult political, economic, and social problems for the world powers interested in these resources through concessions of their nationals, for the countries where the oil is produced, and for the nations dependent on supplies from the Middle East.

To comprehend the importance of Middle Eastern oil resources as an objective of world power it is necessary to survey in broad lines the recent course of world petroleum production and requirements and to indicate future developments.

In 1938, the last full prewar year, total world production of petroleum was 5,485,000 barrels daily, of which 335,000 barrels daily or 6.1 percent were produced in the Middle East, mainly in Iraq and Iran, 4,173,000 barrels daily or 76.2 percent were produced in the Western Hemisphere, and 590,000 barrels daily or 10.6 percent were produced in Russia. In 1945 total production had increased to 7 million barrels daily, of which the Middle East was supplying 7.5 percent or 540,000 barrels, while the output in the Western Hemisphere had reached 5,946,000 barrels daily, and Russian production had declined to about 400,000 barrels daily. The bulk of United Nations petroleum supplies during the war and no less than 90 percent of the additional requirements caused by the war were obtained from Western Hemisphere sources. Nevertheless Middle Eastern oil has contributed a great deal to the winning of World War II. From these fields the British 8th, 9th, 10th and 14th Armies, the Mediterranean and Indian fleets, the U.S. 9th, 14th and 20th Air Force, the U.S. Eastern Bomber Command at Poltava, the Persian Gulf Command, the African and Middle East Service Command, and the China, India, Burma Air Transport Command obtained the bulk of their requirements. In addition, considerable quantities of 100 octane and motor gasoline were supplied from Middle Eastern refineries to the USSR, and the civilian consumption in India, and Middle East, and in large parts of Africa were satisfied from the same sources.

The Middle East derives its great importance in the future balance of world petroleum supplies and requirements from the tremendous size of its proven and semiproven reserves, which according to present plans will be translated into vastly increased annual production in the very near future. Fewer than two hundred exploratory wells have been drilled in the entire area, or not even one-twentieth of the number of wildcat wells drilled annually in the United States; but the size of proven reserves in the Middle East, about 27 billion barrels or 40 percent of the world's proven reserves of 66 billion barrels, is nearly as large as that of the whole Western Hemisphere, and many favorable locations are yet to be tested by the drill. In view of likely further discoveries the reserve figures presented here are subject to continuous changes and must be used only with this qualification in mind. If the trend of new oil discoveries in the Western Hemisphere should not rise sharply, total petroleum requirements of the New World will, in the near future, approach the level of its anticipated production. Ignoring the relatively small production in the Far East and elsewhere, the bulk of petroleum requirements of Europe, excluding the USSR, of Africa, Asia, and Oceania must then be supplied from the Middle East. If Russia should need large supplies additional to its domestic production — a question to which we will revert later — she too must rely on Middle Eastern sources. This, in short, is the statistical picture for Middle Eastern oil.

II. Political Power and Corporate Control
Over Middle Eastern Oil

Another important aspect of the power problems caused by Middle Eastern oil is the ownership control of these oil resources. The development of oil production in the Middle East involves the opening up of hitherto completely undeveloped areas and requires tremendous capital investments. This factor limits the number of corporations which could successfully undertake such developments. It is also responsible for the extraordinary size of the individual concessions because only large concessions can compensate companies for the risks involved. The only big international oil groups in the world were and are British, Dutch, or American controlled, and accordingly, they obtained practically all the concessions of the Middle East. The French participation and the division of the various concessions between British and American interests has been influenced, as will be explained later, by political factors.

Two British, five American, and one French company, plus a small private holding, control the known oil resources of the Middle East. The British share in presently known, proven reserves amounts to about 53 percent, that of the United States to 41 percent, and that of the French to 5 percent.

The Iraq Petroleum Company (usually called the IPC), a joint company in which the Anglo-Iranian Oil Company, the Royal Dutch–Shell Group, the Compagnie Française des Petroles, and the Near East Development Corporation each own 23.75 percent and Mr. Gulbenkian owns 5 percent, holds concessions covering the whole of Iraq and large parts of Syria, Lebanon, Palestine, Cyprus, and of several Persian Gulf sheikdoms. Its proven and semiproven reserves exceed 6 billion barrels. The Near East Development Corporation is an American company in which the Standard Oil Company of New Jersey and the Socony Vacuum Oil Company each own one-half interest. The same group, the Jersey company and Socony, are now negotiating for a 30 and 10 percent participation, respectively, in the Arabian-American Oil Company, or Aramco, a corporation which up to now has been controlled 50 percent by the Standard Oil Company of California and 50 percent by the Texas Company. Aramco owns the Saudi Arabian concession with proven and semiproven reserves of probably over 5 billion barrels. The same American interests control the Bahrein Oil Company with less than one-half billion barrels reserves. The Anglo-Iranian Oil Company has a concession in southern Iran with some 6.5 billion barrels reserve and a 50 percent interest in the Kuwait Oil Company, the other 50 percent of which is owned by the American Gulf Oil Company. The proven and semiproven reserves of the Kuwait Oil Company have been estimated at 9 billion barrels.

The various international oil companies are commercial corporations organized as stock holding companies in Great Britain, the United States and France with a commercial behavior generally similar to that of any other private company. It is noteworthy, however, that the most important British company interested in Middle Eastern oil, the Anglo-Iranian Oil Company, and the French Compagnie Française des Petroles are controlled by the British and the French governments, respectively, with the two governments claiming supervisory functions and special veto rights over their policies. It is of particular interest to summarize the reasons given by Mr. Winston Churchill in the House of Commons in 1914 for the acquisition of a government majority interest in the Anglo-Iranian Oil Company. He stated at that time that it would have been easy to sit still and observe the whole world being woven into one or two great oil combinations, to treat these combinations with utmost consideration, to buy oil for British naval requirements from hand to mouth in the so-called open market, and to pay the great oil trusts what they would consider an encouraging price. But it was up to Parliament to balance the moderate element of a fair commercial risk which is inseparable from any business enterprise against the certainty of overcharge which follows a monopoly. Two gigantic oil corporations, Mr. Churchill continued, stood out predominantly in the world's oil industry. It was their policy to acquire control over sources and means of supply and then to regulate production and market prices. The Admiralty could not afford to be dependent for vital supplies upon a few large corporations whose interests were necessarily cosmopolitan and financial. At least one British company should be maintained with independent control over considerable supplies. The British Navy would continue to draw from many sources, for its dependence on Iran alone would not be wholly satisfactory, but control over the Anglo-Iranian Oil Company would provide protection against natural and artificial restrictions of supply.

The British and French governments jointly with private investors have therefore a direct interest in Middle Eastern oil. In addition, the British Navy has entered into a special supply contract with the Anglo-Iranian [Oil Company], and the French Government is entitled to claim for its own needs a large part of the output of the Compagnie Française des Petroles. The Russian Government will probably acquire similar interests in northern Iran if its negotiations for a concession should be successful. The United States participation consists exclusively in private investments, but the attempt of the government-controlled Petroleum Reserve Corporation during the latter part of the war to buy into the Saudi Arabian concession, or at least to obtain some control over the proposed pipeline to the Mediterranean, indicates U.S. governmental concern over Middle Eastern oil. Moreover, the United States Navy has important supply contracts with the Arabian-American Oil Company, although it is not entitled to any privileges similar to those enjoyed by the British and French governments in their companies.

The oil companies interested in the Middle East represent American and British investments not only in that area where, with the development of production, many hundred millions of dollars must be invested and where their assets in proven oil reserves constitute values of many billions of dollars, but in practically every other country of the world. There is no country, except the USSR, and a few minor markets in Latin America, where the bulk of the nation's oil supply, refining, and marketing is not largely handled by subsidiaries of at least one of the American and one of the British oil groups, and where the subsidiaries in turn do not belong to the largest and financially most powerful corporations of their respective countries.

For all these reasons, many activities of these corporations, even though their motives and performance may follow normal commercial lines, have implications on our foreign political and economic policy, on our security, on our relationships to other countries, and on the political and economic well-being of those countries. With economic units of such importance, government involvement of some kind or other in their foreign activities and, in fact, government responsibility for many of their actions cannot be avoided. It matters not whether the flag follows the commerce or the commerce follows the flag. In any case the flag will be there.

III. Political Power and the Acquisition and Exploitation of Middle Eastern Oil Concessions

A short survey of the political and diplomatic background of the various Middle Eastern concessions will further illustrate the peculiar intertwining between commercial and political operations that characterizes Middle Eastern oil and perhaps international oil.

The world's largest concentration of oil reserves on which most countries outside the Western Hemisphere must rely for their supplies are located in politically, socially, and economically weak countries. Great Britain has treaty rights and mandatory powers in that area and is interested in securing the British lifeline to India. Russia enjoyed important privileges in Iran under the Czars and has for likely defensive as well as offensive reasons a continuing interest in establishing herself in this area and in obtaining warm-water outlets to the Persian Gulf and the Mediterranean. France, whose ties with the Levant go back to the Crusades, was, up to World War II, one of the important mandatory powers. The United States had obtained the right to equality of treatment by special agreements with the mandatory powers and by her insistence on the Open Door policy and nondiscrimination.

The acquisition of concessions by the various British, American, and French companies cannot therefore easily be disassociated from political factors, treaty rights, and other governmental influence, and cannot in fact be judged solely as resulting from the unimpeded competition between private commercial corporations. The political and diplomatic conflicts centering around the acquisition of Middle Eastern concessions show this clearly. The oldest concession, that of the Anglo-Iranian Oil Company, was obtained in 1901 for an area where British political influence was predominant. When the Shah cancelled this concession in 1932, the case was brought before the Council of the League of Nations and was finally resolved by the granting of a new concession in 1933. The new agreement was more favorable to Iran than the old D'Arcy concession. Iran dared risk this cancellation only because she felt confident that her request for new and more favorable terms, if balanced against the precarious British-Russian balance of power in Iran and against whatever influence the League of Nations was able to exercise at that time, would prove acceptable to the British.

In 1943, when Iran was occupied by Britain and Russia, the Standard Vacuum approached the Iranian Government for a concession in southeastern Iran, closely followed by bids of the Sinclair Oil Company, the Shell Oil Company, and reportedly the Standard Oil of California and the Texas Company. While negotiations were still proceeding the Russians approached the Iranian government with a request for a concession in northern Iran extending over 200,000 square miles. Iran then ceased all negotiations and passed a law in 1944 prohibiting all government officials from negotiating oil concessions, reserving this right to the Iranian Parliament.

The story of oil concessions in northern Iran is a further illustration of the relationship between oil and political power. It would take too much time to discuss in detail the various attempts made by American, British, and Dutch companies to obtain and operate concessions in that area. None of these attempts proved ultimately successful, largely for political reasons. As far as Russia is concerned, the czarist regime had established a zone of influence in northern Iran, formalized by the 1907 agreement with Great Britain, and had obtained a number of mining and other concessions. In 1921 the new Bolshevik government formally renounced all Russian concessions in Iran, but stipulated that these concessions should not be transferred to any other interest. In April 1946, finally, in spite of the above mentioned law and obviously not unconnected with the negotiations on the Russian troop withdrawal from Iran, a Russian-Iranian agreement for a joint oil company was announced. A detailed agreement was to be submitted to the Iranian Parliament for ratification before October 24, 1946. As, however, elections to the parliament are just now taking place the agreement has not been ratified.

In Iraq where the predecessor of the Iraq Petroleum Company had acquired incomplete concession rights from the Turkish government shortly before the outbreak of World War I, Great Britain was the mandatory power when the concession was finally granted in 1925.

The American participation in the Iraq Petroleum Company was obtained only after strong protests by the State Department to the British Government, which had originally obtained a 75 percent interest for British companies, allocating to the French in the San Remo Agreement of 1920 the former German share of 25 percent. At that time the United States government insisted on the application of the Open Door principle, urging that every interested party should be entitled to bid for concessions and obtain them if, other conditions being equal, its bid was the most favorable one for the producing country. No monopolistic concession, and no concession covering all the oil resources of a mandated country, should be given to a single party. In line with the Open Door policy, the original IPC concession of 1925 provided that the IPC would obtain directly for itself only a very small concession of 192 square miles and would be obliged to auction off to the highest bidder each year additional parts of the defined area. Subsequently, however, the original State Department policy was somewhat lost sight of. By 1931 and for a variety of reasons the obligation to auction off concession areas was cancelled and an exclusive concession was granted to the IPC, covering an area of 32,000 square miles in the Provinces of Baghdad and Mosul. Further concessions covering the remaining areas of Iraq were obtained in 1937 and 1938. In addition, the IPC acquired oil rights in Syria, Palestine, Cyprus, and other areas of the Middle East, and now controls oil concessions extending over 373,000 square miles.

In three Middle Eastern areas, in Saudi Arabia, Bahrein, and Kuwait, American companies outside of the IPC were able to obtain valuable concessions. In Bahrein and Kuwait, as in other Persian Gulf sheikdoms, Great Britain had treaty rights concerning their defense, their foreign relations, and the granting of oil concessions. Standard Oil of California obtained a concession for Bahrein in 1930 only after protracted negotiations between the American and British governments. Prior to the grant of the concession the Bahrein Oil Company was forced to sign a political agreement with the British government, whose main points were as follows: (a) the company would always remain British, with an office in Great Britain under a British subject as channel of communications to the British government; (b) one director, at least, was to be British and must be approved by the British government; (c) the local representative in Bahrein must be British and must be the only channel of communication to the Bahrein government; (d) as many employees as possible must be British or subjects of Bahrein; (e) the company promises to submit to the influence of the British government and to the wishes of the Sheik and the British political agent; (f) the concession can only be transferred with the approval of the British government; (g) in times of emergency, the company will cooperate with the government, and the government can take over the production of the company at a fair price and can request the company to produce fuel oil for the British Navy; (h) the Sheik is entitled to terminate the concession if the company violates the political agreement.

In Kuwait the Gulf Oil Company obtained an option for a concession. But again the British Government intervened on the basis of its treaty rights and after long negotiations, involving also the State Department, the Gulf Company acquired the concession jointly with the Anglo-Iranian Oil Company. The British Government also insisted on the conclusion of a political agreement similar to that described for Bahrein. Added to this, and designed to protect certain commercial interests of the Anglo-Iranian Oil Company, was an agreement between the American and British partners according to which none of the Kuwait oil should be sold by either partner in countries where the other partner had a market position which might be upset or injured directly or indirectly through such sales.

In Saudi Arabia, too, the British had originally veto rights over the granting of foreign oil concessions, but these rights were cancelled when the country's independence was confirmed by the British in the Treaty of Jeddah of 1927. King Abdul Aziz Ibn Saud, who for political reasons preferred American interests to British ones, granted a large concession to Standard Oil of California in 1932 without any direct political pressure or interference of the United States or any other government.

Most of the Middle Eastern oil concessions were therefore obtained by the various companies only after diplomatic intervention of their governments. While Britain, France, and Russia exercised direct political power and control over this area, the main instrument of United States policy has been the insistence on the Open Door principle and on non-discrimination. Even where American companies obtained concessions, Britain was able to protect her interests by special political agreements with the companies, except in the case of Saudi Arabia, where Britain enjoyed no special privileges. Any grant of an Iranian concession to Russia would be closely associated with the political relations between the two countries, and may well provide the basis for Russian political and economic penetration.

The freedom of most of the countries of the Middle East as far as the granting of oil concessions is concerned has therefore in fact been limited by their political dependence on the big powers. But it must not be overlooked that as a consequence of this very dependence on Great Britain and other Western nations, reasonably stable and peaceful conditions could be established in this area without which no large-scale economic developments could have taken place. These countries would most likely have been unable either to develop their oil resources themselves or to establish a pattern of development by foreign corporations without outside help. The only chance for the improvement of economic and social conditions in the Middle East rests in the development of its natural resources; and it is obvious that in organizing such developments the Western powers will also obtain benefits for themselves. The United States' Open Door principle must be judged accordingly. It is unlikely that this principle was meant to imply that the governments carrying the political responsibility for certain areas should be obliged to throw open the resources of these areas for exploitation by any nation or corporation without considering political factors. On the other hand, the State Department's policy certainly exercised a moderating influence on the use by the mandatory powers of political influence to achieve economic aims. In particular, it prevented a complete monopoly for the exploitation of these resources by any one nation, assured reasonably equitable terms to the local governments, and last but not least, procured a participation, if not for the world at large, at least for American interests.

IV. The Oil Concession Pattern in the Middle East

The actual pattern for producing concessions in the Middle East follows in broad outlines the revised 1931 IPC concession. This concession was as favorable to the country concerned as could be expected, particularly in view of the investment risks involved for the oil companies.

In general, producing concessions are granted for the whole country or sheikdom or for a major part of the territory. They provide for dead rents until production is obtained and established. Usually, the royalty amounts to four shillings gold per ton. The rates are, however, somewhat lower in most of the sheikdoms and size of the return to the country is probably not completely unrelated to the degree of its political independence. The oil companies are usually exempt from all obligations to pay taxes, import duties, etc., against some compensatory payments, usually related to the tonnage of crude oil produced. Oil companies are also exempt from the foreign exchange regulations of the producing countries, are entitled to build communications, and to use government lands and building materials at nominal fees. They are usually obliged to supply domestic requirements somewhat below the world market price.

Pipeline and refining concessions in countries through which oil from producing countries must flow before it can be marketed also follow the IPC pattern. Originally, the San Remo Agreement between France and Great Britain committed France to grant free transit rights for Iraq oil through the mandated territories under her control. Great Britain granted similar privileges for the shipment of Iraq oil through Transjordan and Palestine, which were under her mandate. The resulting lack of direct returns to these countries was criticized by members of the Permanent Mandate Commission in 1931. The U.S. government has recently taken the position that existing and future pipeline and refining concessions in Middle Eastern countries should reflect full recognition of the principle that countries which contribute in any way to the development and commercialization of petroleum resources should receive fair and reasonable compensation for such contribution. Accordingly, the Arabian-American Oil Company has agreed to pay transit fees to Transjordan and Lebanon in its pipeline concession of 1946, though American companies were entitled to the same privileges in mandated and former mandated countries as those given to British and French corporations.

Present concession terms are in many respects more favorable to the producing countries than those included in the first D'Arcy concession in Iran (then Persia), and are in general not inequitable and in line with the general concession pattern in that area. Nevertheless, it is likely that with the political and social advances which these countries will be making, largely as a result of the development of their oil resources by foreign concession holders, the concessionaire will be subject to increasing pressure to grant more favorable conditions in line with the terms prevalent in advanced and politically stable countries.

V. Political and Economic Effects of Oil Concessions on Middle Eastern Countries

The stability of concessions is to no small extent dependent on the general support and interest of the producing countries in the activities of the foreign concession holder. The oil companies are usually the biggest or even the only large scale industrial enterprise in the country.

By 1950, the royalty income from total Middle Eastern production will have increased to between 100 and 150 million dollars and provide a major if not the main source of income for Iran, Iraq, Saudi Arabia, Kuwait, and Qatar.

The labor force needed by the oil companies will greatly increase. At present the Anglo-Iranian Oil Company employs some 55,000 industrial workers in Iran or 30 percent of the country's total labor force. The Kuwait Oil Company will probably absorb over 90 percent of all available labor in Kuwait.

The economic, social, and governmental structure of the Middle East is at present not able to cope with all the problems caused by modern industrial development. This becomes a serious problem the moment large Western industrial enterprises enter such countries. The companies similar to the East Indian Trading Companies of centuries ago are forced, whether alone or through and with their governments, to concern themselves with the political and economic development of these areas. But with the growing independence of these countries, increasing local opposition against the rights and power of foreign concession holders must be anticipated. It would be extremely shortsighted if because of this threat the companies and their governments would use their influence to maintain the status quo rather than to obtain the willing cooperation of the producing country by following a most enlightened and progressive policy.

I want to mention one further problem, that of labor unrest, because of its importance to the stability of concessions. Obviously, no provisions in concession contracts could prohibit strikes. But strikes stop oil production as surely as the cancellation of concessions or physical occupation of oil fields by an enemy force. The recent strikes in Iran and Iraq actually cut British-controlled oil production by nearly 50 percent. They interrupted oil supplies to the British Navy and to the Empire, and if they had lasted much longer, they might have immobilized the British Navy and the British economy. These strikes were beyond doubt instigated by the left-wing Tudeh party which made skillful use of labor's unrest caused by complaints over insufficient wages, lack of housing and of other facilities, conditions which because of the war could not have been improved even with the best will in the world.

As you will recall, Indian troops were sent to Basrah on the occasion of the last Iranian strike in the summer of 1946. British officials stated at that time that should the strikes result in danger to British life and property their troops might have to be used without consulting the Security Council of the United Nations in advance, and a long-drawn-out strike would have surely resulted in damage to property and danger to British life.

Nothing perhaps could illustrate more clearly the interconnections between the operations of the oil industry in Iran and the political relations between Iran and Great Britain, the economic and military security of Great Britain, and the maintenance of peace in Iran and perhaps in the world.

We have discussed the power problems connected with the acquisition and exploitation of Middle Eastern oil and have tried to describe the close relationship between economic and political activities in this particular field. We may perhaps now underline the economic and security aspects of Middle Eastern oil for the various countries, taking account of the changed postwar power relationship between the various nations.

VI. Middle Eastern Oil as a Factor in Great Britain's Power Position and Security

The political control which Great Britain historically exercised over this area has been challenged not only by the growing independence movement in the Middle East, but also by Russia's emergence as one of the Big Three, if not of the Big Two. Russia's aspirations are well known. Militarily, Great Britain might never have been able to protect large parts of the Middle East against direct surprise attacks from the north. Churchill in his above quoted 1914 speech appeared to have been of this opinion. But Britain's position in Europe and her alliances with France and Russia were designed to deter any aggressor. Under present conditions Great Britain must, if possible, seek alliances which will also assure the protection of the Middle East. One means through which she might hope to achieve this is by actively promoting a community of interests with the United States. Great Britain therefore now appears to welcome United States oil interests in this area. Further protection is sought through her support of the United Nations organization.

But under present circumstances and as long as the intentions of the USSR are unknown, Great Britain cannot count on the continued availability of Middle Eastern oil in times of war. Even if physical control over these areas could be maintained, it is likely that oil facilities such as the Abadan refinery will be inoperable and that transportation by tanker out of the Persian Gulf or by pipeline to the Mediterranean will be subject to serious interruptions.

By 1950, close to 60 percent of total British controlled production will be obtained in the Middle East. Production in the Western Hemisphere and the Far East will not be sufficient to cover even the peacetime demand of part of the British Empire. Assuming traditional naval and land warfare over a protracted period of time, Britain, therefore, could not fuel a war with her oil resources outside of the Middle East, and she would be dependent on supplies from American petroleum companies if the oil were available and if they were willing and permitted to supply it. Nothing could illustrate the change in the British power position more dramatically than Churchill's 1914 statement that oil in the Western Hemisphere might be even less securely available to Great Britain in an emergency than Middle Eastern oil.

To sum up, Middle Eastern oil, as was also pointed out by Churchill in 1914, should primarily not be considered under the aspects of war but under those of peace. In peace, British-controlled oil in the Middle East supplies a major part of the Empire's needs and makes probably the largest contribution to the balance of payments of Great Britain in her present economic situation.

VII. Middle Eastern Oil as a Factor in the United States Power Position and Security

Ignoring the advantages which the possession of the atom bomb may or may not give the United States, it will be impossible for us to protect the Middle East against surprise attacks of a nearby world power without maintaining a vast military machine with bases all over the world.

The United States, too, cannot therefore safely rely on the availability of Middle Eastern oil resources in times of war, at least not during an initial period and until we have established ourselves nearer to the enemy and have driven him off those areas which he is likely to occupy at the outbreak of war. The U.S. supply position in an emergency, taking account of these facts, may be presented in a few figures. It is estimated that if war should break out in the near future, total essential requirements of major petroleum products for the Western Hemisphere will rise to over 7 million barrels a day, compared with total requirements of 6.1 million barrels daily by the United Nations in 1945. Western Hemisphere production of crude oil is expected to increase to 6.3 million barrels by 1950 including British-controlled Western Hemisphere production which may or may not be available. The sizable gap between estimated production and requirements may in part be bridged by natural gasoline, benzol, and alcohol, which accounted for over 300,000 barrels daily in 1945. The main contribution to cover this deficit is likely to come, for an initial period at least, from an increase in crude oil production, which might have to be raised over the technically sound level. It is worthwhile to point out that while we started World War II with a reserve producing capacity of nearly 1 million barrels daily, our present production rate exceeds the optimum technical level. Additional supplies will be obtained from stocks and probably from synthetic oil produced from natural gas, coal, shale, and tar sands. It is unlikely, however, that the production of synthetic oil on a large scale will be started in peacetime, and that it can quickly and easily be built up to a very large figure during a war. According to estimates made by the Standard Oil of New Jersey the production of 300,000 barrels daily of synthetic oil, half by coal hydrogenation and half by synthesis of natural gas, would on the basis of 1943 costs require an investment of about $2 billion or as much as that for the atom bomb. Any remaining gap between supplies and requirements will probably be made good by reducing civilian or military consumption; this is likely to affect our military strength less detrimentally than the extension of our military commitments to include the protection of the Middle East.

If the United States had Great Britain or any Western or Far Eastern power as an ally, the problem of assuring oil supplies for them too would be even more complicated.

VIII. Middle Eastern Oil as a Factor in Russia's Power Position and Security

As far as oil is concerned and apart from other considerations, Russia's interest in the Middle East is perhaps based, one, on her desire to protect the nearby Caucasian oil fields against any possible attack on this area and, two, on her desire for the acquisition of Middle Eastern oil for herself since her production declined nearly 40 percent during the war and for the denial of Middle Eastern oil to the Anglo-Americans. The Caucasian oil fields, from which Russia drew in 1945 70 percent of her total production of 400,000 barrels daily, will still account for 64 percent of her total planned output of 700,000 barrels daily in 1950. These oil fields are only a few hundred miles distant from Iran, Iraq, or Turkey and would therefore be vulnerable to air attacks from bases situated in these countries.

According to data published in 1939 in connection with the Third Five Year Plan, Russia's proven and semiproven oil reserves have been estimated at as much as 7 billion barrels, of which some 79 percent are located in the Caucasian area. This figure includes an estimate for reserves in fields which have not yet been surveyed completely. Russia's proven and possible reserves have even been put by the same source at 60 billion barrels, of which some 42 percent might be found in the Caucasian fields. These latter figures are nothing but guesses made on the basis of some geological estimates. Nevertheless, with Russia's production at its present low level, she must be sorely tempted to obtain by whatever means would seem feasible to her a participation in the fabulously rich oil fields of the Middle East which may yield a larger output at an earlier time, at less expense in material, and in a more favorable location than the development of Russian oil fields might promise. Moreover, Russia's petroleum consumption related to the size of the country and its population is exceedingly small. A fast expansion of consumption could probably not be planned on the basis of production likely to be available in Russia within a short time. It is an obvious move for a nation which thinks in power terms to try to cash in on the large oil discoveries of British and American companies, practically at her own door steps.

Russia must also be well aware of the degree of economic and political importance accompanying the control of Middle Eastern oil and of the markets which depend on it. She might feel that for reasons of prestige it behooves a big power to participate in the international oil business. The weakening of the Anglo-American power position which the loss of this oil would entail and the importance of this oil for the balance of trade of any country that possesses it are too obvious to be overlooked. The temptations to Russia to establish herself in the Middle East for any and all of these reasons are very strong, and as long as Russia is engaged in a worldwide struggle for power, continued alertness is necessary to protect our position in the Middle East.

IX. Middle Eastern Oil as a Factor in the Power Position and Security of Consuming Countries

As stated before, the consuming countries of the Eastern Hemisphere must increasingly rely on oil supplies from the Middle East. Their economic well-being depends upon the physical availability of this oil and on the willingness of the oil companies to supply it to them. International settlement of the Middle Eastern power conflict and a guarantee of assured supplies from this area at fair prices constitute probably the minimum policy program of an oil-importing country. Therefore, it may be expected that these countries will sooner or later seek these guarantees through the United Nations. They may perhaps be satisfied with the commitments for assured supplies to all nations at competitive prices as pronounced in the Anglo-American Oil Agreement, and as actively discussed between the British and American governments. The two governments hope this agreement will be ratified in the near future.

As far as their ability to wage war is concerned, these nations would be unable to fuel a major traditional war without Middle Eastern and/or Western Hemisphere oil. It should, however, not be overlooked that Germany with only the domestic European oil resources and her synthetic oil industry at her disposal was able to sustain a large war effort over a period of nearly five years with a production which at its peak did not exceed 300,000 barrels daily, and Russia was able to sustain a very large war effort over a period of three and a half years with an oil production which did not exceed 400,000 or 450,000 barrels daily.

X. Conclusions

The Middle Eastern oil resources constitute an important concentration of economic and political power in the hands of the British and American oil companies and through them of their two countries. However, as in the case of any other concentration of power, international tensions, frictions, and jealousy center around it. The problem is further complicated by the fact that the resources are located in small undeveloped countries and that for strategic and economic reasons part or all of this area is considered by at least two of the Big Three to lie within their strategic zones. We have not yet succeeded, as Mr. [Ernest] Bevin has pointed out recently, in arranging our international relations in such a way as not to make the small countries of the Middle East the victims of controversy between the big allies. We have also not yet succeeded in finding a completely satisfactory solution to the problem of controlling the complex relationship between private commercial activities and foreign political and economic policy.

However, in the world as it is today, power implied in the control of Middle Eastern oil represents an important factor in our policy and constitutes a valuable asset. It is, however, incumbent upon us to use this power in such a manner that it will contribute to the establishment of conditions under which the tension and suspicion centering around it will decrease rather than increase.

This requires a constant awareness and frank acknowledgment of our responsibilities toward producing and consuming countries as a corollary to our control over Middle Eastern oil. It may also require the provision of reasonable guarantees that we will live up to these responsibilities. Our support of international organizations such as the UN and of that envisaged under the Anglo-American Oil Agreement are steps in that direction.[2]

2. The "Agreement"—never concluded—was intended to clarify and protect the interests of American oil companies in the Middle East where and when these were in conflict with British interests in oil.   — Editor

5

Petroleum Under the ECA Program

An early, exacting experience in Mr. Levy's career came with his service as Chief of the Petroleum Branch, Economic Cooperation Administration (ECA), in 1948 and 1949.

ECA was the U.S. instrument for the implementation of the Marshall Plan for the recovery of Europe following World War II. The magnitude of the role of oil—and all of the economic, financial, and political issues involved in its obtaining and financing—was something that the United States and many allied governments were ill prepared to deal with.

At the heart of the problem was the availability of oil from British and American companies coupled with the inability of European states to find the necessary dollar exchange to pay for their imports. It was the purpose of the U.S. Government to assist those governments through dollar funds to purchase the oil they needed. An early and important question was that of price, an issue which Mr. Levy successfully addressed.

A longer-range issue that had to be dealt with simultaneously was the reconstruction of the European refining industry. Another was the issue of the future commercial role of American oil companies in the supply of products against the competition of oil from British companies.

All of these matters were presented by Mr. Levy on two occasions—first on March 8, 1949, to the National Federation of Financial Analysts Societies ("Petroleum Under the ECA Program") and second on April 27, 1949, to the National Petroleum Council (NPC) ("One Year of ECA's Oil Operations"). In these presentations, he sought to emphasize the implications of a Europe that was obtaining more oil from the Middle East than from the Western Hemisphere. This observation led to a conclusion that the price for the oil from the Middle East would be less than that from the Western Hemisphere—an alert that was further discussed in October 1949 (again at a meeting of the National Petroleum Council) in a paper included in this collection.

Lecture delivered before the Conference on the Petroleum Industry, National Federation of Financial Analysts Societies, New York, March 8, 1949, and published in *Financial Analysts Journal*, First Quarter 1949, pp. 50–53. Reprinted with permission.

In two particular respects Mr. Levy presented, in effect, a further dilemma: how to account for the expenditure of U.S. public funds in the
oil aid to European governments and how to discuss oil in terms of
the larger, strategic dimensions of the commodity and the future role
of Europe. How could one address both of these issues and acknowl-
edge the enormous role and future prospects of the private American
sector?

The approach laid out in the April 27, 1949, statement to the NPC
defined the objective. It is included here as a necessary introduction to
the papers that follow.

> . . . while we must help Europe improve its dollar balance to enable it to
> achieve recovery within the next three years, vital United States interests are
> at stake and the mere dollar-saving approach is too narrow in the case of oil.
> Some sacrifices may be required in the process of making Europe self-
> sustaining but I believe it is imperative that no vital interests of the United
> States be jeopardized and that no legitimate business interests be hurt un-
> necessarily.
>
> For a variety of reasons it may be very difficult to carry out this policy ef-
> fectively. Certain factors and developments are, as a practical matter, out-
> side the control of ECA. In particular you must be aware that if ECA refuses
> to finance certain projects, the country concerned may find non-ECA
> dollars to carry out those projects or may even be able to procure all the
> necessary equipment for soft currencies. What can or should the ECA do
> under such circumstances? This question is difficult to answer; and a drastic
> reply to it may not lead to the best or wisest course from an over-all point of
> view. Moreover, should all ECA assistance cease, much less dollar oil would
> find a market abroad and the pressure for expansion of non-dollar oil
> facilities would be even greater.

In dealing with these subjects, Mr. Levy was raising issues that had been
among those of greatest importance to the recovery of Europe and had
come to reflect the natural concerns of a government official responsible
for the use of U.S. public funds in aiding European governments to secure
"dollar" oil. It was an awesome responsibility whose every aspect
underlined the observations of the preceding paper that the United States
did not yet have the process well in hand for dealing with the private
commercial interests of American oil companies in the context of national foreign policy pursuits. Even without that process, it is altogether
correct to write that Mr. Levy's efforts to deal with the issues, which are
made explicit in these lectures, secured his reputation—and altered
substantially the nature of the relationships between government and the
companies, and the ways in which these should be considered,
henceforth.

Where dollars are concerned, ECA comes into the picture. Western Europe consumes about one-third of the oil moving in international trade, the remaining two-thirds going into other parts of the Eastern Hemisphere and Latin America. As a result of the war, Europe is unable at the moment to balance its payments on current account with the Western Hemisphere and thus incurs an annual deficit with the Western Hemisphere of about four to four and a half billion dollars.

When ECA began operations on April 3, 1948, many Western European countries had scarcely a single dollar to pay current obligations. If ECA aid had not been made available immediately, the trade of many of those countries would have been blocked by currency difficulties with the most disastrous economic and political consequences not only to them but also to us. Oil would have been one of the first victims of the trade disorder that would have followed European economic collapse. Your charts on the oil industry would have shown an unexpected change in trend and the change would have been downwards.

. . . The loss of invisible income by European countries as a result of the war, adverse terms of trade, and production difficulties which hampered exports are mainly responsible [for the lack of dollar resources]. . . . According to present estimates, it is more than likely that Europe will still be faced with a dollar problem in fiscal 1953 after Marshall Plan assistance comes to an end.

Now, what is ECA doing about this whole situation? We are, in fact, helping the countries to pay for dollar imports by converting their soft currency into dollars. We do not, and I think this should be stated as clearly as possible, make gifts of any kind to the individual oil importers of the participating countries of Western Europe. For example, when ECA provides dollars to finance the purchase of petroleum equipment, the European oil company must pay the total bill in its own local currency.

ECA assistance is furnished to the government of the country, not to the oil company, on either a loan or a grant basis. If it is a loan, the government will repay the dollars. If it is a grant, ECA makes the dollars available to pay for the imports either directly to the foreign government or directly to the supplier for the account of the foreign government. The importer must then deposit with its government a corresponding amount of local currency. The local currency funds paid to the government are put into a special account which is under the joint control of the government concerned and ECA. These "counterpart" funds are then used by local governments with the approval of ECA for debt retirement or for productive purposes of one kind or another.

In its operations, one of ECA's basic tenets is that, wherever possible and feasible, it rely on private trade channels for the supply and distribution of goods and services.

However, it will be obvious . . . , and I am afraid it is also obvious to industry, that even with the most sincere intentions not to interfere with private channels of trade—and our intentions are sincere—it is absolutely impossible for government, when it undertakes operations of the scope and magnitude of those under ECA, not to disturb from time to time some private business arrangements. The expenditure of government funds poses special and peculiar problems of its own. When such funds are used to finance private trade in an industry as complex as the international oil industry, some transactions even though based on long-established practices are bound to be ineligible for financing. We have all learned that lesson the hard way—the government as well as business.

We not only have our own laws and regulations to observe, and I assure you they are complex, but we also have to apply them against old, established and historically developed, but not always rational, trade practices. If you will consider, for a moment, the ramifications, the complications, the amplifications and the implications of the international oil trade and if you will consider, for another moment, the fact that our American companies very frequently produce, transport and refine crude oil, and then transport and market its products in foreign countries, you will realize that difficult problems are bound to arise if and when a government agency finances any part of these transactions.

Furthermore, since public funds are used for the purchase of commodities and services, our government, in some form or fashion, must be concerned with the prices that are paid in those transactions. As you know, we are not a procurement agency and we cannot bargain for special rebates or special prices as such. Nor, according to the laws and regulations under which we operate, is it any of our business what the profits, costs and, sometimes perhaps, the losses of the supplier are in any particular transaction. However, being charged with the prudent administration of large public funds, we are legitimately concerned that, in general, prices charged on ECA financed transactions should fully reflect the most favorable terms available in the markets which supply the participating countries.

In the ECA program, dollar oil plays a very large role indeed. Total dollar oil imports from American companies will amount to nearly 22 million metric tons valued at more than $550 million in fiscal 1950. If payments for tanker transportation and for petroleum equipment are added to this figure, the total will be somewhere between $800 and $900 million, or more than 20 percent of the total deficit of about $4.2 billion estimated for fiscal 1950 by ECA. . . .

In addition, British companies will supply Europe with nearly 31 million metric tons of crude oil and petroleum products valued at over $700 million, making a total for Western Europe of nearly 53 million metric tons of imports valued at nearly $1.3 billion in fiscal 1950.

The question [need be asked]: "Why not more oil from non-dollar sources and less from dollar sources if Europe is short of dollars?" The answer is very simple. The available resources of non-dollar oil are also needed to supply the world markets of the British oil industry. Any increase in shipments of non-dollar oil to Europe at the expense of non-European markets might result in a serious interference with private channels of trade, causing world-wide confusion. At the same time, it would deprive the British of some of the most needed goods which they are able to get in payment for their oil exports—goods which are not available from the other participating countries.

However, a great deal of European self-help has already taken place in the field of oil and more is planned for the near future. Let me describe this to you very briefly. Europe is and is likely to remain an importer of oil. Its consumption, which is expected to be about 46 million tons in fiscal 1949 compared with about 30 million tons in the pre-war period, is likely to continue to rise by about 6 percent a year for the next few years, reaching a level of nearly 60 million tons in fiscal 1953. However, while two-thirds of Europe's imports were finished products in the pre-war period, next year crude oil will be about one-half of much larger total petroleum imports. A large saving in foreign exchange results from importing less of the more expensive refined products and more of the less expensive crude oil.

By 1953, the individual European countries' unscreened programs call for a refining capacity of nearly 66 million tons. This, I may say is a most optimistic forecast. . . . At the same time, the European oil companies plan to increase their crude oil production outside Europe from about 75 million tons in fiscal 1949 to 114 million tons in fiscal 1953 and their overseas refining capacity from 54 million tons to 72 million tons during the same period.

These expansion figures for production and refining presuppose an increase in the world's requirements for finished products of about 14 percent a year compared with, as I mentioned before, an increase of about 6 percent expected in Europe and an anticipated rise in American needs in 1949 of about the same percentage according to United States Bureau of Mines' estimates. . . .

The expansion of refineries in Europe and of crude oil production controlled by British companies outside Europe is one of the most effective means of reducing Europe's dollar deficit. According to the British . . . an investment of about $2 billion, perhaps 30 percent of it in dollars and 70 percent in sterling and other currencies, will lead to an increase in the annual value of crude oil and refined products output by British companies of nearly a billion dollars by fiscal 1953. Of course, only part of the billion-dollar increment in value will result in dollar savings or dollar income. Even, therefore, if the original plans of the OEEC [Organization for European Economic Cooperation] countries do not completely materialize, as we believe they will not, the contribution which oil refining in Europe and oil production outside Europe will make to recovery will be extraordinary.

From what I have said before about the likelihood of a continued dollar shortage in Europe, even in 1953, and about the expansion program and the expansion possibilities of the British oil industry, it is obvious that grave and very serious problems now confront, and are likely to remain with, our American oil industry. The overall problem is easy to state. How to sell oil for dollars to an importing country which doesn't have enough dollars to pay the bill, or to a country that can buy oil for currencies other than its scarce dollars? Its solution, I assure you, is not quite as easy.

Of course, our sincere hope is that the European countries will continuously improve their balance of payment positions principally by increasing their productivity so that they can export more to dollar areas. However, as I mentioned before, there may not be a complete balancing of dollar accounts by 1953 and you know, as well as I do, the difficulties that will confront European efforts to export more goods to the United States, exports that will be necessary for economic recovery and, at the same time, for the maintenance of European imports from the United States.

Our American oil industry faces a difficult but, in my judgment, a not at all impossible problem of adjustment to existing conditions. It is the problem of maintaining outlets for dollar oil in Europe even though the dollar resources of the importing countries are severely limited and even though sterling oil competes with dollar oil for such outlets. Skillful planning by our American oil companies will be necessary, therefore, during the next few years. It is, of course, in the economic, political and strategic interest of the United States that these companies maintain their oil interests world-wide and obtain fair and equitable treatment in the oil markets of Europe. On the other hand, if Europe is to survive without continuing American assistance, it must increase production for its own use and for the expansion of exports into dollar areas. In this process of making Europe self-sustaining somebody may well get hurt but I believe it is imperative that no vital interests of the United States be sacrificed and that no legitimate business interests be hurt unnecessarily.

It is sometimes charged very loosely that without ECA everything was, and would have continued to be, so much better. Many of my oil friends have said so, and even though they say it jokingly I am sometimes afraid they really mean it. I do not happen to think so. Without ECA, we would have had not only political chaos in Europe of an unheard-of magnitude but the dollars already spent — and what we have spent on oil up to now is a very sizable amount — would not have been spent; the American oil industry would already have lost a major share of its present exports with serious repercussions on our foreign and domestic production and, I believe, on prices.

Moreover, if there had been no ECA and if the countries had been thrown on their own resources with no holds barred, the obvious thing for a country like Great Britain to have done would have been to develop its one great imperial asset, and that is oil, for all it was worth. Without ECA, therefore, the European countries would have had no alternative but to buy British oil to the limit of its possibilities and those possibilities are great indeed. There would have been no chance to work out a solution in good time which would permit the American oil industry, with foresight and judgment, to maintain its important and vital role in the oil production and marketing centers overseas. With ECA, however, I confidently believe that, in cooperation between government and industry, ways and means can be found to solve the problems confronting the American exporter in general and the American oil industry in particular.

6

One Year of ECA's Oil Operations

In this address, Mr. Levy elaborated upon his earlier remarks. The fact should be noted that only seven weeks elapsed between his first and second presentations on the subject of oil and ECA; it is a reminder of the extraordinary attention riveted on the issue of oil supply to Europe.

A little more than a year has passed since ECA started its operations, which are probably the largest in the financing of foreign trade ever undertaken. . . . I should like to review what we have done during the past twelve months.

We have certainly spent a lot of money. We have authorized the expenditure by European countries of about $460 million for crude oil and petroleum products to supply Europe and about $130 million have been authorized for tanker transportation. We have, however, authorized scarcely any expenditures for petroleum equipment. . . . Our petroleum program, including crude oil, refined products, transportation, and equipment for the fifteen-month period for which funds had originally been appropriated, would cost nearly a billion dollars. On a fifteen-month basis, expenditures for crude, products, and transportation, but excluding petroleum equipment, will probably be somewhat less than three-quarters of a billion dollars. If we had authorized the purchase of the petroleum equipment originally included in the program, expenditures would probably have amounted to about $900 million, or approximately 10 percent below our earlier estimate. ECA, therefore, is able to carry out its program at a considerable saving to the United States taxpayer largely as a result of two factors: the decline in Middle East crude oil prices and the easing supply situation, which has not only caused a decline in the prices of nearly all refined products but has also made most products available for purchase at the lowest competitive prices.

Lecture delivered before the National Petroleum Council, Washington, D.C., April 27, 1949.

In actual operations, one of our cardinal principles is to operate to the greatest possible extent through private channels of trade. We have also tried to avoid as much as possible in our operations any harmful impact on the United States' domestic economy. When the program started, as you know, the United States was still short of oil, and we have done our utmost not to aggravate the shortages in the United States or contribute to an inflationary pressure on prices. As a matter of fact, United States exports of petroleum to ECA countries in 1948 declined by nearly 40 percent compared to 1947, while petroleum exports from the United States to all other countries declined only 8 percent. We also have refused to pay premiums over the posted prices for United States crude oil and we were successful in financing the largest part of all product purchases at or very close to the low of Platt's. We have done so without, I hope, taking an attitude at any time which would have led to undue and uncalled for pressure on private business arrangements, and we have done so only on the general principle that government money must always be spent prudently and with safeguards and precautions.

We have always fully appreciated that it is the private industry of the United States operating under a free enterprise system which is producing and supplying the goods which Europe needs; that private industry is entitled to arrange its affairs in line with normal economic, competitive, and commercial considerations; and that the government has a right to interfere in such operations only on the basis of a specific law or of overall principles, the equity of which cannot be denied and which is apparent to everybody.

In this connection, we were faced with the problem of Middle East crude-oil prices, and we have been working on that problem ever since ECA started to finance the purchase of Middle East oil. We have acted on the firm assumption that any solution we suggested for the problem would have to be fair to the public as well as to the oil industry. We have also adhered to the principle that under our law we should under no circumstances, in this or any other field, take an approach based on cost and profit considerations. We felt that, to the greatest possible extent, the industry should be left free to exercise its own initiative and make its own decisions in line with the normal play of competitive and commercial forces operating in a free enterprise system. We felt very strongly that, if any segment of the oil industry were treated under different principles, such discrimination would not only be unfair and inequitable, but it would also put the whole industry in jeopardy.

We have always felt free of course . . . to talk to the companies about our problems in so far as they affected the companies and about company problems if they also affected us. We have also felt free to try to persuade them to adopt certain policies and procedures in the interest of our own government operations and also, I believe, in the long-term interest of the industry. In this connection, I would like to mention a few of the major facts that have entered into the consideration of Middle East crude oil prices.

Tremendous investments have been made by private American capital in the Middle East, and tremendous risks have been and are being run. Most of that investment was made with the intention of finding new sources of oil to supply Eastern Hemisphere requirements. There are reasons to believe that, at the moment at least, investments to supply Western Hemisphere oil requirements could be made more profitably in the Western Hemisphere than in the Eastern Hemisphere. We are also aware that, during the period of shortage last year, Middle East oil was shipped and, in fact, is still being shipped to the United States, mostly, but not exclusively, for the domestic marketing needs of the importing companies. We know, too, that some Middle East oil was sold by companies operating in the Middle East to United States oil companies not affiliated with them. In such transactions there was some freight absorption which led to an f.o.b. price somewhat lower than the price at which ECA has currently been financing shipments of Middle East oil to Europe. The lower f.o.b. price resulting from such freight absorption was necessary in order to permit the oil to compete in the United States with domestically produced oil.

We had to weigh all these factors, plus additional ones, in considering ECA financing of Middle East crude-oil purchases. During 1948 Middle East oil production increased tremendously, and for the whole of 1948 production averaged 1.1 million barrels daily or 34 percent over 1947. In the last few months of 1948 there was enough Middle East crude oil available, or even more than enough, to satisfy Europe's current crude-oil requirements. Western Hemisphere crude oil was still moving into Europe, but the flow was declining and was counterbalanced by somewhat larger Middle East crude-oil shipments into the Western Hemisphere.

The former realized price for Middle East crude oil was based on an equalization of the delivered price of Middle East and of Western Hemisphere crude oil in the importing countries of Western Europe. The basic facts of supply and demand supported, in my judgment, such a price level because Western Europe was at that time dependent on these two sources of supply. However, in view of the increased availability of Middle East crude oil since late 1948, Europe is, in fact, in the process of becoming independent of Western Hemisphere crude oil. Middle East crude oil will, therefore, in due course find its own price level for shipments to Europe. We are in a period of transition during which the change is taking place. The present price on shipments of Middle East oil to ECA destinations is already somewhat below the former price, which was determined by equalization with Western Hemisphere crude oil in Western Europe.

ECA financing may have accelerated the trend to an independent Middle East crude oil price but I believe that such a trend is in accord with a natural economic and commercial development in this field. We have done our best to follow and evaluate these trends. Since ECA began operations, Middle East crude-oil prices have declined by more than 15 percent, completely independent of any change in the United States crude-oil price structure.

A few figures will indicate the importance of this decline to our program. Currently estimated crude-oil imports from dollar sources in the Middle East into Europe during fiscal 1950 would have cost, at the prices prevailing last April [1948], about $20 million more than they will cost at prices expected to prevail during the year. If we were to finance purchases of Middle East crude oil at prices permitted under the law, which sets a formula by which maximum prices for ECA-financed transactions may be determined, the estimated cost of Middle East crude-oil imports from dollar sources into Europe during fiscal 1950 would be approximately $35 million more than we, in fact, expect it to be.

I should like to discuss another problem with you: the present and future position of American oil in European markets. There is no doubt that the American oil exporter is going through a difficult period but his problems would have been more difficult if there had been no ECA. His future problems will be even worse if ECA is not successful in its endeavors to make Europe independent of foreign assistance by 1952.

The basic facts are very simple. Total European exports of all kinds of merchandise to the United States in 1948 were valued at less than $1 billion and total European imports from the United States at more than $4 billion. These figures exclude shipments of dollar oil from offshore sources to Europe which would add nearly another half billion dollars to Europe's total dollar expenditures.

In prewar years, the dollar gap in the European merchandise balance was closed by European dollar income from invisible items such as investment, insurance, shipping, etc. As a result of the war, Europe has lost nearly all such income. Therefore, if we want to maintain our exports to Europe without continuing dollar assistance, which in fact means taking money from the United States taxpayer in order to finance the United States exporter, Europe must increase its dollar earnings very greatly, mainly by exports to the United States. Otherwise our exports to Europe could not be paid for. It is as simple as that. It is meaningless to charge European countries with trade discrimination and unfair trade practices if they do not have dollars to buy American goods.

Europe tries to reduce its dollar expenditures for oil in two ways. On the one hand, it is trying to build up a big refining industry in Europe. On the other hand, it hopes to develop the crude-oil production and refining facilities of companies of participating countries in overseas areas. It is obvious that such a program cannot be carried out without affecting exports to Europe from the United States and exports from American-owned offshore sources of oil to Europe. It is also obvious that the dollar shortage of importing countries introduces a new and very disquieting competitive element in the international oil trade which may override in importance considerations of price, quality, trade relationships, and historical trade patterns.

What makes the oil problem so peculiar and so important is that American national and security interests are closely interwoven with commercial operations. There exists, I believe, a definite American national interest in a healthy and strong United States oil industry in both its domestic and its far-flung foreign oil operations. Huge American investments are at stake not only in the United States but also in the foreign areas of production and in the European importing countries.

A reasonable and effective protection of such national interests poses very vexing and difficult problems. There exist some mitigating factors which, I believe, will help to solve these problems in a fair and equitable manner. There is, first, the great driving force and ingenuity of the industry. It possesses powerful home bases in the United States and in the Western Hemisphere. It has gone through a period of great expansion and strengthening during and after the war. Even now, it is participating to a remarkable extent in the present refining expansion program in Europe. There exist, moreover, many possibilities of adjusting the operations of the industry to the strained currency situation by which, in fact, the dollar burden of oil imports into Europe might be minimized and by which the dollar income of such countries might even rise to such an extent that they could afford a larger volume of dollar imports than before.

Once the obvious is stated, that American companies should maintain a substantial stake in the European oil business, the present trend of minimizing the dollar expenditure for the imports of dollar oil by the construction of American-owned refineries in Europe is, of course, of great value and importance. If, coupled with that, the American companies concentrate on minimizing the dollar drain on Europe and, at the same time, create new dollar exports by using European facilities and European equipment, it should be possible to assure that American-owned refineries in Europe will continue to serve as outlets for crude oil produced by American companies. It should also be possible in certain well-defined circumstances to assure American companies against unfair competition based on currency considerations, especially as in many cases the real dollar savings made possible by switching sources from dollar to non-dollar suppliers might in fact be small or even nonexistent. It should also be possible, in spite of currency difficulties, to maintain European markets for products of special quality which cannot easily be matched. On the other hand, a healthy expansion of the European refinery industry, which may mean fewer exports of finished products for American suppliers, appears to be desirable for Europe. The fact that trade patterns will change so that some suppliers gain markets while others lose markets is not necessarily a national disaster.

Nor will it be a national disaster if Western Hemisphere oil is no longer needed in Europe to the same extent as before. However, it would be a national disaster if, at the end of the Marshall Plan, Europe were to find itself in as helpless and as exposed a position as it was at the beginning of ECA. Europe must be enabled to maintain a reasonable standard of living. To achieve that end, an expansion of the European oil industry at home and overseas is justified and necessary. That cannot be denied.

It is often charged that ECA is responsible for the problems that are facing our export industry at the present time and that without ECA the American exporter would have had no problems and would be much better off. Obviously, a direct opposite viewpoint is correct. Without ECA the American oil business in Europe would already have been shot to pieces. Many of the most important European oil markets had exhausted their total dollar resources a year ago and without ECA aid they would have been forced to cut their oil imports from dollar sources to the barest minimum. The British would have had to build up their oil industry with the greatest possible speed to furnish an alternative source of supply.

It is further charged that ECA creates problems by supporting oil developments in Europe and overseas. Here, too, I feel strongly that the charge is not justified. ECA's attempts to help Europe achieve recovery through increased production and exports would be unnecessary only if the American people desire to make continuous dollar grants to Europe and if Europe were willing to accept such grants.

We are committed to help Europe achieve recovery by the end of 1952. Increased production in Europe and more dollar exports are essential to achieve the goal. Nevertheless, while we must help Europe improve its dollar balance to enable it to achieve recovery within the next three years, vital United States interests are at stake and the mere dollar-saving approach is too narrow in the case of oil. Some sacrifices may be required in the process of making Europe self-sustaining but I believe it is imperative that no vital interests of the United States be jeopardized and that no legitimate business interests be hurt unnecessarily.

We believe that the oil industry will ride with this storm as it has ridden with many others. Everything will not and, perhaps, should not go its way but everything will not go against it either. Europe will undoubtedly increase its refining capacity and its overseas production, and Europe will also find it easier to trade in sterling than in dollars. Sterling oil will be easier to market in Europe and elsewhere than dollar oil, especially since European oil companies can rely on their governments to convert their income, regardless of the currency in which it is received, into sterling or dollars as needed. We must not forget, however, that the European oil industry must expand if Europe is to recover. We must also realize that the European oil companies must plan their expansion programs as commercial ventures because ECA makes dollars available to the governments concerned for the use of the European oil companies for their equipment purchases, only to the extent that the oil companies make payments in local currency.

*   *   *

. . . [T]he United States has undertaken a tremendous job in helping to support the economies of the participating countries. I believe that the demonstrated ability of the United States to produce enough goods to maintain the highest standard of living in the world for its own people and, at the same time, to produce $5 billion worth of goods to help maintain a minimum standard of living for nineteen other countries is extraordinary proof, if such proof were needed, of the vitality of the American system of private enterprise. It is a remarkable undertaking for the United States to help restore the productivity of other countries thereby enabling them to compete more fully and more effectively with us. But I sincerely believe that, if the United States had not followed this course, the world would have been threatened with political chaos and economic disruption which would have jeopardized not only the economy of Europe but also the American system of free enterprise in which we all believe wholeheartedly.

7

The Role of American Oil in the World

The sole purpose of the National Petroleum Council (NPC) in 1949 was to counsel the secretary of the Department of the Interior on issues relating to petroleum or the petroleum industry. It has long been a prime source of industry advice to officials with highest energy responsibilities. Consequently, its meetings are designed to inform participants—from government and industry—on major issues of oil supply. The meeting held on October 25, 1949, was in this tradition. "The Role of American Oil in the World," Mr. Levy's subject, had two aspects that were central to the presentation: the magnitude of the role of American oil companies in supply and in the terms on which oil could be obtained.

Mr. Levy reminded the NPC that the United States remained the world's largest producer and consumer of oil and consequently was a determining factor in the setting of oil prices "in every market of the world." However, the United States was no longer the leading exporter or the major source of supply for the rest of the world's importers, and it no longer possessed the world's largest concentration of reserves.

If the impact of this change did not become fully appreciated until the supply emergencies of 1967 and thereafter, when the U.S. inability to be the residual crisis supplier of last resort became patent, there could be no mistaking the warnings to the NPC of nearly twenty years earlier.

Central to the observations about supply was Mr. Levy's explicit discussion of how the price for oil was still being set by a formula based upon the "U.S. Gulf" plus transportation to Europe, whether the real origin of the crude (or product) was in the U.S. Gulf or in the Middle East. In making these points, he was reflecting an earlier concern that this concept of pricing could not survive the dramatic increase in lower-cost oil production from the Middle East. Having held these views while in government, Mr. Levy would not say otherwise when in private life.

At the same time that conditions (opportunities and risks) in world oil challenged American oil companies, emphasis was also given to the national interests served by the astonishing magnitude of the American

Lecture delivered before the National Petroleum Council, Washington, D.C., October 25, 1949.

companies' investments in oil—four-fifths of all American investments overseas.

I believe that our industry is going through a very interesting and difficult period. I also know that many in the industry wish it were less interesting and less difficult. As an economic consultant, I, of course, do not quite share their wish. I feel, however, that it is useful to go back to the fundamentals of the problems we are confronted with, in order to understand and evaluate them better.

The American oil industry is at present uncertain about its role in the world's oil industry, and somewhat fearful of the impact which foreign production, marketing, and general economic developments may have on its future. Let me say first that the American oil industry has been and still is the leader of the world oil industry—the leader in more than a nominal or limited sense. The United States is still the largest producer of oil, accounting for about 60 percent of total world production. The United States is still the world's largest consumer of oil, accounting for about the same percentage of the world's oil consumption. And finally the United States still is, but not in the same manner as before, the determining factor for the oil prices in every market of the world.

However, some of the underlying conditions have changed. The United States is no longer the leading exporter of oil. The United States no longer includes within its boundaries the world's largest concentration of proven reserves.

What has happened is that outside the United States very large oil resources have been discovered, accounting now for 70 percent of the world's proven reserves. Since the actual rate of production in those foreign areas amounts only to about 40 percent of the world's total, there exists an apparent and obvious trend to increase the rate of production in foreign producing areas.

There are added political and economic pressures which tend to push the rate of production of foreign countries upwards, such as the terms of foreign concession, the desire of foreign countries to develop their resources, and of course the necessity for foreign oil companies to provide an increasing production in order to obtain a higher foreign exchange income for the foreign exchange hungry treasuries of their countries.

What does all this mean to American oil? It seems to imply that in one field of leadership the role of the United States is coming to an end. Oil from the United States is no longer the major source of supply for the rest of the world. However, the American oil industry has not been idly watching this development. It has developed and acquired interests in many foreign concessions and plays in fact a most important role in foreign developments. Moreover, the leadership of the United States oil industry, as representing by far the largest single world market, is one that has been maintained and will be maintained, I believe, for many years to come or even for as long as oil remains an essential commodity. The role of the United States as the largest single consumer results from our predominance as the world's largest manufacturing center and as the country with the highest national income and the highest standard of living. This role has, I believe, been established firmly and securely.

The World Oil-Price Structure

Further, the leadership of the United States in determining world market prices for oil, which was based formerly on the export capacity of this country, will be maintained, I believe, in a somewhat changed form because this country still does and will continue to represent the world's largest market for oil.

As long as the United States was a major supplier to all the other countries of the world, the delivered price from the United States and from most foreign sources of supply was calculated as the U.S. Gulf price plus transportation from the U.S. Gulf to the destination. Now that the United States is no longer the world's most important supplier, economic laws and forces will, I believe, determine the world oil price structure in the following manner.

In the case of Middle East crude oil, as Middle East production is in fact now sufficient to cover Eastern Hemisphere crude-oil requirements, prices will normally fluctuate between a high and a low — a high that will be a price which will just permit Western Hemisphere crude oil to be shipped to Western Europe, and a low which will just permit Middle East crude oil to move into the Western Hemisphere. As a matter of fact, on the basis of present tanker rates the current Middle East crude oil price is near the low of this range. In the case of refined products, as Western Europe still needs large supplies from the Caribbean area, Middle East refined products will usually be priced in such a manner that the delivered price in Western Europe equalizes with that of Caribbean oil. Crude oil from the Caribbean which moves in sizeable quantities to the East Coast of the United States will be priced in the Caribbean in such a manner that it will be able to compete with United States oil at the East Coast, and this will also in general be the Caribbean price which will be charged for shipments to the Eastern Hemisphere. This is the price structure as it has evolved already or as it will, I believe, evolve in the near future.

Devaluation and Oil Prices

I do not believe that devaluations or currency manipulations or any arbitrary government rules and regulations could substantially and for any length of time interfere with the sensitive mechanism of world oil pricing. Any such attempts would run counter to normal economic forces and would soon prove futile.

Moreover, British oil includes a very sizeable dollar cost element not only for production in the Western Hemisphere where both royalties and operating expenses are paid for in dollars, but also in the Middle East where royalties, which are a fixed sum per ton of oil produced, are calculated on the basis of the gold standard. Further, as Iran did not devalue its currency, British operating expenses there have gone up by the full amount of the British devaluation. Finally, the British oil industry purchases a large amount of equipment from American manufacturers. As a result of the devaluation its costs have therefore gone up very considerably.

But, even more important, the importing countries of the world need oil from British as well as from dollar sources in order to satisfy their requirements. If the British were to offer oil at a sterling price lower than the corresponding dollar price on the basis of the new sterling rate of exchange, they would lose dollar and other foreign exchange income and would establish an untenable two-price system for oil. It would not and could not last long. To try to keep oil prices after devaluation down to their former level would be, as the London *Economist* put it so aptly, "nonsensical in the circumstances."

The Development of Foreign Oil Production and Refining

As I mentioned before, one of the great changes that is confronting the American oil industry is the discovery of large oil reserves in foreign countries, particularly in the Middle East, and the resulting increase in foreign production. A recent report published by ECA on the companies' programs for the development of foreign production and refining is most informative. According to this report, foreign crude oil production would increase from 3 million barrels daily in 1948 to 4.6 million barrels daily in 1952, and foreign refining throughput from 2.4 million barrels daily to 3.8 million barrels daily. I want to stress as strongly as I know how that this report does not represent an ECA program or the program of the European countries as such, but is the total of all the programs of the various oil companies — American, British, Dutch, French, and so on. The report has been compiled and published to permit everyone concerned to evaluate the combined company programs and to reach conclusions on the desirability of their scope and size. On the basis of these figures ECA, the European countries, and the interested companies must obviously make their final investment decisions, and in particular they must decide whether adjustments are called for.

The Threat of Overexpansion

It is interesting to note that while the total figures in the ECA summary for foreign crude-oil production in 1952 are only 4 to 5 percent higher than the so-called McCollum figures in the "Report on the Long-Term Availability of Petroleum" of November 1948, the figures for the Eastern Hemisphere, outside Eastern Europe, are nearly 25 percent higher than the corresponding McCollum figures and those for the Western Hemisphere, outside North America, nearly 20 percent lower.

It is also interesting to note that if the working assumptions are made that the world's oil requirements outside the United States would increase by about 6 or 7 percent annually during the next three to four years, and U.S. consumption by about 4 to 5 percent, while U.S. domestic production would expand in accordance with the average of the McCollum figures and U.S. exports would decline by about 40 percent, there would be a surplus of foreign crude-oil production of about 150,000 to 350,000 barrels daily and a surplus of foreign refined products of about 350,000 to 500,000 barrels daily. Because of the great dollar shortage in nearly every one of the consuming countries of the world, it is likely that the total surplus that would exist would have to be absorbed by American oil; or to put it differently, foreign companies could sell all that they plan to produce for soft currencies at the expense of outlets for American-owned oil. If that situation should arise, American-owned foreign production would have to remain at or even fall below the 1948 level, while foreign oil companies would supply not only their own market share but also the total increase in all foreign requirements.

This would be the conclusion on the basis of the assumptions stated here. These assumptions appear to me to be reasonable and probably err on the side of overestimating the rate of increase of demand. In particular, devaluation has made oil more expensive in all countries that have devalued, thus probably exercising a retarding influence on the expansion of consumption. On the other hand, devaluation has also made dollar equipment more expensive to those countries, and that will probably affect adversely the expansion program.

If, however, the general economic recovery in Europe and developments in the rest of the world should support a higher rate of increase in consumption, the conclusions on the required rate of production and refining expansion in the Eastern Hemisphere must, of course, be adjusted accordingly. It is therefore necessary to review the whole situation continuously in order to be able to make any called-for adjustments in the capital expansion program timely enough to cover adequately the needs of the Eastern Hemisphere.

U.S. National Interest in American-Owned Foreign Oil

The figures just cited indicate a potentially very serious situation, not only for the American oil industry as such, but also in terms of our political and strategic position. The stability of our concessions and the economic and political well-being of those countries where our companies operate would obviously be put in jeopardy if American oil developments are stymied at a time when British projects in the same or neighboring countries proceed at an unprecedented rate.

The foreign operations of our industry are an integral part of our defense system. For our defense we must be able to count not only on a sound and healthy domestic oil industry but also on U.S.-owned foreign oil resources. This is obvious in terms of Western Hemisphere oil. It is no less correct in terms of Middle East oil. Imagine for a moment what it would mean to the economic and political position of the United States if the oil resources of the Middle East were controlled by a hostile power on whose good will all the Eastern Hemisphere countries would then depend for their essential oil supplies.

I need not elaborate on how this would affect our security; nor need I dwell on the positive contribution which Middle East oil in fact made to the Allied cause during the last war and is likely to make again in any future emergency.

Moreover, in terms of U.S. foreign economic policy, United States private foreign investments are the keystone in the [effort to assist in further economic recovery and development]. The U.S. oil industry represents in fact by far the largest source for foreign capital investments. It provided . . . four-fifths of the private investments made by American interests abroad last year — totaling $1.5 billion. If this source of investment is cut off or the productivity of past investments curtailed, the whole . . . private investment program will be put in jeopardy.

Conclusion

The world's oil economy is undergoing far-reaching structural changes as a result of the development of Middle East oil and the refinery construction in the Eastern Hemisphere. Such changes obviously will affect our U.S. oil economy as well as that of foreign countries. It is also true that there will be an interplay of forces between Western Hemisphere and

Middle East oil, with each acting as a somewhat controlling and balancing factor on the other. Such an interplay of economic forces is the direct result of the free enterprise system which has succeeded without fail in assuring supplies for the ever-increasing oil requirements of the world.

Thanks to the free initiative of all segments of our industry, the leading role of the American oil industry in satisfying such world demand from their domestic and foreign sources is still maintained. There is no doubt in my mind that when the storm has blown over and when things have settled down again, the American oil industry will still be the leading oil industry of the world.

8

Europe in the Oil Economy
of the Free World

With the recovery of Europe well underway, the prospect was of the continent again becoming a large and growing consumer of oil with implications both to other importers (including the United States and Japan) and to oil-exporting countries. If Europe had not yet adopted the course of rapidly accepting oil while drastically reducing its consumption of coal, that time was fast approaching. To the economic needs for oil were now being added the requirements from rearmament.

The principal ingredients in Europe's oil economy and the key problems in obtaining supply were the subjects of a paper Mr. Levy delivered to the French Society of Petroleum Technologists on June 7, 1951. At that time, he noted that self-sufficiency in oil was hardly likely and that governments and companies should pay closer attention to diversifying sources of crude and product.

The impact on Middle East countries of a surge in European demand was clearly something to be taken seriously. It was foreseen to be a prime cause of further instability and insecurity in the region – at the same time allowing oil-exporting states to benefit more fully from the sale of their resource in terms of their own greater economic development.

A failure on the part of Europe to pay close attention to the strategic dimension of its now major supply of oil – the Middle East – could gravely impair its own security and that of the free world. In this paper are references to all the political and economic strains yet to come whose advent in the mid-sixties would occur with such speed and would so thoroughly transform the control of oil.

Within the framework of the free world Europe occupies an essential role. Its Western orientation, its vast industrial power, and its strategic position make it so. To help rebuild Europe's industrial power and its overall economic strength, the European Recovery Program (ERP) was

Lecture delivered before L'Association Française des Technicians du Pétrole, Paris, June 7, 1951.

undertaken. Now, some three years after the initiation of that program, we are doubly aware of how important the strengthening of the European economy has been to the free world. The expanded rearmament and military preparedness programs must be based on a strong and buoyant European economy. Therefore, there is little room for a letup in the rapid economic progress which Europe has achieved in the last few years, for the force of international events has placed additional burdens and responsibilities upon it.

Within the framework of the European economy, oil plays a vital role. Its availability in abundant quantities contributes significantly to the growing level of industrial production. Now the European economy, straining under the impact of the rearmaments program, requires even greater quantities of oil than heretofore.

Consumption

Outside the United States, Western Europe is the world's most important oil-consuming area. During 1950 it consumed about 350 million barrels or approximately 11 percent of the oil produced in the free world during the year. The United States consumed 72 percent; other countries of the Western Hemisphere, about 11 percent; and the rest of the free countries of the Eastern Hemisphere, about 6 percent.

Oil consumption in Europe, accelerated by the fast rate of reconstruction and increased industrial activity, has grown rapidly since the end of the war. From 1947 to 1949 it rose at a rate slightly below 10 percent; from 1949 to 1950 the increase was somewhat about 11 percent. Increases were recorded in all countries, with the most notable ones occurring in France where consumption rose by about 18 percent from 1949 to 1950.

These rapid postwar increases have helped Europe to make up for the low levels of consumption suffered during the war. It is interesting to note that the long-term rate of growth in the period from 1930 through 1949 indicates that oil consumption in Europe progressed geometrically at an annual rate of 4 percent compounded. This same rate was also recorded in the Far East and in the Western Hemisphere, excluding the United States. In the prewar period from 1930 through 1938 the rate of increase in Europe was 6 percent per year compounded.

European consumption is now far above the depressed level at the end of the war and, in view of Europe's expanded industrial activity, stimulated by the demands of the rearmament program, we may expect it to continue its increase. However, it is probable that the rate of increase, barring unforeseen developments or the outbreak of another international war, will taper off gradually in the future.

Production

That the oil industry has met the ever increasing oil requirements of the world is, of course, axiomatic. Crude oil production in the free world, at 3.3 billion barrels in 1950, was double the 1938 rate. Moreover, the increase in production from 1946 to 1950 — which amounted to about 910 million barrels — was almost equal to the current level of consumption in all areas of the free world outside the United States. At the present, however, the high level of demand has placed added strains on the industry. Refineries the world over are operating at or near capacity and threatened shortages of materials only serve to make a tight supply and demand position even tighter. Any sudden interruption of the flow of oil from one of the major producing countries would have serious repercussions on the free world's supply and demand position.

Europe, despite the sharp increases which have been registered in the Netherlands and in Western Germany, produced only 14 million barrels of crude oil in 1950, or about 4 percent of its consumption. It thus contributed only a very small fraction of the free world's crude oil supplies. The United States, the largest producer, accounted for about 57 percent of the production in the free world, a relative decline from 1938 when it was responsible for 70 percent of the world's crude production outside Russia and the satellite countries. The other two main producing centers of the free world — Venezuela and the Middle East — now account for much more of the free world's petroleum supplies than they did before the war. Venezuela's share has risen from 11 percent in 1938 to 16 percent in 1950 and that of the Middle East has increased from 7 percent to 18 percent.

Thus, among the major powers of the world, the European countries are "have-not" nations, when it comes to oil. Europe must, therefore, import almost all of its oil needs. During 1950 Russian crude oil production, together with the satellites' output, was of the order of 280 to 315 million barrels, having increased about 20 percent from 1938. The other principal power — the United States — produced about 2 billion barrels of oil in 1950. In addition, the United States is also the world's largest single importing country. Last year its petroleum imports alone were approximately the same as total Russian and satellite production or nearly as large as the total inland consumption of all participating countries. However, the fact that the United States and Europe must import large quantities of oil from abroad should not be considered a sign of weakness. On the contrary, the expanding American and European oil imports are a reflection of the increasing economic and industrial strength of the free world. In Russia and those countries within its orbit, however, consumption is held down to the prevailing level of crude oil production.

Refining

In contrast to its position as a producer of only small quantities of crude oil, Western Europe has now a large proportion of the free world's oil-refining capacity outside the United States. Before the war, when Western European refinery capacity was about 140 million barrels, France was the only country which approached self-sufficiency in refining. Now, however, Italy, the Netherlands, and Western Germany—in addition to France—obtain most of their oil supplies from their own refineries. Within the next few years the United Kingdom and other European countries will also satisfy most of their requirements from local refinery output.

In addition, the development of a petrochemical industry on the basis of Europe's increased refining capacity should become of considerable importance to the area. In the United States many chemicals are being derived from oil to an increasing extent. The petrochemical industry has established itself firmly, and the supply of raw materials to the chemical industry at a low and stable cost has contributed significantly to industrial expansion in the United States. The European oil industry has just begun to open up to the European economy the same new vast possibilities which have been provided by the American petrochemical industry for the American consumer.

Refining capacity in the free world has increased about 50 percent from the prewar level and now amounts to about 530 million tons. Sharp increases have been recorded in almost all areas. The Middle East has doubled its capacity as has Venezuela; in the United States the increase has been of the order of 40 percent. None of the principal refining centers of the free world, however, have recorded more striking increases than Europe. The rate at which the reconstruction of war-damaged refineries, the expansion of existing ones, and the construction of new facilities has taken place in the postwar period is, indeed, remarkable. Western Europe's refining capacity is now more than double the prewar level and will reach 60 to 70 million tons in the near future. Accordingly, it possesses almost one-quarter of the free world's refining capacity outside the United States, in contrast to about 15 percent before the war.

European Oil Trade Problems

This large-scale expansion in European refining capacity is the result of Europe's decision to import crude oil rather than refined products. Owing to the vast divergence between European consumption and local crude-oil production, Europe must import practically 95 percent or more of its oil requirements. To Europe this fact alone poses many problems in the fields of finance, commercial policy, and strategy. The problems of where Europe must draw its oil supplies and in what form are also of outstanding importance to Europe as well as to the world oil industry. Since Europe fulfills such a significant role in the framework of the free world and since oil has become increasingly important in Europe's maintenance of that role, European oil requirements must be satisfied efficiently and sufficiently. Without oil the rapid economic development recorded in Europe during the last few years can hardly be expected to continue, and without its continuance the free world's stability and security would be seriously endangered.

Before the war Europe's oil requirements were satisfied, in the main, through imports from the Western Hemisphere — the United States and Venezuela and the Netherlands West Indies, in particular. The majority of its imports were in the form of finished products. In 1938, for example, Europe drew over 75 percent of its supplies from the Western Hemisphere and only 23 percent from the Middle East. In the same year refined products made up about 65 percent of the area's total imports.

These shipments, while involving a substantial outlay in dollars and sterling, did not, generally speaking, upset the balance of payments of the European countries. European oil imports from the Western Hemisphere, like other imports, were paid for not only by exports of commodities from Europe directly, but by shipments of raw materials from Europe's overseas possessions, by invisible income items like shipping, insurance and the tourist trade, and by earnings on Europe's large foreign investments. In cases where European countries decided to erect refineries and to import crude oil the motivating factor was, in most instances, not so much the desire to save on foreign exchange as that of independence from a particular source of finished-products supply in case of war.

Postwar Expansion of Oil Consumption

This situation has drastically changed in the postwar period. At the end of the war Europe, ravaged by long years of fighting, destruction, and enemy occupation, was faced with the tedious task of reconstruction. Economic prosperity and social and political stability could be restored only with outside aid, which took the form of the European Recovery Program.

As the result of European self-help and American assistance, European industrial production had by the middle of last year reached a level 25 percent above prewar and is today 38 percent higher. The recovery and expansion has been accomplished by means of a great increase in output per man, based on the use of more and better machinery. This in turn has meant the use of more and better sources of energy in a more efficient manner.

Compared with the highly mechanized industries of North America, per capita oil consumption in Europe is still low — about one-fourth that of the United States. By 1948 it had reached the prewar level and has since then surpassed it substantially. The overall figures do not, however, bring out the changing role of oil in the energy pattern nor the changing importance of the various sectors using oil.

Following a similar long-term trend in the United States, the share of oil, and to a lesser extent of hydroelectric power, in total European energy consumption has been rising at the expense of coal. It has not yet gone nearly so far as in the United States, where energy derived from oil now exceeds that from coal. In 1950 it constituted about 10 percent in the OEEC countries compared with almost 40 percent in the United States. Nevertheless the trend is very marked. Since coal production has still not risen above the prewar level, the other sources, oil and electricity, have made up the gap and also supplied the full increase in energy use. It is expected that by 1953 the share of petroleum products in European energy consumption will be 15 percent, roughly double that of 1938.

It may here be interesting, perhaps, to relate this advance of the share of oil in total energy use to that in the national output which is a gauge of both the demand for energy from all sources and of the volume of production achieved with the help of the indicated energy. In Europe such a comparison is possible for the OEEC group of countries, which constitute the bulk of the European market outside the Communist-controlled area.

Industrial production in Europe between 1938 and 1949 has risen at a compounded annual rate of 2.3 percent. This growth has been supported by a volume of energy from all sources which increased at only one-half that rate, 1.2 percent per year. The slower growth in energy use has been due in large measure to a shift to more efficient sources, particularly oil. In addition, the smaller increase in energy requirements as compared with industrial production indicates that the effects of technological progress have made possible the more efficient use of energy. This relation between the increase in energy requirements and industrial production holds for all geographical areas of Europe. It is also to be noted that the more rapid advance in the use of oil, compared with total energy, applies to each of these areas and has, therefore, taken place regardless of the local availability of coal or hydroelectric power.

In addition to the greater share which oil has attained in the total energy picture, it is also significant that a much larger share of oil than before the war is today used for essential productive purposes. Data for eight important . . . countries indicate that the volume of oil consumed in industry and in agriculture has increased two and one-half times since 1938. The proportion of oil used in private transportation, on the other hand, has dropped from 21 to about 9 percent. Consumption in this group is the only one which has not regained and far surpassed the prewar rate.

In line with this change in end-use pattern, the product distribution of oil consumption in the OEEC countries has also undergone significant changes. The use of gas, diesel, and heavy fuel oil has risen most, while that of gasoline was in 1949–50 still below prewar. The middle and heavy products consequently constituted almost 64 percent of the major products consumed last year, compared with less than 50 percent prewar.

Effect of Rearmament Program

The impact of the mobilization program which the Korean conflict has set in motion is likely to be felt to an increasing extent during the immediate future. The rearmament programs of the Western nations is raising the demand for energy from all sources more rapidly than had been anticipated, and present expansion programs are considered to be insufficient to meet future requirements.

European coal is again becoming tight, and output is unlikely to be raised substantially in the near future. Output of hydroelectric power is far above the prewar level. As the result of the rearmament effort, however, presently planned additions to electric generating plants based on coal or water power will not be large enough to meet the requirements of both the civilian sector and the expanding military demand.

Under these circumstances it is likely that the bulk of the future expansion of energy consumption, as in the past, could only be met from oil, provided, of course, that political or other developments will not interfere with the free flow of oil from the producing to the consuming countries. This expectation is based on the trend during the past decade, both in the United States and in Europe. It is reinforced by the strain on existing resources imposed by the rearmament program. The advantage of using oil rather than local energy sources is particularly great because of the fact that the large production investments required are made by the international oil industry, thus freeing the resources of the consuming countries for the purchase of additional oil-using equipment. This in turn makes possible an accelerated development of other sectors of the economy.

Postwar Trade Problems

As a result of the rapid increases in the requirements of European industry, serious balance-of-payments difficulties have arisen in a number of European countries. Not only is the demand for foreign exchange larger, but the destruction caused by the last war left many European productive facilities damaged and the normal fabric of trade broken down. Many of the goods which Europe needed, both for immediate consumption and for restoration of its producing capacity, could be obtained only from the dollar area, where production had not been impaired by the war but had greatly expanded. Europe's low level of production, however, made it impossible for her to export in sufficient quantities to pay for this increased flow. Moreover, much of Europe's overseas investments had been liquidated to pay for the war and earnings from this and other "invisible" sources of foreign exchange were far below the prewar level.

To solve this problem, as mentioned before, the European Recovery Program was initiated. It was essential, within the framework of the program, that the dollar gap should be closed. In this gap, oil was a particularly important item, for two chief reasons. First, shipments of oil, measured in terms of both value and volume, are the largest of any commodity moving in international trade. Second, as American and British oil companies, with the exception of the French participation in the Iraq Petroleum Company, are nearly the world's only oil producers and exporters, practically all oil shipments must be paid for in dollars or pounds sterling. Because of its importance the flow of oil is not only affected by international currency developments but oil in turn exerts a strong influence on the latter. In view of the rapid increase in European production which was possible only by using a greater volume of energy, and the increasing share of oil in the total European energy supply, European oil imports were likely to exert a very large and increasing pressure on the scarce supply of dollars. The European countries were, therefore, faced with the necessity of obtaining oil in sufficient quantities and at the same time of keeping their dollar expenditures on oil, as on other imports, to the lowest possible level.

Three alternative ways of reducing Europe's dollar expenditures for oil presented themselves. First, Europe could cut consumption or prevent it from expanding during the postwar period. Second, it could stress the purchase of sterling oil at the expense of dollar oil. Third, it could attempt to increase the soft currency content of dollar oil.

The first method, reducing consumption, would obviously have been harmful to the European Recovery Program, since oil plays a vital role in any modern industrial system. The substitution of sterling for dollar oil would have led to only limited dollar savings, since no substantial quantities of surplus sterling oil were available during the tight supply conditions of the last few years. In addition, "sterling oil" produced in the Western Hemisphere involves, in general, a higher dollar cost than "dollar oil" produced by American companies in the Middle East.

The third alternative, that of raising the soft currency content of dollar oil, involved three phases, (a) a shift from the Western Hemisphere to the Middle East as Europe's principal source of oil supply; (b) the expansion of European refining capacity, so that future imports would consist chiefly of the cheaper crude oil rather than the more expensive finished products; and (c) the purchase by American companies which supply oil to Europe of equipment and services in the soft currency area.

The replacement of Western Hemisphere by Middle East oil in the European market has been a natural development during the postwar period. While production in the Middle East has expanded greatly compared with prewar, the United States has become a large net importer of oil. U.S. oil exports to Europe are no longer as important as before the war, except for a limited quantity of specialized products.

This same transition to Middle East oil is also being facilitated by the construction of large refining capacity in Britain and on the Continent. After the completion of present plans, in the next one to two years, Europe will in general no longer be dependent upon the output of refineries in the Western Hemisphere (or elsewhere) but will be able to import most of its oil needs in the form of Middle East crude.

The policy of lowering the hard currency content of dollar oil in the two ways discussed above is, therefore, preferable, from every point of view, to the alternative means at Europe's disposal in its efforts to save dollars. This policy, unlike a cut in oil consumption, is in harmony with the economic recovery program. It also is least in conflict with the policy of liberalizing the flow of international trade, in contrast with the alternative step of excluding dollar oil from Europe.

The agreements between the American oil companies and the British and also other European governments have, therefore, made a substantial contribution to the economic recovery of Europe and a freer flow of trade. By the terms of these agreements the oil of the companies concerned will not be subject to substitution by sterling oil, since the dollar content of the oil will be greatly reduced. This reduction is being accomplished by increased purchases of equipment and materials used by the oil industry in the soft currency areas and by the acceptance of larger portions of the royalty payments in local currency or sterling. In the case of shipments to nonsterling soft currency areas Britain is in some instances serving as the banker, with the oil companies accepting sterling for dollar oil and using the sterling to purchase supplies in the United Kingdom. A similar effect is caused by producing countries accepting sterling or other soft currencies for royalty and other payments from the companies.

The measures taken under ERP, the devaluation of the currencies, and the large raw material purchases by the United States resulting from the Korean war, all have helped to achieve a marked improvement in

Europe's international payments position. In the fourth quarter of 1950 the trade gap of the OEEC countries with the United States was only about $100 million monthly, compared with $200 million per month one year earlier and almost $500 million monthly during 1947–48, before the Marshall Plan began to make itself felt. At the same time Europe's deficit with other countries, which had also been substantial immediately after the war, turned into a small surplus during 1949. Accordingly, Europe's gold and short-term dollar reserves, which had decreased more than 25 percent below the prewar level, have shown a substantial rise and are now close to the prewar level of over $10 billion.

Investment

The rapid expansion of European and world oil consumption and of the change in the direction of the international oil trade have required vast new investments by the companies which supply the European and world markets. The production potential needed to meet this additional demand was available only in the Caribbean area and the Middle East.

As between these two areas a number of factors pointed clearly toward the Middle East as a basis for Eastern Hemisphere supplies. The area was known to have the world's largest reserves, practically untapped. It had relatively low production costs, because of the richness of its deposits. Local consumption, unlike that in the Western Hemisphere, was a minor quantity which was not likely to absorb the bulk of increased output. The fields were favorably located for the European market, especially if pipelines to the Mediterranean were to be built. Lastly, the producing countries of the Middle East were in the soft currency area and purchases from there would not constitute as heavy a drain on Europe's scarce dollars as would delivery from the Western Hemisphere.

The development of the Middle East required very large investments by the British, Anglo-Dutch, and American companies holding concessions there. The countries of the Middle East had scarcely been touched by modern industrial trends and the oil companies, in developing a large new industry, had to build from the ground up.

Accordingly, the arrival of the oil industry changed the way of life for the local inhabitants; it brought with it training of the people in the use of machinery, elementary education, and health and sanitary facilities. In addition, the companies incurred large expenditures for housing; they frequently provided the necessities of life at low cost and built roads, railroads, port facilities, and even whole cities. All this was done in addition to establishing and operating the industry proper which included prospecting and production of crude oil, construction and operation of large refineries, transportation—either by tanker around the Arabian Peninsula or by pipeline through perhaps 1,000 miles of desert—and storage and loading facilities. Lastly, there was the vast investment in expanding refining facilities in the European consuming countries themselves. American companies, for instance, spent nearly $500 million in the Middle East, between 1946 and 1949, and the cost of the European refining program is close to $1 billion.

As a matter of fact, the oil industry accounted for more than 75 percent of the total foreign investment of American private companies made in the postwar period. As a result, production of United States companies abroad is, by 1953, expected to reach nearly four times and refining capacity nearly three times the prewar level.

No comparable figures are available for British and Anglo-Dutch companies. However, investment was probably only slightly less than that of the American companies; 1953 crude production is expected to rise to two and one-half times the prewar level, and refining capacity also will be very substantially greater.

As a result of these large investments, a new source of oil production has been opened up in the Middle East and damaged facilities in the Far East have been restored. Also, production in the Caribbean has increased over 160 percent since prewar to total over 515 million barrels in 1950.

Europe's Dependence on Middle East Oil

The extent to which the Eastern Hemisphere relies on the Middle East as a source of oil supply, the vastness of the area's reserves, and the size of the investments made by the oil industry all serve to bring out the importance of Middle East oil to the free world.

The Middle East supplies at present about 40 percent of the free world's oil outside the United States. The continued availability of oil from this source for the needs of Europe and other areas in the Eastern Hemisphere is vital, and any event which might interfere with the flow of this oil would have far-reaching repercussions throughout the free world.

Yet this area is peculiarly insecure in a world where insecurity is prevalent everywhere. It is insecure economically because its population has a very low standard of living—lower than in any other important area except South Asia. The bulk of the population is no longer content with such conditions and will no longer accept them as inevitable. There is a clear and growing tendency among these nations to follow the lead of any power which promises them economic betterment. The area is politically and socially unstable. Lastly, its geographical proximity to potential enemies of the free world make its position very tenuous from a strategical point of view.

On the other hand, oil is indivisible and the effects of an interruption of supply from anywhere will be felt everywhere. The effect of economically unsound and technically inefficient operations anywhere will have repercussions everywhere.

This interdependence is dramatically illustrated by the conflict between Great Britain and Iran in connection with the Anglo-Iranian oil concessions. If, for any reason, the present flow of oil from Iran should be curtailed or interrupted, the effects will be felt all through the free world. I believe, however, that with goodwill and cooperation on all sides the worst consequences to the prosperity and security of the Eastern Hemisphere could be avoided. Of the 210 million barrels produced in Iran, some 42 to 56 million barrels are shipped in the form of crude oil, mostly to Europe. Any such loss could be made up from other sources. Of the 154 to 168 million barrels of Iranian refined products, only perhaps one quarter goes to Europe and the remaining quantities to East of Suez markets. Grave problems would arise particularly in the East of Suez area if this supply were to be curtailed, but I believe that the combined efforts of the free world may result in covering perhaps two-thirds to three-quarters of such a loss through the utilization of all existing production and refining facilities to the utmost, and by increasing imports from the Western to the Eastern Hemisphere by perhaps 5 to 10 million tons. With wise and timely planning by government and industry, I am convinced that a catastrophe can be avoided.

Even more important, with the political orientation of free Europe to the West and the dependence of a large part of the free world on the oil supplies of the Middle East, potentially dangerous frictions and strains have arisen, which the Western world must try to solve wisely before they result in serious damage to its prosperity and strategic position. Nor can the solution of these problems be delayed safely or undertaken on a half scale. The force of the powers which have been unlocked is so great that immediate and visible results are called for.

Revenues from oil form very large shares in the income of the producing countries of the Middle East and in most instances represent the only source of funds which could be set aside for economic improvement. Moreover, they provide, in many instances, the major or only source of foreign exchange. The expansion in oil production and the recent revisions in the royalty payments of several concession contracts will result in large increases in the revenues which may, utilized wisely, go far toward giving the area a basis for greater prosperity and social and political stability.

Conclusion

. . . There is an intimate relationship between the prosperity and security of Europe and the continued availability of oil supplies. Without sufficient oil European industry cannot operate and Europe's economic and political stability would be gravely threatened. The free world's economic and military strength would suffer a tremendous, and perhaps fatal, blow.

Europe depends, however, for the bulk of its oil supplies on a few small underdeveloped countries in an area with a high degree of strategic, economic, and political vulnerability. If the flow of this vital oil should fail, no readily available alternative sources could be drawn upon on short notice. Europe's minimum needs could, and undoubtedly would of course, be obtained from the remaining supplies of the free world, in particular, the Western Hemisphere. Any such shift could not be made without a tremendous effort involving, probably immediately, rationing in the free world and, over the long run, tremendous new investments to create the required additions to producing and refining potential.

To prevent such a contingency from ever arising must therefore be one of the most important economic, political, and strategical policy goals of all the nations of the free world. It involves a progressive and well thought out economic development program in the oil-producing countries of the Middle East based largely on the development of their oil resources.

The economic progress and security of the oil-producing countries of the Middle East is thus closely linked to the prosperity and security of oil-importing countries of the Eastern Hemisphere and, in fact, to that of the whole free world. The oil economy of our free world is indeed indivisible.

Part 3
WESTERN OIL POWER

Introduction

The years of the fifties were those in which the demand for oil in the free world escalated from 9 to about 18 million bbl. per day.

By the end of the decade 25 percent of all oil in international trade came from the Middle East. It was a period in which the importing nations were not totally aware of how their oil needs involved a broad array of their separate and collective interests nor of how the signals emanating from oil producers as to impending changes should be interpreted, much less responded to.

The fifties were a decade of phenomenal increases in oil consumption – to be followed by a comparable surge in the next ten years – but they were also a decade of extensive political change. The European imperial reach was no longer a profound force; retreat, or accommodation to war-induced weaknesses, provoked an increase in nationalism, especially among those who had been part of the British and French systems. Political freedom alone was an insufficient goal; economic power must also be present. While these views pervaded the then colonial world, their effects upon the international oil system were detected and discussed in the following papers.

Two events in particular accelerated change. One was the abortive effort by Great Britain, aided by France, to reassert its presence and control over Suez through the invasion of Egypt in 1956. Although it is doubtful that the British forces could have prevailed in any case, U.S. determination to end the engagement made defeat of British-French objectives certain. Both the attack, and the U.S. reaction to it, were widely regarded in the Middle East as marking the end of a Western imperial presence. Henceforth, political and economic forces no longer felt constrained by the possible arrival of Western military forces to restore order. Aspects of the crisis are discussed in Chapter 10, in Mr. Levy's article from Foreign Affairs, "Issues in International Oil Policies," April 1957. By 1956 the dependence of Europe on Middle East oil was already so large that the actions of oil producers in response to the Suez attack virtually deprived Europe of all its imports from the region – a singular warning of the potency of the "oil weapon." No other region in the world could replace that embargoed oil.

Another event – with which Mr. Levy was closely involved as adviser to Governor W. Averell Harriman, who was sent to Iran by President Harry S

Truman to assist in the resolution of the Anglo-Iranian controversy—was the 1951 disintegration of the British oil arrangements with Iran, centering upon the role of the Anglo-Iranian Oil Company (now British Petroleum). The enormous oil and financial stakes of Britain and that company had long made Iran a place of special importance. When Iranian political movements caused the collapse of the existing systems, the predictable response was to make clear that Iranian oil was not an irreplaceable source; a blockade, in effect, of nationalized oil by the international community and its oil companies was put in place.

The loss of revenue to Iran, as a consequence, was sharp and devastating. Negotiations recommenced and a large but by no means full restoration of British interests was the immediate result. In fact, little satisfaction could have been obtained for no durable settlement was possible in view of the fundamental political forces that had emerged. The winds of change, as discussed by Mr. Levy, were beginning to take their toll. Nevertheless, the international oil system was given an extension, force was avoided, and a compromise was struck that lasted for much of the decade. In these complicated rearrangements, Mr. Levy played an important and widely acknowledged role.

On November 15, 1951, in a presentation on "The Impact of Oil on the Political, Social, and Economic Development of the Middle East" before the members of the Council on Foreign Relations, Mr. Levy discussed a perspective on the region different from that to which most of the audience were probably accustomed. It should have been a disturbing experience. The fact of the immense oil reserves of the Middle East was well established, and the implications to importing societies were appreciated. The effect of these reserves on the region itself, however, was rarely discussed. The extremely complicated interests of governments of the importing states, oil companies headquartered in London, Paris, and New York, and the governments in the region were assessed by Mr. Levy.

All of these interests had to be considered by the companies whose own concerns must have seemed to them straightforward. Yet the companies functioned in an ever more stressful milieu in which they were in competition for concessions, while their governments, generally in support, still had their own larger purposes to be secured. At the same time, the governments of the Middle East had their own perspectives and pursuits. Among them, oil was never so much a unifying factor as a cause for competition. In a later paper, delivered January 14, 1953, to the Philadelphia Committee on Foreign Relations, Mr. Levy spelled out these complications with regard to oil transactions; he did so in a manner which he adopted on many other occasions by referring again and again to the separate but interdependent relationships of producing and importing governments and the international oil companies. Over the years he built both a conception of their interests and of their differences, and elaborated upon their prospects:

... Foreign oil operations are subject to a series of conflicting economic and commercial considerations which, in their turn, have frequently important political aspects and repercussions. To illustrate, one may perhaps review an oil transaction from a producing field in the Middle East to the market in Western Europe or the United States.

The producing country would like to obtain a maximum income from its oil. It is therefore interested in the largest possible royalty and also a high price, as such price would increase the profit of the operating company subject to its taxation. The country would, for the same reason, insist on maximum production and sales of its oil and also on the quickest feasible development of its reserves. Such pressure for production and sales may easily conflict with the desires or needs for outlets of other producing countries. It may also exceed the practical possibilities existing for the present operators to provide the necessary capital and markets, and it may interfere with their commitments in other producing areas. The producing country would also prefer to have its oil refined locally as this would increase the value of exports and result in additional employment and industrial activities. It would, further, like to receive its income to the greatest extent possible in hard currencies. Finally, it would be concerned with the destination of its exports, at least to the extent that such trade might affect its political or commercial interests.

The transit countries through which the pipelines from the Persian Gulf to the eastern Mediterranean are laid and through which the oil will pass are making another series of requests of the operating company or the operator of the pipeline. They would ask for a maximum income from the pipeline operators; they would want their oil needs to be covered on favorable terms; and they, too, would try to establish some measure of control over the destination of exports, in accordance with their own political considerations.

The consuming and importing countries, in turn, would like to obtain the oil at the cheapest possible price. They would prefer to receive it as crude oil rather than as finished products in order to save foreign exchange and to provide employment and industrial development in their countries. In nearly all instances they would like to pay a minimum amount of hard currency and a maximum amount of soft currency. They would also be interested in procuring their oil from a variety of sources rather than from one producing country or company, in order not to become too dependent on a single supply basis.

The operating company, with responsibilities to all parties in the chain, must seek an optimum basis for its entire operation. This involves obtaining and maintaining the necessary freedom of control over all its activities, receiving an equitable return on its investments at each operating stage, and securing conditions and financial arrangements that will be conducive to

*maximum efficiency and optimum production efforts and sales oppor-
tunities.*

*Finally, the parent country of the international oil company is interested
in the continuation of the operation and prosperity of its companies, the
safety of their foreign investment, and the general degree of prosperity and
security which their operations provide for peace-loving nations.*[1]

*Moreover, as is pointed out in Mr. Levy's presentation, oil and the in-
terests of great powers impinged on a region where governments were
generally weak and unavailing, subject to forces endemic in the area, and
ill equipped to deal with the phenomenon of the modern, external states'
geostrategic interests.*

*In this period, companies and their governments were strongly inclined
to preserve the existing systems in the Middle East. Nevertheless, the
author clearly foresaw the nature of the changes that were coming in the
region as nationalism began to light fire after fire in an incendiary area.
This view of the impending changes was expressed thus by Mr. Levy:*

*Arrangements between Middle East Governments and the oil companies
must be flexible enough to adapt themselves to changing circumstances and
must be firmly rooted in equity. The acknowledgment of the concept of the
sanctity of contracts is all important, but this acknowledgment must be
coupled with a deep appreciation that conditions and concepts change,
particularly during as long a period as concessions contracts are usually concluded for. The concepts of payments of income taxes by the concession
holder, of currency, export and import controls exercised by the big trading
nations of the West, of the equity of profit division between a producing
country and the company, all developed during the last twenty years or so
had obviously an effect on Middle East oil countries. In order to maintain
the concept of sanctity of contracts, it is necessary to be willing to adjust
contracts by negotiations and mutual agreements in order to meet new conditions.*

*There is no telling how such an approach, adopted earlier, might have
altered the situation in the years to come. Arguably, it could have greatly
affected the course of adjustment which, in time, was forced upon the
companies. The later comment that "oil operations in the Middle East
[have an] intense political character" was almost an understatement.*

*Finally, Mr. Levy wrote compellingly of the distractions and corruption
that are visited upon a society overwhelmed by a sudden profusion of
what is, for the bulk of the population and its government, "unearned
wealth." One can suppose this remark was regarded then as superfluous*

---

1. The last two paragraphs of this quotation are extracted from Chapter 9, "Interdependence as the Foundation for World Oil Operations."

and, indeed, gratuitous. Read today, it was an urgent and early warning of a possibly fatal weakness in the societies of most producing countries of the Middle East.

Yet, as these references make clear, repairs to the system, and even some basic changes—the better to cope with what was happening—would not suffice. The gray clouds, which were gathering, are discussed in all these papers—culminating in a storm that was finally to break in the early seventies, as described fully in Part 4.

9

Interdependence as the Foundation for World Oil Operations

At the Fourth World Petroleum Congress (June 1955), Mr. Levy presented a paper on the theme of interdependence of interests and relationships among all parties to oil as the fundamental explanation of the astonishing expansion in its supply. He described the situation as one made possible through recognition by each party of the opportunities it made for itself and the others, while also recognizing the constraints existing on each other for unilateral action or disregard of the interests of the rest.

It was an accurate depiction of a process which, had it continued, would have greatly improved upon the prospects for the 1980s. But, in a real sense, the situation it described was already disintegrating, perhaps beyond recall.

Introduction

During the last few decades all nations have become increasingly dependent for their prosperity and security on continued access to ample oil supplies. At present 30 percent of the world's energy is supplied by oil and its share is steadily advancing. The bulk of the future expansion in energy requirements, at least until the use of atomic fuels has been commercially developed, is likely to be met from oil. In many of the countries where it is produced, meanwhile, oil has become the major basis for economic development.

Since oil is thus of vital concern to all nations, it is frequently a major subject of national and international policy. It is hardly surprising, therefore, that any conflict of interest centering around oil always makes news. However, much less attention is paid to the fabric of cohesive forces that is essential to the continuous functioning of the world oil economy. An analysis of the play of these forces which provide the essential link in the uninterrupted chain of oil operations, from production

Lecture delivered before the Fourth World Petroleum Congress, June 1955 and published in *Proceedings of the Fourth World Petroleum Congress*, Sect. IX/B, pp. 31–38, Carlo Colombo Publishers, Rome. Published with permission.

through refining and transportation to distribution, will form the subject of this statement.

The Participants in the World Oil Economy

To establish the necessary basis of a review of these cohesive forces, it may be well to consider first who are the various participants in the world oil economy and what are the salient features that have given rise to their characteristic role in international oil operations. Functionally, there are four principal types of participants: producing and exporting countries, international oil companies, consuming countries dependent on oil imports and, on a slightly different level, parent countries of the oil companies.

Regarding the *producing countries,* the world's very large known oil deposits are concentrated in four major areas: the United States, the USSR, the Caribbean and the Middle East. The first two of these areas, since they constitute important industrialized countries, are also large oil consumers, utilizing virtually all of their available production within their own borders. Accordingly, most of the world's oil exports originate in the producing centers of the Caribbean and the Middle East, where a limited number of relatively small and industrially underdeveloped countries account for the bulk of the world's proven oil reserves. These two areas and, more specifically, five countries (Venezuela, Saudi Arabia, Kuwait, Iraq and Iran), provide over 75 percent of total current crude-oil production and about 90 percent of the proven reserves outside the United States and the USSR. The share of these countries in the world oil trade amounts to almost 85 percent excluding, and to over 75 percent including, the U.S.A. and Eastern Europe.

The *consuming and importing countries,* in contrast to the producing areas, are very numerous. They comprise first of all the industrialized countries of Western Europe, which is the world's largest oil-importing area. Secondly, substantial and growing oil import requirements exist in virtually all countries of Latin America, Africa, Asia and Oceania. Finally, the United States, even though it is the world's foremost oil producer, is also an importer of very large quantities.

Turning now to the third group of participants in the world oil economy, the bulk of worldwide development, refining, transportation and distribution of oil, outside North America and Eastern Europe, is undertaken by a relatively small number of international *oil companies* of very large size. The foremost reasons for this concentration are perhaps the huge capital investments and the extraordinary technical and managerial skill required in international oil operations.

The large investment requirements in turn are based on three factors.

First, the oil industry is engaged in a commercial activity involving very large investments in fixed specialized equipment at each stage of operation, both in actual amounts and relative to other productive factors such as labor. Secondly, most countries (outside North America) have preferred to grant to the companies oil exploration and exploitation rights over very large areas at one time. Finally, oil operations, particularly the development of production in remote regions, involve an extraordinary degree of risk which only companies with exceptional financial strength have been willing and able to assume. In order to minimize this risk factor the companies had to diversify their interests by engaging in oil operations in several of the major areas of the world. Moreover, in order to assure themselves of access to markets, on the one hand, and availability of supplies, on the other hand, they had to build up a completely integrated chain of operations, from exploration and production to refining, distribution and marketing. Only in this manner could the companies be reasonably certain that their vast investments would be continuously, and therefore profitably, employed at all times.

The fourth and final group of participants in the world oil economy, although playing a role which differs somewhat from that of the other parties, consists of the *parent countries* of the international oil companies. For a variety of historical, political and economic reasons these companies are all of U.S., British, British-Dutch or French nationality. Among the most important of these reasons has been the long-established predominance of the parent countries in world industry and commerce. This leading role was accompanied by very large capital formation, the development of economic and technical skills and, in the case of the United States, the early establishment of large-scale oil operations at home. On the basis of such a strong foundation, the companies of these countries were willing and able to risk the vast sums of capital and to supply the specialized technical and managerial know-how required for successful international oil development.

The Relationship Among the Various Participants

The Basic Play of Forces

As presently constituted, the world oil economy is thus composed of a considerable number of parties, i.e., five very sizeable producing countries (outside the United States and the USSR), seven or eight very substantial international oil companies, a very large number of importing countries and three or four parent countries of the international oil companies. These parties stand in a variety of relationships to one another, which may be conveniently divided into two basic types. First, there exists a functional or "vertical", relation between the various participants in any one chain of operations, from production through refining and transportation to distribution, on which the continuity of the operation depends. Secondly, as there are a number of producing countries, oil companies and importing countries making up the world oil economy, there exists also a distinct interplay of forces between the participants in any one chain and those engaged in other chains of operations.

Both these sets of relationships are of relevance in an analysis of the cohesive forces responsible for the continuous functioning of the world oil industry. Accordingly the basic relationship of the participants within an individual vertical operating chain, i.e., that between the four participants making possible an effective operation, will be discussed first. This will be followed by a review of the interplay of forces which exists among participants of different operating chains as such forces also affect the relationship between the participants in any one particular chain.

The Respective Contributions and Benefits

The functioning of world oil operations is based on the joint endeavors and the continuous contribution of all the participants. In and by itself, neither the oil in the ground in a producing country, nor the availability of a market for oil in an importing country, nor the investment and the managerial and technical skill of an oil company can create or maintain effective world oil operations. Only if all the parties concerned make their full contribution toward a functioning world oil economy will an otherwise unused resource or unsatisfied need or unutilized investment or latent managerial and technical skill be fused into a new and valuable economic asset.

Examining the respective contributions which the individual participants in any one chain of operations must make in order to fulfill their function, the *producing country* furnishes of course the oil resource itself. This implies that it must provide not only physical access to the oil located within its jurisdiction but, equally important, a general framework suitable for the operations of the oil industry; that is, economic and political conditions in the country must be such as to make it possible and attractive for the oil companies to establish large-scale operations within its borders. Specifically, such factors as respect for assumed obligations, a stable political and social environment, favorable tax and currency legislation, and noninterference with vital managerial functions may be mentioned.

The *country dependent on imports* makes its contribution to the continuing functioning of oil operations by permitting equitable access to its market. This implies that no unwarranted or discriminatory restrictions on imports must be imposed, that appropriate means of payment must be made available, and that the use of oil must not be prohibited or greatly discouraged by quantitative controls or excessive taxation.

The *oil company's* contribution lies in the field of capital and skill. It must make huge investments to provide most of the facilities from production to distribution involving, particularly in the early exploration stages, very great risks. In addition, the company applies its technical know-how and managerial skill to the whole chain of oil operations.

Finally, the *parent country* of the oil company must facilitate the task of the company by basing its policies on principles favorable to capital formation at home and to the flow of investment and expansion of trade abroad, including those of the "open door" and of free competitive access to the world's raw materials. Moreover, the parent country supports and encourages the operations of its company by exercising a generally constructive and stabilizing influence in the community of nations.

The division of basic responsibilities between the various participants as it has developed in the past is not arbitrary. With oil resources concentrated in a few areas and import requirements distributed world-wide, a link had to be provided. The economically underdeveloped producing countries lacked the capital and know-how to develop the resources and distribute the oil; these essential tasks could be carried out only by the oil companies. In this manner, under present conditions, the existing division of functions has resulted in a most effective overall performance by the oil industry. In every case when any one of the participants attempted to interfere unduly with the respective functions and responsibilities of the other participants, the efficiency of the oil economy was gravely affected; in some notable instances operations even came to a virtual standstill.

Since the contribution of each of the participants is required for the continuous success of the operation, it must of course be matched by certain benefits to each of them so as to assure that his essential contribution will be forthcoming.

The major *producing countries* expect to attain a high level of oil operations, counting on these operations, which generally represent their most important industrial activity, to provide them with large government revenues and a high foreign exchange income. The entire economy of most producing countries is based on such receipts.

The *consuming countries* depend on continued international oil operations to provide them, under equitable conditions, with an assured supply of fuel vital to the development and operation of their industry and transportation and thus to their prosperity and security.

The *oil companies* rely on the unrestricted functioning of the world oil economy for the continued ability to fulfill their production and supply commitments in the many countries of the world where they operate. On this ability depends the security of the companies' investments and their commercial success, if not survival.

The prosperity of their nationals will naturally also be of benefit to the *parent countries* of the oil companies; in some instances this may well be a decisive contribution to the parent countries' economic prosperity. In addition, of course, the continued progress of world oil operations is essential to the well-being and security of the entire world in which the oil companies' home countries, in view of their world-wide position and responsibilities, have a unique stake.

*   *   *

These various, and to some extent divergent, interests of the various participants in the world oil economy carry, of course, the seeds of serious potential conflict. Nevertheless, with only a few notable exceptions, oil operations in general have been carried on smoothly. What, therefore, are the factors that have been responsible for reconciling any apparent conflicts of interests and for establishing and maintaining a balanced, workable relationship among the various participants?

The Process of Adjustment and Reconciliation

The effective adjustment and reconciliation of the respective interests of the various participants require a complex and delicate balancing of many essential considerations. They affect a number of nations at different stages of economic development, with diverse political, social and legal systems, and they involve problems of the relationship between sovereign powers and private commercial interests.

However, the very fact of the continuous functioning of the world oil economy proves that these problems can be solved. There are perhaps three major sets of conditions relevant in this connection, which will be reviewed separately. They are: a. the recognition of interdependence; b. the force of competition; and c. the threat of countervailing power.

The first essential factor, the *recognition of interdependence,* implies the realization that the contribution of each of the participants is vital and that each one of them, at all stages of any bargaining process or operation, must be able to obtain certain benefits if his cooperation is to be forthcoming.

It is obvious, therefore, that each participant must abstain from exercising such pressure that others would be discouraged from making their necessary and legitimate contribution to the world oil economy, or would be prevented from receiving those benefits that are essential to them.

There are thus basic limitations on the conduct of each participant in his relation with the others. In particular, no participant can with impunity attempt to:

    a. obtain for himself a return from world oil operations that would destroy the inducement of others to produce or consume oil in ever-increasing quantities;

    b. interfere with the continued possibility for equitable commercial development and investment, and thus jeopardize the continuous functioning and competitive strength of the oil economy;

    c. deprive any of the participants of effective and necessary control over his own operations within his sphere of responsibility, and thus interfere with his contribution and efficiency of performance;

    d. extend his own legal concepts or economic philosophy beyond his legitimate sphere of power, and thus impose his own system of law and economics on the other participants.

The *force of competition* and free choice in the marketplace represent the second set of conditions that are essential to the equitable balancing and adjustment of the various divergent interests involved. Each of the participants is obviously aware that, on every level of transactions, there exists a variety of alternatives which is available to the trading partner.

Thus the producing country, at the time of contract negotiations, is fully cognizant that the oil company has investment opportunities in a number of other producing countries. Moreover, even after a company has acquired a concession, it still has a choice of where to make additional capital expenditures, since there are other countries which offer favorable prospects for the development of production. Finally, the producing country also realizes that any oil importer can draw on different sources for his oil supplies.

The oil company, in its turn, is confronted by competition from a number of other firms on each level of its operations. For instance, when the company negotiates with a producing country for oil concessions it must obviously be prepared to meet the competition of other commercial enterprises. Similarly, only if its supplies to oil importers are offered under competitive terms will the company be able to maintain its sales in the market place.

Competitive access to sources of production as well as to markets is thus essential in the process of maintaining effective checks and balances among the various participants. If any one participant, or any combination of them, were ever to attempt to monopolize any one phase of operations, or to interfere with the free competitive choice of the other participants, the continued effective functioning of the world oil economy might well be jeopardized.

Finally, there is cognizance by all participants that oil operations involve the security and vital interest of nations, and that, therefore, any attempt by any one party to exert unwarranted pressures beyond the point of basic equity would bring into play *countervailing powers* that are ever-present in the world oil industry. It may suffice to point out that in any extreme case, where the continuity of oil supplies to any nation would be seriously threatened, such severe tensions might be created that the economic stability and peace of the world might be endangered.

The Guiding Considerations

In accordance with the continuous interplay of all these forces, the various participants in a functioning world oil economy must therefore pursue a course of conduct that is based on:

a. the recognition that they all depend on each other's contributions for the realization of essential benefits;
b. the understanding that there must be an equitable relationship between their respective contributions and benefits;
c. the awareness that not only their own vital interests but also those of the others are involved;
d. the acknowledgment that, therefore, each of them must, in the exercise of his own prerogatives, take into account the effects of his actions on all others and must be willing to limit the exercise of his political, economic or legal power accordingly; and
e. the realization that, as the survival of nations might be at stake, the alternative to operations based on free consent may well involve the use of force.

To sum up, each of the participants must accept freely as his guiding and limiting consideration the pursuit of his enlightened self-interest based on the recognition of mutual interdependence and founded on the respect for his own obligations and the basic rights of others.

The Recognition of Interdependence and the Recent Progress of World Oil Operations

While there have of course been some temporary setbacks in individual instances, the concept of enlightened self-interest, based on the recognition of mutual interdependence, has found an ever wider acceptance by all the participants in world oil operations during the last decade or so. A few recent developments may be cited in support.

Petroleum legislation in many Eastern and Western Hemisphere countries has been designed specifically to attract foreign private investments and to make possible the introduction of foreign technical and managerial skills. Guaranties against expropriation, arbitrary controls over management, restrictions of currency transfers, and other impediments to effective operations have been increasingly provided for. The financial arrangements between producing countries and oil companies have in general been based on the so-called 50-50 principle. Agreements for equitable local taxation and the avoidance of double taxation have been made by many countries. In practically every instance where such favorable conditions were established the response of the oil industry was immediate; large new investments were made, technical skills and know-how were provided and new oil developments were initiated.

All participants have extensively and increasingly cooperated to assure a continuously expanding flow of oil from the producing countries to the importing countries. Particularly difficult problems were encountered and solved during the period of severe currency stringency after the second World War. The solution of these problems involved great shifts in the oil supply basis for many countries, the refining and transportation of oil, the provision of equipment and services for the industry, and the trade and currency policies of many nations.

Against this background of basic progress in the fundamental recognition of interdependence in world oil operations, there has been an unprecedented performance by all participants. Oil production, particularly in the Middle East, was developed at an extraordinary speed, a large refining industry was created in Europe, tanker and pipeline transportation was expanded most rapidly, new equipment and service industries were built up in many soft-currency nations, and the pattern of the world's oil trade and of the industry's supply and services was drastically adjusted to meet newly evolving conditions.

*   *   *

In summary, the participants in world oil operations have indeed succeeded in assuring a continuously expanding production to meet ever-growing world needs, furnishing large revenues to producing countries as a stable basis for their economic development, and providing uninterrupted access to supplies and markets through all contingencies. In short, they have been able to make a unique contribution to the prosperity and security of all members of the peace-loving world.

10

Issues in
International Oil Policies

Following the British and French attack upon Suez, Mr. Levy wrote a paper for Foreign Affairs *(April 1957) that set forth the principal long-term effects of that attempt. "Economic considerations, important as they are to the relatively impoverished countries of the area, become insignificant when confronted by political necessities or political pretensions." After Suez, nothing could ever be the same again.*

The necessity of the United States and Europe to reconsider not only the implications of Europe's dependence on the Middle East in particular, but also the ramifications of dependence on imports in general, led the author to stress the now critical need for the United States to adopt the following priorities:

1. *Obtain assured access to foreign oil sources for the United States, its allies, and friends on an equitable basis (by which the author meant in circumstances and on terms favorable to both consumers and producers of the oil);*
2. *Assure that the flow of oil (sources and volumes) would be in accordance with basic policy aims and strategic necessities (excessive dependence on some sources would increase the nation's vulnerability);*
3. *Encourage and support effectively the foreign oil operations of American companies; and*
4. *Collaborate with other nations whose companies are also engaged in foreign oil operations.*

These considerations are then spelled out by Mr. Levy. Particular stress was placed on the need to emphasize and buttress the community of interests between Middle East suppliers and the West (and thereby limit any opportunities the USSR might perceive to extend its influence among the suppliers). Especially important was an urgent requirement on oil importers to minimize their vulnerabilities to interruptions of the flow of oil,

Reprinted with permission from *Foreign Affairs,* April 1957.

thereby increasing the bargaining position of the West with respect to any particular producer.

Also important (in view of subsequent events) was the author's emphasis on the need for strategic petroleum reserves by importers and the creation of a program whose elements came to be the principal ingredients in the present emergency program of the International Energy Agency. That agency was founded in 1974 for the chief purpose of improving the capabilities of importers to withstand sudden shortages.

Finally, Mr. Levy's concern over the relationship between governments and oil companies was expressed.

> *Our policy requires, of course, the closest cooperation between the oil companies and their own national governments. This involves special responsibilities on either side. It also creates new problems of communication and of chain of command between government and the companies. The demands and responsibilities which have devolved on our international oil companies go far beyond the normal concerns of commercial operations. Public and private responsibilities become increasingly intertwined. Our existing arrangements for government-industry relationships in this new unchartered area appear to be inadequate to cope with the broad range of new problems. At present neither party knows quite how to proceed, who should act, and who must take responsibility for decisions; serious misunderstandings have thus been inevitable. The problem deserves the most urgent and careful study if our government as well as our companies are to play their proper roles.*

Over the past decade, the economic growth of the industrialized West has been based in large measure upon a prodigious expansion in sources of energy. Oil has made the largest single contribution to that expansion; and the stepped-up consumption of oil has been especially marked among basic industries engaged in production and transport. In consequence, Western industry has become increasingly dependent upon an uninterrupted flow of oil. Since the end of World War II, Europe has been drawing more and more heavily upon Middle East oil to meet its requirements. But mounting tensions in the Middle East, arising from aggressive nationalism, the deterioration of British political authority and Soviet expansionist tendencies, put Europe's access to these critical supplies in jeopardy. The Suez crisis has driven these points home as no argument or previous circumstance could.

I. The Suez Crisis and Europe's Oil

Just a few figures will highlight the proportions of the current crisis for Western Europe. Europe's oil requirements last year were running at about 3,000,000 barrels daily. Imports from the Middle East amounted to 2,100,000 barrels per day, or 70 percent of European requirements. In contrast, crude oil production in Western Europe itself came to a bare 200,000 barrels. The balance of its needs was largely met by crude and product imports from the Western Hemisphere.

These oil supplies accounted for almost 20 percent of the total energy utilized by Europe. The relative importance of oil as a source of energy varies, of course, from country to country. The United Kingdom, for example, with relatively high coal production, relies on oil for only 13 percent of its energy needs. Sweden, on the other hand, depends on oil for about 45 percent of its energy needs. For Europe as a whole, each 5 percent shortfall in its oil supplies is the equivalent of a 1 percent decline in total energy availability.

When the Suez Canal was blocked following the British-French military operations against Egypt, the normal flow for 1,350,000 barrels daily of Middle East oil was cut off. When Syria blew up the pumping stations of the Iraq Petroleum Company, delivery of 550,000 barrels of Iraq oil came to a halt. Thus, 1,900,000 barrels, out of total shipments of 2,100,000 barrels per day, were lost. All that remained of Europe's normal receipts from the Middle East were 200,000 barrels per day moving from Saudi Arabia via Tapline.

Tanker tonnage, which was already fully engaged in mid-1956, was obviously inadequate to long-haul the same volume of Middle East oil to Europe around the Cape. Europe was obliged, therefore, to turn to the Western Hemisphere for a maximum contribution of both crude and essential black oils. Tanker priorities were given to the movement of supplies from Gulf and Caribbean ports; remaining tonnage could be assigned for liftings from the Persian Gulf around the Cape.

As a result of the U.S. supply effort and its own stock withdrawals, Western Europe was able to maintain over-all oil consumption at about 80 percent of normal. In terms of total energy, the 20 percent oil deficiency amounted to an over-all energy shortage of about 4 percent. All countries, of course, made every effort to meet their more urgent industrial requirements. In general, the minimum needs of railways and basic industries were maintained. Distillate and fuel oil supplies for other industries ranged from about 80 to 90 percent of normal. Gas and diesel oils for heating were more severely restricted; and gasoline consumption was reduced by rationing devices.

The economic impact of the Suez crisis extended, of course, beyond the direct effects of these oil shortages. In two broad areas, that of dollar exchange and of investment potential, the economic consequences of recent months set Western Europe back considerably. European balances of trade—especially those of the United Kingdom and France—were seriously disturbed. Britain's currency position deteriorated badly, and France's was equally precarious.

II. The Problems Ahead

When Europe emerges from the present crises, it will still have to face up squarely to two stern realities. First and foremost, there is its continuing and even increasing dependence upon Middle East oil. And set against this dependence is the seriously compromised position of the Western Powers—and of the international oil companies—throughout the Middle East.

*   *   *

This increasing dependency provides Middle East nationalism with its most effective weapon. The dynamics of that nationalism make existing oil arrangements an inevitable target for attack. Nor can the West rely on the importance of uninterrupted oil operations and oil revenues to Middle East governments as a deterrent to hostile actions. Economic considerations, important as they are to the relatively impoverished countries of the area, become insignificant when confronted with political necessities or political pretensions. Syria provides a striking example. Last October, the Iraq Petroleum Company [I.P.C.] dropped its plan to construct a new pipeline through Lebanon to Tripoli (which would have meant a considerable gain in revenues) because of its dispute with the Lebanese Government over taxes. The new line was instead scheduled for Syria. Yet Syria, the impending beneficiary from the dispute between Lebanon and I.P.C. over transit revenues, wantonly destroyed I.P.C. pumping facilities. Under the circumstances, there is little chance that Syria will be regarded as a better risk than Lebanon.

Meanwhile, British political authority, which has contributed so much to the stability of institutional arrangements in the Middle East, has been on the decline and has now practically disappeared except perhaps in the Persian Gulf sheikdoms.[1] In 1951, [Prime Minister Mohammed] Mossadegh nationalized the properties of the Anglo-Iranian Oil Company.

---

1. This exception was removed in December 1971 when the United Arab Emirates came into existence and the traditional British presence among the Trucial states came to an end.   —Editor

Europe weathered the crisis by virtue of expanded crude production in other areas of the Persian Gulf and product exports from the United States. But American and other non-British participation in the operating consortium represented an obvious derogation of British status in Persia. In 1954, Britain acceded to the evacuation of the Suez territory, with only pro forma recognition of its vital interests in the Canal itself. More recently, Jordan evicted British military advisers and then voided the long-standing treaty with Britain. Cyprus is in revolt. Yemen now stirs up trouble over Aden. Even in Kuwait and Bahrein, Britain has been faced by local disturbances.

Under the pressure of increasingly aggressive Middle East nationalism, local forces have frequently concentrated their attacks to disrupt existing oil arrangements. At the same time, the Soviet Union is in a position to exploit every tension in the area. It can conspire with rulers or conspire to subvert them. It can make political capital out of the explosive Israeli situation. It can support one power bloc against the regional grouping that the West relies on for support in the cold war. In this situation, no institutional arrangements into which Western governments or oil companies enter may long be secure.

Finally, the commercial dominion of the international oil companies has been increasingly impaired. Development of the area's oil resources had been initiated under the umbrella of British political authority. The countries themselves were underdeveloped, often with no prior contact with the Western world; their political and social institutions had scarcely been exposed to modern Western influence at the time when international oil companies started their operations. Concessions were secured by large international oil companies—three of them European and five American—mostly in the inter-war period. These concessions were usually framed on the broad basis, giving the companies development and export rights.

In the ten years following World War II, international oil companies invested $2.5 billion in Middle East development. These investments were undertaken under concessions and contractual arrangements that seemed to offer a substantial measure of security, and the oil companies could pursue commercial operations relatively freely. Production, pricing, and sales all fell within the province of company operations and could be worked out in the context of world resources and requirements.

In recent years, however, oil companies operating in the Middle East have found themselves increasingly circumscribed by political considerations. The threat of expropriation is ever present; and the precedents of Iran and Suez can hardly be reassuring. Under that threat, terms of concessions are constantly revised in favor of the Arab governments; and one revision is scarcely completed before new demands are presented.

What appear to be minor impositions gradually add up to pretty basic changes in the circumstances under which companies operate. Local government representatives gain participation in management of company affairs; headquarters have been transferred to the producing countries; 50-50 profit-sharing arrangements are used by the local government to obtain a voice in commercial decisions. Control is exercised over destination of exports and attempts are made to control tanker shipping. In the end, the international company is being required to behave as though it were solely a national organization.

The companies are also confronted by attacks from quite the opposite direction. While Middle East governments may argue that prices should be higher, the Secretariat of the U.N. Economic Commission for Europe suggests that those prices might well be lower. In the United States, oil companies are under indictment for violation of anti-trust laws by virtue of their foreign operations; they are, on the one hand, asked by our Government to limit imports, and, at the same time, charged with manipulating prices by not importing more.

In sum, the commercial operations of companies are exposed to conflicting political pressures. The companies are no longer able in all circumstances to assure supplies from the producing countries to various consuming nations. Frequently they cannot balance and reconcile their interests in various producing and consuming countries effectively. Also, they may no longer always be able to implement effectively the policy decisions of their home governments.

In view of the deterioration of the arrangements under which a large part of the international oil trade is carried on, we must define the broad goals of our oil policy and find effective ways to implement it.

First, our international oil policy must assure access to foreign oil resources for ourselves, our Allies and other non-hostile nations, no less during troubled times than during peacetime.

Second, it must provide for access to foreign oil on an equitable basis.

Third, it should so far as possible provide that the flow of oil from the various producing countries where our corporations and those of our Allies operate will be in accordance with our basic policy aims and strategic necessities.

Fourth, our international oil policy should offer encouragement to the foreign oil operations of American companies. It should protect the concessionary arrangements and operations of our companies against undue and illegal interference by the governments of foreign producing countries; and it should assure non-discriminatory treatment of our corporations engaged in refining and marketing operations in consuming countries.

Fifth, it should include friendly collaboration with other Western nations whose companies are also engaged in foreign oil producing operations.

III. Limitations of International Agreements

We are now facing a challenge to every single aim and aspect of our international oil policy. The range of alternatives through which we might seek effectively to implement our major goals is broad. They narrow down considerably, however, when we measure them against the unpleasant realities that we have just reviewed. For example, to secure uninterrupted Western access to Middle East oil, several proposals have been made involving new international agreements, providing either guarantees of access or guarantees for private foreign investments, or both. While such agreements may well represent a step forward in the evolution of international law, it is nevertheless important to recognize their inherent implications and limitations.

To be effective, the principle of assured international access would have to involve also agreement on the terms under which oil would be made available. But the interests of consuming countries in access to supplies on "equitable" terms would be countered by the interests of producing countries for guaranteed access to markets at "reasonable" prices. This would seem to suggest the need for an international oil authority. But such a development would probably put our companies and those of our Allies into the position of being subject to regulation as international public utilities, and it is unlikely that it would either provide effective protection for the terms under which our companies presently operate or assure their management control. In the Suez Canal case, Egypt has actually taken over the management and control of the Canal, and it is noteworthy that during all of the negotiations no effective consideration was given to the reestablishment of the old Suez Canal Company.

Nor is it clear what effective sanctions could be invoked if free access to oil resources or markets was refused by a producing or consuming or transit country. The most prominent and perhaps the only example of an international treaty assuring free access to an international facility is the Constantinople Convention of 1888. This Convention worked reasonably well so long as it was not subjected to intense conflict of national interests. However, it broke down during the two world wars. It also was ineffective when Egypt believed that overwhelming political or strategic considerations warranted closing the Canal to Israeli shipping.

If effective sanctions cannot be established, it follows that an agreement on free access will break down whenever any participating country becomes engaged in overt dispute with another signatory country. In the midst of cold war, and while the world is disturbed by Soviet machinations and subversive activities, the effectiveness of such an agreement must remain in doubt.

It has also been suggested that an international agreement be concluded which would assure respect for private foreign investment. Such an investment treaty might imply that an international body would also have the right to adjudicate disputes arising out of various agreements under which foreign investment is undertaken. It might also imply that there would be machinery for adjustment of contractual terms, particularly where contracts had been concluded for periods of 60 to 90 years.

While such a charter might cover the case of expropriation and provide arbitration machinery for disputes over compensation, it should be noted that the way international law has been interpreted during the last 20 years, expropriation with adequate, prompt and effective compensation has not been successfully contested. No effective test has ever been made of the case where expropriation actually involved unilateral cancellation of foreign concessions and breaches of contractual commitments by a sovereign. The sovereign, by refusing to permit an international tribunal to pass upon his conduct, closes the door against any international legal recourse.

Equally unresolved is the question of how such a charter could deal with a progressive erosion of concession rights. Changes in concessionary terms undermining the position of the foreign investor may be as harmful as expropriation. Without in fact openly nationalizing the property, governments may infringe on management rights, establish local political control over operations, impose increased taxation, and enact troublesome labor laws. Similarly, the establishment of production and export controls under what countries may claim are their sovereign rights, the submission of the operations to their own foreign policy considerations, and a host of other devices would effectively limit and might even destroy the value of foreign investments.

In the final analysis, neither an international agreement providing for free access to oil nor an international charter guaranteeing the security of foreign investments can by itself meet the basic needs of an international oil policy. Both would probably lead to the establishment of new and complicated international machinery which would interfere with the functions and flexibility of private operations. They would fail to provide ultimate security against interferences with oil supplies or violations of investment rights precisely because the West would still have no practicable recourse against such moves when they are spawned by nationalistic determination or Soviet machinations.

There is also some reason to doubt whether the West could at this time rely on the United Nations for the establishment of a policy that would effectively protect its interests in Middle East oil. The United Nations is not an impartial judiciary body; its power often depends on the support of voting blocs with sectional interests; it would have no practical means of enforcement when either the United States or the Soviet Union opposes its decisions. We could expect the USSR to support any move against the West which would interfere with Western political, economic and strategic interests. The Soviets would naturally frame all oil and Middle East political issues in terms of "Western imperialism and oil monopolies," and try to unite the voting strength of their own satellites with that of members of the Bandung group and of other underdeveloped countries.

Considerable thought has been given to the possibilities of a European Oil Community, designed to improve Europe's bargaining position vis-à-vis the Middle East oil producing countries, on a commercial as well as political level. The Community could, in the view of its advocates, more easily integrate Europe's oil supply within the framework of Europe's over-all energy economy. In case Middle East oil were unavailable or obtainable only on the basis of unreasonable terms, the Community could take joint steps either to regain access to the oil or to make alternative provisions and divide the burden of any shortfall equitably among its members.

In evaluating the potential effectiveness of an oil community, however, it is essential to keep in mind that in contrast to the resources of the Coal and Steel Community, oil reserves are located outside Europe, in an area of political unrest and subject to constant Soviet interference. A combination of European consuming countries that tried to enter into negotiation with any oil producing country would most likely provoke the creation of a bloc of Middle East producing countries. There are, of course, distinct trends toward a unified oil policy by the Middle East producing countries. But political problems and economic rivalries have up to now prevented its effective establishment. Nothing would give it greater impetus than a combination of European consuming countries. It is to Europe's interest, however, to avoid as long as possible the establishment of such a Middle East bloc; and certainly to do nothing that would provoke its early creation. Once consuming bloc and producing bloc confront each other, each separate grievance of individual countries is likely to be embraced by all. Each oil problem would then tend to become an intergovernmental and political problem and the great flexibility inherent in private oil operations would be lost. Accordingly, under present conditions the oil problem is more apt to be aggravated than eased by an open combination of European consuming countries. This of course does not imply that the countervailing power of consuming countries does not provide an essential contribution to the implementation of international oil policy.

IV. Implementation of International Oil Policy

While international agreements may fall short of guaranteeing Europe secure oil supplies, they may in certain instances help toward the evolution of principles of international behavior and procedures for the international settlement of disputes. And in spite of its limitations, the U.N. within certain areas may determine at least a minimum basis of common interest and exercise a moderating influence.

However, it would be dangerous to rest our national security on the expectation that international agreements will insure international performance. To be successful in protecting our essential interests and those of our allies in the Middle East, an oil policy for the United States must proceed simultaneously along three lines:

1. Emphasize the community of interest between Middle East states and the West, and minimize thereby the opportunities for Soviet intrigue.
2. Minimize Western vulnerability to the interruption of the flow of Middle East oil, and increase thereby the bargaining position of the West.
3. Support effectively the rights of private companies which are prerequisites to continued investment and development.

No one of these goals by itself will result in absolute Western oil security; together they hold out the promise of restoring stability to the international oil trade.

As to the first, we must try to establish with as many of the major producing and transit countries as possible a continued relationship that would tie them more firmly and more securely to the Western side so that they will be immune to Soviet interference and Soviet temptations which are likely to persist as long as the East-West struggle lasts. This will require an effort to accommodate at least the major political and economic aims of the Arab countries.

Such a policy would inevitably involve some identification of the Western world with at least the most essential aims of Arab national aspirations—the development of their economies and improvement of standard of living. The major emphasis of such a policy must be on the enlightened self-interest of all the parties concerned and on awareness that a breakdown of their relations with the West would be catastrophic, perhaps even more so to them than to the West. The prerequisite for Western cooperation must be some basic commitment by Middle Eastern countries of their own national resources and efforts to their national purposes.

Arrangements with the governments of Middle East countries would not necessarily be all that is required to assure the security of our oil operations. A great deal would depend on the popular support which these governments command. To achieve a measure of popular support is the more important as Soviet attacks on our position in the Middle East are clearly designed to appeal to popular prejudices against our oil companies. Their propaganda repeats monotonously that the companies are out to "plunder" the Middle East's natural resources and export their oil without adequate compensation to them, and that "oil monopolies" in the United States dictate U.S. foreign policy to assure the most "colossal superprofit" to these monopolies.

We cannot, therefore, ignore this issue, and must try to see to it that the benefits from our oil operations and our economic aid as well are spread reasonably fairly throughout the economy. This is easier said than done, but it would be helped along if Western governments were to provide greater encouragement to those countries whose governments act responsibly.

We should also try to encourage a spirit of competition among the various producing countries for attracting investments and securing outlets. The development of their oil industry should, to the extent possible, be a measure of their own cooperation. We should further do our utmost to dissuade producing countries from the notion that because the international oil companies control production in other areas and have refining and marketing affiliates all over the world they can always be assured of a market outlet by applying pressure against the companies.

The problem of the degree to which the United States and the West can accommodate themselves to Arab policies and national aspirations is of course a most serious one. We cannot give up vital principles, policies or economic interests. We must not be blackmailed into taking a position contrary to basic equities because Arab countries threaten to cut off our access to the oil, or take over our companies, or join the Soviet bloc. Such policies would be self-defeating in the long run.

There are plainly certain political issues on which we simply cannot satisfy the Arabs. In the first place, the Middle East is so lacking in intraregional unity that certain of our decisions might be acceptable to some countries and completely unacceptable to others. In particular we cannot afford to refuse support to the friendly nations of the Baghdad Pact and yield to pressures or threats of other Middle East countries hostile to us.

Secondly, we cannot ignore certain vital interests of Britain and France which have run counter to Arab national ambitions and have led to friction between our Allies and the Middle East. The maintenance of the NATO alliance imposes upon us the obligation to protect their vital interest as well as ours. Moreover, in our oil operations throughout this area our companies are nearly everywhere closely associated with European companies. We cannot (and in general must not even try to) escape the concomitant responsibilities of our Western alliances. Popularity in the Middle East may be quickly acquired and even faster lost; it provides no reliable basis for Western policy.

Finally, we cannot agree to the continued corrosion of essential rights of our own and allied corporations, not only because unilateral and arbitrary breaches of commitments are contrary to basic Western principles, but also because they would increasingly jeopardize Western access to the oil. Behind our willingness to accommodate ourselves to Arab national aspirations there must also be the willingness and ability to resist unjustified requests and threats. Our Middle East policy must thus be based on friendship backed by strength. For on the realities of power at any given moment rests the effectiveness of diplomacy.

Let us now turn to the question of how we might minimize the West's vulnerability to interruptions in the flow of oil from the Middle East. Since our strength to resist undue pressures in that area will rest in large measure upon our success in minimizing our dependency upon its oil, we must put ourselves in a position in which we are at least able to cope with a temporary interruption of supplies. If that can be done, it will be apparent to the Middle East that Europe could survive a temporary cut in its oil supplies without too much danger. At present, continued availability of Middle Eastern oil is so urgent that no interruption can be borne. In contrast, the dependence of some Middle East countries on the income they obtain from the sale of oil is of a different order of urgency. Many of them could absorb a reduction of their royalty and tax income for some period of time by drawing on accumulated funds or by reducing less essential expenditures. By redressing this balance it might be possible to drive home to the Middle East its dependence on income from sales of oil.

Wherever allied companies are in a position to do so, it would seem essential to encourage the development of excess productive capacity. This would include the oil-producing countries of the Middle East, for it is possible that in an emergency our access to production in some of them might be maintained. Excess productive capacity in the Western Hemisphere and in the Eastern Hemisphere outside the Middle East would, of course, be particularly desirable. In addition, the development of other sources of energy should be pursued as rapidly as economic considerations permit.

There should also be a greater flexibility in the provision of transport and refining facilities. We need a maximum build-up of tanker capacity and should avoid wherever possible the construction of pipelines from oil supply sources through third countries, especially if tankers can be made to do the job. Further, we should encourage the building of refining facilities in consuming rather than in producing countries or other areas which are likely to be subject to political disturbances.

Finally, provisions must be made to accumulate substantial strategic reserves in the United States as well as in Europe. During periods of ample availability, arrangements might perhaps be made to produce and ship crude oil from the Middle East to suitable consuming countries for storage for an emergency. The target for such a program might well be on the order of nine to twelve months of European crude oil requirements.

If such a broad program were carried out, our Allies could do without Middle East oil for a limited time, particularly if we were prepared not only to make excess production and stocks available to them, but also to share in the shortage, if necessary. Our bargaining leverage with the Arab world on all vital issues would be enhanced and the security of Europe's oil supplies greatly increased. It would provide us with alternatives either to yielding to completely unreasonable requests of the Middle East countries or to using more drastic and probably less effective means such as economic sanctions or even force to impose our will. Even a temporary ability of Europe to support its economy with alternative oil supplies might be of decisive value in the play of forces with which we are confronted. With wholehearted cooperation between the United States and Europe, this program can be realized at a total cost of less than our present peacetime military expenditures for a few weeks.

We have already dealt at length with the increasing disabilities to which our oil companies have been subjected. It is becoming imperative that we insist more energetically that the rights of our corporations be respected and that disputes be arbitrated rather than unilaterally resolved in favor of Middle East governments under the threat of expropriation. In particular, we should not leave our corporations without advice and protection against arbitrary decisions of Middle East governments. Our corporations, with their world-wide interests and responsibilities, must not be coerced into becoming, in fact, instruments of the foreign or strategic policy of Middle East producing or transit countries. The framework of international oil operations and international investment would be torn apart if we are not able to put a halt to such local pressures.

In lending support to the companies in their foreign operations, Western governments must be prepared to recognize (as must the companies themselves) the legitimate interests of producing and transit countries. But Middle East governments must in turn recognize that their oil as a resource has been developed through international participation; and its value hinges on international trade which brings producing and consuming countries together; and that oil's role in future economic expansion depends on continued capital investment on a massive scale in production, transport, refining and marketing facilities. International oil companies have undertaken the costs and responsibilities in each of these areas — but the flow of private capital and the effectiveness of commercial operations can continue only if the security of investment against political depredations is assured.

*   *   *

Within the framework of our international oil policy we must unequivocally state our intention to assure Western access to Middle East oil and our readiness to protect the equitable rights and basic position of our companies. If our interests can in due course be fortified by treaties so much the better; if not, we must nevertheless undertake to support them with all the power at our command. They involve basic issues of international comity and behavior and our prosperity and security depend on the respect they command.

11

Western Security and International Oil

In his June 1958 remarks before the Council on Foreign Relations, Mr. Levy reexamined and elaborated upon the security dimension of oil supply. He warned that the ramifications were so important that governments should be alert to the probability that a threatened loss of supply could turn a limited engagement into general war. Conversely, having secure sources of oil might be decisive in the ability to limit a war. In words which have been applied to the Gulf region in more recent years, Mr. Levy said: "We must . . . avoid a situation where because of oil shortages that would vitally cripple our allies, we would be forced to redress the balance by the threat or even the use of force."

Turning his attention to American oil strategies, Mr. Levy criticized the oil import policy and found it seriously wanting—an issue that was to plague government and industry and affect the national interest for many years yet to come.

Mr. Levy reviewed the increasing threat to the durability of existing concession arrangements and the problems inherent in maintaining these concessions over many years. These problems would arise in circumstances in which extensive political changes and a more equitable share in the benefits from the exploitation of oil would have to be reassessed in order to avoid increasing instability in oil supply.

The significance of the global logistics system is emphasized in the mutual interest of suppliers and consumers of oil. Its possible impairment, as a result of tensions between governments and companies or as a consequence of oil producers acquiring ever greater control over key decisions, would have to be watched carefully.

Again, emphasis was given to the cardinal points in oil security presented in the earlier paper but now elaborated upon: domestic resource development, Western Hemisphere sources, surplus producing capacity, and diversification of sources; strategic oil stocks; spare tankers and refining capacity.

Lecture delivered before the Council on Foreign Relations, June 11, 1958.

Mr. Levy concluded by stating that unless governments and oil companies understood each other's respective areas of responsibility,

> a divergence between Western security policy and commercial interests in foreign oil would nearly inevitably reflect a deterioration of the commercial position of our companies and it would usually also result in a weakening of our basic power position. What is badly needed, therefore, is a determined effort by government and industry to collaborate now on all the measures that would enhance our basic security and commercial strength in international oil. Such a community of purpose alone holds out any real promise of averting a fatal breakdown in contractual and political relations in international oil, which if it were ever permitted to occur would gravely jeopardize Western Security.

It was the author's balance and objectivity in discussing such matters that led John J. McCloy to write of his association with Mr. Levy that it had been "highly advantageous . . . in arriving at . . . conclusions in respect to the entire energy field." Nevertheless, in light of differences of view, not all oil executives or government officials agreed with his suggestions nor do they now. But as Sir Eric Drake, formerly chairman of British Petroleum, recalls (with particular reference to the tumultuous years of the early fifties—the Mossadegh crisis), "while recognizing [Mr. Levy's] massive grasp of the economics of the problems, I was by no means convinced of the validity of some of his ideas as to what ought to be done . . . but in the years since . . . I have had increasing respect for our friendship with Walter which I deeply value." Consider these words in the light of Mr. Levy's effort in the following paper to assess the significance of the accomplishments of the international oil companies and their importance to Western security—in the context of sweeping political change.

Recent developments—in Indonesia, the Middle East, Algeria, and Venezuela—make it imperative that we reassess the significance of international oil to Western security. Old issues have been inflamed and new issues posed for the world oil trade and for Western foreign policy. It is particularly important, therefore, to review our foreign and economic policies against our security requirements. In present circumstances, we dare not be burdened with unnecessary or wrongly conceived objectives. The issues are too great; the consequences of mistaken policies, perhaps even of misunderstood policies, might well be disastrous.

The first question that arises is why oil should raise security problems at all. In this connection, we might first consider the issues of oil and war; and then the more complex and vexing issues of oil and peace.

Oil in War

Total war between major powers now means atomic war, which would be fought out on the basis of military forces in being. In such a war, our international oil position would hardly be relevant to the outcome. The status of general industrial activity after an atomic attack, and the condition of oil refining and transport facilities, would obviously limit severely the use of oil. Whether or not we would then have continued access to large domestic or foreign oil resources would most likely be of little relevance. What is vital is that we have readily available in stock the necessary supplies of oil and weapons to support the deterrent and retaliatory power of our nuclear forces and of our strategic air command.

It is also obvious that neither the U.S. nor its allies in Europe is preparing to fight a massive and protracted nonnuclear war of attrition. We do not undertake such military preparations because we are not willing to underwrite their economic cost. It would, therefore, make very little sense to incur the cost of such preparation in a specific economic field such as oil, when for reasons of economics we are not preparing ourselves for such a contingency in the overall military field.

There is still, however, the constant and real threat of limited hostilities. Such warfare might be limited in its theater of operations or in its objectives—and would presumably involve the use of tactical forces rather than the unleashed destructive power of nuclear weapons. In general, we are entitled to assume that in a limited war, even of protracted duration, full U.S. mobilization would not be required. By the very nature of a limited war, it is likely that some if not all channels of international trade will remain open except in the direct combat area.

It is unlikely, however, that such hostilities could remain limited if they occur at our boundaries in Latin America or in Western Europe. The U.S.-Canada-Mexico-Caribbean area we would certainly assume to be a home base which must be kept open and free; the survival of our European allies should be of equal importance. A war in those areas, therefore, would most likely be either of short duration or turn out to be a major war.

It is quite possible, however, that a limited war could occur in the Middle East, for example. The problem we would then face is Western dependence on Middle East oil and the consequences that might result from an interruption in the availability of such oil. Any position the enemy would gain during such a war he would probably maintain thereafter, if his dislodging required the use of atomic weapons and his advantages were not of decisive importance. In this situation, our Western European allies in particular might well be deprived of the oil supplies that would be essential to their future prosperity. To the utmost extent possible, therefore, it must be the goal of security policy to be able to face and survive (from an oil supply point of view) a limited war that would involve the Middle East.

Should the West fail to achieve a degree of independence from vulnerable sources of foreign oil, then threatened loss of access to that oil — which would in fact prevent us from maintaining our economies and fighting forces — would probably turn limited hostilities into all-out-war. We must assume that neither side in a limited war could accept a loss that undermines its basic security. We had concluded earlier that there are strategic areas where hostilities would probably explode into total war. Here we find that oil, as a strategic resource, could be an equally decisive consideration. In this context, therefore, the continued availability and accessibility of large quantities of oil, in the final analysis, may be decisive not so much for victory or defeat as for the ability to limit a war.

Oil in Peace

From the standpoint of national security, we have also to consider the critical role of oil in meeting the energy requirements of the free world during an uncertain peace. In order to win this cold war, we must maintain our own economic and political strength and also that of our allies. We must gain the support of the noncommitted nations, and hopefully pray that in due course our way of life will attract to us the support of the present satellites of the Soviet Union. In this manner we could weaken the strength of our potential enemy or at least take the edge from his aggressive power and intent.

We need not on this occasion review in detail how important a contribution oil makes to the economic strength of ourselves and our allies; how essential oil income and foreign exchange earnings are to the balance of payments and financial standing of the U.K.; how basic it is for the economic development of the producing countries. We need not dwell on the fact that the large oil reserves outside the U.S. and USSR are mainly concentrated in the less-developed countries, the Middle East, Indonesia, and Venezuela. As mentioned already, unrest in each of these areas raises grave questions with regard to the durability of the country's political fabric and at the same time implies in some instances a most serious inroad of Soviet influence and thinking in the government's own circle.

During this period of cold war, the Western nations depend for their prosperity and security on access to oil on reasonable terms. And for those powers who in fact control such access, oil provides a great degree of economic and political power in their relations with both the oil-dependent nations and the producing countries. We must therefore, if at all possible, avoid a situation where because of oil shortages that would vitally cripple our allies, we would be forced to redress the balance by the threat or even the use of force.

The issue of oil and security thus involves, in the first instance, sufficient flexibility in sources of supply so as to cope with the dangers of limited hostilities in areas where oil resources or channels of transportation might be affected; and secondly, the problem of access to oil supplies during a period of cold war so as to maintain the economic viability of the free world. Within this broad framework of targets set for guarding against limited war and conducting and winning the cold war, the problems centering around oil are of grave importance on all levels—strategic, political, and economic.

Control and Access

Beginning with the ideal case, Western control over oil resources is obviously the best means of assuring access. Control means, of course, that Western government policy can, if necessary, be effectuated by government authority. It would include the ability to make available or withhold supplies, and insure delivery over essential transport routes. It would include the ability to impose economic or even political terms for those supplies. Our most desirable security target, therefore, would be to establish a position so that we can assure sufficient quantities of oil for our own needs and those of our allies during a period of cold war and limited hot war, and withhold supplies from our enemies. Conversely, it would be an essential target of our security policy that no force hostile to us, be it local or foreign, should gain control over the oil-producing countries or the transit and transport routes and be able to withhold oil from us or our allies or to impose terms which are either economically or politically unacceptable.

It is in fact no longer possible to achieve and maintain this kind of control over the oil resources that we and our most important allies are now drawing on. Much of the free world's oil is located in areas outside our direct political province or power sphere, or even worse, in areas which are torn by internal strife and where communistic or Soviet military power can easily destroy or at least severely impair our supply bases and transport routes. This would not apply to North America itself, and perhaps not to the Caribbean, but from a strategic and worldwide point of view, there is very little to be gained from our own relative independence of foreign oil if all our allies are desperately dependent on insecure supply sources.

The problem turns, therefore, from one of establishing control over oil to one of securing access to oil. Access to oil would basically involve a dependable physical flow of oil from producing areas to consuming countries. This would require that no hostile forces control either the producing areas or transit routes from producing to consuming areas. It would mean that the terms under which oil can be obtained do not involve economic, commercial, or political conditions that would make it undesirable or impossible for the user to accept such terms in order to obtain his oil. It would imply further that the oil is obtained with sufficient technical efficiency and that a coordinated program is carried out which would provide the necessary flows of oil in the desired quantities and qualities. Secure access to foreign oil would thus be based on a friendly or at least a nonhostile relationship with the governments and local powers that control the oil producing and oil transit areas, and a sufficient power position of the West to deter the Soviet Union from any kind of interference in the flow of oil.

It is obvious that the producing centers in the Western Hemisphere, particularly in Canada and perhaps less so in the Caribbean, are likely to be safest for Europe as well as the U.S. It is also obvious that oil supplies from the Middle East and Indonesia, while accessible at this time, might not be accessible when needed, either because of hostile control over the producing areas or over the major transport facilities; or because of local unrest and strife which would make producing operations impossible; or because of conditions that interfere with technically efficient operation of the fields and refineries and their transport lines (be they pipelines or the Suez Canal).

U.S. Oil-Import Policy

From everything that has been said, a critical review of our present oil import policy would seem to be required. The current import program has tended to alienate our Western Hemisphere oil-producing neighbors, particularly Canada and Venezuela. If it should be maintained, and become really restrictive against the oil exports and production of our neighbors, it is bound to handicap badly our future relations with these vitally strategic countries.

At the same time, U.S. import policy is based on considerations of national security and designed to protect incentives for exploration and thus the productive potential in this country. The necessity for it, as we have seen, is based not so much on the needs of a major war as on the requirements of economic strength in a cold war or under limited hostilities. On the basis of present replacement costs, it would appear that unrestricted imports, drawn from the "bottomless" reserves of the Middle East which have already been discovered, might badly affect the U.S. oil-producing industry. This would in fact mean that a large and growing part of our oil supplies would be based on uncertain availability from the Middle East.

If we accept the need for some control over imports for the stated reasons of national security, it is obvious that we must under no circumstances tie ourselves to a policy which could harm our neighboring oil industry to the north and to the south and make us decisively dependent on faraway sources such as the Middle East. As a matter of fact, the natural outlet for Middle East oil in the Eastern Hemisphere is of such magnitude and growing at such a rate that the support of Middle East economies should at this time not require large expanding sales in the markets of the Western Hemisphere. Indeed, with the abundance of low-cost oil in the Middle East, a strategic import policy should take account of the fact that important Western Hemisphere oil resources may require protection against the potential competitive impact of Middle East oil. The security of our country should not be left to the accident of competitive strength of particular oil resources.

Further, the present "voluntary" U.S. import control system raises most serious problems for our companies. Obviously, it is undesirable to have the government enter private business or control normal private commercial operations where it can be avoided. However, the present so-called voluntary system in fact brings the government right into the oil business; and even worse, it involves private enterprise in the affairs of government.

On the one hand, a target figure for foreign oil imports is translated into permissible quotas among companies according to a somewhat arbitrary and often-changing yardstick. Not only does an executive authority determine quotas, but it sits in judgment over companies who appeal against or apply for quotas, and exercises a measure of police power over those who do not comply with the voluntary system. This may well raise grave constitutional questions.

On the other hand, companies are free to determine the source of their permissible imports. But this means that the companies carry the responsibility of determining the pattern of oil flows into this country and the onus of explaining the impact of restrictions to foreign governments. Obviously, the normal commercial profit motivation of the importing companies would not necessarily result in a distribution of imports from the various foreign sources that would also be in accordance with our security needs.

Finally, this method of voluntary oil import control, as developed in the last year or so, might not raise such troublesome issues if it were only a temporary measure. However, if it should be maintained in this form for any length of time, which in the absence of any new supply crisis now seems likely, it could well represent a danger to the maintenance of inter-governmental commitments. It certainly represents a precedent under which any government that is committed to certain policies in its foreign relations might require its citizens and corporations to follow a different course of action, on a "voluntary" basis. It is not a broad jump from "voluntary" import restrictions asked of our corporations by our government to "voluntary" export restrictions or say "voluntary" tax or national contribution which may be demanded of producing companies to effectuate the national and security policy of foreign governments. Once governments embark on such a course, there is no way of predicting where it may lead and how it will undermine international arrangements and foreign relations.

The Role of the International Oil Companies

The subject that now warrants a most searching analysis is that of the position and role of the Western international oil companies within the framework of Western security policies and goals. The companies today are operating in an essentially hostile environment, not only in many producing areas, but also in many consuming countries. In part, this is inevitable. The very nature of their operations involves them with conflicting economic interests and subjects them to economic [and] political pressures—as among producing countries, between consuming and producing areas, etc. In addition, their operations have become a target, in the cold war, of both Soviet and local nationalistic attacks.

The companies must, of course, try to protect their economic and commercial interests. They will naturally resist any infringement of rights that have been acquired under concessionary or contractual terms, and must utilize all means at their disposal in doing so. It should be recognized, however, that it is by no means certain that it would be in accord with our security interests to give our companies under any circumstances all the support they might need—economic, political, or even military—in their legitimate pursuit of commercial interests, particularly in the event that friendly relations between the companies and a foreign government have broken down. The Suez Canal nationalization highlighted this possible divergence between the rights and interests of a nationalized company, the economic and commercial considerations of transiting nations and companies, and the policy of the U.S. Government and of the Western world.

Suez as a Precedent

Nationalization certainly deprived the old Suez Canal Company of its concession; but it did not ipso facto reduce the security of the West with regard to the utilization of the Suez Canal. Once Western bases had been liquidated in Egypt, the security of communication through the Canal did not rest so much on the position of the French concessionary company as on the ability and desire of Egypt to maintain transit or interfere with traffic.

It is significant that while nationalization had taken place under circumstances that make its legality doubtful; while it provoked the most serious but ineffective opposition, particularly in Britain and France; while the oil companies, because of the precedent it might set for their own interests, would naturally oppose the cancellation of a concession in Egypt which was in this instance even protected, at least in some manner, by a formal treaty—despite all these, the Suez Canal was freely used by the European consuming countries, by oil corporations, and shipping companies. This meant in fact making arrangements and agreements with the Egyptian national authority which had taken over the Canal by force even before compensation was agreed upon or paid to the private owner.

Our compelling interest in the Canal was and is that it remain open and available to the Western powers on terms that are reasonable for the traffic that can economically be shipped through the Canal. It is essential, therefore, that Egypt remains at least neutral in the East-West struggle and that we do nothing which would drive it into the Soviet orbit. This experience with the whole Suez affair is particularly important as it might well set a pattern if and when any new nationalization of concessions should be undertaken, and in particular in oil concessions in the Middle East. The lesson would not be lost on the various countries of the Middle East and it should be carefully evaluated by the Western powers, as well as by their international oil companies.

The Soviet Threat

The USSR, of course, is always prepared to play upon dissatisfaction and political passions. Again and again it stresses that "monopoly profits" from the oil concessions under our control vastly exceed our help and contribution to underdeveloped areas, and that our economic and political interest in such areas is in fact only an interest in protecting the "exploitation profits" of our corporations. Our concern for the stability of governments in the Middle East they interpret as a determination to protect old-fashioned and outdated government. The West has no interest in progress and economic development, they say, because this might prove to be upsetting to its economic concessions in the countries. At the same time, the Soviets argue in the various consuming areas, particularly the underdeveloped countries east of Suez, that our large corporations exercise a stranglehold over energy supplies and exploit the people by overcharging them for the oil they have to purchase in order to cover their needs.

For themselves, as the Russian delegate at the recent Afro-Asian People's Solidarity Conference in Cairo put it, their only concern is "their readiness to help as brother helps brother, without any interest whatever, for they know from their own experience how difficult it is to get rid of need." It is probably no overstatement to say that this Russian propaganda has proved extremely effective in the Middle East producing countries, in Indonesia, and elsewhere; and in many, many of the consuming countries where our oil companies operate. It has proved effective not only among the people, but also among government officials who should and could know better if prejudices, emotions, and extreme nationalistic—or socialistic, as the case may be—tendencies, did not control their reasoning. Above all, the actual and potential Soviet threat to world peace tends to neutralize our own position in those noncommitted, underdeveloped areas of the world and provides the power background for the ever-increasing nationalistic pressures against Western interests.

Erosion of Company Positions in Producing Countries

The trend toward nationalism in the Middle East and elsewhere is inevitable. Foreign investment in that area—particularly where it involves large raw material resources, where it provides nearly all of the foreign exchange needs and budgetary income of a country, and at the same time yields large profits to the foreign operator—is a natural target of jealousy and attack. The still-lingering hate of colonialism and imperialism is only too easily translated into opposition against foreign investment, and a strong drive to control it wherever possible, to take it over whenever feasible. Moreover, because of the size of the oil resources that have been found, and the stated dependence of so many nations on its continued availability, the countries concerned have become all too clearly aware of the economic and political leverage that would go with their control over this resource.

Within this framework, the danger of nationalization is always in the fore; or the threat of nationalization as a means of coercing significant changes in concessionary arrangements or enforcing ever-expanding local governmental controls. The international oil company is obviously interested in maintaining the concessionary and institutional arrangements under which it operates in the various countries. It is therefore greatly concerned with the sanctity of contracts as a necessary basis for continued international investment and international oil flows under its commercial control. The U.S. Government and its allies are, of course, no less concerned with the sanctity of international obligations and the legality of national conduct as it affects international relationships. But the issue of legality is not always posed as clearly as in the case of nationalization.

While the ultimate destruction of concessionary rights via nationalization is always a danger, there are many subtle encroachments on the prerogatives of our international oil companies that pose perhaps even more vexing problems and may ultimately turn out to be equally damaging to them. It is essential to size up these pressures, to evaluate their causes, and to assess their effects on the countries as well as on the companies in order to obtain a clear understanding of the proper relationships among commercial, political, and security issues.

The major threats to the operations of our companies as they manifest themselves against the backdrop of Soviet support, particularly in the Middle East area but also increasingly elsewhere, can be summed up as follows. First of all, the concessions usually are very large, often encompassing a large part or all of the oil-bearing territory of the country, so that there is only a small number of companies which can undertake the development of these oil resources. The local producing companies, on the other hand, are owned by a few international oil companies with producing interests in many other countries. The international companies must, of course, balance production and development in various parts of the world. But this foreign control by parent companies is often considered to be hostile or at least nonsympathetic to the specific needs and policies of the producing country, which naturally tends to look exclusively at its own position and potentialities.

Further, these concession arrangements were usually concluded for very long periods—for forty years and upward. At the time they were concluded the position of the two partners to the agreement was perhaps far from equal. The producing country, in particular, may have been subject to political pressures from Western governments. Or, its understanding of the oil business—the technology, economics, and politics of oil—may have been exceedingly limited, particularly where the company had been dealing with governments or autocratic rulers or sheiks without any Western political or commercial experience.

At that time, too, neither the company nor the country concerned had any realization of how big in fact the oil reserves would prove to be in some of the areas, exceeding by far anything that had previously been found or known. Now that the companies have discovered reserves which far exceed the immediate possibilities of production, the countries concerned believe that little more is necessary in the way of technical knowledge or investment risk in order to maintain and expand production for many years to come. They would feel that they could easily take over production operations themselves; and with demand increasing at a rapid rate, that they could also sell their oil in world markets and secure for themselves not only 50 percent of the profit as at present, but a much higher percentage.

Add to this the desire of producing countries to exercise the political and economic power that control over oil would imply, and the degree of unrelenting local pressure on the companies becomes obvious. As a result, the companies have lost much of their basic position and strength during the last few years. Perhaps nothing illustrates this decline as drastically as the change from royalty payments to the producing countries of 4 shilling gold per ton of oil produced to a 50-50 profit participation. The earlier system in fact reflected the "extraterritorial" character of the operations of the oil industry. The 50-50 system not only submits the company to local taxation, but also thereby to a local check on profits, prices, expenses, and so on. And by specifically naming it "50-50," there was an implication of a partnership arrangement between the country and the company which is now used by the producing country to claim increasing control over management functions and operations.

The international parents have thus increasingly been asked to organize companies subject to local national jurisdiction, to transfer their top management to the various producing countries so as progressively to separate the subsidiary from the control exercised by the parent company, and to install government representatives on the board of the local producing companies. In addition, demands are made for forward integration of local producing companies into transportation, refining, and marketing on a worldwide basis to secure a further transfer of power from the international oil company to the local government. At the same time, the necessary administrative and technical talent is rarely available in the producing country, and Western concepts of commercial conduct are simply not understood or properly appreciated in many instances.

A weakening of the organization and central planning of integrated company operations could easily destroy the efficiency and dependability of supply operations—and, incidentally, undermine the source of government income, which so depends on successful production in the country. The importance of integrated company operations for continued access to world oil must not be treated lightly. Consider for a moment the coordinating and planning functions of the parent companies—the heart and sense of integrated operations. This coordination and planning links widely separated areas, by programming production in far-flung corners of the world. It links producer with consumer, by a chain of transportation, refining, and marketing facilities. It links the present with the future, by investment now to provide the capacity for years ahead.

The operations of the international companies thus assure that worldwide oil requirements will be met by drawing on various worldwide sources of supply. At the same time, they assure market outlets for the production of various countries, making for efficient development and substantial oil revenues for those countries. To do all this, the companies must be able to conduct world trade through dollar and/or sterling currency systems. They must possess the physical and financial resources to match supplies with requirements in practically all foreseeable contingencies and to develop and distribute oil resources during periods of prosperity, depression, and crisis. Above all, the companies must balance sensitive political, strategic, and economic considerations—in producing countries, consuming countries, and in countries through which major oil movements pass.

The only alternative to the coordination and planning function that has given the integrated oil company its remarkable efficiency would probably be the conclusion of intergovernmental oil agreements. It is however extremely dubious whether such agreements, even if negotiable in the present state of world affairs, would not hamper rather than aid the progress of the world oil economy, and whether therefore from a Western point of view it would not be ill-advised to attempt to proceed along these lines at this time. What might, however, be the subject of a broad company policy review are the problems of how best to cope with the issues that are being raised in at least one of the Middle East producing countries with regard to joint ownership of Middle East concessions by several of the international oil companies. While the establishment of such companies resulted from genuine commercial—and in some instances, partly political—considerations, complaints are now being voiced that a joint company is governed by decisions of anonymous home office committees set up by the various owners, and that it can, accordingly, take actions only on the basis of the lowest common denominator. This, it is charged, is hampering the progress of a jointly owned producing company.

While obviously to the greatest extent possible we must attempt to take account of pressures and legitimate complaints, one thing is clear: we cannot afford to have the present efficiency of corporate and institutional arrangements in world oil replaced by chaos. For instance, a concept of competition in the sense of Adam Smith would be unworkable in economic as well as political terms. It would both interfere with the assured flow of world oil and also affect the economic prosperity of the producing countries. Cutthroat battles for market outlets between oil from the various producing countries might bring prices for crude oil down drastically, because crude oil supplies for many years to come are already available in the form of proven reserves and actual production costs in certain areas are a fraction of market price. A low-cost producer, such as Kuwait, could be the major surviving supply source. Most others, particularly those in the Western Hemisphere, might well be unable to compete even in their closest markets. Government revenues in many producing areas would tend to vanish, and the balance among producing areas and between production and consumption requirements that an integrated industry has been able in general to assure would be irretrievably lost.

Finally, the entry of new producing groups is almost certain to pose new difficulties for existing concessions. Not only the Italian and Japanese firms in Iran and Saudi Arabia, but a large and responsible American company, Standard Oil (Indiana), have entered upon new concessions with the governments of the producing countries that go far beyond previous arrangements and are designed to give the producing country increasing power in the world oil industry. The international oil companies, of course, would be reluctant to accede to such new arrangements as would jeopardize the terms under which they now operate. But the large profits that have been made on foreign crude-oil production have obviously acted as an incentive to newcomers and provided the inducement for them to "improve" on the old terms. For their part, the producing countries have a keen interest in taking in such new companies, both because new concessions to the international group that already possesses tremendous proven reserves would not seem to promise any rapid increase in the country's total production; and because the establishment of new arrangements as to profit sharing and national participation in the broadest scope of oil company operations provides new controls and powers as well as additional leverage in their demands upon the established companies.

Only time will tell whether the new companies will find oil — and once they find it, whether they will be able to develop and market it profitably. But the danger to existing arrangements remains, I believe, whether or not the new ventures succeed. As a matter of fact, if they fail, the pressures on established companies for improvement of concessionary terms could well be intensified. In their case, the success of exploration has already been proven and as some of the countries' government officials have put it, the original risk money has been returned to them manyfold.

The Attacks on Oil Companies in Consuming Countries

The issue of prices and profits, in particular, has also affected relationships between the oil companies and many consuming countries.

Especially in some of the underdeveloped countries of Asia and the Far East, there has been a strong feeling that they have been asked to pay much too high a price for their oil supplies. Similar resentments have been expressed even in Europe from time to time.

As in producing countries, such feelings have been intensified by the fact that supplies and distribution of oil in most of the consuming areas is undertaken by foreign-owned subsidiaries, which in most instances belong to very large U.S. and British corporations. Thus they become an easy target of suspicion. And in consuming countries, too, the desire is for greater national participation — for local refining, a locally-controlled transport and tanker industry, for centralized planning and coordination of the various available energy resources, for oil exploration in their own country — and the feeling is widespread in these countries that the foreign oil companies are not really interested in such national aspirations.

[In addition], price developments in U.S. as well as foreign oil have for one reason or another resulted in a higher profit element in crude-oil production than in refining and distribution. With huge reserves proven in the Middle East for Eastern Hemisphere needs, Middle East crude-oil prices and profits have naturally received a great deal of attention. The consuming country accordingly feels that an undue part of the total profit from oil operations is made outside the consuming country and beyond its taxing power. Finally, the Suez crisis, when price increases and other measures were subsequently reflected in increased profits of some of the companies, coupled with the indictment by a U.S. grand jury on charges of price collusion among many important U.S. oil corporations, will tend to undermine foreign confidence in the industry, however unwarranted the present unproved charges would ultimately turn out to be.

The Threat of Foreign Domination

As it is working out, the widespread interests of the international oil companies in the production of many countries, and in refining and marketing operations in most of the consuming areas of the world, may actually be used by some important foreign producing countries to carry out their own policy. Their demands may cover not only affairs in the producing country itself, but also in other areas where the companies operate and where the producing country, for political or other reasons, desires the company to handle its business in a manner different from the way the company itself would act. We need only refer to the Suez Canal crisis when the Middle East producing countries prohibited exports of their oil to Britain and France; or to other requests or suggestions where the producing country attempts to exercise some control over the conduct of the oil company and its affiliates in third countries and exercise pressures with regard to concessionary arrangements, supply policies, pricing, etc. in such areas.

The political control by producing countries over the operations of oil companies would thus be extended in depth and scope. While local affiliates of the international companies have obviously to conform to the national position in each of the various countries where they operate, the danger exists that not only the foreign subsidiaries but even the parent companies might be under pressure to act in the interest of such countries where their important affiliates operate. Obviously neither our companies nor our government could ever yield and become hostage to the economic policies and strategic necessities of foreign countries where vital interests of the U.S. or of the corporations are involved.

Commercial Interests and National Security

It would appear, therefore, that if the present arrangements in international oil, that have contributed so much in terms of technological, logistic, and commercial efficiency, are to be maintained, the companies must succeed in convincing the many producing and consuming countries in which they operate of the mutual advantage of continued association. But it must be realized that however reasonable the arrangements between the international oil companies and the countries where they operate may prove to be, the companies would still have to cope with many of the problems and pressures which have previously been referred to. The ultimate protection, therefore, of the commercial position of the companies as well as of Western security interests would not necessarily or perhaps even primarily depend on the equity of the various oil arrangements, however essential such mutually beneficial arrangements would obviously prove to be.

The real and lasting basis, in addition, of course, to the equity of our oil arrangements, for our security, as well as for the bargaining power and ultimate commercial strength of the companies, would rest on the ability to get along without the production of any particular country and still maintain adequate supplies to various market areas. If, however, the oil companies are unable to make up for the loss of supplies from any particular producing area, the inducement for the producing country to use or misuse its strength would be nearly irresistible. Similarly, the consuming countries, if they could not obtain their essential requirements from the companies, would be sorely tempted to make independent arrangements with the producing country where the production is available. The situation as it developed with regards to the Suez Canal stands out sharply. Then every country and company very rapidly made its own arrangements with the Egyptian Authority which had nationalized the

Canal company. On the other hand, the producing countries need outlets in Western markets. The ability to provide such markets without being dependent on any particular source of supply is the only really effective position of strength for our Western companies. If we are able to establish this position clearly and decisively then we will also be able to protect effectively our essential commercial and security interests. Once the oil companies are in a position to supply the essential needs of their major customers on reasonable terms even when a particular producing area should no longer be available, it is that much less likely that the consuming country will make its own deals with the producing country and it is that much less likely that the producing country will risk a showdown with the company. When this bargaining power is a fact, and after the expenses to provide it have been incurred, only then will it probably be unnecessary ever to make use of this power.

Basis for a Security Policy

If we are not to be dependent for our oil on any particular country or transport facility where interruptions would endanger our survival, then patterns of oil operations and oil flows, and the policies of government and companies that affect them, must be analyzed most carefully. Some changes in emphasis on the future utilization of capacities may prove advisable, or the establishment of alternative supply facilities, in the event that present patterns are disrupted. In general, the following would seem to be basic considerations in a security policy:

- The greatest reliance that is feasible on domestic resources, together with those in other Western Hemisphere countries.

- A buildup of some excess producing capacity in the Western Hemisphere, and also in the Middle East, so that, for example, operations in Iran could be expanded should operations in Arab countries be impaired, etc. Development of new producing areas, including the Sahara if that should prove politically and economically feasible.

- Establishment of oil stocks in Europe and other important consuming areas of sufficient size to bridge the gap until flows can be readjusted, should present supply sources be cut off.

- Availability of tanker and refining capacity sufficient to cope with minimum adjustments resulting from interferences with normal transportation or operations in producing areas.

- Provisions so that sufficient strategic surplus capacity as may exist and will be needed to assure minimum supply flexibility will be maintained over time and in a manner that would not be economically and commercially destructive. This is particularly relevant at present when there is sizable surplus capacity in world oil, giving us a great degree of flexibility at this time.

Acceptance of some of these considerations among the various companies has perhaps been slow. There may well have been, at least up to a short time ago, a basic misapprehension, among some companies as well as Western governments, of our strength and basic power relationships. In this connection, I need only refer to the recent governmental and company interest in a large new Middle East pipeline from the Persian Gulf to the eastern Mediterranean, based on the unrealistic hope that such a pipeline could be effectively protected by international treaties which would provide that all disputes would be adjudicated by the International Court. However, it should be noted that the U.S. excludes International Court jurisdiction over domestic matters, with the U.S. being the sole judge whether or not such matters are domestic, and the United Kingdom excludes such jurisdiction in all matters affecting national security. At best, therefore, one would have to expect that Middle East countries would insist on similar clauses which would greatly reduce the effectiveness of international treaty protection, even if otherwise they might have provided some measure of security. On the other hand, the construction of such pipelines would have reduced future tanker needs. This would have further impaired the companies' bargaining position by providing a new facility which would have been subject to Middle East political control, in contrast to the flexibility that is provided by tankers. It would have been possible for the producing countries to lay down vastly increased quantities of oil right at the eastern Mediterranean in case their relationship with the companies should ever deteriorate.

Some of the companies, too, have shown a great deal of reluctance in going along with the concept of an increased European strategic reserve against interruption of supplies from the Middle East, such as occurred during the Suez crisis. They are naturally disinclined from a commercial point of view to maintain surplus capacity in transportation or any other level of operations except perhaps in crude-oil reserves. They are inclined to discourage the growing concern of European governments with regards to the security of their energy supplies from abroad or the desire of some for a coordinated energy policy, including oil. In fact, some of them prefer to keep their producing operations completely outside the sphere of interest and concern of their European customers and other countries. In doing so, they may well be depriving themselves of a most important partner and of a basis of potential strength in their relations to producing countries.

It would appear, therefore, that the whole range of company policy with regard to its bargaining strength in producing areas and its standing and position in consuming countries [should] be given most careful study by the Western governments as well as the management of the international oil companies. The protection of commercial interests is, in the first instance, the concern of the companies themselves. As it turns out, however, the measures that contribute most to the bargaining position of the companies are essentially the same as those that would contribute most to the security interests of our governments during a cold war and serve as a contingency against limited war. There is, therefore, a great community of interest in the policies that may appropriately be undertaken so as to guard against eruptions of issues that would upset world oil supplies. But that community of interest is not without its limits.

Once a company finds itself in conflict with a foreign country, the first reaction of its home government is naturally to lend its protection and to assist in arranging for a solution of difficulties on an adequate and equitable basis. However, as the problems and issues become sharper, the home government must consider whether it wishes or can afford to get involved in all of the commercial conflicts that seem to threaten international oil operations. By so doing, it might risk that the foreign country would turn for support to the Soviet Union, which could thus acquire a new power position, and in the end might deprive us of essential access to oil or force the outbreak of a major war. This was one of the basic problems in the Suez Canal crisis. The security interest may thus require the government to take an independent position in its foreign policy under certain conditions, irrespective of commercial interests or the effect upon U.S. foreign investment.

A point of critical conflict could be reached in the affairs of our international oil companies where considerations of national security would diverge from the commercial interests of the companies. If that point is reached, the companies would find that their own governments are obliged to take a foreign policy line that would run counter to the companies' commercial interest. On the other hand, there may be issues even though they may ostensibly be posed as infringement of commercial rights that raise such grave policy and security issues that the government must intervene, even if the company should not request or desire such intervention. The test would in the final analysis be whether or not continued Western access to sufficient oil supplies would or would not be put in jeopardy.

Part 4
WORLD OIL IN TRANSITION

Introduction

In the tumultuous decade of the sixties and on into the early seventies, an unprecedented shift in power occurred over the disposition of a strategic commodity of immense importance to all industrial economies and to an increasing number of developing societies. What may be most remarkable about this transfer of power was that it occurred without recourse to force by those losing control or gaining it—despite the serious political, economic, social, and security implications of an alteration in the balance of oil power.

The papers in this part deal with the effects of the ongoing process of change and its many facets. The first two papers deal with the shift in power, the next two are concerned with policy implications, and the final paper introduces the problems facing developing countries that lack oil and thus must find the ways and means of fashioning suitable policies to meet the challenge of cost and adequate volume.

The Economist, in one of its rare signed articles, published Mr. Levy's general review of the world oil situation in its issue of August 19, 1961. He chose to highlight the current situation, summarizing the principal actors in international oil, the trends in their relationships, and the prospects for the future.

Mr. Levy's basic assumption was that there were adequate reserves of petroleum worldwide to meet the anticipated increases in demand. Whether there would actually be enough oil produced would be another matter.

The international oil system was in a further stage of its transition, as seen by: (1) the increase in the role of producing governments in determining volumes, prices, and profits; (2) the entry of so-called "independent" companies (companies lacking the large, integrated functions and generally dependent on a few sources of crude in producing areas) often, by superficial comparisions, offering better deals for producer governments than the agreements with the "majors"; (3) the establishment of refining companies also without other functions; and (4) the birth of the Organization of Petroleum Exporting Countries (OPEC) in 1960 and the possibility of coordinated strategies amongst producers. The interests of the giant international, integrated companies—which were essential to the system—were being challenged by these factors and by the reemergence of the USSR as a major source of exports—a source of concern to Western and Middle East security.

12

World Oil in Transition

The world oil industry has just rounded out 15 years of unprecedented expansion. In this time, petroleum provided for most of [the] rapidly rising energy requirements—supporting the postwar industrial reconstruction and subsequent economic growth. Behind all this was a prodigious exploration effort to search out crude-oil reserves; refinery construction to provide the many petroleum products used for light, heat, and power; and development of transport and distribution facilities linking widely scattered producing areas with markets in all parts of the world.

Looking ahead, the next 15 years will present an even greater challenge to the world oil industry. Energy requirements will be mounting, not only in the industrialized West, but especially among underdeveloped areas. The ability to achieve higher living standards obviously depends on constant improvement in the productivity of labor. So capital formation becomes a crucial factor; with it, the availability of energy. And for most countries, increasing energy requirements will have to be met by oil.

Over the next 15 years, for example, oil consumption outside North America could mount at the rate of perhaps 7.5 percent per annum. Together with North American consumption this would mean free-world oil requirements of around 14 billion barrels a year by 1975, against about 6.3 billion barrels now. Fortunately, huge proven resources are available to meet these future requirements. Eastern Hemisphere reserves are at present conservatively estimated at 196 billion barrels, accounting for some three-quarters of the free world's established oil resources and representing 30 years' consumption for it at current rates. And huge new reserves are certain to be proved—in view of potentialities in the Middle East and North Africa and widespread exploration elsewhere. It would appear, therefore, that Eastern Hemisphere resources should be adequate to meet the area's rapidly rising requirements plus whatever the Western Hemisphere needs to import, and still leave ample reserve-to-production ratio in 1975, even at the very high rates of production that would be reached by that time.

Reprinted with permission from *The Economist,* August 19, 1961.

But between retrospect and prospect there is a troubled present — with world oil operations beset by economic uncertainties and political tensions.

The prolific oil reserves offer an assurance of adequate supplies to meet mounting requirements in the future, but pose serious difficulties today. What stand out are the disruptions brought about by a surplus of oil in the free world and the intrusion of Soviet oil. But the oil industry has worked through periods of surplus before; and a previous episode of aggressive Soviet competition, in the 1930s, coincided with an earlier glut of oil on world markets. It is not so much the immediate economic dislocations alone that are cause for concern, as the continuity of effective commercial arrangements and the political situation in key oil areas.

The Impact of Nationalism

Foremost among the critical factors bearing on world oil operations in recent years is the upsurge of nationalism and the urgency for economic advance in underdeveloped areas. Governments in some of these countries are increasingly concerning themselves with oil operations that had until lately been the function of private companies. In some instances — e.g., Brazil, India — the governments enter directly upon oil operations: in exploration where prospects appear to be favorable, in refining, and even in marketing. In Ceylon and some other countries the governments interpose themselves on established oil operations, affecting significantly the conditions under which the industry can continue to function — both in producing and in consuming countries. Superimposed on these, the cold war exacerbates any difficulties between the companies and local governments. The Russians, whenever the subject of international oil is raised, immediately refer to "monopoly profits," charging the companies with having exploited the national resources in countries from which they export and the consuming public in countries where they market.

The essential function of the internationally integrated companies — to program production among diversified areas and to match supplies with world requirements — is thus complicated by changes in the structure of the industry and by politically inspired limitations on both their freedom of disposal and their freedom of supply. Nowadays subsidiaries of international oil companies are coming under pressure to consider simply the national interests of the countries in which they happen to operate. International coordination of investment, of production among various areas, and of supplies for various markets would in such circumstances have to yield to whatever political imperatives are most urgent. Withal, the major international companies have to meet the competition of the

TABLE I
FREE WORLD CRUDE OIL

| | PRODUCTION | | | RESERVES | | | |
	1950 '000 barrels per day	1960 '000 barrels per day	Percent	1950 Billion Barrels	Percent	1960 Billion Barrels	Percent
FREE WORLD.........	9,579	17,672	100.0	88.3	100.0	264.3	100.0
Western Hemisphere.....	7,451	11,281	63.8	38.4	43.5	60.4	22.9
United States........	5,408	7,030	39.8	25.3	28.7	31.6	12.0
Canada.............	80	526	3.0	1.2	1.4	3.7	1.4
Venezuela.........	1,498	2,844	16.1	9.5	10.8	18.5	7.0
Other W. Hemis.....	465	881	4.9	2.4	2.6	6.6	2.5
Eastern Hemisphere(a)..	2,128	6,391	36.2	49.9	56.5	203.9	77.1
Middle East..........	1,755	5,264	29.8	48.0	54.4	183.2	69.3
Iran.............	664	1,067	6.0	13.0	14.7	35.0	13.2
Iraq.............	136	966	5.5	8.7	9.9	27.0	10.2
Kuwait...........	344	1,622	9.2	15.0	17.0	62.0	23.5
Saudi Arabia.......	547	1,246	7.1	10.0	11.3	50.0	18.9
North Africa(b)......	...	184	1.0	...	...	7.2	2.7
Indonesia & Br.Borneo	217	510	2.9	1.3	1.5	10.0	3.8

Sources: Production -- U.S. Bureau of Mines.
Reserves -- Oil & Gas Journal; World Oil; American Petroleum Institute;
Canadian Petroleum Association.
(a) Includes countries not listed separately.
(b) French Sahara for production; French Sahara and Libya for reserves.

many "newcomers" who are now active in foreign production and of independent refining and marketing companies with access to low-cost crude from a variety of sources.

The world oil trade plays a central role in the economic life of many nations. The economic strength of the industrialized West depends on uninterrupted availability of oil at reasonable terms. But foreign oil is largely concentrated in areas that are the focus of political tensions, and the cold war points up the danger inherent in Western dependence upon sources of supply that may not always be securely available. Access to foreign oil is essential to consuming countries; access to markets is essential to producing countries. And the conditions of trade are vital to each—from both economic and political standpoints.

This interdependence, even though it is the keystone in the whole structure of world oil trade, has not been adequately appreciated by all concerned. Each participant must obtain certain benefits; at the same time, each must realize that the contribution of others is vital. Accordingly, each participant may take as a guiding consideration his enlightened self-interest; but must also accept as a limiting consideration the basic interests of others. It has been through the operations of an internationally integrated oil industry that these diverse, but interdependent, interests have been accommodated. But the world oil industry today is confronted by a number of issues that go right to the heart of its economic rationale, its institutional structure, and its relationship with both producing and consuming governments.

The Middle East

A fact of overriding importance in the current oil environment is the large size and relatively low cost of reserves discovered in recent years in a few Middle East countries. Proven reserves in this area are conservatively estimated at around 175 billion barrels, enough to support production at current rates for nearly 90 years. In effect, the economics of Middle East oil production more nearly resemble those of a manufacturing operation than of exploration with its normally uncertain finding costs and results. From a physical as well as from a cost point of view, Middle East oil could presumably replace a substantial proportion of the oil that the free world produces elsewhere, as well as a large part of the output of competing energy sources, such as coal.

There are compelling reasons, however, why Middle East output has not expanded at such rates. The producing countries' governments are interested in a relatively high level of prices because their revenues largely depend on an income tax levied on the producing companies' profits. Similarly, the governments would prefer to see less of their oil sold at higher prices than more at lower prices, as long as their revenues would remain unaffected. They would obviously wish to enjoy the benefits from oil revenues over as long a period as possible and to recapture for themselves at the end of the concessions the highest possible proportion of the oil in place.

International oil companies, too, because of their geographically diverse production interests would not all benefit equally from cheap Middle East oil. Moreover, all of the companies are dependent for part of their requirements on more expensive sources of supply. The economics of past investment thus lead to the maintenance of production in other areas than the Middle East. Significantly, too, any concentration of production in a few Middle East countries would undermine the national economies of higher-cost oil-exporting countries.

Diversification of production has been undertaken to assure that expanding world requirements would be met and also to provide against any possible interruption of supply lines—which could occur with unforeseeable swiftness and for unpredictable reasons. This diversification is also essential for the companies to retain bargaining strength in their relations with the various producing countries (of which more later).

Many consuming countries possess some local energy supplies. Local production of energy may be more costly than imported oil; but strategic, economic, or social considerations often lead governments to develop such national energy sources and to protect them in the home market.

But there are continuing pressures to produce more and more, both in the Middle East and elsewhere. Concessionary companies have a strong inducement to step up output as rapidly as is feasible. For one thing, their concessions, although generally running for another 40 years or so, are still of limited duration. Reserves already proven in some of these countries, such as Kuwait and Arabia, would in some instances sustain production at levels rising above present offtake for more than the full period of the concession. And the sooner a barrel of oil is produced, the more valuable it is to the company in terms of cash income.

Too Much Crude

The pressure rapidly to expand output of crude oil is particularly acute for "newcomer" companies. Their financial resources generally do not match those of larger, established rivals. The need to recover exploration and development expenditures is thus correspondingly greater. They generally have no extensive investments in refining and marketing to protect and may thus be less reluctant to resort to intense price competition to gain outlets for their oil.

In spite of the state of crude oil markets, major oil companies as well as newcomers continue looking for more oil. Established international companies spend large sums on the search for oil each year. One reason is that they have explicit or implicit commitments to meet minimum drilling programs in various concession areas. Also, contagious competition impels companies with far-flung markets to carry on continuous exploration—to protect indigenous hydrocarbons, to achieve greater diversification of supply sources, as a protective measure to forestall rivals from preempting an inordinate number of promising locations, and to maintain the continuity of their organization and staff.

In recent years medium-sized and smaller companies, especially American, which had previously limited their search for oil largely to their home countries, have been attracted into foreign exploration, partly by the lure of the big strike, which is always a potent factor in oil ventures. They have also been attracted by the profits earned in successful producing operations during the postwar oil boom. And they were concerned over their future supplies—particularly American companies facing the high and rising cost of adding to their domestic reserves.

National policies have also played a growing role in the expansion of exploration. Many countries have encouraged the search for oil within their own borders and abroad, in order to save foreign exchange, gain greater security, or enhance their national prestige. And countries which are already major producers have opened up additional areas to concessions, in part because sharp competition among bidders promised handsome terms in the form of initial bonuses as well as future revenues.

In sum, on the supply side, there are obviously strong and continuing incentives to produce and market extra low-cost crude from prolific producing areas. In addition, there is the increasing importance of new sources of supply, of newcomers to foreign production, and of government demands for expanded output in virtually every producing country.

Focus on Narrow Markets

On the demand side, surplus production tends to focus upon relatively narrow markets. This aggravates the pressure both on the price of crude oil and on the price of oil products in such markets. It gives rise to an increasing prevalence of discounts off the posted price and of investment in refining and marketing facilities in order to gain or protect crude-oil outlets. In general, independent crude producers sell only to refineries that are not affiliated to any of the major groups. Since these refineries themselves have limited outlets for their products, the independent producers of crude are often obliged to make very steep concessions to dispose of supplies during periods of surplus. These may take a great variety of forms in addition to, or in lieu of, direct discounts from posted prices. Profit sharing arrangements, low-interest loans, refining and/or transportation below cost—all may be resorted to on one occasion or other. Established suppliers naturally fight to keep their customers from the independents. Having access to very low-cost crude on a large scale, being under strong pressure to produce additional quantities, and possessed of large financial resources, they are usually able to match, and often better, the offers of independent suppliers.

The pressure of surplus crude oil has led to considerable investment in refining and marketing that would not have been made under more normal conditions. New refineries are built in markets that might more economically be served from existing capacity. Established companies do so to protect their crude sales; newcomers, to provide a "home" for their production.

Access to low-cost crude from a wide range of sources, in turn, permits independent refiners (or marketers, through the use of processing arrangements) to sell finished products very cheaply, at times in direct competition with the refining or marketing affiliates of companies that supplied them with crude. Even though the quantities involved may not be very large relative to the size of the market, they may still be sufficient to force major marketers to lower their prices in order to hold existing customers. Depressed product prices, in turn, affect the earnings of these affiliates, at times even to the point of causing substantial losses in their accounts.

At the same time, potential market outlets are constricted by the efforts of many important oil-consuming countries to develop their own sources of supply, at home or in associated areas. Argentina and France are cases in point. Japan may soon have access to substantial "national" oil production from an offshore concession in the Persian Gulf. In the United States the imposition of mandatory controls over oil imports has left various American companies that had ventured into foreign oil production with limited access to domestic refineries. In consequence, the pressure of surplus tends to be focused on a few accessible marketing areas.

All these factors have robbed posted prices of a great deal of their sensitivity to changes in supply and demand. For a balance between supply and demand in the short run to be achieved through the price mechanism, oil prices would have to fall to an impossibly low level—below the operating cost of all production except from a very few prolific sources. This would mean abandoning or destroying large segments of the petroleum industry—and of other energy industries, notably coal. Incentives for exploration and development would be impaired; current consumption at ultracheap prices would be at the cost of future supplies; and overall this would involve the economic waste of scarce resources.

In fact, economic adjustment through a destructive play of market forces is manifestly intolerable, being harmful to all parties involved. The petroleum industry and the governments of oil-producing countries are naturally concerned to avoid such severe consequences. The governments of oil-producing countries, for whom posted prices serve as the basis for determining their tax take, have indeed increasingly resisted any price reductions by the companies. Many consuming countries, too, are determined to avoid the disruption of their domestic energy industries. To the economic forces that are typically expected to shape and adjust the activities of an industry there are added in oil not only the interplay of physical and commercial factors, but institutional, political, and strategic considerations as well.

Soviet Oil

The pressure of surplus on various markets is further aggravated by the reappearance of Soviet oil as an important factor in international trade. Oil exports by the Soviet bloc to the free world rose from 35 million barrels in 1955 to about 161 million barrels last year. It is estimated that the Russians could export in 1965 twice their exports in 1960. Russia's substantial oil reserves are likely to be developed, along with increasing volumes of natural gas liquids, and the planned expansion of natural gas production there would also release oil supplies for export.

With substantial production coming from relatively new fields, the average cost of Soviet oil is apparently quite low. Second, because the bulk of Soviet production moves to protected markets in the U.S.S.R. and its satellites, the cost of incremental production for export is still lower. In addition, Soviet cost accounting obviously differs from Western commercial practice; the Russians are in a position to charge costs according to a politically determined scale of values. Finally, it would appear that oil exports are an especially attractive source of foreign exchange earnings, involving relatively small capital and labor inputs as compared with the goods that the Soviets may expect to receive in exchange.

The Russians are accordingly in an advantageous position to compete aggressively in terms of price, and price cutting has become common in the Soviet oil trade whenever it is required and promises to be successful. At the same time, the Russians can be selective in pricing policy: within their own bloc, prices are often considerably higher than for exported oil delivered to distant markets.

Where price competition alone may not succeed, the Russians conclude government-to-government arrangements to place their oil. Soviet willingness to accept payment in soft currencies and bartered commodities carries an obvious trading advantage in countries with balance of payments problems — such as most of the underdeveloped countries of Asia, Africa, and Latin America.

The market impact of Soviet oil, coming at a time of already serious surpluses, is far greater than the volume of shipments alone might indicate. And the problem is not only one of commercial competition. The Russians have made it quite clear that they regard oil as an instrument of national policy. They are prepared to intrude it where it is likely to disrupt relations between Western industry and various governments or to withhold it where it serves their political purposes. Within the framework of stated intentions toward the West the Russians are bound to consider, in addition to whatever commercial advantage it may give them, their international oil activities as an ideal weapon in the cold war, even though sales of Soviet oil would contribute to Soviet economic strength.

Any buildup of Soviet exports that leads to undue dependence on the flow of such supplies or tends to undermine the economics of commercial oil operations would pose a very real problem of continued availability. Nor is it a matter that involves just the countries that happen to be substantial importers of Soviet oil. Should the Russians decide to cut off their exports (e.g., in conjunction with a political crisis that may also affect access to other oil sources), the responsibility for maintaining essential oil supplies would eventually become a common concern to the entire Western community.

In the major oil exporting areas, oil companies have generally acquired their production rights through long-term concession contracts over very large areas. The companies have normally been promised freedom from government interference in the determination of such matters as levels of production, size and destination of exports, setting of prices, and the disposal of foreign exchange receipts. Government revenues are at present generally defined as 50 percent of production profits at posted prices, though in Venezuela the government's share of earnings actually reached 69 percent in 1960. These concessions offer the companies contractual protection that was asked for and freely granted at a time when they were undertaking heavy investment at considerable risk. For the major oil producing governments, the concessionary arrangements have yielded oil revenues that are far beyond what they might have expected.

Yet the budget accounts and foreign exchange resources of some of these countries are precarious and most are not satisfied with their rate of economic and social progress. They now criticize the very arrangements that have contributed so much to the progress they have made. And local dissatisfaction can easily and conveniently be directed against one target — that is the "rich and powerful foreign-owned oil companies."

Terms of Concessions

Producing governments also often complain that the concessions were negotiated when their countries were under colonial administration, or when they were ignorant of the value of the resource and were otherwise unable to secure equitable terms. Many concession areas, they argue, are too large and cannot be properly explored by the company in the foreseeable future; the concessions, they complain, extend too far into the future. And they feel the present 50-50 arrangement tax gives them too low a share. Recent concessions that include new features add to the pressures even though the improvements in terms generally reflect the fact that the prospects of finding oil appear much more favorable mainly as a result of earlier discoveries nearby. In the late fifties large bonuses were paid for the acquisition of new concession rights in oil countries such as Venezuela and Iran. When certain American, Italian, and Japanese companies acquired new Middle East concessions, they agreed to pay more than 50 percent of profits to host governments or allow governments a share of profits on subsequent refining and distribution operations in consuming countries. Further, they admitted the possibility of purchase by the producing government, at cost, of up to 50 percent of the corporate interest in the new producing venture (in addition to the 50 percent income tax) once oil was discovered in commercial quantities. In the most recent concession granted to Royal Dutch–Shell for uncommitted offshore Kuwait rights, a Kuwaiti-owned company holds the option to acquire at cost up to a 20 percent interest in the venture if successful. Shell also binds itself to purchase the 20 percent share of oil production enuring to its Kuwaiti partner at not less than 10 percent below posted prices and to give it other business assistance. Even though some of the arrangements between governments and private companies in the newly formed ventures appear to be impracticable, the direct participation of producing countries in oil production seems to reflect the trend in their expectations and demands.

Most of the existing concessions, formally, would run beyond the end of this century. In point of fact, the companies have been in practically continuous renegotiation with producing governments over the years and the provisions of their contracts have been fairly regularly adjusted to contemporary conditions. But revisions in the concessions' fiscal and operating arrangements have frequently resulted in only temporary accommodation between companies and governments.

But if sovereign power is imposed against the companies' contractural rights to the point at which essential management prerogatives are eroded, the results will defeat the purposes of the producing countries themselves. Consideration might perhaps be given to a new approach for the settlement of major issues that may go unresolved through protracted negotiation over long-term concessionary arrangements. In such instances, and where relations between companies and government may be seriously disturbed by inability to arrive at a modus vivendi, it might be possible to agree on independent arbitration arrangements. The intent would be to arrive at a reasonable balance of inherent merits, taking account of the respective legal rights under the concession and also of other compelling circumstances.

There would be both limitations and difficulties in such an approach. Certain issues, involving most fundamental interests of either company or government, might not be arbitrable. On the other hand, negotiation of outstanding issues might become more difficult—demands more peremptory, agreements more reluctant—if recourse to independent arbitration were available. However, the critical state to which industry-government relations may be brought, and the far-reaching consequences of a breakdown in confidence, suggest that the possibility of arbitration on a much broader scale than is usually conceived warrants serious consideration.

OPEC

The creation of the Organization of Petroleum Exporting Countries (OPEC) in 1960 was obviously related to the policy goals of producing governments. While the first aim was to gain a voice and possibly even control over posted prices for crude oil, OPEC's resolutions have included also the possibility of production or export controls. Agreement on such controls presupposes that the various producing countries would be ready to exercise self-restraint. This would not appear to be the case today, as witness the frequent demands by various countries for stepped-up production. In the event, abstention of a few of them would render any attempt at controls ineffectual.

Yet the concept of international prorationing remains attractive to some producing governments—as a means of containing potential surplus production, preventing price weakness, of conserving an exhaustible resource, and, in particular, of gaining a greater measure of control over oil company operations. It is suggested that such prorationing would simply follow the pattern of conservation as practiced in the United States. However, this fails to take into account an important distinction between prorationing within a country such as the United

States, where domestic production is used internally, and prorationing that would affect the export operations of a producing country and thus involve the varying and often conflicting interests of a large number of countries, as well as companies. Such controls as might be administered by a few producing countries could not fail to have disturbing implications for the security of supplies and the terms at which oil would then be available to the free world.

Any system of controls over international production or exports, no matter how broadly based, would give producing countries inherent incentives to advance their interests by maneuvering within the limitations of the system. To improve their positions, all countries would try to build up their reserves or productive potentials, depending on the statistical criteria that were adopted in such an allocation scheme. And companies with only limited access to supplies in prorated areas would be induced to intensify the search for oil elsewhere. All this would tend to add to, or at least prolong, the oil surplus.

Moreover, oil stands in sharp contrast to many other primary commodities moving in international trade, for which production, prices, and employment have fluctuated violently within short periods of time. Oil, on the other hand, has enjoyed a rapid and steady growth in demand, relatively stable prices, and has made an unparalleled contribution to the revenues of producing governments. For all these reasons and also because of the difficulties in resolving a range of political issues, it is unlikely that any effective prorationing scheme will be established in the near future.

Western Oil Companies Now

The bulk of oil reserves and production in the free world outside North America has been developed under long-term concessionary agreements by a relatively small number of internationally integrated oil companies of American, British, British/Dutch (and French) nationality. These same companies have also undertaken the transport, refining, and distribution of oil in practically every country of the free world and they have come to supply the greater part of the world's oil requirements. The effectiveness of their operations is due in large part to the fact that they are *international* and *integrated* companies.

These major companies undertook most of the highly uncertain and risky search for oil. They put up the capital for pioneering oil ventures in numerous areas where geography, climate, and terrain made operations difficult and expensive. Later, they spread their risks, and the financial stability of their operations no longer depended on the success or failure of any individual effort. Exploration in many areas, allied with their international integration of transport, refining, and marketing, enabled the companies to finance uncertain ventures, bear the cost of repeated disappointments, and to accept the heavy cash drain often involved in the development of new producing areas.

Most significantly, the companies' scope of information on trends and developments in many geographic areas and on all phases of oil operations enables them to coordinate the timing, location, and scale of their investments and thus to plan far ahead for future needs. And it ensures an ample range of petroleum products at attractive terms in all parts of the world—undoubtedly one of the most important factors contributing to the striking growth in oil consumption and production. As a result, the oil companies have been able to maintain orderly and efficient operations from which they, together with both producing and consuming countries, have benefited greatly. For the most part, output has been continuously increased, prices have remained relatively stable, local government revenues from production have expanded, and rapidly rising demands in consuming countries have been equitably satisfied. Assisted in their foreign operations by the international prestige of their home countries, the companies in turn have assured the flow of essential oil supplies in time of war and crisis.

There is now a threat that the companies may be more and more handicapped in maintaining the efficiency of their world-wide operations. Recent trends are toward the "Balkanization" of world oil. While the technical contributions of these companies are clearly essential to effective oil operations in virtually all sectors of the industry, they would tend increasingly to take on the character of service organizations if this were the limit of their contribution. The danger is that the world oil surplus acts to obscure the contributions they make in their basic operating functions of producing, refining, marketing, and the financing of investment.

As noted previously, however, mounting world oil requirements will require a great and uninterrupted expansion in proven reserves and in the facilities to translate reserves into petroleum products in the hands of consumers. For all this, the internationally integrated oil industry is uniquely in a position to make essential contributions. These include forward programming, in exploration and also in refining and distribution; diversification of risk, as among areas and functions; and the internal generation of capital, to finance necessary investment without undue capital demands upon individual countries. But the continued effectiveness of industry operations will depend on how well it can cope with the strains to which it is currently subjected and on the policies of governments in matters intimately affecting world oil trade.

In this respect, it is of paramount importance that expanded opportunities, and improved procedures, should be provided for consultation, on critical issues, between the oil companies and their home governments. Western policy is closely concerned with developments in all areas where the companies have operating responsibilities. Nor is it merely Western oil policy that is involved. It is essential, therefore, that company decisions be made with full regard for the far-reaching political and economic consequences that may be involved. It is equally essential that the companies' position be strengthened and appropriate ways found for the companies to consider in concert those broad problems that bear on the entire industry's vital position, without running foul of an interpretation of American antitrust laws that in such instances might be self-defeating or harmful to the basic interests of the free world. Otherwise the companies cannot be expected to carry out their commercial functions effectively, the while acting as a buffer between conflicting government interests.

By 1975, the share of oil in energy consumption outside North America will have increased to over 50 percent. Petroleum products are becoming more and more important in a wide range of uses, including essential and strategic industries that have hitherto depended on local energy sources. In consequence, the economic effects of interruption in the flow of oil become more severe, and there is a risk that this very vulnerability might become the target of hostile maneuver.

Security of Supplies

In the interest of the prosperity of the free world as well as its security, oil operations need to be kept as far as possible on a genuinely commercial basis. Should the provision of supplies come to be determined more by political than economic or commercial considerations, the dependability of supplies would be seriously impaired. By the same token, the terms under which oil can be obtained must not involve economic, commercial, or political conditions that would make it impossible for the user to accept them.

Viewed from this perspective, the nations of the free world, and especially the industrialized countries, must aim for as balanced an energy supply position as possible—drawing on the availability of low-cost energy, but promoting the diversification of sources that would ensure adequate supplies at reasonable prices over the long run. This involves concern both for the security of oil imports and for the viability of domestic energy industries. Consuming countries would continue to draw ever-increasing quantities from the oil resources of the large producing areas, which would thus be assured of expanding production and revenues. But consuming countries would also try to avoid an undue measure of dependence that would leave them totally vulnerable.

Maintenance of diversity—and security—in one's sources of energy would likewise provide continuity between present and future. By support of diversified oil-producing sources and of reasonably economic domestic energy industries, it would ensure the maintenance of capacity that could contribute significantly to energy requirements over the years ahead.

There is no simple formula to determine the requirements of oil security. However, a general approach might be somewhat as follows. If oil supplies were to be interrupted from one or several important producing areas, or become subject to unacceptable terms, then remaining sources of supply together with extant stocks should be capable of sustaining essential activities for a prolonged period, until the potential loss of revenue and the possible economic and political repercussions had become matters of serious concern to the producing country. If this were appreciated in advance, any threat of interruption might well be avoided, and if it came to pass, the consuming countries would be in a position to withstand it.

The greatest measure of security undoubtedly rests in the diversification of producing areas from which oil supplies can be obtained. Here the internationally integrated oil companies contribute very considerable diversification through the development of production in widespread areas of the world. In their established operations, these companies have been singularly successful in meeting unexpected increases in demand or disruptions in normal patterns of supply. Recent years have also witnessed a greater emphasis on the exploration of new producing areas. And the number of companies engaged in the search for oil has increased sharply. If these developments have contributed to the present world oil surplus, they have also promoted increased diversification of supply which in the long run would help to ensure a continued flow of oil.

Oil policy in the United States is also an important factor bearing on the potential security of other oil-importing countries. Import restrictions, instituted in July 1957, seem to an American to have a twofold effect. The United States avoids dependence on the same sources of supply as go to meet European and other Eastern Hemisphere requirements. And protective measures taken on behalf of the American producing industry help to sustain a large "resource base." This represents capacity in being, to which other countries could also turn in an emergency, should normal sources of supply be disrupted.

Reasonable provision for ready stocks of crude oil and products within consuming countries, as is already the case to a substantial extent, also contributes to security. An obvious problem is the cost of stockpiling—to provide storage facilities and to carry oil inventories. The oil companies themselves are certainly aware of the importance of carrying stocks in consuming areas, but obviously they cannot be indifferent to the burden which such costs impose on their commercial operations. On the other hand, consuming industries also have an interest in the ready availability of oil supplies, and national governments too. Under the circumstances, stockpiling would properly involve some reasonable apportionment of costs among suppliers, users, and governments.

At the same time, indigenous energy industries would warrant support, wherever they can produce under reasonably economic conditions. This does not necessarily mean that local fuels need everywhere and at all times meet the competitive prices of imported energy. In world oil commerce, for example, it has not been the case that petroleum requirements were met entirely from lowest-cost producing areas. If it had, a few producing areas might have preempted the world oil trade; productive capacity elsewhere would then have been abandoned, and the search for oil cut back sharply. In the event, the conditions of world oil trade might have become subject to a one-sided dependence on the small number of producing areas that remained. As a result, and with the natural exhaustion of the few producing fields, the trend in oil prices might soon have been sharply upward.

Perhaps the most that can reasonably be expected during these difficult times of economic uncertainties and political tensions is some sort of uneasy equilibrium among the various conflicting interests centering around international oil. This equilibrium would be sensitive to developments on all sides, but one hopes that none need endanger it. It is true that in the future nothing is apt to be as secure as in the past. But the free world can cope with uncertainty and a lack of tidiness in world oil affairs, as it must in all others. The problem should not be abandoned wholly to governments merely because a simple or neat settlement appears unlikely.

There is a tendency now for many countries to secure their own interests in this business solely through political devices. Whatever the intentions or merits in individual instances, it is important to avoid such a proliferation of barriers as would undermine the rational allocation of resources and the efficient performance of oil operations. It is an unfortunate reality that government interposition in producing countries tends to beget a political reaction in consuming countries, and vice versa. The danger is that every oil problem, commercial or otherwise, would tend to become an intergovernmental affair, or subject to a tug-of-war between political blocs, or an issue in the East/West struggle.

Lessons of Interdependence

What may be called for is not so much a solution to the difficulties of the moment as comprehension of underlying realities. One is the basic and continuing interdependence of all parties to the world oil trade.

There is a real danger that a few producing countries, because they have physical control over huge resources, might believe that they have special power over the world oil equation. In fact, producing countries depend to an extraordinary extent upon the countries that are responsible for the development of their resources and the marketing of their production. In the Middle East, for example, government oil revenues have risen from less than $200 million to about $1.3 billion a year in the past decade. On the other hand, importing countries likewise depend on the major producing areas for the energy that is essential to their continued prosperity.

Inevitably there will be marked changes in world oil arrangements, through the renegotiation of concessions or different approaches in new agreements. But the recognition of interdependence should prevent either side from asking too much, or attempting to achieve its ends through unilateral action. And whatever new arrangements might evolve, they must not destroy the incentives for continued investment; they must provide for reasonable stability of operations; and they must assure the companies of sufficient managerial control for the planning and coordination of their worldwide responsibilities toward producing as well as importing countries.

But while the difficulties of the present are substantial, the prospects for the future are impressive. As noted earlier, oil consumption in the free world could reach almost 14 billion barrels by 1975 of which more than half would be in the Eastern Hemisphere. Over the fifteen years, Eastern Hemisphere production could aggregate almost 70 billion barrels – to meet the area's own needs and to fill the import requirements of the Western Hemisphere. The oil resources should be available to meet these rapidly rising requirements. But great investment will be needed.

It is precisely here that the international oil industry will have to play a pivotal role. In consideration of demand among all oil-consuming countries, it will have to provide for increasing production in existing areas and maintain exploration in widely scattered regions. In anticipation of future demand, it must plan now to provide the necessary facilities. To do [this] the industry must be left with reasonable freedom to plan its investments and to manage its affairs. If nationalistic, political and "cold war" pressures tear our world asunder, the international oil company can hardly remain alone as a cohesive and constructive worldwide enterprise. Given a modicum of law and order the industry will be able to function in a rapidly changing world, though many of the changes may not be easy or attractive. But in any rational evaluation of future prospects, its contribution should be no less essential than in the past. And a period of huge expansion in oil demand and production should offer untold opportunities to all if only industry and governments can tackle constructively the problems of transition.

13

Basic Considerations for
Oil Policies in
Developing Countries

In early 1962 the United Nations convened an interregional seminar on the techniques for petroleum development, and Mr. Levy was invited to discuss the basic consideration for oil policies in developing countries. In doing so, the United Nations was reaffirming a particular interest in the special prospects and problems of energy that confronted societies whose fuel requirements were increasing at a high rate but whose resource base, finances, and lack of technically trained personnel militated against mobilizing the requisite efforts to obtain greater supply.

In his contribution, Mr. Levy reviewed the principal ingredients in an oil policy and the ways in which developing states could generate for themselves, most profitably in association with the private oil companies, the assets needed to explore for domestic oil or, as in the case of refineries, could begin to move on a limited basis into the processing of imported crude. Recognizing that political considerations might make links with Western oil companies difficult, Mr. Levy discussed how these considerations might be handled in light of the changing circumstances of the international oil system. Virtually every part of this paper could be read as usefully today as it was then, two decades ago.

The oil policies of any country would reasonably reflect its own unique circumstances—geophysical, economic, and ideological. At the same time, to be effective, a nation's oil policies must recognize the inherent problems posed by oil operations. It is this latter subject which I would like to discuss with you today. My remarks will be centered around two questions. What are the basic considerations involved in a national oil

Paper prepared at the request of and presented to the United Nations Inter-Regional Seminar on Techniques of Petroleum Development, January 23–February 21, 1962, New York City. Published in *Techniques of Petroleum Development: Proceedings of the United Nations Inter-Regional Seminar on Techniques of Petroleum Development* (1964), pp. 323–330. Reprinted with permission.

effort? And what are the implications for the oil policies of developing countries? All of your countries are putting forth a maximum effort on many fronts — to improve agriculture, to diversify industry, and to provide the facilities for health, education, and welfare of your peoples. Hence, there are many essential and competing demands upon all the available technical and financial means. For any country looking toward oil development, the crucial problem is how to mobilize the scarce technical and financial resources now so as best to meet its petroleum needs for the future.

Oil and Energy Needs

I might begin with just a few words about oil's role in meeting future energy needs. Fifteen years ago, at the war's end, oil accounted for 25 percent of world energy requirements. Today, oil accounts for 35 percent. Fifteen years hence it will have to provide 45 percent or more of all energy consumed. More significantly, for most developing countries, rapidly mounting energy demand is going to be translated largely into demand for oil. In very few areas are there substantial coal or other energy resources that can be counted on.

What does this growing world dependence on oil mean for your countries? First and foremost, you are undoubtedly concerned whether there will be enough oil on hand to meet your country's needs over the years ahead; and what the cost may be. Second, as developing countries, you probably want to participate more actively in this vital energy industry.

You might hope to assure at least some part of your oil requirements by developing your own resources, insofar as prospects seem to be favorable. Local production would provide a secure source of supply, and it would be free of direct foreign exchange costs. But the results of exploration are uncertain; they can be evaluated only after considerable time and effort have gone into testing them. The question then arises: how to go about stimulating an oil search? On the other hand, the chances for domestic oil discoveries may appear slight. Yet the nation may still hope to participate in oil operations through establishment of local refining. Here again, the question is posed: how to go about it? I would indicate briefly the problems that are inherent in these operations and then suggest various approaches to oil development that ought to be considered in setting national oil policies.

Future Oil Requirements

Before turning to the question of world oil availability, I would first like to refer for a moment to the physical quantities of oil that are going to be needed in the years ahead. At present, oil consumption in the Eastern Hemisphere is at the rate of 9.4 million barrels daily. Future growth could be at an average annual rate of perhaps 7 to 8 percent, which means consumption of around 28.5 million barrels daily by 1975. Similarly, in Latin America, oil requirements could mount from 1.6 million barrels daily to 4.8 million barrels daily by 1975. In North America, where per capita oil consumption is already at relatively high levels, the rate of growth will be appreciably slower; still consumption may mount from 10.5 to 16.2 million barrels per day. Adding all these together, we get a striking expansion in world oil requirements, from 21.5 to 49.5 million barrels daily—with total oil consumption aggregating some 190 billion barrels over the 15 years, 1960–75.

I call your attention to the especially striking rates of growth that are projected in those areas of the world where developing nations are embarked on new and determined economic programs. These figures may be good or bad, as forecasts. But they serve to focus on this critical consideration: to the extent that you successfully move toward your economic goals, your countries will have to call on oil as your source of energy; and together you will be taking an even larger share of the world's oil production.

Future Oil Availability

Against these prospects for tremendous gains in demand, what about potential supply? North America will almost certainly have to draw increasingly upon imported oil to meet its expanding needs. To a large extent, these imports will be drawn from Latin America's substantial resources, but as that area's own requirements increase the Western Hemisphere will be turning more and more to the Eastern Hemisphere for its supplies.

In the Eastern Hemisphere, the development of oil resources is being pushed in North Africa, in the Soviet Union, and, of course, in the Middle East where huge quantities of oil have already been proven up. Reserves in that area are at present conservatively estimated at some 200 billion barrels—enough to support production at current rates for nearly 90 years. Additional large discoveries are to be expected as the area's potential continues to be probed. All in all, Eastern Hemisphere resources should be adequate to meet the area's own rapidly rising requirements plus whatever the Western Hemisphere needs to import and still leave ample reserve-to-production ratios in 1975, even at the very high rates of production that would be reached by that time.

The picture that emerges is a relatively few export centers contributing significantly to the energy needs of the rest of the world—with a very large and vital world oil trade linking producing and consuming countries. Despite the dimensions of our expanding world oil economy, there is little question but that the oil will be there, in a physical sense.

From Reserves to Markets

This ample availability is a promise for the future—but it is also the problem of the present. I do not want to dwell on the economic dislocations arising out of current world oil surplus. But it would be most misleading if the circumstances of the moment were to blind us to the magnitude of the job that remains to be done—to translate physical availability of oil in the ground into the diversity of products that will have to satisfy all sorts of future requirements in all corners of the world. It is easy now to take this all for granted—the huge proven reserves in producing countries, a seemingly assured flow of products in consuming countries—and to ignore what went into this. The forward planning, the research and technical competence, and the huge capital investment!

To be able to draw upon the world's oil reserves at the rates indicated by expanding world demand will require the most impressive construction and installation of equipment. For every additional barrel of oil per day that is to be produced out of our underground reserves, we will have to have added transportation facilities (pipelines, tankers, barges, trucks, and railroad cars), refining facilities (for distilling crude and processing increasingly varied and efficient products), and distribution facilities (storage tanks, depots, stations). Put these all together, and what we're talking about is further capital-investment of some $3,500 per daily barrel of consumption, apart from what is invested in production itself.

In terms of overall capital outlays, it has been estimated by the Chase Manhattan Bank that some $90 billion were spent in the past decade on oil facilities outside the Soviet Bloc. Over the next decade, expenditures could run to $140 billion. These numbers are striking; more significantly, they focus on an essential feature of oil operations that is especially relevant for developing countries. It is the combination of petroleum resources and capital facilities that is required to transform crude oil hidden in the ground into the energy that will support a nation's economic efforts—and the technical experience and competence that makes it all possible.

Participation in National Oil
Exploration and Production

Turning now from the question of overall world oil availability, I would discuss with you what might be involved in testing and developing your own oil potential to meet your growing energy needs. To begin with, there are the inherent problems attached to oil exploration. If exploration were taken on by the government itself, how would these devolve upon the state entity? Alternatively, what contribution might private enterprise make, operating either by itself or in cooperation with a national company, within the framework of a national oil program? Each country's oil policy must ultimately reflect its own determination of values. My comments, therefore, will not be directed to ideological considerations, but rather to what seem to be significant realities about oil operations.

Inherent Nature of Exploration

Uncertainty. Oil exploration in new areas is an undertaking that requires costly effort, but promises uncertain rewards. At the outset, the geologist and the geophysicist can seek out likely source beds. But even with the most advanced techniques and professional competence, the most that can be said is that oil-bearing conditions would seem to be present in an area. Thereafter, the drill must probe from selected locations to specified depths; and many wells may have to be completed before oil is found or the search is abandoned.

The record is marked with evidence of the uncertainty that accompanies the search for oil. Persistent and costly exploration, backed up by advanced technical skills and proven managerial competence, has been carried out in promising areas, and turned out futile. Prolific structures have gone undisturbed for years until one group ventured where others had passed by. And there have been instances of striking success in areas that had been worked over previously and then abandoned. But for every Burghan, Ghwar, or Agha Jari there are literally thousands of determined efforts that result only in dry holes. I would cite a few examples from the many that fill the record.

- In Ecuador, two major oil companies pursued the search from 1938 to 1950, when operations were suspended without success. In the interim, $47 million had been spent on their exploration efforts.

- In Peru, some 12 companies obtained exploration rights in the Sechura Desert under the 1952 petroleum law. Between 1953 and 1956, 22 wells drilled at an estimated cost of $20 million, but no commercial production was established.

- In Australia, exploration has been underway for more than a decade. To aid in the search, the Government has been subsidizing certain drilling costs—currently at the rate of up to $4.5 million annually—and has provided certain tax concessions on exploration expenses.

All told, more than 30 different companies have spent more than $150 million on exploration. It was not until late 1961, however, that the first really encouraging oil strike was made—and this by a relative newcomer drilling his third well in Australia. Many further tests will be required to determine whether Australia has commercial oil potential.

Capital Investment to Establish Production. Thus, there is inevitable risk involved in any exploration program. At the same time, initial capital outlays are large. By way of illustration, consider the experience of Nigeria where exploration has proved successful.

Oil operations were initiated in Nigeria just prior to World War II. In one venture, that of Shell-BP, some $168 million had been spent on oil exploration by 1960. The first commercially-producible oil was discovered in 1956. Production began on a very limited scale in 1958; it climbed to 64,000 barrels daily in 1961; it is expected to reach perhaps 90,000 barrels per day by the mid-1960's. But at best the company does not expect yearly cash receipts to cover cash expenditures before 1964. And, according to company estimates, it will be during the 1970's at the earliest before the accumulated deficit can be wiped out.

Continuing Financial Requirements. The risks inherent in exploration for oil and the very large capital investments that are normally required to establish production both stand out in the record. What is less commonly appreciated is the fact that substantial outlays must be maintained after a commercial discovery has been achieved. This continuing investment has to create the facilities—wells, gathering lines, storage tanks, etc.—through which production potential can be realized. It has to finance further exploration to replace reserves and to sustain production. Finally, it has to provide a progressive expansion in reserves and facilities—if production operations are to remain viable and grow along with the rising trend of oil requirements.

In consequence, the successful oil effort is likely to involve a prolonged cash drain, before current revenues from production begin to cover current expenditures. Only in the case of a really prolific find can it be anticipated that the cash flow from production will exceed expenditures in the short run. This rather striking fact is illustrated in the experience of many new producing regions where exploration has been successful, and has been accompanied by a build-up of reserves and of output. Producing operations in such regions can be favorably regarded, yet the companies involved have had to sustain substantial cash deficits for a considerable span of years, while production revenues have fallen short of current outlays.

The Canadian oil industry is an example of a relatively young operation that has witnessed significant growth in the postwar period. Following the initial major discovery at Leduc in 1946, reserves rose rapidly; by

1959 they totalled 3.5 billion barrels. In the same period, there was a striking expansion in production—to over 500,000 barrels daily.

The financial concomitants of this growth have been documented by the Canadian Petroleum Association. Cash income rose rapidly as operations expanded; at the same time, however, the industry's cash outlays consistently ran ahead. And the combination of exploration and development costs, together with production expenses, has kept total cash outlays well ahead of cash income. Over the 12 years, exploration costs amounted to around $2,200 million. Development costs came to $1,100 million—half again as much as was spent on the oil search itself. Production expenses were $510 million. Together, these outlays of $3,900 million exceeded cash income by $1,600 million.

These inherent problems of exploration are evidenced in many parts of the world—where wildcat operations are pursued in the hope of discovering new oil sources; where the productive potential of newly-established petroleum reserves is being developed; and where a viable industry is engaged in maintaining and expanding its resource base and increasing its producibility to meet future requirements. The problems being common to oil operations everywhere, they have to be faced in the course of any oil program. Against this background, we can consider the implications for a developing country that decides to go it alone in oil exploration.

Oil and the Task of a State Monopoly

When a government entity is charged with the entire responsibility for national oil operations, the many inherent tasks associated with oil activities devolve upon it.

Technological Capabilities. An obvious problem is that of assembling competent personnel to carry out the oil program. Such personnel would include, first, the top administration echelon, then the scientific and technical specialists having both requisite training in their fields and the experience that is so essential to effective performance.

A government oil entity often runs into very real difficulties in staffing its operations. Invariably it is obliged to rely largely on nationals. Indeed, such a policy is often among the very objectives of the government's program. And in the long run, the policy can be expected to up-grade employment opportunities, insofar as successful oil operations would provide more jobs in a wide range of occupational classifications. But it takes time and exposure to develop the number of technically trained people that are required to launch and direct oil activities.

In the interim, the availability of technicians is circumscribed. Thus, skilled personnel are likely to be scarce if not completely unavailable, and the burden on these correspondingly heavy. In many instances, these few may be required to discharge responsibilities for which they are not yet fully prepared—which would be as unfair to the individual as it is unfortunate for the organization.

Further, the government organization often finds itself outside the main stream of technological progress. At least, it is not likely it would participate fully in the world-wide flow of newly acquired knowledge or methods. These difficulties are, of course, usually on a consulting basis. But the consultant, however competent, is no real solution to a basic personnel problem. His stay is brief. He can only make recommendations, which may or may not be accepted by others. The point is that responsibility for decisions does not and cannot rest with him.

Centralization of Judgment and Decision Making. This leads to a basic question, whether the centralization of judgment that is inherent in a government oil monopoly is the best means to successful oil operations. It is not just the possibility of political intrusion into operations that should be rigorously oriented toward maximum effectiveness. The problem goes much deeper. It would still exist, even if the government oil entity were set up as a quasi-independent body with safeguards against outside interference. It would exist as well under private operations if one company alone exercised a monopoly in operations.

In contrast, diversified perspectives among many companies, each spurred by competitive considerations, have contributed to the effectiveness of world-wide exploration. A government oil entity, on the other hand, is almost inevitably forced to be circumspect in its approach. In a country of vast prospective but untested areas, it may require a very large-scale exploration program to assess the true potential and disclose the most promising acreage. The official who commits public capital has to consider the many dry holes that could result, the prolonged period of apparently fruitless search—and the consequent effect on his budget and future appropriations. On balance, intensified development of proved areas may be regarded as the more attractive decision, because it promises immediate pay-off in increased production at the rate of hundreds or thousands of barrels per day, despite the nation's long-run need for millions of barrels of added reserves.

Capital Requirements and National Budgets. We have emphasized the important role of capital in oil operations. Capital is today a scarce factor in virtually every country that is looking toward the development of its economy. And the search for oil can indeed impose an awesome financial burden. Earlier, I cited the experience of several exploratory efforts—both successful and unsuccessful—as illustrations of the large capital sums that are essential to an intensive oil search. Bearing in mind that tens to hundreds of millions of dollars may be involved, can young countries afford to take on the burden of testing their oil potential completely on their own? Considering the uncertainty that attaches to exploration, there is always a danger that scarce capital diverted from other pressing needs will be dissipated in unsuccessful ventures. The cost of one dry hole, for example, may have paid for the construction and staffing of several schools. And even where the search for oil is successful, the costs of development are likely to mean continuing cash deficits for many years, at a time when government budgets are hard pressed to procure essential services.

Thus, the very substantial capital requirements for a major exploration effort would entail expenditures on a far larger scale than most national budgets could support. The alternative is apt to be a more modest effort in which resources are allocated to exploration by dint of sacrifice elsewhere. But where prospective areas are vast, chances of success are increased by thorough survey and extensive testing. A very limited program, constrained moreover by the single judgment of one government organization, can hardly be expected to yield the best results.

Foreign Exchange Commitments. As we noted earlier, a major impetus to government oil operations often stems from the need to conserve foreign exchange balances. Where oil prospects are promising, the development of local production would provide a measure of self-sufficiency. But the process of oil development itself involves heavy foreign exchange costs. Equipment, facilities, installations – all or a large part of these may have to be obtained abroad. In consequence, foreign exchange outlays are apt to rise in this early period, when such imports are added to the continuing importation of the nation's oil requirements. A government oil entity that is charged with full responsibility for national oil development would have to cope with the foreign exchange difficulties that so often cumulate until oil operations are firmly established. To some extent, foreign credit from suppliers of material may ease the burden, but these are usually for relatively short-term. And for countries just embarking on oil operations, the annual rate of investment by the state entity is likely to be large relative to its total assets, which naturally would tend to limit the amount of credit it might expect to obtain.

In reviewing these problems, it is not my intention to discourage a national effort, but only to help you assess realistically the choices that lay before you. In that respect, I would now like to say a few words about the role of private enterprise in oil development, and particularly about the many different ways in which private undertakings have been adapted to the interests and orientation of various countries.

Oil and the Task of Private Enterprise

Bearing the Risk. A basic function of private enterprise in undertaking investment is that it bears the risk of failure while anticipating the

rewards of success. As already noted, uncertainty is inherent in oil exploration, and the incidence of failure is high relative to success. But
each instance reflects an individual company's evaluation of oil-bearing
potential and production prospects. Thus, the worldwide explorations of
the international petroleum industry encompass the individual decisions
of a large and growing number of firms.

Two factors that are essential to a successful search for oil are thus
brought into play—diversification of judgment and technical competence drawn from wide experience. Diversification of judgment is
essential if prospects are not to be rejected or pursued on the basis of a
single evaluation, especially since evaluation of oil-bearing potential rests
on so many geological and geophysical considerations, each subject to a
multitude of interpretations. It is the very multiplicity of judgments
within the oil industry that provides the broad scope and intensive effort
entering into world exploration. Technical competence reflects the training and experience that is built up only in the course of repeated operations in many areas and under all possible conditions. Past failures, as
well as successes, have contributed to a fund of technical knowledge: and
each new area that is opened to exploration benefits from previous experience.

Financing Oil Operations. On the financial side, I would stress two
vital contributions of private enterprise—in providing essential capital
and subsuming foreign exchange costs. As noted earlier, the flow of
capital required to finance oil operations is very large indeed. Within the
international oil industry, funds generated in the course of established
operations provide for replacement and expansion. They also flow into
the exploration of new areas; and they support the development of
resources and construction of facilities until these can become self-
financing. In effect, world-wide operations of the industry enable companies to draw on their earnings in established areas to finance exploration and development elsewhere.

At the same time that the flow of private investment in the course of
international oil operations serves to supplement national funds in
capital-short countries, it provides essential foreign exchange for
machinery and equipment imports where international payments positions might otherwise be adversely affected. On both counts, private
operations enable a country to benefit on a scale that neither its own
capital nor foreign exchange resources might permit.

Many instances can be cited by way of illustration. I would here note
briefly the experience of two countries that have recently been opened to
exploration by private companies. The contribution of private enterprise
in these cases should be measured according to the investment and
physical effort being made; the results have been quite different—which
is part of the point of the story.

In 1955, Guatemala enacted an oil code conducive to foreign investment in exploration. By mid-1959, concessions had been granted to more
than 30 companies, covering more than two-fifths of the national territory. More than $50 million has been spent by these companies in
Guatemala over the past five years. While sums thus far invested in
Guatemalan oil exploration are not unusually large compared with
outlays that have been incurred elsewhere, it is noteworthy that oil company expenditures in 1957–58 amounted to more than 10 percent of
Government income from all sources. Thus an exploration program was
launched on a scale considerably beyond the country's own financial
resources. The capital requirements (and foreign exchange) being provided by the various private companies, the risk of failure is theirs alone.
Results have been generally disappointing, but the burden of unsuccessful explorations has not fallen on the country.

A contrasting example is Libya. The oil possibilities of the region
aroused only minor interest prior to the initial successes in Algeria in the
early 1950s. Then, a comprehensive oil law was adopted in 1955 which
was obviously designed to attract substantial investment. By the end of
1960, 18 companies held exploration rights on some 390,000 square
miles, or nearly three-fifths the national territory. After six test wells, oil
was discovered in commercial quantities early in 1958. Now at least 25
oil-producing structures have been found in 17 concession areas. The
most important find is Esso's Zelten field, where production has begun
and is expected to average 125,000 barrels daily this year. Behind these
results was a prodigious flow of private capital into an early exploration
effort, an estimated $300 million.

Although the striking discoveries in Libya stand in sharp contrast to
disappointing results in Guatemala (and in so many other areas), the
countries were faced by a common set of problems in getting an exploration program underway. Turning back just six years, there was virtually
no oil search going on in either of the countries. While each contained
large sedimentary areas that might be conducive to oil formation, the
existence or extent of oil deposits was completely unknown. Local financial and technical resources were obviously inadequate for any significant exploration effort. In consequence, each country chose to encourage private investment in exploration by adopting a liberal
petroleum code. The governments looked forward to an extensive assay
of their national oil-bearing potential and rapid development of production if prospects warranted. And in each case, a large number of companies took up the initiative, providing the financial and technical means
for the exploration effort.

Use of Foreign Aid. With respect to the question of availability of
capital for a national oil effort, one final thought. Even where foreign
aid is available for economic development, in the form of governmental

grants or loans and of technical assistance, a country is still confronted with the decision whether and to what extent such foreign aid should be used in the search for oil. It seems to me that two considerations would have to be most carefully weighed. First, the fund of international aid is obviously limited—certainly in comparison with the wide range of social and economic programs in developing areas. Second, private investment may be available in certain economic sectors, such as oil, and could thus share the burden of development. In these circumstances, the allocation of resources becomes a key question—whether foreign aid should be used in the search for oil for which foreign private capital might otherwise be attracted, or rather concentrated on development projects that inevitably depend on public investment.

The Wide Range of Possible Cooperation Between a National and Private Oil Effort

Many countries that have had national oil operations have found it advantageous to accept the participation of private enterprise in order to secure, also, the advantages that private enterprise brings to an oil search, under arrangements that are compatible with their own national oil policies. The impetus stems from a desire to enlarge the base of exploration—technologically and financially—and speed the pace of local oil development beyond what could be expected of a government organization itself.

In developing countries with their lack of local savings and risk capital, it is perhaps inevitable that private participation would in large measure be foreign participation, at the outset at least. The question of foreign investment may well raise ideological or political issues in some countries. On the other hand, it is significant that many countries have arrived at a *modus operandi* for private, foreign participation in their oil development; and feel strongly that in doing so they have not compromised either their national or social objectives.

We live, after all, in a rapidly changing world where the institutions and relationships of the past are everywhere being re-examined and modified in line with the new economic and political realities. The international oil industry is itself undergoing rapid change. Today, an increasing number of firms, drawing their capital from many different countries, is engaged in oil exploration, production and refining in widespread areas. A country seeking private assistance in oil projects can thus look forward to attract a number of applicants of diverse size, interest and nationality.

Similarly, the arrangements under which oil operations are carried out—in both producing and consuming areas—have become increasingly flexible. Certain features are generally considered essential to newly-drawn arrangements. From the standpoint of government, diligence on the part of operating companies in searching for and developing oil reserves is a primary consideration. The country needs and looks for a maximum contribution from its own oil resources to its energy requirements and its economic progress. To this end, oil rights are often granted to many different companies, each to prospect on a limited portion of the national area. Minimum work obligations and provision for the relinquishment of parts of the area over time are also often stated as a spur to rapid exploratory work. And the term of the contract is set for a limited period, after which producing assets are to revert to the government. At the same time, the country may ensure that it receives financial contributions in keeping with the value of such resources as may be discovered and developed.

There are also essential prerequisites to private investment. These include foreknowledge of company rights and obligations during all phases of operations, security with respect to arrangements that are concluded, a clear-cut understanding as to managerial prerogatives, and the possibility of attractive compensation for risk and effort if the oil search should prove successful.

A few illustrations will show the variety of ways that have been found by which the interests of government and industry have been accommodated within the framework of national oil policies.

In Turkey, for example, the search for oil was initiated in the 1930's by a state agency. Between 1935 and 1954, this agency spent $20–24 million and established productive capacity of around 6,000 barrels daily. But demand was far greater and growing rapidly, with a commensurately heavy foreign exchange drain. In 1954, state operations were reorganized and a liberal petroleum code was adopted to attract private capital. By the end of 1959, 20 companies held exploratory permits. In all, more than $70 million has been spent since 1954 by the private companies. After four years and 39 dry holes, oil was discovered in commercial quantities. Significantly, one company found oil on its fourth try; another company decided to withdraw after 11 dry holes and the loss of $20 million. These experiences illustrate dramatically the importance of a large and diversified approach to the search for oil. Meanwhile, the state oil entity stepped up its own drilling program in selected areas and has been rewarded by several promising finds.

The case of Argentina is of particular interest. For many years Argentina had reserved virtually all exploration and production to a state organization. Despite considerable expansion of reserves and production, demand grew at a still more rapid rate. In consequence, import requirements and foreign exchange costs continued to mount. In 1959, the Government turned to private industry to supplement the State effort.

Exclusive and autonomous rights of the State over national oil resources were reaffirmed. Private participation was to be on the basis of contracts with the government's oil entity.

In course, a program of oil exploration and development has been launched that holds forth promise of early self-sufficiency for Argentina. Production has tripled — from 82,000 barrels daily in July 1958 to 248,000 barrels daily in July 1961. Half of this increase was provided for by the state entity, half by private firms under contract to the Government. Whereas, in 1957 Argentina had to import more than 60 percent of its total consumption, imports dropped to 35 percent of demand in 1960 and to about 8 percent in 1961. In all, private companies have invested close to $160 million in Argentine exploration and production since 1959.

While arrangements such as in Argentine have proved effective, we do not suggest that they are in any sense models that should be copied elsewhere. Many ways have been found in which the state and private enterprise can work together to test the oil potential of developing areas. I might cite, as further example, the cases of Bolivia, where certain areas are reserved to the state entity, with private companies allowed to explore elsewhere, or even in the reserved area under special arrangements; and of India, which has established government participation with private enterprise in jointly-owned ventures. Clearly, each country has to be guided by its own special values and circumstances in working out its national oil policy.

As a final note, it should be emphasized that private participation, by its very terms, is limited in tenure. Upon completion of contract or concession, a going oil operation reverts to the country — to be continued under state or private auspices, according to the dictates of national policy. In the interim, the country has had its oil potential proved and disproved. If production has been established and sustained, the country can count on training and experience in oil operations, which are so essential to effective performance! In the meantime, it can apply its own limited financial resources to the many vital efforts for which foreign capital could not so easily be found.

I might refer, at this point, to a study that we prepared at the request of The International Bank for Reconstruction and Development, *The Search for Oil in Developing Countries: A Problem of Scarce Resources and Its Implications for State and Private Enterprise*. In that study, we review in detail the many problems that I have touched on today, together with a rather comprehensive description of the alternative ways that have been worked out for cooperation in oil development between national and private efforts.

The Establishment of a Local Refining Industry. Up to now my remarks have dealt primarily with problems which developing countries are apt to face in testing their own oil potential. At the same time, local refining may be considered as a follow-up to a successful oil search in the national territory. Or it may appear attractive in any case as a means of reducing the cost of imported oil supplies and saving foreign exchange. In general, the problems of national refining are less intransigent than those of exploration. Still there are realistic considerations that must be carefully weighed before embarking on such a venture.

To begin with, construction of a new refinery, even one of relatively small size and limited facilities, involves substantial capital investment. To the extent that the necessary equipment and technical skills would have to be drawn from abroad, foreign exchange costs could also be high. These funds would have to be committed far in advance of any product output. In time, of course, sizable savings in foreign exchange can be anticipated in the switch from refined product imports to crude imports (or locally produced crude oil). But in the meantime the country would have incurred a debit against its scarce capital and foreign exchange resources — in excess of its annual bill for product imports only.

A developing country might hope to overcome these (and other technical) problems by inducing foreign enterprise to bring in the capital and foreign currency required for the project. In time of oil surplus, as at present, oil companies are particularly active in seeking outlets for crude production. Newcomers are anxious to break into markets; established companies must try to protect the outlets they have built up. In this environment, many companies have been willing to invest in refineries in consuming areas under a wide variety of special arrangements, including local government and private participation.

What must not be lost sight of, however, is a very basic principle — that refinery economics will ultimately govern the costs of refined product output, and hence the country's energy costs. A key consideration would be the size of total demand and its allocation among the various oil-products, both currently and as projected for the future. If demand is small or unbalanced, real costs are bound to be higher as a consequence. And while the viability of a specific refining venture may be protected — by preferential supply rights for crudes and/or for marketing products, or other advantages — the country inevitably must pay the price for such protection over the longer term.

In sum, there is an obvious attraction in local refining insofar as it promises to reduce the cost and foreign exchange burden of a country's oil supplies. And there may be further considerations, including the possibility of other industrial development centered around refining. But these should be weighed carefully, in the light of the country's own product requirements and hence refining economics. And the immediate capital and foreign exchange costs of such an undertaking to the developing country would have to be balanced against the prospect of future savings, along with the potential contribution of various domestic as well as foreign sources of investment if the decision is taken in favor of local refining.

Conclusion

In conclusion, I should like to emphasize several points. Developing countries are going to witness a sharp upsurge in their demand for energy, and particularly for oil in the decades just ahead. The outlook for oil supplies to meet this rapidly growing demand is excellent, provided that investment in the range of facilities needed to bring oil products to the consumer is forthcoming in a coordinated and timely fashion.

Against this background, there is naturally a strong desire on the part of every country to test and develop its oil potential so as to participate in this vital energy industry. For a developing country with limited capital and foreign exchange availability and a host of pressing and competing needs, the problem is how best to mobilize the financial and technical resources for the task.

In looking to the development of its potential oil resources, a country has to consider the initial capital outlays with attendant risks, the early foreign exchange costs, and the continuing cash drain that may persist for a considerable time.

To vest all oil development in a government monopoly would mean the use of scarce capital and would inevitably circumscribe the national oil effort, even if results were favorable. To enlarge the scope and speed the pace of local oil development, many countries have encouraged the participation of private capital. For most developing countries this, of course, means foreign participation. On the other hand, established oil companies are constantly looking to expand and diversify production in order to meet growth in oil consumption. Existing operations generate internally a substantial part of the capital that has to be reinvested in the continuing search for new resources. And the results of continuous enormous research efforts and wide experience with exploration in many parts of the world and under diverse geological conditions can be brought to bear in each new venture. Significantly, too, the world oil industry embraces a large and increasing number of firms from many countries that may be expected to compete aggressively in the search for oil.

The question of foreign investment may pose ideological or political issues in some countries. But it is significant that many countries have arrived at a *modus operandi* between local national effort and private foreign participation and are obviously convinced that they have not thereby compromised either national or social objectives. Times are changing rapidly, as developing countries well know. And the world oil industry, for its part, has shown a striking ability to accommodate operations to national oil policy and to contribute to national oil development when circumstances are sufficiently attractive for investment.

In the final analysis, of course, each country must set its own policy in line with its own desires and its own values. But for any decision to be well based, thorough consideration ought to be given to the inherent problems of developing an oil industry and to alternative paths that might be followed in order to achieve the optimum progress for the economy of the country.

14

Oil Power

The tortuous course of "negotiations" between OPEC governments and oil companies was grave news to anyone concerned with the vital requirement of assured supply. The very pace at which "agreements" were made and unmade warned of the collapse of the traditional international oil system. The consequences for companies, oil-exporting states, and importers were sensed but not truly comprehended.

In Foreign Affairs for July 1971 appeared an article by Mr. Levy titled "Oil Power." That article may be rightly regarded as the forerunner of a series that served to bring to the policymakers of governments and companies the central issues and concerns of "oil power" with which we have to grapple (unsuccessfully, to date). It dealt also with the erosion of the international supply process, which has been the greatest achievement of the private international oil companies, largely due to dependable performance.

Yet, in making this last point, analysts generally paid little attention to the underlying political forces which helped propel the oil producers to pursue the tactics which they adopted: each had, in one way or another, been part of the "colonial world." Mr. Levy did not make that mistake.

The article asks "What went wrong, and why?" and "What remedies may there be especially for the importing world in a situation which was well into its transformation?"

The same questions continued to haunt governments and companies. They led Sir Donald Maitland, now permanent under-secretary of state (energy) and then deputy under-secretary of state (economic affairs) in the Foreign Office, to comment that it had fallen to him

> to supervise the U.K.'s reaction to the oil price rise and our contribution to setting up the eventual International Energy Agency. It was in this capacity that I met [Mr.] Levy . . . [for] discussion about the problems facing the industrialized world, not only over oil supply, but also over price and over the OPEC countries' rapidly accumulating balances. [His] reading of the situation . . . was authoritative and wise. . . .

Reprinted with permission from Foreign Affairs, July 1971, pp. 652–668.

I

In the brief period since the late summer of 1970, Tripoli, Caracas, Tehran, and then Tripoli again have witnessed unprecedented demands upon the international oil industry by major oil-producing countries, dramatic confrontations with threats to withhold essential oil supplies, and far-reaching "settlements." As a result, the economic terms of the world trade in oil have been radically altered. The balance among oil-producing and exporting countries and oil-consuming and importing countries, and among oil companies themselves appears, at least as of now, to have shifted decisively in favor of the producing countries.

The winds of change for the oil industry that have been stirring throughout the decades since 1950 have now risen to hurricane proportions. The aim of major oil-producing countries in this vortex is clearly to maximize their governments' "take" out of the value of their oil production and to obtain increasing control over oil operations. To achieve this, these countries — already formally joined in the Organization of the Petroleum Exporting Countries (OPEC) since 1960 — have now effectively combined to wield the economic and political power of an oil monopoly.

For their part, consuming countries are faced with appreciably higher prices for their oil imports, which for most constitute by far the major part of their total energy supplies and energy costs. Foreign exchange outlays are thus mounting rapidly. And the traumatic experience of confrontation between the industry and the producing governments raises new questions as to the security of essential oil flows against interruption. Clearly, a very real challenge to the historical structure and operation of the internationally integrated oil industry is emerging — at a time when demand for oil is increasing swiftly.

The figures are dramatic. Oil consumption in the non-Communist world increased from 10 million barrels daily in 1950 to 39 million in 1970 and will reach 67 million in 1980; U.S. oil consumption increased from 7 million barrels daily in 1950 to 15 million in 1970 and will reach 21 million in 1980; Europe's consumption shot up from only 1.2 million barrels daily in 1950 to 12 million in 1970, close to that of the United States, and will reach 23 million in 1980, exceeding that of the United States; while Japan's consumption zoomed from 100,000 barrels daily in 1950 to 3.7 million in 1970 and will about triple to 10 million in 1980. The hoped-for economic and social progress of developing countries will also depend upon accelerated oil consumption.

As for the supply of petroleum, world production parallels consumption. Western Hemisphere production about doubled, from 8 million barrels daily in 1950 to 18 million in 1970; whereas Eastern Hemisphere production increased about tenfold, from 2.1 million barrels daily to over 21 million. On the basis of present data, U.S. reserves have a life span of perhaps 12 years; that of the combined reserves of the Middle East and North Africa at least 60 to 70 years. The output of OPEC members was 22 million barrels daily in 1970 and their oil exports accounted for nearly 90 percent of total free world oil trade.

Despite discoveries in the North Sea, Far East, and elsewhere, it is clear that the Eastern Hemisphere will continue to depend decisively on OPEC oil to meet mounting oil requirements. With its surplus productive capacity largely gone, the United States, too, will probably have to increase its oil imports. As of now, this country draws 55 percent of its total oil imports, equivalent to about 11 percent of U.S. oil consumption, from OPEC members, notably Venezuela. These figures could go up appreciably in the next ten years or so, even taking into account Alaskan production.

II

Within this context, the recent dramatic confrontations between the oil companies and the producing countries, which started in Libya last summer, assume great importance. In the short span of the 1960s, Libyan production rose from zero to almost 3.7 million barrels daily, rivaling the output of the leading Persian Gulf producing countries such as Iran and Saudi Arabia. The competitive urge among concession-holding companies to take advantage of the location and quality of their Libyan oil for European markets caused reserves to be rapidly drawn upon, as compared with major Middle East producing countries, apparently resulting in some overproduction of fields.

Europe looked upon Libyan oil as a valuable source of diversification, because of its west-of-Suez location—particularly after the 1967 closing of the Canal; by 1970, about 30 percent of European oil requirements were being met from Libya. Whatever the tacit reservations of companies or European governments about the corruption of King Idris's administration, apparently they gave little forethought to the consequences of any radical change in the Libyan situation. And while the price had been in dispute during the period of the monarchy, the revolution, of course, profoundly affected government-industry relations. The companies' postrevolutionary offer of an adjustment of six to ten cents over time was not enough, although a somewhat more substantial offer of perhaps 15 to 25 cents probably would have been acceptable as late as the spring of 1970. During that summer various factors, including a break in the pipeline in Syria and a sharp increase in European demand for oil, abetted the attempt to coerce concessions from the companies. In addition, Libya cut back its production in the name of conservation and threatened to cut off totally companies that did not accede to its escalating demands.

Capitulation came in September 1970. The companies agreed to increase posted prices by 30 cents per barrel, with 2 cents per annum escalation through 1975, and generally greatly increased tax rates, ranging from 54 to 58 percent.

Inevitably, the very substantial price and tax increases were bound to become goals which other OPEC members not only aspired to but were compelled to emulate. What ensued was a crescendo of demands, backed by threats to withhold production from companies that did not acquiesce. In December 1970, Venezuela enacted an increase in its statutory tax rate from 52 to 60 percent, and in March 1971 substantial price increases were imposed.[1]

Against this background, an OPEC session convened in Caracas in December 1970 and set forth a broad range of demands, enjoining the oil companies to come up with an acceptable offer within a provocatively short period and threatening prompt joint action otherwise. With the scene shifting to Tehran, negotiations proceeded between OPEC and a joint industry group bargaining on behalf of all. By February 1971, the Tehran agreement was whacked out, under constant threat by OPEC of joint-government legislative enactment of its demands and stoppage of production for any company that did not conform. Roughly, the posted price for Persian Gulf production was raised by 35 cents (compared with Libya's 30 cents), and would escalate thereafter by about 11 cents per annum through 1975. The tax rate was increased from 50 to 55 percent. The governments conceded that there would be no leapfrogging of Persian Gulf demands on the basis of the next round of negotiations for Mediterranean oil and that the agreement would hold through 1975. Withal, it was publicly asserted by spokesmen of producing countries that the higher government payments need not require higher consumer prices, in view of product price increases already in effect, and it was implied that stability of tax arrangements would thereupon depend on the future course of world market prices.

Through all this, Libya was setting out a whole new set of demands (supported by the OPEC organization only to the extent that they conformed to the December resolution, but with less qualified backing from

1. It should be noted that the value of Venezuelan oil had in fact risen owing both to the advantage in location as tanker rates increased and to accelerated demand and price increases for heavy fuel oil in the U.S. market, especially in the latter half of 1970—which for one reason or another had scarcely, and then only belatedly, been reflected in Venezuelan f.o.b. prices and tax revenues.

its various members). Finally, in April, Libya obtained a further increase in posted prices of 90 cents, to $3.45, with escalation through 1975,[2] and the Libyan tax rate was uniformly fixed at 55 percent plus some additional payments on retroactive claims.

It remains to be tested over time whether the agreements so painfully concluded will hold up.[3] Even though integrated earnings on Eastern Hemisphere operations have been long depressed, an upturn in world market prices and substantial increases in company profits or changes in the relative value of Western currencies, especially the dollar, could trigger renewed pressure from producing countries for increased per-barrel take.

III

The most obvious effect of the recent round of oil agreements is the striking increase in producing country revenues from $7 billion in 1970 to around $18.5 billion by 1975. (Without the new terms, OPEC members' oil revenues would have increased to $10 billion in 1975.) The impact upon consuming countries will be correspondingly awesome. The cost of European oil imports amounted to around $9.5 billion in 1970; by 1975, the increased cost to Western Europe of the new OPEC settlements will be as much as $5.5 billion; for Japan the increase will be over $1.5 billion (the oil import bill was on the order of $2.5 billion last year). For the developing countries, whose oil import costs were around $2.1 billion in 1970, the cost of the OPEC advances will be about $1 billion for 1975; for these countries, the higher costs threaten to aggravate further chronic adverse balances of payment.[4] Unlike the industrialized countries which may at least expect some increased export trade with oil-producing countries and additionally substantial inflow of financial funds through their banking system, the less-developed countries will be hard put to offset the drain on their resources.

Patently, the economic terms of the world oil trade have shifted radically. And the occasion has been marked by an equally dramatic shift

2. Of the increase, 25 cents was linked to the Suez closing and the tanker rates; that amount presumably may be rescinded in the course of time.
3. Settlements with Iraq and Saudi Arabia over eastern Mediterranean exports are still outstanding at time of writing, with a sticky and potentially even unsettling issue of quality valuation raised by Iraq and also now posed by the OPEC Secretary General as applicable elsewhere in the Persian Gulf.
4. In this respect, it is noteworthy that the agreed escalation of posted prices through 1975 was related to OPEC complaints that the international purchasing power of their oil revenues was eroded by persistent inflation in the prices of industrial goods which they have to import. Now oil-importing developing countries face the prospect both of higher prices for manufactured imports and for oil imports — a depressing outlook for the poor developing countries as compared with the oil-rich developing countries.

in the institutional and political positions of the industry and of producing and consuming countries. The question now arises, what should or
can constitute a Western oil policy? The major concern is oil availability — on acceptable commercial terms, strategically secure, and not
subject to political blackmail. These require bargaining leverage and
countervailing power.

Concessionary arrangements and international agreements can be
depended on as long as all parties are convinced that they serve their interests, and that a breach would be more harmful to their side than to the
other. For example, a producing government will be less prone to impose
unreasonable demands upon oil companies or to threaten expropriation
if the turmoil of a confrontation might threaten expropriation if the turmoil of a confrontation might threaten its regime; more secure governments may be less inhibited. Again, if a producing country can only afford a relatively short interruption of its oil revenues, while consuming
countries can survive an oil embargo for a longer duration, the oil embargo will probably not be used as a weapon.

Despite their new position of power, the attitude of the oil-producing
countries still reflects a lingering heritage of emotional resentments
against former colonial administrations and concessionary circumstances.

OPEC was established in 1960 to protect the member governments' oil
revenues against erosion, when declining competitive oil prices were
threatening further to pull down posted prices on which taxes were
calculated. OPEC did succeed in preventing further cuts in posted prices,
and in 1965 it won a relatively modest improvement in tax arrangements.
Interestingly, the companies then argued and OPEC accepted that the
full burden of the new arrangements was more than the industry could
bear all at once; a time schedule for effecting the new arrangements was
agreed upon, reducing the immediate impact from about 11 cents per
barrel to half of that.

Since then, however, the margins of profit of oil companies in the
Eastern Hemisphere have continued to narrow, and rates of return are
now barely in line with competitive rates in other industries or with the
capital requirements to meet rapidly expanding oil consumption. The
producing countries now appreciate that they are no longer bargaining
for a share of profits; they are now weighing in on world oil prices. By
raising tax-paid costs, they leave it to the industry to look after its profitability. Although statements of producing governments made in Tehran
are meant to reassure consumers that the recent settlements do not require higher prices, there can be no question but that the increased cost
of oil payments to producing governments will eventually have to be
reflected in consumer prices.

OPEC's agenda for the future, laid down in its Declaratory Statement of Petroleum Policy of June 1968, includes: (1) a program of relinquishment of concessionary acreage, with government role in selection; (2) tax rates and tax-reference prices to be unilaterally determined by governments; (3) participation of the producing country in existing concessions, justified by *clausula rebus sic stantibus,* that is, by reason of a fundamental change of circumstance.

Of these, the last — participation as a device in lieu of nationalization — is potentially the most threatening. "Participation" is a grand design not only to effect a more active and direct role in world oil trade for the producing countries, but in the thinking of the Saudi Arabian petroleum minister at least, to bind the interests of the oil companies with those of producing countries, to prevent competition among producing countries and companies as sellers in the open market, and make it difficult for any producing country on its own to insist on an abnormal increase in production.

In any such partnership arrangement with a producing country, the oil companies would be destined to become completely subservient to their host government, as somewhat ironically is now happening to the French oil interests in Algeria. Major producing countries already have direct access to their own production, through joint ventures, etc., and the volumes will undoubtedly increase over the years ahead. There is nothing to prevent them from actively entering into world oil competition and from integration downstream by investment in tankers, refineries, and marketing. But this is precisely what many of the countries do not want — to compete. Participation is a device to achieve all these objectives without competing; or to put it bluntly, to restructure the oil trade so as to give expression to producing country interests through the good offices of the oil companies.

Even if the participation issue does not come to a head in the near future, it could become pressing by the latter 1970s. The shah insists that the Consortium rights will terminate in 1979, ignoring company options to extend the duration. If Iranian participation in the Consortium should then be imposed, Saudi Arabia and others will surely not be far behind with their demands. Many of the large concessions in Venezuela expire in 1983-84 and here, too, alternative arrangements will have to be worked out.

IV

A major decision that the oil companies will be facing over the years ahead is to what extent and for how long they can be held hostage by their resource interests in producing countries. Will they, together with consuming countries, be able to moderate the ransom, or, alternatively, would it be better to abandon the hostage?

Meanwhile, what is important for the long run is not so much *what* the producing countries wrested for themselves, but *how*. The political effectiveness of OPEC unity, of unilateral action, and of the threat of an embargo—these are the realities to which companies and consuming governments must now begin to address themselves.

The companies now find themselves in a very real bind. How far can industry resist the pressures of producing countries? To what extent can the industry expect to recoup its higher costs in consuming countries? And since "industry" is really only a catchword—made up of an increasing number of commercial, governmental, and quasi-public entities based in an increasing number of countries—how do the oil companies as a group define their self-interest and go about pursuing it?

Called to Tehran to negotiate OPEC demands, the oil companies involved tried to take a common approach. The companies posited all-embracing representation for the company side and requested simultaneous settlement with all member governments as an essential condition of negotiation. This was a complete reversal of the company position in previous OPEC negotiations in 1965, when the OPEC representative was held by the companies to speak only for his own government (Iran); the reason now, of course, was the immediately preceding experience of having been whipsawed by Libya.

In fact there could be no universality on either side. Even among American producing companies, some did not align themselves, having diverse problems in their arrangements with producing governments; Arabian Oil (Japanese), ELF-ERAP (French), and ENI (Italian) were also conspicuously absent. On the other side, it was soon clear that governments controlling Mediterranean oil would not agree to be bound by a Tehran settlement for Persian Gulf oil. Neither would Indonesia, and Venezuela had legislated her own settlement in any case.

As noted, tax settlements tend now to be reflected in market prices, but the question is always, how soon and to what extent? Competition in oil, as elsewhere, can work either way—competitively to weaken prices or competitively to strengthen prices. The latter occurs when cost increases are made to apply generally to the whole industry, hence, the natural concern of oil companies that all of them be uniformly exposed to higher tax costs.

The oil companies also have ultimately to consider that if producing countries withhold production from "recalcitrant" companies and if the resulting shortage of oil supplies becomes unduly onerous for consuming countries, the latter may in time feel compelled to accept the producing countries' invitation to come and purchase the oil, bypassing the companies entirely. In a crunch, neither oil company control over tankers nor refineries could be pivotal; these would be mustered into service if consuming governments as a matter of policy decided that a breakdown of negotiations was threatening intolerable economic consequences for their nations. And even the parent governments of the oil companies could not effectively object without jeopardy to the Western alliance.

Therefore it has to be at least considered whether the ultimate riposte of the industry—faced with "impossible" demands and backed by consuming countries—may be to turn away from their reserves and reappear as competitive buyers of crude from the producing countries. From the company standpoint, its purchasing power would derive from past investment in and current control over transport, refining, and marketing facilities—the power to dispose. And they could expect that producing countries eventually would compete for export volume since captive concession-holding companies would no longer be at their behest. For established major oil companies, the crux would be the loss of control over reserves. Downstream position, historically, has been related to preeminence in resource position. If that is replaced by a bargaining situation, with all buyers haggling over crude price advantage, it is doubtful that refining and marketing shares will remain as is. While efficiency in refining and marketing could be expected to count, the companies will probably still prefer to hold on to the competitive edge of "low-cost" reserves as long as possible, no matter how high the producing governments may push up that low cost.

How to balance risks and interests in producing versus consuming countries? The refining and marketing investments of companies in oil-consuming countries tend to be regarded as much safer than their resources. In the circumstances, the oil companies may naturally be inclined to be more yielding to producing countries' demands so as not to jeopardize their irreplaceable resources.

The companies have normally been disinclined to invest in capital-intensive, low-profit, oil-related enterprises (such as petrochemicals) in producing countries; such investment does not readily achieve a competitive market position and is further tied to one unique resource base in an unstable area. Withal, the companies are increasingly pressed to commit part of their operating profits not only to these but to projects of general social or economic interest to the producing country and not directly related to the companies' business activities. There is an obvious financial risk in making the investment, but perhaps a greater risk to their concessionary position if they do not.

Then the companies must balance short-term competitive interests against longer-term appreciation of company/government relations in negotiating concessionary terms. If a company can obtain especially favorable terms it will find it difficult not to accept them—since competitors may seize the opportunities it has refused—even if the oportunity results from ignorance or corruption on the part of local officials. But taking such an advantage might prolong the heritage of ill will with which the industry has already to cope. Considering past experience with the unilateral imposition of more onerous terms in so many countries, the companies are apt to be reluctant to agree to more generous terms, except under governmental pressure or threats. This might be so even if changing circumstances make adjustments reasonable and equitable.

The companies must also try to reconcile commercial criteria with the pressures from both producing and consuming governments everywhere for them to identify with each one's national interest. Realistically, their various affiliates are often among the largest corporate entities in the countries where they operate and of overwhelming importance for energy supplies, foreign exchange balances, budgetary revenue, and industrial activity. Obviously the company's and the nation's interests cannot always be wholly reconciled, and lip service has often to be paid to the company's constructive national role. In a crisis situation, the company may then be charged with deceit as well as activity contrary to the national interest.

In the long run, however, much as the short-run interests of oil companies may seem to be allied with producing countries, it should now be recognized that their position as an internationally integrated private industry depends on a closer relationship and better understanding with consuming governments. Obviously, the consuming countries are apt to suspect the companies of being too much concerned with protecting their positions in producing countries. To establish confidence among consuming countries, these should be involved on a continuing basis with company actions relevant to them. In the past, consultations have taken place so late in the day that options are few, and the time when government policy might weigh in the balance has largely passed.

V

Despite the great efficiency and impressive results of the international oil industry's management of its affairs in the past, the present attacks on its fundamental position make a frank analysis of past actions and future prospects utterly necessary. What went wrong and why? This is not only essential to the continued effective performance of the industry, but for the security of the Western world which so intimately depends on the uninterrupted flow of oil.

Such is the challenge which the top management of the companies and the governments of the consuming and parent countries must squarely meet, indeed, cannot possibly avoid. The international oil industry functions effectively by virtue of its private competitive strength. Nevertheless, because of its massive impact on the economy, security, and foreign relations of its parent countries and the producing and consuming countries where it operates, it must also cope with the difficult challenge inherent in its involvement in and responsibility to diverse public interests. This was highlighted in the Tehran and Tripoli negotiations, when most of the oil companies with foreign oil production decided to negotiate as a group with the OPEC producing countries as a group, on matters that would vitally affect the tax-paid cost and oil supplies of about every oil-importing country of the free world.

As oil progressively replaced other energy, notably coal, in the postwar period, Western oil policy could be stated simply: to obtain as secure a supply of imported oil at as low a cost as possible. But relatively little was done to implement those objectives by many governments whose countries were most dependent on imported oil. Rather, it was left to the industry—particularly the major international oil companies—to effect. And this the industry did, over many years, by virtue of competition and diversification.

The assurance of inexpensive and secure oil supplies is now cast in doubt by recent events. But the sole responsibility can hardly be laid upon the industry; consuming countries must bear a large part of the onus for their present exposure. Remember that the initial impetus to the 1970–71 events was Libya's unilateral demands on the oil industry. And Libya's ability to impose her conditions reflected not only the unique circumstances of the time, but the progressively increasing dependence of Europe on Libyan oil—accepted without demurrer or provision for alternatives by the governments most concerned. Now consuming countries are provoked to ask what counterbalance they have to the increasingly effective posture of producing countries and what influence they really have through the oil companies in negotiations with producing countries.

The U.S.-Canadian situation is somewhat different from that of other consuming countries whose dependence on imported oil seems to be unavoidable. The United States must now be convinced that control over oil imports and support for indigenous energy resources is vital to its security and credibility as a world power. If implemented, the recommendations of the Cabinet Task Force on Oil Import Policy—to replace the present import control system by a tariff system and allow domestic crude-oil prices to decline so as to take economic advantage of low-cost foreign oil—could have been a disaster.

The issue was, and is, not higher imports and lower oil prices, as so often bruited. This nation can and probably will accept higher import volumes. How domestic oil prices may work out over the long run, compared with foreign oil prices, will still depend largely on the costs of developing North American energy supplies. The issue is whether we are prepared to expose ourselves to undue dependence on insecure oil imports, or whether we will keep import volumes under restraint and foster a domestic energy environment with adequate incentives to continuing exploration and development. If we choose the latter, our import requirements during the next five to ten years should not exceed danger levels. Frontier areas such as Alaska and offshore hold out great promise. A mutually advantageous and dependable arrangement with Canada should be possible. And we can reasonably count on substantial supplies from other Western Hemisphere sources, despite recent problems and irritations in various countries.

Moreover, an accelerated atomic energy program will make a rapidly increasing contribution to our power supplies. With some governmental inducements of manageable proportions, we could develop a sizable hydrocarbon production based on the huge coal, shale, and tar sand resources of North America. Within the foreseeable future, to which current planning would reasonably be directed, there thus need be no danger that the United States would become unduly dependent upon insecure sources for its oil supplies.

Other consuming countries, notably Western Europe and Japan, but also developing countries, have an even more urgent need to reassess their positions. In spite of promising developments in the North Sea and expanded exploration in other areas, most consuming countries of the Eastern Hemisphere will not be able to avoid continued dependence upon imported OPEC oil for the foreseeable future. And with oil reserves so heavily concentrated in a handful of developing countries of North Africa and the Middle East, it is inevitable also that these countries will use to the utmost their control over the resources—certainly for their economic advantage, but also where possible for political purposes.

In this connection, the role of the Soviets is also of concern. Basically, the Soviets will be able to obtain the oil they need from their own sources. Nevertheless, in their present position as a world power the Soviets will almost inevitably insist on a presence in the eastern Mediterranean, Persian Gulf, and Indian Ocean. They will not, however, be able to take over the constructive role of Western oil companies in developing and marketing the production of major Middle East oil concessions nor would the Arabs want them to. They will instead offer technical and financial assistance to willing Arab recipients and deal for limited volumes of oil in repayment of loans, or otherwise largely in barter transactions. Their main objective thereby will be to support their overall power position, undermine Western standing in the area, and fortify nationalistic groups hostile to the West. Their physical or political ability to interfere significantly with the actual flow of oil will depend on the broad balance of power between the United States and the Soviet Union, but any interference that would really jeopardize Western oil security might risk a big-power confrontation that all parties, on the evidence, are trying to avoid.

A more effective relationship with the industry is essential to the longer-run interests of all consuming countries. Their governments have already indicated that they intend to involve themselves with many aspects of company operations within their countries, including the relationship among the industry's costs, taxes, prices, and profits. An example is the new Common Market policy to obtain information regularly on the oil industry's supply and investment programs.

From the standpoint of security, there is a range of policies that will be considered or reconsidered. It is questionable whether the industry alone can provide security through its diversification of oil sources or whether policy guidelines may not have to be laid down by the countries most concerned in order to prevent risky overdependence on any one or few particular sources of supply. A proposal is already pending before the Common Market which would give it the right to exercise surveillance over proper diversification of supplies.

As a practical matter, probably the most persuasive undertaking of consuming countries to protect their interests would be increased mandatory stockpiling. During the 1970 crisis, Europe had only some 60 to 65 days supply at hand (which has now been raised to a target of 90 days); Japan and the developing countries had even less. Realistically even a 90-day stockpile begins to lose its assurance after 20 to 30 days of withdrawal have taken place. More ample stockpiles will probably be required if they are to have any real security value in improving the bargaining position of both countries and companies. The cost of such stocks would be very high indeed, but experience has shown that the cost of exposure could be even greater.

Costs of storage facilities, beyond normal commercial requirements, might properly be charged to the country concerned. On the other hand, it would not seem unreasonable for the industry, which would also benefit from stockpiling, to supply storage at cost and to forgo any profit margin unless and until the oil supplies enter into consumption.

Similarly, the countries should investigate the adequacy of tanker tonnage available to them, under abnormal as well as ordinary supply conditions. One approach, possibly more appealing in terms of natural control than meaningful in security of supply, would be for operating affiliates to own or charter their tankers — not necessarily under their own flag.

The tanker situation may well go through full cycle over the five odd years ahead. Major new pipelines and expansions are projected from the Persian Gulf to the eastern Mediterranean, notably by the U.A.R., Israel, and Iran. The added pipeline capacity would ease tightness of tanker tonnage commensurably. But in due course, oil companies will have to align their tonnage to their reduced transportation requirements to maintain competitive efficiency, and thereafter, if the pipelines are disrupted, tightness in tankers could again cause a crisis in oil delivery. The challenge for the industry and for consuming countries will be to prevent dissipation of tanker tonnage and to conserve sufficient transport capacity against another future emergency.

Meanwhile, consuming countries should again consider the importance — economically and strategically — of indigenous energy sources. The exploration and development of oil resources in "safe" areas such as the North Sea will be pushed to the utmost. Nuclear power will look better; so will even neglected coal. And while no single energy source by itself is likely to alter dependence on imported oil, taken together they may somewhat reduce the degree of dependence and the margin of risk. So long as oil flows are threatened by unstable terms of trade or political interruptions, consuming countries are likely to evaluate these various alternatives on a new cost-benefit basis, where the costs may now appear less onerous and the benefits more imperative than heretofore.

Some consuming countries may also be tempted to embark on an independent course that would bypass the "uncertain" role of the internationally integrated industry: on the one hand, by stepping up protection of their national oil companies in internal refining and marketing; on the other, by increasingly supporting and subsidizing their own companies in foreign exploration and development. Neither has been notably effective where attempted. The difficulty with government sponsorship, protection, and subsidy is that they sap the competitive thrust; once government-supported undertakings have been embarked on, there is a tendency to impose the consequences upon the country's economy rather than to write off unattractive ventures, as a commercial enterprise would be forced to do.

Further, various consuming countries may be enticed into attempting direct oil negotiations with producing countries. OPEC and the Organization of Arab Petroleum Exporting Countries (OAPEC), its wholly Arab offshoot, have put out this siren's lure. And the attraction is reflected in a recent statement by a Spanish government official. He complained that consumer countries were not represented in the Tehran negotiations and warned that Spain would try to get more oil through official agreements with Middle East and North African governments—thus bypassing the companies—and pay with increased exports to those countries. However, it must be appreciated—emotional responses to 1970–71 notwithstanding—that direct negotiations between consuming and producing governments have not been attractive either as to terms of trade or security of supply, as witness the experience of France with Algeria. Further, there would always be the danger in such negotiations for otherwise commercial differences to devolve into political confrontations between governments—which could be doubly disruptive to the vitally important oil trade.

For the industrialized oil-consuming countries, there is, however, the possibility of developing closer overall economic ties and thereby a hopefully stabilizing community of interest with producing countries through acts of association, as contemplated by the Common Market. The rapidly increasing oil revenues and accumulating financial reserves of major producing countries already vest them with an interest in the stability of international trading and financial arrangements. To the extent that industrialized countries may step up investment in the economic development of oil-producing countries, relations between the two groups may be conducive to a better balance in the negotiating position of the industry, and producing governments may become less prone directly to confront industry and indirectly to put to consuming countries take-it-or-leave-it demands.

The French, of course, have not had a happy experience in their economic association with Algeria; however, special circumstances there have been operative. And it would be ironic if industrialized countries were to direct a substantially increased proportion of investment for development to those countries that are already best off owing to their oil resources. None the less, a strengthening of two-way economic ties between industrialized oil-consuming countries and developing oil-producing countries may be a positive factor in the future direction of international oil trade relations.

In the final analysis, it would appear that despite repeated crises and uncertainties the internationally integrated oil industry will continue to play a pivotal role: in linking relatively distant producing centers with widely dispersed consuming areas; in linking the present with the future through technology and risky exploration efforts in many areas, as well as through huge worldwide investments in facilities; and by providing a firm basis of commercial decision making in the politically fraught world of oil. The shape of the industry will surely be changing with the advent of more companies and with a broadening of national origins in both consuming and producing countries. Most importantly, industry will be dealing with a much greater degree of involvement on the part of consuming (as well as producing) countries in oil operations that affect their economy and security.

The challenge of today's stark realities is whether, at a time when producing governments are weighing in so heavily to further their own interests, the oil policies of Western governments can help restore a more viable balance among all factors, thus providing the consuming countries with reasonable assurance of security of supply on manageable terms.

15

An Action Program for
U.S. Energy Policy

On November 14, 1973, in the midst of the oil and political crises and
war in the Middle East, and the ensuing fivefold increase in oil prices and
sudden loss of control by the oil companies, an address was presented by
Mr. Levy to the American Petroleum Institute (API). The subject was the
policy and program imperatives for the United States during the seventies.

Nearly a decade later, all of the elements in the current U.S. energy effort are to be found in Mr. Levy's remarks to the API. The paper is included in this collection for two particular reasons. The first is to serve as
a reminder that everything we have been urged to act upon by energy
analysts in more recent years was specifically listed in the 1973 address.
Mr. Levy's remarks may or may not have been the genesis of most of what
came later from other analysts, but there can be no disputing the com-
prehensiveness of the challenge described at the API: the need to re-
examine the issues of energy price, laws, and regulations which hindered
exploration, development, and production—all with the objective of
reducing the national vulnerability. The links between refining capacity
and security, tanker controls, the need for synfuel incentives, conservation, nuclear power (especially for Europe and Japan in order to reduce
their dependence on the Middle East) and, once again, coordination of
the policies and practices of the Organization for Economic Cooperation
and Development (OECD) nations are all considered in Mr. Levy's address. The signal failure came in the nation's not acting urgently on its
energy options.

Soon came the flood of changes which finally overwhelmed the hitherto self-contained, private international oil system as oil power passed
into the hands of the producers.

This transfer of oil power was, in effect, foreseen in all of the earlier
papers selected for this volume. The second reason, therefore, for
publishing the following paper is that it warned the OECD world in very
explicit terms of the impending strain upon financial systems already

Lecture delivered before the American Petroleum Institute, Chicago, November 1972.

assailed by the requirements of importers to meet large increases in oil prices and by the flood of petro-dollars which followed.

> The large and continuously growing surpluses of foreign exchange funds that would accrue to the treasuries of a few Middle East governments, and to a small number of their privileged citizens, will far exceed any accumulation of foreign-held funds ever before experienced. Realistically, such funds could probably not be placed into long-term or short-term investments year in year out without risking severe international repercussions and potentially extensive restrictions on the free flow of capital. It is most unlikely that we or any other developed country would permit continued massive foreign investments on a scale that would progressively result in foreign takeovers of important companies and industries. Moreover, the reverse flow of dividends and interest would soon add an additional unmanageable balance of payments burden to the oil import bill of the key countries. Nor could the short-term money markets handle such excessive and most likely very volatile funds without undermining the world's monetary arrangements. Needless to say, the oil-short developing countries would face even more insoluble problems with regard to the cost of their oil imports.

I. The Setting for an Energy Policy

. . . Many very competent studies have been devoted to the present and prospective position of energy supply and demand of the United States, as well as that of our allies abroad.

I do not plan . . . to repeat this analysis or to burden my presentation unduly with figures. I will only refer, as a point of departure, to the practically unanimous conclusion that from now on — certainly until the early Eighties — U.S. energy requirements can be met only by very substantial increases in oil imports. If present policies and trends are left to take their course, oil shipments from abroad will advance from some 4 million barrels per day in 1971 to over 11 million barrels per day in 1980. The oil imports of Europe and Japan combined are estimated to advance during the same period from 17 million barrels daily to 30 million barrels daily.

The preponderant part of all these imports would have to come from Middle East producing countries. Their output would rise from 16 million barrels daily in 1971 to an estimated 32 to 35 million barrels daily in 1980. The share of Middle East production in total U.S. oil imports would, in 1980, amount to about 50 to 55 percent; and for Western Europe and Japan, to about 75 to 80 percent.

The USSR will probably remain self-sufficient in covering its oil and other energy requirements and may, on balance, continue to be an exporter of oil and natural gas.

Let me cite one more set of data that is most relevant for the formulation and urgent implementation of U.S. energy policy. The revenues likely to accrue to Middle East producing countries by 1980 can tentatively be estimated at about 30 to 40 billion dollars annually, with Saudi Arabia alone accounting for as much as perhaps half of this total. In some of these countries, such as Saudi Arabia, a large part of these funds could not possibly be absorbed in their internal economies.

So much as a prologue for defining the magnitude of the problem that we, as well as our allies, will have to face if we do not establish new policies with regard to our developing energy supply and demand situation. I should stress that the line of reasoning, and the course of action I am going to suggest reflect solely my own evaluations and assessments. Many of you will doubtless agree with at least some of what I have to say here, but probably none of you will agree with all of it. That is a pattern with which I am fully familiar.

It is, I believe, obvious that the U.S., as a major world power, simply cannot afford an ever-increasing over-dependence for its oil supplies on a handful of foreign countries, especially as there are realistic and economically manageable alternatives. Otherwise, its security in a narrow sense, as well as its prosperity and its freedom of action in foreign policy formulation, will be in jeopardy.

Even though such alternatives may now look expensive, the cost of foreign oil imports is likely to escalate continuously, and will sooner or later — and probably sooner rather than later — exceed the cost of alternative sources of supply that could be developed in the United States.

*   *   *

Any international restrictions on capital or short-term movements of funds would, in and by themselves, be most harmful to our monetary system. In the affected Middle East oil and capital-surplus countries, any restrictions on their investments abroad would probably be accompanied by restrictions on the output of oil; obviously, if the income of oil-producing countries were to be "sterilized," it would be more advantageous and completely rational for them to limit their oil exports. This would then further aggravate the world oil supply position. However, controls over the level of oil production are unfortunately likely to be introduced anyhow, even without any hostile political or economic motivation of the producing countries, for reasons of conservation and wise resource management — at least in some of the major oil-producing countries — and certainly as soon as their production-to-reserve ratio begins to decline noticeably.

A recent pronouncement of a top Middle East oil official has clearly suggested such a course of action. Significantly, his statement was coupled with the suggestion that in order to assure continued supplies, oil imports from his country be given a privileged position in the U.S. market. We could obviously not accept such a proposal without jeopardizing our relations not only with all other producing but also consuming countries.

As of now, continuing dependence of Europe and Japan on Middle East oil appears to be inevitable. And the build-up of Middle East oil revenues will reflect that. But the U.S. does have an alternative—and that is to point its energy policy toward accelerated development of its large domestic resource potential.

II. The U.S. Energy Resource Base

Fortunately, all authoritative studies of the U.S. energy resource position have demonstrated that our nation has the potential for large additional hydrocarbon discoveries and production, and that we also possess huge reserves of coal and oil shale. Moreover, we can count with some degree of confidence on reasonable access to the tremendous tar sands reserves in Canada. Technology for the production of oil from shale, tar sands, and coal, and of gas from oil and coal is in hand, at a cost which—even though substantial—is certainly manageable within total U.S. economic capabilities. In addition, we can with near certainty expect substantial advances in the technology and the economic attractiveness of existing or of newly-to-be developed processes through continued research. Nuclear energy based on secure uranium resources is a reality, and with further substantial research, economic improvements in presently applied processes and the development of commercial breeder reactors and of fusion techniques would appear to be an attainable goal.

However, in order to make investments for finding and developing additional hydrocarbon resources or for producing synthetic oil and gas commercially attractive, the prices for oil and gas would in most instances have to be substantially higher than those presently prevailing. Likewise, the cost of the research required for the whole range of improved and new technology far exceeds the amounts that private companies could be expected to spend for an effort whose ultimate technical success and commercial attractiveness under existing conditions are not certain. Moreover, because of the time lag involved between expenditures for research—or even the start of construction of new process facilities—and the completion of such projects, the uncertainty of future developments in energy technology and economics weighs heavily in the balance. Finally, the successful conclusion of a major research effort in these fields would not uniquely benefit any firm that would undertake such research, but would be external to it, and would provide more or less similar advantages to competing companies, even though they had not contributed to the research effort.

III. The Crucial Price Problem

In the light of all relevant circumstances, the question may well be asked: how did we get into a situation where we are now facing a potentially dangerous or unmanageable oil import gap, with its related deleterious effects on our security, political, economic, and balance of payments position?

The causes can be traced to several major factors. Among them, the most important one is probably that for broad economic as well as other reasons, the price mechanism has not been working effectively either in crude oil or in natural gas commerce.

Prices of U.S. oil and gas resources have reflected primarily current supply and demand balances rather than expectation of shortages some years in the future. Current price levels have just not adequately responded to the fact that oil and gas reserves were beginning to run down during the past few years. In the case of natural gas, Federal Power Commission pricing for interstate supplies clearly did not react promptly to emerging shortfalls between demand and supply or to distortions in the disposition of available gas and the interplay between gas and other fuels in competitive markets. Crude oil prices also remained largely unresponsive to developing supply imbalances. Neither industry pricing nor government policies as they affected prices effectively responded to the changing relationship between current supplies and future requirements.

Oil import policy was designed to protect the U.S. oil industry from a flood of cheap foreign oil and thereby to prevent U.S. crude prices from declining to the substantially lower level of delivered foreign crudes, with resulting detrimental effects on U.S. oil exploration and production activities. Under our import quota system, the differential between domestic and foreign prices has accrued to the U.S. refining industry. This has not, however, resulted in "windfall" profits for the industry. Instead, quota values have reduced the average crude costs to U.S. refiners; and since the refining/marketing function in the United States has certainly not evidenced returns in excess of competitive rates, such savings have largely been passed on to the consumer through lower refined product prices.

The effects of U.S. tax policy, especially the depletion allowance, have been mixed. By the very nature of competitive enterprise, depletion allowance could not provide for the crude oil producing industry over any length of time "excessive" after-tax rates of return—i.e., rates of return out of line with similarly situated industries. Depletion benefits taken in isolation have undoubtedly attracted larger amounts of capital into the oil and gas industry than would have been forthcoming absent depletion, but at the same time they have resulted in crude oil prices that are lower than they otherwise would have been—although still providing essentially the same rate of return as higher crude prices without depletion.

However, a significant portion of the benefits of depletion has been passed on to land-owners, both government and private, in the form of higher lease bonuses and larger after-tax royalty income.

It should perhaps be noted that both import quota benefits and depletion allowances have probably in part also supported uneconomic allocations of resources by the industry, such as inefficient refining or marketing operations. Doubtless they have also made a contribution to larger investments in producing ventures, but this was neither necessarily nor probably in fact the major utilization by the industry of such additional funds. For the future, we obviously have to be concerned that both the protection provided by the oil import policy and the incentives of tax policy are more sharply focused on the purposes for which they are intended.

IV. An Agenda for Action

The Broad Principles

It will be a cardinal principle for all of these recommendations to try to provide for a maximum use of the pricing mechanism, realizing that it must inevitably be influenced by government policy designed to achieve our country's security, political, and economic objectives. We must also recognize that prices should reflect the true cost of energy in the light of such policy goals. Within these limits, the program should allow for the optimum contribution of private enterprise to our energy supply effort.

To achieve these objectives, new governmental policies for the development of domestic conventional and synthetic oil and gas resources and of nuclear energy, and a review of our policies on imports and taxation, are an absolute necessity.

To the extent that this would require changes in governmental policies, they should be phased in over time, while previous policies that either may have been misconceived or are no longer valid are being phased out. Equitable consideration should be given to investments that have been made in good faith in reliance on older policies. But in view of the overriding national interest, fundamental policy changes cannot be delayed too long and some hardships and even inequities may not always be avoidable.

As an introductory comment applying to the whole range of measures required to cope with the energy problem, it cannot be emphasized too strongly that it is essential to resolve environmental problems expeditiously and with common sense, based on broad-gauged cost-benefit analyses of the overall national interest. Accordingly, a rational balance between environmental and energy goals, and a realistic timetable in terms of securing essential energy supplies, must be established. Within this framework, I firmly believe that what is really essential for our energy resource development is also essential for our nation.

Expanding Conventional Hydrocarbon Resources

The nation's hydrocarbon resources cannot be significantly expanded without opening up new prospective areas to exploration. The leasing program for federal lands for hydrocarbons on and offshore, including the Outer Continental Shelf, must be regularized and expedited. The environmental and any other roadblocks presently delaying or even preventing leasing arrangements—and pipeline construction as in Alaska—must be overcome by applying reasonable yardsticks through executive and, if necessary, legislative action.

In order to channel a larger portion of available exploration funds into productive activity, it would appear advisable to move toward a leasing system based on production bonuses alongside or perhaps even instead of the present method of initial lease bonuses. There must be due safeguards to limit bidding to technically and financially responsible parties who are able to undertake the necessary exploration and development, and thus avoid unnecessary costly speculation by promoters. Royalty bidding would not be desirable, because high royalties would tend to make production prematurely uneconomic.

State oil prorationing for conservation purposes and/or in accordance with market demand has tended to support domestic prices. In any case, prorationing served to maintain a U.S. reserve productive capacity from which, until its disappearance a short time ago, we and our allies have benefited so greatly during emergencies. It would be essential, if a reserve production potential were to be reestablished, to maintain, where applicable, the institutional framework for market prorationing of production.

In line with the principles and goals heretofore outlined, I submit that specific inducements should be provided to encourage the lagging investment effort for the discovery and development of our still-ample natural hydrocarbon resources. The depletion allowance in its present form, with its depressing effect on crude oil prices, is only an indirect and perhaps not very efficient incentive for exploration. A shift to the concept of earned depletion, under which depletion tax benefits would have to be reinvested in exploration, would reorient tax policy more closely in line with the nation's vital needs for resource development.

The most effective incentive for investments would probably be provided through a special tax credit for exploration, and for secondary and tertiary recovery. Such a proposal was turned down by the Senate in November, 1971, by a vote of 65 to 22. However, if as tax credits are being introduced, the depletion allowance were to be phased down, government revenues would not be detrimentally affected and the depletion tax benefits would be directly applied to the expansion of our hydrocarbon reserves. Without such trade-offs, investment allowances for the producing segment of the industry are unlikely to be politically acceptable—if even then.

As far as natural gas is concerned, a carefully designed decontrol program for gas prices is being considered; but it cannot in all fairness, and to be really effective, be limited solely to newly committed gas. The inherent equity of reviewing also gas contracts that were concluded when price controls limited the freedom of the sellers is obvious—provided the vital interests of the buyers are protected.

However, in the light of the severity of our gas problem, we should also look to a more rational use of gas in overall energy balances. For instance, about half of our total gas consumption is used under boilers in industry and electric utilities and over 10 billion cubic feet daily are burned in Gulf Coast facilities alone. The substitution of oil or coal for gas in "inferior" uses could, within a reasonable time, set free large additional quantities of gas for "premium" uses in residential and commercial markets. This would, of course, presuppose that old contracts for the very large quantities of gas sold in intra- or interstate trade for burning under boilers were also to be opened up, leading to some equitable adjustments between buyers and sellers.

In the meantime, the FPC [Federal Power Commission] has been reviewing proposals for the importation of liquefied natural gas, especially from Algeria, under which the landed price of gas would be very substantially higher than that of domestic natural gas, and involving also huge government subsidies for U.S.-built LNG tankers. Additional requests for permission to import large quantities of LNG are already before the Commission and others will undoubtedly soon be presented. Most of this gas will be available only in a number of years. Various proposals for the manufacture of synthetic natural gas from selected imported liquid feedstocks or from coal are also being considered. These SNG plants could apparently make gas supplies available within a comparable or even a shorter time span than many LNG projects, and would involve somewhat lower costs than LNG. There is some question whether the decisions that are being taken now are really based on a complete evaluation of the various alternatives still open to us, especially the possible availability for priority uses of gas consumed currently in intra- and interstate trade for burning under boilers.

Moreover, projects for the development of Soviet-Siberian gas resources based on U.S. credits or guarantees of several billion dollars for the development of the fields or the facilities and to be repaid over very long periods through LNG sold to the U.S. market at high prices beginning several years from now, are currently being discussed. It would seem to be extraordinary if the United States should get involved in such huge financing schemes for the future development of Soviet or some other country's gas resources — which by no stretch of the imagination could be described as a safe source of supply — where the financial risk may largely be borne by the U.S. Government, the supply risk is carried by the U.S. consumer, and the financing burden is passed on to the U.S. purchaser through prices far in excess of the domestic price level — without at least applying first and foremost comparable measures of support for the development of domestic energy resources. It would appear that with investments of similar magnitude, and gas prices lower than the projected laid-down costs of offshore LNG, large quantities of domestic natural gas and synthetic gas from coal or oil could be procured with greater security of supply and a smaller drain on our balance of payments.

Changes in Oil Import Policy

With respect to oil imports, what is now urgently required is a clear statement of policy and a program that is consistently aligned with that policy. It must, without fear or favor, be administered in a rational manner, designed to secure a reliable domestic resource base, and not be influenced by extraneous political, social, or economic goals that have in the past led to "special" quotas for certain interests or certain areas, unrelated to achieving the major objective.

As to policy, it is essential that the volume of imports of foreign oil be under continuing control so long as the price of foreign supplies is or could be below the price at which domestic oil resources could be developed.

In the short run, import volumes obviously should not be less than necessary to supplement current domestic availability. Over time, import volumes would be limited according to the trend in domestic availability, considering reasonable rates of production from domestic resources and taking account of such standby capacity as is deemed desirable from a security standpoint.

Given the import volumes that are compatible with near-term requirements and long-term security, an import program should aim for maximum flexibility in the integration of foreign oil into the nation's energy economy and hence for the optimum efficient utilization of domestic and foreign energy supplies.

If the interested industries (petroleum, chemical, and gas) and the many companies within these industries have access to permissible imports on reasonably comparable terms, investment initiatives and competitive pressures would conduce over time toward a more rational allocation of available domestic and foreign supplies. In contrast, ad hoc administrative decisions have in the past so often been made either in isolation or in response to special pressures. They have dealt not only with how much foreign oil should enter our country, but where, to whom, and for what purpose. They have led to confusion and uncertainty in a never-never land of exercise of administrative discretion.

What has frequently been lost sight of is that if security is the basic purpose, that can best be served by controls over total import volumes, so as to ensure continuing incentives in the domestic environment, and by generally proportional access to permissible imports, so that maximum competitive pressures bear on domestic price relationships.

How then to allocate permissible imports? Via tariffs would be altogether impracticable. Frequently changing tanker rates and built-in or competitive adjustments of f.o.b. prices for foreign crudes would have to be accompanied by frequent changes in tariff levels as determined by a newly established Tariff Authority, which would in fact also have to be entrusted with the task of establishing the proper level of domestic crude prices. Further, no tariff that would permit foreign oil to enter competitively could effectively control the volume of foreign oil that could surmount the tariff. Finally, with "participation," the volume of foreign oil at the disposal of foreign producing governments will be rising sharply. A tariff that, however carefully designed, takes into account the tax-paid cost of private companies producing abroad would be irrelevant to the companies' host governments, whose true costs would be reckoned in pennies, and who could, if they so desired, shade their prices in order to preempt the U.S. market.

Via quota auction has the attraction of siphoning off ostensible import profits and of generating government revenues. And of course, we do have, in effect, a quota auction, through the quota exchange market. It has to be appreciated, however, that the transfer to government of the cost advantage of importation by the auctioning of quotas would mean correspondingly higher prices for consumers.

There would also be a range of complications in an auction program. Who could enter into the auction would have to be carefully determined, or here also the foreign national oil companies might effectively dominate the import trade through acquisition of quotas. Separate auctions would probably have to be established for Districts I, V, and II–IV; possibly also because of the different security and cost implications for Western Hemisphere and Eastern Hemisphere supplies. This would be even more problematical if, to begin with at least, the auction system were for practical and political reasons applied only to incremental import quantities.

A system under which import quotas would be given directly to crude producers with the intent of inducing thereby increased drilling activities or of maintaining unused productive capacity, as has sometimes been suggested, is much too complex; it would probably also not be effective in maintaining an expanding and readily usable crude oil production basis.

On balance, it would appear that the most practical alternative would be a simplified and expanded quota allocation program for all refiners and other processors of domestic crude and synthetic feedstocks, and also of Canadian, if energy policy moves toward increasing imports of oil and synthetics from Canada, as is likely. Each processor would share in the access to foreign oil, reasonably proportionate to his total crude-oil and synthetic-feedstock requirements. Competition among industries and among firms would establish the exchange value of quotas and would determine the quantities of foreign oil that would be used for the processing of imported crude into fractions for refinery products, petrochemical feedstocks, or SNG feedstocks. In the circumstances, the cost of imported LNG could be properly evaluated as compared with the cost of SNG, and both with the cost of fuel oil and coal in competitive end-uses.

Initially, so long as certain product imports are free of restriction, such as residual fuel oil, a separate and equivalent import right for crude oil should be available to any domestic refinery or processing facility that produces such product. That would enable domestic facilities economically to supply domestic requirements which now have to depend on offshore capacity.

In due course, however, unrestricted imports should probably be brought within the control program and special import allocations should certainly be phased out. It just does not make sense for our Government, through special exception and allocations within the import program, to decide that foreign oil should move disproportionately into certain uses, certain areas, or to certain special interests; not by administrative fiat. If such allocations represent a more efficient utilization of foreign oil, competitive pressures will do it.

The nation can hardly afford less than optimum utilization of imports when the volume may reach 11 million barrels daily, as is indicated for 1980.

In sum, oil import policy should ensure a domestic market for domestic energy resources; and an evolving import program should aim toward reasonably proportionate allocation of permissible imports among all who process domestic crude or synthetic feedstocks, be they refiners, chemical companies, SNG plants, or any combination of them. This approach would provide the best guarantee against windfalls and for the most efficient integration of foreign oil into the domestic energy economy.

The Domestic Refining Capacity and Tanker Gap

The present erosion of our domestic refining position must also be dealt with because of its potentially serious effects on our security and balance of payments position. The free imports of fuel oil into District I have undoubtedly contributed greatly to the "export" of fuel oil refining capacity. Moreover, this has aggravated the supply problem for low-sulfur fuel oils which could have been produced from the amply available low-sulfur U.S. crudes, while corresponding quantities of high-sulfur imported crudes could have been used in our refineries, largely to obtain other refined products. Obviously with the investments made on the basis of the existing import system—and in the light of foreign crude and foreign and domestic refining availability, and also the revenue needs and employment especially in Venezuela and in some Caribbean refining countries—any imposition of restrictions on imported fuel oil would require most careful consideration.

In any case, as discussed, the right to an equivalent import allocation for domestic refiners who produce products such as residual that are now unrestricted, would conduce toward expansion of capacity at home instead of abroad. And in time, proportionate access to a rising volume of permissible imports would provide the basis on which industries and companies could make investments in future capacity with reasonable confidence as to the rules of the game—decisions which have been unnecessarily delayed because uncertain import policy compounded problems of location, technology, and feedstock selection.

However, in addition to the "export" of refining and crude processing capacity resulting from our import policy, we are now facing a further substantial emigration of capacity because of environmental restrictions that have stymied the expansion of our crude processing industry. It is absolutely essential to halt this trend of shifting capacity to foreign environmental havens, by a more considered application of environmental rules. Presently, not one refinery is under construction in all of the United States—but many are being planned or actually built abroad for product shipments to our country.

With producing countries becoming more and more insistent on the establishment of national tanker fleets, as reflected in many resolutions of the Organization of Arab Petroleum Exporting Countries, and perhaps further spurred by the recent action of a producing country which simply decreed that 50 percent of its oil exports must be carried under its national flag, the U.S. should review its policy position on tankers. Any shift of effective control over tanker tonnage to the producing countries would obviously further affect the security and foreign exchange position of the U.S. It would appear to be necessary for the U.S. to provide the essential support for obtaining a firm stake in sufficient tonnage that could transport competitively—and "competitively" is the operative word here—a substantial amount of our oil imports.

Synthetic Oil and Gas

An urgent program of providing incentives for the production of synthetic oil from shale, coal, and tar sands, and of synthetic gas from coal and oil, should be initiated forthwith. Coupled with it, an accelerated major joint government-industry research effort, substantially supported by the government, on new technology and process improvement including the development of commercially feasible measures for sulfur-emission controls, should be pursued. Effective cooperation with our allies in such a research effort should be instituted. Leasing policies for shale and coal lands should be established so as to permit large-scale commercial operations. With responsible regard for environmental factors, restrictions imposed and the delays involved must be kept to an absolute minimum.

To enable private industry to make an optimum contribution in these fields, the government should freely permit technical and commercial cooperation between various firms, because the expense of the research and the investments required for many of the ventures far exceeds the technical and financial capabilities of individual companies.

As referred to previously, it should be obvious that our Government should at least be willing to do for the development of our own oil and gas resources what it is ready to do for the development and imports of foreign LNG. The Government should be prepared to encourage the production of synthetic oil as well as gas through provisions for:

a. an investment credit. This would, in effect, lower the capital cost of such ventures, and apart from reducing losses, would enhance the potential return on risky investment where the venture may prove marginal.

b. a relatively rapid amortization of investment—if for no other reason than the possible obsolescence of present technology over a relatively short time.

   c. an option for the investor — if justified — to obtain a guarantee for
      a profit margin that would assure an adequate return on the in-
      vestment at risk.

   This approach may be relatively easy to implement for synthetic gas
that would be used by a public utility, with its assurance of a rate of
return and its rate-making opportunities. But it is equally possible for
synthetic oil. The amounts involved in the profit guarantee would in fact
largely depend on how the difference between the cost of synthetic oil
and the prevailing market price for competing oil of comparable quality
would develop over time.
   By initially limiting the profit support to projects firmly started during
a certain period of time, and perhaps prescribing also a date by which in
general the plant must at the latest be completed, it is most likely that an
optimum private effort for the production of synthetic oil and gas will be
initiated.
   At the same time, the Government together with the AEC must accelerate greatly the implementation of a nuclear energy program, accompanied by a maximum effort of government-supported research on
safety problems, new and improved processes, and environmental issues
that have held back developments. In addition, government-industry-
sponsored research on a battery-powered car and atomic-powered ships,
and perhaps some provisions for their gradual introduction looking
towards the period when nuclear power will be the mainstay of our
energy supply, are called for.

V. Conservation

   As far as conservation of energy is concerned, in addition to the usual
measures to prevent waste, the principle should be established that
whoever for reasons of his own convenience prefers to use a dispropor-
tionate amount of energy should contribute also to the disproportionately higher cost of supplemental energy supplies. In practice, this might
mean a substantially higher and escalating excise tax on motor cars,
depending on horsepower; a rate for gas and power used in households,
escalating on a unit basis when a certain reasonable level per applicable
unit is exceeded; and perhaps a special tax on the use of scarce energy
resources, if there are other amply available forms of energy that could
be consumed, etc.
   The major principle underlying all such measures should be not prohibition or end-use control, but an equitable burden-sharing if some
users prefer "conspicuous" consumption of energy or the use of certain
more expensive supplies. However, care would have to be exercised so

that measures would not discourage energy consumption by industry which could contribute to higher productivity.

It would of course be only prudent with the inevitable increase in our import dependence, to have in readiness a rationing scheme that could quickly be applied if we were ever faced with an emergency. Also, within reason, we must have some build-up of our storage above ground so as to provide some cushion, even though, because of the size of our demand, the only effective reserves we can accumulate are a prosperous and operating oil industry's proved reserves in the ground.

If all the actions suggested in this presentation were to be taken with utmost urgency, our dependence on total energy imports by the early nineteen-eighties might be limited to perhaps around 20 percent — instead of somewhat over 30 percent if present trends were permitted to take their course. Our oil imports at that time would be substantially lower — perhaps about one third — than they would otherwise have been, and probably would not exceed the "danger" level.

VI. Concluding Comments

As far as our allies are concerned, they would, except for the promising developments in the North Sea, and the unknown potential in Japanese offshore waters or in other "safe" areas, have in general much more limited, if any, possibilities of developing dependable energy supplies. But even with the most optimistic estimates for North Sea developments, their dependence on Middle East supplies will inevitably increase greatly during the seventies and early eighties.

Any U.S. program that would lower American dependence on Middle East oil and thereby reduce the competitive bidding up and depletion of Middle East resources is thus a constructive contribution to their position.

It is apparent that Europe and Japan must much more than up to now concentrate on the development of nuclear energy because of the political, economic, and balance of payments problems posed by their ever increasing dependence on Middle East resources. Moreover, they must prepare themselves for the period after the Eighties when Middle East oil availability may begin to decline. After all, even the Middle East oil reserves have a finite limit.

In sum, the program for achieving a reasonable degree of energy independence for the U.S. not only is a sine qua non for the maintenance of our political and economic independence, but also makes an essential contribution in preventing a destructive competition for oil supplies between the U.S. and the rest of the Free World. Moreover, the basic strength of Western oil companies in producing countries would be further weakened if their parent countries were desperately dependent on the oil supplies of those producing countries. Likewise, the position of American companies in consuming countries would suffer if the latter came to fear that the United States, through these companies, would, so to speak, put a first mortgage on the available foreign oil resources — and even worse, say buttressed by special deals with producing countries, claim for themselves a privileged position in the major Middle East producing areas.

Europe and Japan thus must share with the U.S. the deep concern about the physical availability, the terms of trade, the balance of payments impact, and the investment and monetary consequences of heavily increased oil imports; but only the U.S., as one of the two or three world powers, carries the additional responsibility of safeguarding its position in the concert of nations, especially since the Soviet Union and, for that matter, the People's Republic of China, are not similarly situated.

There is a most urgent need for coordinated planning and actions, not only by the United States Government and the American industry but also by the Government of the U.S. together with its Western allies. This should lead to a concerted effort by the Western governments and their industries to try to protect as best they can their security and prosperity, which depend so decisively on energy availability on acceptable political and economic terms. It must be made obvious to all concerned that the Western world could and would not sit by completely passively if the flow of international oil and the world's monetary arrangements were to be jeopardized by arbitrary conditions or unacceptable political and economic pressures. The mere awareness that there are practical limits to the exercise of "Oil or Money Power" by the producing countries may well prove to be the most effective deterrent to its misuse.

As far as the U.S. is concerned, it is long overdue to move from the generalities of pronouncing the need for a coordinated energy policy to the field of specific actions. Inevitably a coordinated energy policy and measures designed to achieve optimum energy security for the U.S. would lead to a much greater involvement of the U.S. Government in industry affairs, with all that this may imply. But there are no realistic alternatives, and the time for action is now, if not yesterday.

16

An Atlantic-Japanese Energy Policy

In the following year (March 1973) Mr. Levy addressed the Europe-America Conference in Amsterdam. In his text he reiterated the common dependence of the Atlantic community on imported oil to meet much of its energy requirements. Instabilities in the Middle East would be both traditional ones and, further, those caused by the increase in revenues obtained from its oil.

Next, the paper introduced and enlarged upon a theme that runs throughout the rest of this volume: the essential requirement of a joint or coordinated strategy on the part of Europe, the United States, and Japan to better assure supply and to cope with the financial aspects generated by increased oil prices. Note that these remarks preceded the shocks to international oil in 1973–74. Nothing would have been changed in the text, the editor believes, could the events of that winter have been known in full detail. Those fateful events were certainly anticipated, hence the urgency with which the omens were addressed.

Mr. Eugene V. Rostow, former under secretary of state and now director, United States Arms Control and Disarmament Agency, wrote of the origin of the request to Mr. Levy to prepare the following paper: "with the help of Emilio Collado, I took the position that [Walter Levy] was the only man . . . who could say what needed to be said, and might be heard. . . . When I read his draft, I wrote him that his paper alone justified the conference, and relieved me of my guilt for forcing him to take on the assignment."

In this respect, the inclusion of Japanese energy interests in a Europe-America meeting set a precedent which became of increasing importance as the global consequences of the oil revaluation became apparent.

There can be no doubt but that the argument and proposals which were the core of Mr. Levy's paper laid the foundation for the subsequent creation of the International Energy Agency (IEA), part of the OECD, and for its program that has been, in most respects, a near mirror image of what was suggested by him. The single—and important—exception has

Reprinted with permission from *Foreign Policy*, Summer 1973, pp. 159–190.

been the inability to date of the IEA to become that common negotiating forum in behalf of importing countries that Mr. Levy called for.

The prosperity and security of the whole free world depend on sufficient availability of energy on satisfactory economic terms.

During the next 10 to 20 years, oil will provide the mainstay of the world's energy supplies. In practical terms, because of the size of known reserves and the lead time for finding and developing new oil and other energy resources, the world's growing needs will be supplied predominantly by huge increases of oil imports from the Middle East — mainly the Persian Gulf area.

Directly connected with this, the consuming countries will face the following:

- The cost of oil imports will rise tremendously with extraordinarily difficult implications for the balance of payments of many consuming countries;
- Foreign exchange accumulations and the international use of such funds in the case of some of the major oil-producing countries, such as Saudi Arabia and Abu Dhabi, could cause serious problems;
- A complete change is developing in the relationships between the oil-producing, importing, and home countries of international oil companies and the national oil companies of producing and importing countries.

The formulation of a realistic energy policy for the oil-importing countries cannot be limited to the Atlantic nations but must include Japan. It should also encompass other developed nations and should take account of oil-importing developing countries in Latin America, Africa, and Asia.

But the primary responsibility for the formulation of policy and organization inevitably belongs to the Atlantic group plus Japan — and their need for action is urgent.

Basic Data on Energy Supply and Finance

If present U.S. policies and trends are left to take their course, oil shipments from abroad will advance from about 4.7 million barrels per day in 1972 to over 11 million barrels per day in 1980, while the oil imports of Europe and Japan combined are estimated to advance during the same period from 18 to 30 million barrels daily.

The preponderant part of all these imports will have to come from the Middle East. Their output will rise from 18 million barrels daily in 1972, to an estimated 35 to 40 million barrels daily by 1980. The United States will, for the first time, compete with Europe and Japan for major oil supplies from the Middle East, whose share in total U.S. oil imports will, by 1980, amount to about 50 to 55 percent and in those of Western Europe and Japan to about 75 to 80 percent. There is little doubt that Middle East oil reserves are sufficient to cover these requirements, but without very large new discoveries this situation might change during the 1980's.

The U.S.S.R. will most likely remain self-sufficient in its energy requirements and may continue to export oil and natural gas.

Two more sets of data are most relevant for the formulation and urgent implementation of energy policy. The total value of U.S. net imports of energy materials, mostly oil, may, according to U.S. Department of Commerce data, easily reach $18 to $24 billion annually by 1980, those of Europe $23 to $31 billion and those of Japan $12 to $16 billion—as compared with $2.3 billion, $8.5 billion and $3.1 billion in 1970, respectively. The revenues likely to accrue to Middle East producing countries can tentatively be estimated at about $40 billion annually by 1980—as against $9 billion in 1972—with Saudi Arabia alone accounting for as much as perhaps half of the 1980 total. In some of the countries, such as Saudi Arabia and Abu Dhabi, a large part of these funds could not possibly be absorbed internally.

The United States simply cannot afford an ever-increasing over-dependence for its oil supplies on a handful of foreign, largely unstable, countries. Otherwise, its security—and that of its allies—as well as its prosperity and its freedom of action in foreign policy formulation will be in jeopardy. But the United States does have a realistic and economically manageable alternative—accelerated development of its large domestic resource potential for conventional and synthetic hydrocarbons and nuclear energy.

Even though such alternatives may now look expensive, the cost of foreign oil imports is likely to escalate, and eventually approach the cost of alternative sources of supply that could be developed in the United States.

If all realistic actions to increase its domestic energy supplies were to be taken with utmost urgency, U.S. dependence on total energy imports by the early 1980's might be limited to perhaps around 20 percent—instead of somewhat over 30 percent if present trends were permitted to take their course—and probably would not exceed the "danger" level. But, as of now, continuing dependence of Europe, Japan, and the United States on Middle East oil appears to be inevitable.

Power Structure Changes of International Oil

In the immediate postwar period, the international oil companies effectively supplied the bulk of the ever-increasing energy requirements of the free world. From 1946 to about the late 1950's, the companies—on the basis of their rich Middle East oil concessions and at least indirectly benefiting from the immense power of the United States—were able to dispose of their oil reasonably freely and on favorable commercial terms.

Moreover, the United States itself was on balance independent of foreign oil imports and possessed a sizeable reserve productive capacity from which our allies benefited substantially during the Iranian and, with some short delays, during the first Suez crisis.

By 1960, when the Organization of the Petroleum Exporting Countries (OPEC) was established, the relative power position of the United States was beginning to decline as Europe, Japan and the U.S.S.R. acquired new strength. It was also the time when the developing countries began to play a more important role in world affairs. OPEC's ever-growing influence in international oil operations was beyond doubt at least in part the result of a certain inability and inflexibility of the international oil industry and their home governments to anticipate, assess and adjust to the changes that had begun to erode their paramount position of political and economic influence in oil-producing countries.

During the next 12 years, from 1960 to 1972, OPEC and its members succeeded in achieving, to begin with, minor increases in the government take of oil-producing countries, and since the early 1970's, in enforcing a quantum jump in the royalty and tax payments levied on their production, capped in 1972 by the so-called participation agreement. Assuming present arrangements are implemented, participation means an immediate 25 percent interest for the Arab producing countries in the Persian Gulf in existing concessions, leading to 51 percent control within nine years. National oil companies of the major Middle East producing countries will thus become the largest sellers of crude oil. Algeria, Libya and Iraq have already taken over a very substantial part of the previously foreign-owned production, and the current Indonesian oil contracts also leave the Indonesian National Oil Company free to dispose of a substantial part of the oil discovered by foreign oil companies.

During the same period, the U.S. domestic oil outlook underwent drastic changes and its reserve productive potential began to disappear. By 1972, with imports of close to 5 million barrels per day, we had become one of the largest importers of oil.

Power of the Major Oil-Producing Countries

There is little doubt that the major oil-producing countries, especially of the Middle East, have acquired an immense potential for power — as long as at least two of the more important producers are able to maintain a reasonably united front. Saudi Arabia alone will soon have a pivotal role in supply.

Their power will in due course derive not only from their effective control over immense oil resources, but also from their control over unprecedented financial resources which they will be able to extract from the oil purchasers. Moreover, large monetary reserves will give them the freedom to restrict their oil production for political or any other reasons.

The control which the producing countries will be able to exercise over their oil production and exports is not only based on their participation in the national oil producing companies, but also stems, perhaps even primarily, from the exercise of their sovereign power over companies operating in their countries. There is ample precedence for such use of power with the reluctant acceptance of the oil companies and their home governments: the Kuwaiti and Libyan restrictions on production; the prohibition of exports to certain countries, including in certain circumstances even the parent countries of the oil companies; the Venezuelan oil legislation establishing practically complete control over oil operations, which were totally under foreign private ownership. This list could be extended to foreign oil activities in almost any of the major producing countries.

To all intents and purposes, fiscal arrangements and payments to the producing countries are subject to nearly unilateral determination by the producing countries, as reflected in the Tehran and Tripoli "dictates."

Preemptory demands for national ownership of tanker transportation, reinvestments in oil exploration, refining, petrochemical and other related industries are bound to be made. The establishment of levels of production and the size and direction of exports are also "recognized" methods of controls.

In this connection it is noteworthy that the development of the tremendous oil resources of the Middle East does not really reflect any extensive industrial involvement of the economies of their countries or any important contribution by their people. The oil-producing industry operations in these countries are limited fundamentally to a small enclave.

Even though, under recent arrangements, a substantial part of the national companies' entitlements will be sold back to their foreign partners, it is only a matter of time before the national oil companies will dominate the market for non-integrated third party sales of crude oil. They will become major suppliers to national oil companies in many of the importing countries of the world and will probably also deal directly with the foreign refining and marketing affiliates of the international oil companies. In fact, effective competition in crude-oil sales between the producing affiliates of the international oil companies and their partners, the national oil companies of the producing countries, may become very difficult if not impossible, as the producing countries' governments might not only establish the levels of production but also determine the tax-paid cost and the prices at which the greatly increasing quantities of crude to which their companies will become entitled will either be sold back to their foreign partners or to their own customers.

Coupled with the expansion of crude oil sales, the national oil companies of some of the major producing countries will obviously work out deals for joint refining and marketing in importing countries. Likewise, the producing countries, by taking over ownership or control of an ever-expanding tanker fleet to carry their oil exports, will not only increase their revenues, but further enhance their power over the international oil trade.

With Saudi Arabia unable to absorb its vastly expanding oil revenues in its local economy, it is quite possible that by the early 1980's the surplus funds annually available to it may be on the order of $15 billion plus. The large and continuously growing inflow of foreign funds that would accrue to the treasuries of a few Middle East governments, and to a small number of their privileged citizens, will far exceed any accumulation of foreign exchange holdings in modern times. Realistically, such amounts could probably not be placed into long-term or short-term investments year-in year-out without risking severe international repercussions and potentially extensive restrictions on the free flow of capital. It is most unlikely that the United States, or any other developed country, would permit continued massive foreign investments on a scale that could conceivably result in foreign takeovers of important companies and industries. Moreover, the reverse flow of dividends and interest would soon add an additional unmanageable balance-of-payments burden to the oil import bill of many countries. Nor could the short-term money markets handle such excessive and volatile funds without undermining the world's monetary arrangements.

The dilemma confronting us is acutely disturbing, as any proliferation of international restrictions on capital or short-term movements of funds would, in and by themselves, be most harmful to our financial markets and monetary system. In the affected Middle East oil- and capital-surplus countries, any restrictions on their investments abroad would probably be accompanied by restrictions on the output of oil. Obviously, if the income of oil-producing countries were to be "sterilized," it would be more advantageous and completely rational for them to limit their oil exports. This would then further aggravate the world oil supply situation. However, controls over the level of oil production are unfortunately likely to be introduced anyhow, even without any hostile political or economic motivation of the producing countries, for reasons of conservation and wise resource management — at least in some of the major oil-producing countries — and certainly as soon as their reserve-to-production ratio begins to decline significantly. A recent pronouncement by the Saudi Arabian Minister of Petroleum has clearly suggested such a course of action. Interestingly, his statement was coupled with the suggestion that in order to assure continued supplies, oil imports from his country be given a privileged position in the U.S. market.

Some of the major Middle East producing countries will thus become two-pronged power centers; both as suppliers of oil and as extraordinary accumulators of capital — with the latter further strengthening their ability to withhold oil from importing countries over a considerable period of time by drawing on their financial reserves for their budgetary and trade requirements. There is little doubt that this accumulation of oil and of money power — obtained like "manna from heaven," and, at least for the time being, not accompanied by any substantial contribution in political, managerial, or technical competence — would bring with it tremendous and lopsided shifts in the balance of power of a potentially explosive character.

Not the least of the dangers posed by this extreme concentration of oil power and "unearned" money power is the pervasive corruptive influence which this will nearly inevitably have on political, economic, and commercial actions in both the relatively primitive and unsophisticated societies of the producing countries and the advanced societies of the dependent industrialized nations.

Further complicating factors must be taken into account. Within the area itself there are many deep-seated conflicts such as those of Iran versus Iraq, Iraq versus Kuwait, Saudi Arabia versus Abu Dhabi, Libya versus the traditional Arab countries, and so on. Also, there is an underlying rivalry between Iran and the Arab States of the Gulf for hegemony in the area, which may sooner or later erupt into an open power struggle implicating also the Communist and non-Communist allies or sponsors of the various Middle East countries. In addition there are the explosive implications of the Israeli-Arab issue.

All these actual or potential confrontations fundamentally affect the oil companies. When the activities of the companies extend to several of these countries, they will most likely be drawn sooner or later into any local area conflicts. Moreover, the producing countries will hold them responsible for their home government policies and expect them to support the producing countries' political, strategic or economic interests. The companies will nearly inevitably be asked to match any arrangements which either their affiliates or any of the other international oil companies (or sometimes even any newcomer company) make with governments of most other Middle East oil countries. And with the underlying rivalry between the Arab countries and Iran, either of them could feel compelled to be able to claim that it has struck the most advantageous bargain with the oil companies. National pride and jealousy are bound to provoke a one-upmanship that would lead to endless escalations and no end of trouble. This is exactly what is happening as a result of the simultaneous negotiations on participation with the Arab nations on the one hand and on a differently structured deal with Iran on the other hand—and also in connection with developments in Iraq concerning the nationalization of the Iraq Petroleum Company. Accordingly, the outcome in Iran and Iraq, any potential repercussions on the participation agreements with the Arab countries, and especially whether or not and, if so, how long the companies will be able to keep any equity interest in their various oil-producing arrangements are, as of the time of this writing, still undetermined.

Finally, it must not be forgotten that none of the national governments is really stable and that the societies involved are still largely backward; there are always serious doubts whether any existing arrangements would survive the end of any current regime.

Limitations on Oil Companies in Producing Countries

It is clear that participation is mainly a device through which the oil-producing countries plan, by arrangements with the international oil companies, to obtain complete control over their countries' oil operations.

It represents a grand design by the producing countries to forge an alliance with the oil companies in which the producing countries, while pursuing their national objectives, would still be able to take advantage of the large distribution outlets, the investment capabilities and the technical know-how of the oil companies. This is reflected perhaps most succinctly in the pronouncements of Mr. [Ahmed Zaki] Yamani, the Saudi Arabian Minister of Petroleum. His whole approach is based on the assumption that the oil companies would one day turn out to be the natural allies of the producing countries. As he explains it, he wants participation because the weight of the national oil companies in producing countries should be combined with that of the oil companies so as to:

1. protect the concessions from nationalization by providing an en-during link between the oil companies and the producing countries;

2. gain control over the oil operations while maintaining the flow of foreign capital and expertise and obtaining marketing outlets for the output;

3. prevent competition between producing countries as sellers of crude in open market, which would lead to a drastic drop in prices and producing government revenues;

4. maintain thereby price stability, and through the implementation of participation even secure an immediate increase in world crude oil prices from which the producing countries would benefit;

5. achieve through this combination a position of influence in the oil markets;

6. make it difficult for any producing country to insist on an "abnormal" increase in production.

As the Kuwaiti Finance and Oil Minister plainly put it, "What we called phased participation is in fact phased nationalization. This is precisely the situation and its implications."

It must be clear that even though the producing countries will start initially with a minority ownership, they will have a powerful voice on investment, production levels, size of exports and their destination. As corporate partners representing at the same time the sovereign, they possess all the power they need to control and direct the companies on all phases of the operations in the producing country and probably even on many phases of their operations abroad, holding their local interest in oil production as hostage.

Perhaps sensing this, an American top executive of an international oil company in an early statement on participation demands said that the key role of the international oil companies, to satisfy the needs of both the producing and consuming countries, is

> best performed when the commercial enterprise is freed from the pressures of conflicting ideologies and of the clashing political systems. These differences inevitably arise when governments of producing countries have a direct participation in running the oil industry or when government-to-government negotiations are substituted for the company bargaining with the host government.

The commercial framework of operations "would be subverted if we were to adopt an alternative of serving either group of nations exclusively." A top executive of one of the largest European international oil companies stated that a position of 51 percent participation by the producing countries would be "almost intolerable" as the oil companies would have almost all the operating responsibility without any freedom of investment and without control of production levels.

Subsequently, another top executive referred more positively to the new participation agreement with some of the oil-producing governments in the Middle East as an example of building "more stable future relationships," though he conceded, "I won't pretend this was an easy adjustment."

I am afraid that the earlier pessimistic evaluations and reactions of the oil companies' executives to the participation demand will prove to be the correct ones, notwithstanding the firm assurances by the present Saudi Arabian government that Middle East oil should and will be viewed solely commercially and not politically. This is certainly not the position of most other Middle East producing countries and cannot realistically be depended on. A cold-blooded assessment of the real power relationships of the international oil company with the various countries where it operates must lead to the conclusion that its oil production, on which the continued operations of its upstream and downstream facilities are completely dependent, is now or will be soon under the effective control of the producing countries. At the same time, the producing countries will probably deliberately arrange their and the companies' affairs so that the industry's single most important after-tax profit center will, as in the past, be located in the producing countries.

There is thus very little doubt about the change in the role of the oil companies from a bridge between producing and importing countries to what may in fact turn out to be that of junior partners of the producing countries. The oil companies will thus be unable to continue to act as an independent-intermediary commercial force in international oil relations; instead, the producing countries will tend to treat them as service companies under their control that will undertake admittedly essential worldwide logistic, technical, financial, production and distribution operations.

What we are facing, therefore, is a shift of the major center of power over international oil from the home countries to the producing countries. Whether the companies like it or not, they will be compelled to protect their huge interests in the producing countries by adjusting and coordinating their policies and actions with the directives and policies of the producing countries, hoping that their operations in their home countries and the importing countries will not be seriously upset.

The role which the oil companies will be able to play in any of their future dealings with producing countries is thus inevitably severely circumscribed. They cannot be expected to take a strong and determined stand in such negotiations with the sovereign of the country on which their whole prosperity depends and whose national companies are their partners and will in due course acquire the controlling interest in their operations. Moreover, they will have to argue that as long as they are able to secure the availability of supplies to importing countries – even at steeply escalating costs – they also serve the interest of their customers by not risking a confrontation that could lead to interruption of supplies; and as long as the companies are able to recoup such costs from the consumer, they would also protect their own commercial viability. The companies, as private organizations and under the terms of reference applicable to commercial corporations, cannot possibly be expected to carry by themselves the burden of protecting not only their own interests but also those of their customers.

There are thus serious doubts whether the kind of negotiating problems we are facing now can be handled effectively solely through a common posture of the companies or by any other kind of intercompany arrangements. The approach followed in earlier negotiations, when most of the oil companies with foreign production negotiated as a group with OPEC producing countries on matters that will vitally affect the tax-paid cost and oil supplies of almost every oil-importing country of the free world, must thus be subjected to a most searching review. In particular, it would appear that a broad understanding on energy policy among the various importing and home governments involved is absolutely necessary to avoid misuse of bargaining power by the oil-producing countries.

New Role of Importing-Country Oil Companies

The international oil companies continue to be a most important factor in the refining and distribution of oil in practically all of the countries of the free world, based on their predominant investment position in all phases of the local oil industries. They will also represent the most diversified single source of crude oil supplies, even though ever-increasing quantities will be sold in the international oil trade by the national companies of producing countries. The international oil companies will also continue to make perhaps the most important contribution to diversified exploration, to technology, and to expanded investments.

A course by the United States that would, through the exploitation of its domestic energy resources, lower American dependence on Middle East oil and thereby reduce the competitive bidding-up and depletion of Middle East oil reserves would, however, be a constructive contribution to the oil position of the free world.

But beyond that, the United States has additional possibilities to put a "first mortgage" on some of the richest oil resources in the Middle East. Saudi Arabia controls by far the largest known reserves developed by American oil companies; and the Saudi Arabian government has already evinced its interest to conclude special deals with the United States for increasing oil deliveries. No doubt, Iran would be keen to do likewise. However, acceptance by the United States of preferred treatment would be extremely disruptive to its relations with other countries.

The reactions of other importing countries to the Saudi offer is reflected in a statement by the French state-owned oil company ELF-ERAP. In referring to the worries that such a policy would cause, it comments: "What an inducement to the raising of crude oil prices if the money paid by Europe and Japan should be invested through the producing state in the country of origin of these companies strengthening their power. Who would still be able to maintain that the companies which produce in Arabia are impartial intermediaries between these countries and the European consumer?"

Along the same line of reasoning Italy's national oil company ENI suggests that the Common Market conclude direct oil supply agreements, in return for cooperation in the producing countries' development plans, to prevent a supply monopoly of the major international oil companies, especially because American and European interests are not identical. Positions expressing similar reactions have been taken by several other major importing countries.

This prevailing fear is perhaps best summarized in a 1972 draft recommendation unanimously approved by the Western European Union but apparently not endorsed by the Council of Ministers:

> . . . much of the oil imported by Europe is shipped under the American flag. The Middle East oil question is therefore mainly a commercial matter for the United States.
>
> For Western Europe, on the other hand, it is a vital matter and the interests of consumers do not tally with the interests of the international companies. Increased participation in the capital of petrol companies by the Arab States or even nationalization would not necessarily be a catastrophe for Europe.
>
> A European oil policy should take account of these factors and in no case be linked with the international oil companies. This means Europe could reach agreement directly with oil-producing countries, help them to develop a national oil industry and purchase the oil thus produced. . . . Europe has no interest in becoming involved in a vain conflict for defense of the oil companies; its interest is to collaborate closely with the Arab states. . . .

But whatever their motivation, the national companies of importing countries will, in any case, greatly expand their foreign supply operations. While such diversification might provide a modicum of added supply security, any new such ventures would be subject to the same kind of political and economic risks as those of the international oil companies.

Also investments by the producing countries downstream in importing countries are unlikely to take place or to be permitted on a really massive scale; but even if this should occur, these investments are unlikely to provide a much higher degree of oil supply security if the producing countries, for reasons of their own, should decide to withhold oil supplies. Their downstream investments would not constitute an effective hostage in the hands of the importing countries because the latter's continued dependence on oil supplies would be of much greater urgency than the threat of expropriation or the loss of current revenue from such investment.

Moreover, foreign crude secured by a national oil company of an importing country would most likely be given a preferred position in the home market. If so, its dependence on what would most likely be a rather limited number of sources of oil imports would make it even more vulnerable to interruption — and to unilaterally imposed cost increases. If the importing countries would follow a course of "go it alone" in a *sauve qui peut* spirit, each one of them would also become the target for potential political and economic blackmail, such as some of them have already experienced. They would run the grave risk that their policies and actions would be subverted by considerations of securing or protecting their access to foreign oil; ultimately such an approach will prove to be futile, and the price for the oil and the political or other terms under which it could be obtained might easily become untenable.

Obviously a continuous process of yielding valid rights, not through genuine bargaining but under threats by the producing countries and a general posture of subservience by the oil companies and the importing countries — as has occurred in recent international oil "negotiations" — must undermine not only the prestige of the importing nations and of the companies but equally the respect for any arrangements concluded with them. Only a coordinated approach to energy policy by the relevant importing countries could really prevent such harmful consequences.

The Interests of the Home Countries
of the International Oil Companies

The change in power relationships affecting the operations of the international oil industry also has a far-reaching effect on the position of the companies in their home countries. The interests of the home countries in their international oil companies have in the past centered around their supply capabilities for their own country and its allies, their support of the power position of the home country that was implied in control over international oil resources, the contribution of the companies to the balance of payments, and their essential role in meeting ever-increasing worldwide oil requirements.

The ability of the companies to provide secure supplies because of their investment in foreign oil is now no longer absolute and assured. Experience during the first Suez crisis in the case of the United Kingdom and France, and during the Six Day War in the case of the United States and the United Kingdom, has shown that even U.S., British, or French-controlled foreign oil could be and was—even though for a short period only—embargoed for shipments to home countries. While in earlier years the United States was only a marginal importer of Middle East oil, in contrast to the United Kingdom, in the future the United States will become one of the largest single importers of such oil. On the other hand, with the development of the North Sea resources, the United Kingdom—if it could under Common Market rules effectively reserve its domestic oil production for its own use—might be able to achieve a substantial lessening of its dependence on Middle East oil imports.

The same questions hold for the extent to which Anglo-American ownership provides supply assurance to our allies. As a matter of fact, some of our allies fear that American ownership of foreign oil might endanger their supply if there should be conflict between the United States and the producing countries.

In the past, control over the international oil companies could be and was used as a political instrument by their home countries in their relationship to importing countries, such as the United States apparently did during the first Suez crisis or say for oil trade with Cuba, and so on. This possibility, to use the control over foreign oil for political-strategic purposes of the home countries, is disappearing fast.

The contribution of the international oil industry to the balance of payments of their home countries is indeed substantial, but relatively more important for the United Kingdom than for the United States. In the future, with large increases in U.S. oil imports and the continued need for reinvestment abroad, the balance-of-payments concern of the United States with regard to international oil may be directed more towards the huge and escalating foreign exchange costs of oil imports rather than to the benefits of profit transfers from international oil operations. In the United Kingdom, on the other hand, the development of the North Sea resources may relieve its oil trade bill sufficiently so as to maintain a predominant interest in the profit transfers from British international oil companies.

In sum, therefore, the fundamental interest of the United States is moving somewhat closer to that of an oil-importing country. On the other hand, the United Kingdom might, for the reasons cited above perhaps, pay more attention to the profit pattern of its companies from international oil operations.

There are, however, important additional qualifying factors affecting the security position of the home countries and especially the United States with regard to their oil supplies — independent of their position as home countries of worldwide oil companies.

What is relevant now is not so much any influence which the international oil companies may or may not be able to wield in producing countries, but the interest which producing countries have in maintaining an effective relationship with the United States. After all, the United States is the most important political, economic, and military power of the free world which, incidentally, also presents the highest priced and one of the largest markets for imported oil. This, above all, explains Saudi Arabia's and also Iran's interest in trying to conclude special oil supply arrangements with the United States — not the investment of U.S. oil companies in their country, which, as far as Iran is concerned, would anyhow be a minority interest. Moreover, the United States offers the most important potential outlet for their capital investments and constitutes one of the largest sources for capital equipment, consumer goods, and military hardware.

Finally, the United States is the only power that can effectively assure protection against Communist — Soviet as well as Chinese — external and internal incursions. It is the one country which the traditional regimes of the two most important oil-producing nations of the Persian Gulf — Iran and Saudi Arabia — believe they can depend on for the maintenance of their governments, and also for the security of the Persian Gulf area.

In the light of the U.S. possibilities for developing its domestic potential in conventional and non-conventional hydrocarbon and energy resources, and its opportunity for establishing a special oil relationship with the two most important Middle East oil producers, there is little doubt that if it so desires, the United States could go it alone.

With the development of the North Sea oil fields, the United Kingdom will be less dependent on Middle East oil than any of its Common Market partners. Nevertheless, apparently the United Kingdom, in the Paris Summit Meeting of October 1972, was pressing for an early formulation of an energy policy for the [European Economic] Community [EEC] guaranteeing certain and lasting supplies under satisfactory economic conditions.

This policy suggestion must be evaluated within the context of today's stark realities; that unilateral and diverse policies of the various

European nations and of Japan cannot provide real supply security or contain the financial problems connected with the international oil trade; that the international oil companies can no more guarantee supplies to any of their customers in a crisis; that these companies no longer possess the bargaining strength, if left to themselves, to be effective negotiators with producing countries with regard to the availability and cost of oil; and that such a state of affairs would provide the most cogent reason for the importing countries to work together toward an energy policy.

But the ultimate interest of the most important producing countries in the Middle East that have not fallen under Russian domination is bound to remain the protection of their independence, and that can only be achieved by close and friendly relationships with the United States. The United States will thus continue to be the dominant factor in world oil, not because of the foreign oil interests of its companies, but primarily because of its standing in the world balance of power. An energy policy applying solely to the Community would, I believe, be only the first step toward a really effective policy.

The Need for an Atlantic-Japanese Energy Policy

Beyond doubt, U.S. relations with Europe and Japan are in disarray. There are many outstanding unresolved problems.

Perhaps instead of establishing a grand design which would encompass a resolution of all major contentions and areas of conflicts, it might be more fruitful to proceed pragmatically on an issue-by-issue basis and tackle first those problems where the chances of an Atlantic-Japanese policy, or at least of an agreed upon coordinated approach, would seem to be most promising. (The European Common Market was preceded by the establishment of a much more limited joint effort, the European Coal and Steel Community.)

The problem of the future energy position of the Atlantic-Japanese complex of nations is one of the most important issues confronting each country individually and as a group.

What is likely to induce the various countries to agree to cooperation and mutual adjustments is the existence of a severe outside threat to their security and prosperity, resulting from their dependence on oil supplies from a few foreign sources coupled with the potential danger of a flood of foreign funds that could harm their own economies and the world's monetary system.

The weak and unstable foreign political societies where the world's oil and money power centers are located could, for reasons of their own or stirred up by the potentially adversary policies of the Russians and even perhaps the Chinese People's Republic, create great difficulties for the various countries of the free world. The United States as well as the United Kingdom would — shortsightedly to be sure — by themselves probably be able to resolve their energy problems, partly at the expense of other importing countries. But as mentioned before it is to the United States, more than any other nation of the free world, that pivotal producing countries look for their political and strategic security; and this advantage could redound to the benefit of all oil-importing countries. Neither the Common Market nor Japan alone or in combination could provide a comparable total package of advantages for the well-being of the major Middle East oil-producing countries.

If, therefore, the United States abstains from any attempt to try to obtain unilateral benefits, however short-lived they might prove to be, and is willing to participate in an energy policy in a new Atlantic-Japanese partnership, it might thereby provide protection for its partners against potentially very serious oil supply emergencies. Obviously, the latter too must then forego the temptation of looking only at their immediate self-interest without regard to others; a policy that they could in any case not pursue successfully over any period of time. Only then would it be possible for the importing countries to pursue a rational policy for their energy imports and avoid bidding against each other or being played against each other with ever escalating political and economic demands being made upon them. Only then would it be possible for Atlantic-Japanese and especially U.S. power to become an effective countervailing factor in international oil.

The need for a joint or at least coordinated policy is urgent because any delays in which conflicting approaches to producing countries are made by the individual members of the Atlantic-Japanese group of nations will accelerate not only the disintegration of the partnership, but will further encourage arbitrary and dictatorial demands of the producing countries. Moreover, as some of the producing countries accumulate large surplus reserve funds, it might become much more difficult, if not impossible, for the importing countries to influence their policies.

It would appear therefore that Europe and Japan need something from the United States which is in the interest of the United States to give, i.e., its adherence to a coordinated Atlantic-Japanese energy policy, in, as the game theorists would call it, a positive sum game through which all sides would gain.

This does not imply that any of the partners should necessarily be inhibited from pursuing separate diplomatic and economic initiatives within the broad spectrum of developing Middle East relationships and the framework of an Atlantic-Japanese energy policy.

The OECD Oil Committee has for many years served as the most significant international organization encompassing the Atlantic-

Japanese group of nations, providing a basis for the exchange of information and coordination and expert analyses on oil developments. Most important, it has established policies for emergency stockpiling and, within certain limits, for the emergency apportionment of oil supplies in the OECD European area; and during oil emergencies it has in fact served as a clearing body to achieve an equitable division of available supplies among its members.

The Common Market is presently engaged in a slow and difficult effort to establish an energy policy for its members. But national policies of the individual members could severely slow up the establishment of a Community policy, as long as there is no overriding conviction on the part of its members that the Community countries in combination would decisively add to their individual bargaining strength.

In the light of the changed power relationships of today, an effective energy policy of a new Atlantic-Japanese partnership must inevitably go further than either the OECD or the Common Market have advanced so far. Obviously, however, such a policy would build on the valuable achievements of the OECD and the Common Market.

Fortunately there is a substantial consensus on the need for a coordinated or even joint approach to the energy problem in the United States as well as the Common Market and Japan. It is reflected in many official pronouncements during the last year or two.

The United States, in a 1972 statement before an OECD Council Meeting, officially expressed its readiness for such cooperation:

> It is imperative for the world's major consumers of oil and other forms of energy to take joint and coordinated action, starting now, to increase the availability of all types of energy resources; to lessen, to the degree possible, an overdependence on oil from the Middle East, to coordinate the response of consuming countries to restrictions on the supply of Middle East petroleum, and to develop jointly and cooperatively a responsible program of action to meet the possibility of critical energy shortages by the end of this decade.

The OECD itself is again engaged in a study of the world energy situation, hopefully leading to concrete recommendations for action by the member governments. The Common Market Commission considers it necessary to substitute or extend liaison in the energy field between the Community and other energy-importing countries in order to provide a better exchange of information and produce common solutions.

Japan, through its Overall Energy Council, an advisory body to the Minister of International Trade and Industry, recommended in 1971 that, while it was necessary for Japan, in order to assure stable oil supplies at low cost, to behave independently of any foreign influence in all aspects of her oil industry activities, it must cooperate with other consuming countries.

> To this end it is necessary for Japan to promote with them and their national oil companies exchange of information and mutual understanding and to explore possibilities for constructive cooperation on the part of oil consuming countries toward the formation of an organization in which debates are held among the countries with international oil companies and the oil-producing countries on the basic policy concerning the world oil situation.

As the Natural Resources Survey Mission, sponsored by the Japanese Foreign Office, put it in its report published in 1972, Japan must engage in active participation in international cooperation with advanced countries on oil matters and "must refrain from being passive as has been the case thus far. It must take full advantage of opportunities such as an OECD Oil Committee meeting where industrially advanced nations meet, through which Japan could clarify her oil policy on international cooperation before the OECD member countries."

Outline for an Atlantic-Japanese Energy Policy

The major goal of an energy policy for a new Atlantic-Japanese partnership must be to try to cope with the common problems of the security of oil supplies and the financial issues related to it. While nobody can guarantee that such a policy will lead to a completely satisfactory resolution of all the problems, it should at least be possible to contain them. Future bargaining in international oil would no longer be lopsided, i.e., between the producing countries as a group and the oil companies (be they the internationals or the national companies of importing countries) with the latter "negotiating" under the threat of being treated as virtual captives of the producing countries—but would also engage the extraordinary political, strategic and economic power of the Atlantic-Japanese group of nations.

If such "countervailing power" to OPEC should really become a factor in international oil, which indeed it must, there is some reasonable hope that international oil and financial arrangements could be set up on a rational and manageable basis; and that OPEC would no longer be able, as Mr. Yamani put it in October 1972, through its coordination and unity to "prove time and time again that it can enforce its demands."

Some fear has been expressed that such a grouping of oil-importing countries might unnecessarily provoke a confrontation with the producing countries. But circumstances have significantly tipped the balance of power during the last few years. It was the producing countries which, through the establishment of OPEC, created an organization which formulates policy guidelines for major producing countries, and through the threat of withholding supplies to companies that would not submit to its demands and through other means, provides enormous power and overwhelming bargaining leverage for each of the producing nations. Moreover, the Organization of Arab Petroleum Exporting Countries (OAPEC) has stated its intention to establish official relations with countries of the EEC, either collectively or individually. To this purpose, it announced in 1971 that it is setting up a committee to coordinate the relations of its member countries—in the Arabian Gulf, represented by Saudi Arabia, and in North Africa, represented by Libya and Algeria—with the EEC countries.

The subject matters to be covered by the energy policy could be put in the following broad categories:

1. Develop a program for optimum diversification of supplies, based on a study and review of energy demand and supply, including tanker, pipeline, and refining availabilities.

2. Develop new energy sources, especially atomic energy and energy from unconventional sources, through a joint research program.

3. Create national and multinational incentive, investment, and guarantee programs for the development of new energy sources.

4. Establish broad terms of reference and parameters acceptable to oil-importing countries for oil supplies from producing countries, which cover purchases, service contracts, concessions, and so on.

5. Set up a contingency system for stockpiling, rationing, and equitable sharing of imports between all members, to be put into effect in case of an over-all or specific country emergency.

6. Set up a joint and coordinated research program that looks into all methods of conservation of energy, including research on battery-powered cars, nuclear fueled shipping, savings in motor car transportation, and so on.

7. Review and coordinate programs of economic development and technical assistance for producing countries.

8. Review prices, costs, and the balance-of-payments effects of oil imports of member countries and of developing countries, and set up a program for support and adjustment if necessary.

9. Review the government revenues of major oil-producing countries and their impact on world trade, world capital flows, and

short-term money markets, and set up a program of financial cooperation — if necessary.

10. Review the dependency of Middle East producing countries on the exports from the free world's oil-importing countries of industrial and agricultural goods and military equipment, and technical knowhow, shipping and services. Assess in light of this the mutual interdependence and the means that might be available to cope with an oil or financial emergency.

The administration of the energy policy might be entrusted to a special new level International Energy Council, composed of member states with a top-level permanent staff with generally recognized and incontestable professional and practical experience. The timing and method of its establishment, its organizational structure, the range of its executive and/or advisory powers, the procedures on voting and the rules governing ratification and implementation of its decisions and its relationship with the various member countries and their oil companies would of course be determined in a process of give and take through international negotiations. It will, obviously, be very difficult indeed to achieve any such agreement; but it may well be the only remaining chance to attempt to safeguard the interests of the importing countries, the home countries, and those of their oil companies. Whatever the odds, it must certainly be tried, and there is no time to be lost.

The above proposal presents of course only one of several possible approaches to an Atlantic-Japanese energy policy and its implementation. In particular, a great deal of thought must be given to the problem of whether or not it would be feasible and advisable to restructure the present OECD Oil Committee or its High Level Committee so that the conclusion and implementation of an Atlantic-Japanese energy policy could be handled within the framework of the Committee. While this might require substantial changes in the powers and functions of the OECD Oil Committee, it might be more expeditious and easier to reach an agreement on a revision of an existing international organization concerned with the oil policy of importing countries rather than to start from scratch and establish a completely new international body.

The competence and functions of the International Energy Council, however it were to be set up, as well as those of the member countries and those of the oil companies, must of course be clearly delineated. The policy framework established by the Council would set the limits within which the countries as well as the oil companies would handle their affairs, taking into account their changing responsibilities and capabilities.

At the same time it would try to provide an effective basis for protecting the supply security of the oil-importing countries through encouraging the development of added supplies, diversification, investment incentives, research, assuring sufficient tanker and refining availability, etc. Through stockpiling, coordination of rationing policy, and especially through an emergency import-sharing agreement among all members, an oil embargo by producing countries against selected countries would become much more difficult, if not practically impossible; in such circumstances the producing countries would have to be prepared to cut their oil supplies to all member countries — with unpredictable, dangerous consequences to them.

The conclusion of an effective arrangement for emergency import-sharing between the Atlantic nations and Japan would presuppose that each member country, including, of course, the United States and Japan, would be prepared to share with its partners its own import availabilities in an equitable manner on the basis of agreed-upon principles. The establishment of substantial stockpiles of oil by the various importing countries, again including the United States and Japan, would provide them in case of emergency with time for possible supply-demand adjustments, for efforts to resolve equitably any underlying conflicts with the producing countries or, if everything else fails, for initiating whatever measures are required to protect their security. Arrangements on sharing of import availabilities and stockpiling applicable to all nations of the new Atlantic-Japanese partnership may well prove to be the touchstone and provide the foundation for a broadly conceived energy policy such as outlined above; they may well be considered as the essential initial step on which it should be possible to achieve more easily an early international agreement.

Likewise, a joint or coordinated policy on dealing with supply, trade, and financial problems related to oil would have the best chance to lead to rational and manageable solutions of the very difficult issues that are bound to arise. The producing countries could no longer, so to speak, pick out consuming countries one by one; OPEC itself has, in its own resolutions, introduced similar measures of solidarity among the producing countries.

Moreover, the companies in their negotiations on prices and payments to producing governments which will come up for revision by 1976 at the latest — and which OPEC's Secretary General has already described as the next major issue — would no longer be as exposed to unilateral dictates as in the past. Their negotiating stance would be based on broad terms of reference such as recommended or formulated by an International Energy Council similar to the practice OPEC is applying in suggesting the basic position for producing countries. There need no longer be the hectic and somewhat improvised discussions and confrontation between oil companies and producing countries, as experienced between 1970 and 1972 in the Tripoli-Tehran and participation arrangements, brought about by ultimatums of the producing countries rather than through genuine negotiations.

Under current conditions, as pointed out earlier, there would be very little if any bargaining leverage left with the oil companies if, in their negotiations with the producing countries, they were to depend solely on their own strength. Only a firm backing by all major oil-importing countries could provide the necessary countervailing power which would permit the oil companies to establish a credible negotiating stance. The companies, acting within their terms of reference and within the framework of a coordinated energy policy, could thus count on such backing that should enable them to handle international oil negotiations and their implementation.

In this connection, an additional factor in the assessment of the respective bargaining leverage by either side would undoubtedly be the awareness that there is a limit to which the oil companies, together with the importing countries, could be held hostage by a threat to access to reserves in producing countries; that it might in certain circumstances be preferable to abandon the hostage and to turn away from the reserves and reappear as competitive buyers of crude from the producing countries. Since captive concession-holding companies would no longer be at their behest one might expect that OPEC unity would erode and that producing countries would eventually compete with each other for export sales to the companies whose purchasing power would derive from past investment in and current control over transport, refining and marketing facilities — the power to dispose.

The importing countries, through extending economic and technical cooperation to the developing producing countries, should contribute to the advance in their standard of living, the diversification of their economic activities and the expansion of their general import and export trade. Hopefully, the producing countries will in due course become such an integral part of the world economy that they would be much less tempted to take radical measures which might sever these links. If the dependence of the producing countries on continued oil revenues, flow of trade and friendly political and economic relations with the free world is such that they could not risk more than a very short interruption, then and only then will the producing countries act with circumspection and probably be sufficiently discouraged from attempting to impose an oil embargo.

In particular, the producing countries would be constrained to exercise great caution not to confront importing countries or their companies — if firmly backed by all major importing countries — with unreasonable demands if the turmoil resulting from a confrontation is likely to undermine the regimes of the oil-producing countries, or if they would have reason to fear that their actions might provoke dangerous international repercussions affecting their integrity and security.

Moreover, the producing countries are fully aware that if their relations with the major importing countries should deteriorate gravely, they may have to rely on Russian support, which not only could not provide anything comparable to the benefits they are enjoying from dealing with the free world, but would also confront them with grave political and other risks.

Obviously too, the more essential oil supplies from the Middle East become, the more attractive a target it would offer for Russian subversion and control. For the Communist world, the concentration of oil and money power in a few small countries in the Persian Gulf, at their back door, presents an enviable opportunity to attempt to undermine the political and economic strength of the free world by "peaceful means" through encouragement of all the nationalistic and centrifugal tendencies that already exist in the area. However, any serious threat to Middle East oil supplies could, in such circumstances, easily lead to a confrontation between the major powers. Only friendly relations with the free world, including the United States, can hold the Russians at bay. A united or coordinated Atlantic-Japanese posture with regard to oil provides the most persuasive safeguard for the security, prosperity and integrity of the importing as well as producing countries.

What I am suggesting, therefore, in proposing the establishment of an Atlantic-Japanese energy policy, is not designed to lead to escalation of international oil problems, as a prelude to a confrontation with OPEC, but it is, I believe, *the only way to avoid confrontation*. Also, while taking account of the changed role and power of the oil companies, it will strengthen them in their relations with producing countries, rather than leave them and the importing countries at their mercy.

This approach presents the most effective means to make obvious to all concerned that the Atlantic-Japanese group of nations could not and would not sit by passively if the flow of international oil and the world's monetary arrangements were to be jeopardized by arbitrary conditions or unacceptable political and economic pressures. The mere awareness that there are practical limits to the exercise of "Oil or Money Power" by the producing countries may well prove to be the most effective deterrent to its misuse.

There is an urgent need for coordinated planning and action by the government of the United States together with its Atlantic partners and Japan. Inevitably, a newly established Atlantic-Japanese energy policy and measures designed to achieve optimum energy security for the free world would lead to a much greater involvement of governments in what had previously been considered to be industry affairs, with all that this may imply. But there are no realistic alternatives, and the time for action is now, if not yesterday.

Part 5
WORLD OIL IN TURMOIL

Introduction

Among the papers in this part one finds ever more explicit statements of energy imperatives confronting the Organization for Economic Co-operation and Development (OECD) states and less-developed countries (LDCs) as a consequence of past profligate consumption, price actions of OPEC states, and the consequent staggering oil-import payment problems. There is, moreover, no compelling evidence of an effective co-ordination of policies and programs by key consuming states that Mr. Levy believed was a prerequisite for coping with the stresses engendered by the practices of OPEC states. Beginning with the seventies, the key oil importers were "helpless giants" in an unfamiliar and even frightening situation of inescapable oil import dependence. To the extent that any one of the importing countries moved to improve its lot, it did so through attempts to reach special deals with a producer, a practice which the author warns against repeatedly lest it further divide importers.

Throughout the years the special position of the United States has carried with it unique responsibilities — as leader of the free world coalition and as the single largest consumer and producer of energy. Mr. Levy has remarked that the ability of the United States to go without Arab oil (at severe cost) is not shared by Europe or Japan; Japan is warned of a special need on its part to do more regarding energy supply and to remain alert to the factor of oil in the alliance.

The concluding paper in this part, "The Years That the Locust Hath Eaten," may be among the author's most compelling, with its definition of issues so far unmet and others that surely must be dealt with — especially the anticipated realization by the oil producers as to how much had been received in revenue, how much spent, how resources had been drawn down, and how very difficult the years ahead would be. Would this realization lead to a concert of interests of the oil producers and consumers — in effect, to prolong the oil era for their separate reasons but in their mutual interest?

17

World Oil Cooperation or International Chaos

The essence of the argument presented in this paper rests on the observation that the international oil companies can no longer assure continuity of supply or price of oil in international trade. In this situation, uncertainty breeds tension; as governments find it necessary to involve themselves more deeply to try to obtain greater assurance of supply, larger economic, financial, and political questions increasingly affect supply. The remedy—to fashion means for effective coordination of energy policies—has not been pursued, and, without it, chaos is probable.

There remains, however, a lingering hope that oil prices will be manageable, that instability in the Middle East will not worsen, and that the oil companies, somehow, can meet at least one more crisis.

Emphasis is put on conservation, the development of alternative energy sources, and the creation of strategic petroleum stocks (and contingency plans for their use) against a deepening concern that the oil-importing nations may still prefer to find their own ways, individually, rather than collectively.

To do all that has yet to be done, time, more time, is needed. But if granted, little enough may be done without austerity and commitment. Meanwhile, producer nations are increasingly aware of the parlous state of their own development achievements and prospects and of the weaknesses of their societies in dealing with the impact of vast revenues. In 1970, the oil income of the Middle East was $4 billion; in 1972, it was $9 billion; and in 1974—the year of the following article—it was $60 billion.

I

Rarely, if ever, in postwar history has the world been confronted with problems as serious as those caused by recent changes in the supply and price conditions of the world oil trade. To put these changes into proper

Reprinted with permission from *Foreign Affairs*, July 1974, pp. 690–713.

perspective, they must be evaluated not only in economic and financial terms but also in the framework of their political and strategic implications.

I need not dwell here on the overwhelming importance of oil for the energy requirements of every country in the world; nor do I plan to elaborate on the fact that except for the United States, the Soviet Union and a small number of countries that are, or will become, self-sufficient—most of the nations of the world will, at least for the foreseeable future, depend almost entirely on imports from a handful of oil-exporting countries, with an overwhelming concentration of oil production and reserves in the Persian Gulf area of the Middle East. Among those countries in the Gulf, Saudi Arabia is predominant in terms of reserves, production, and most important, in the potential to provide significant expansion of supplies. Inevitably, producing decisions by Middle East governments, especially Saudi Arabia, will play a pivotal role in future world oil availability and pricing.

Over the last three years or so, oil-producing countries have in fact taken over complete control of the oil industry in their countries. They have coordinated their efforts through the Organization of Petroleum Exporting Countries (OPEC) which was established in 1960. Since 1970, producing governments have imposed in rapid succession changes in previous agreements that had been negotiated and renegotiated with their concession-holding companies, predominantly affiliates of the Anglo-American international oil companies. These changes were arrived at under the threat that if the oil companies would not acquiesce, the producing countries would legislate such changes unilaterally or expropriate the concessions. In October 1973 the last vestige of negotiations was abandoned and producing governments unilaterally set posted prices on their oil.

In the exercise of this power, Middle East producing countries have raised their government oil revenues from taxes and royalties from about 90 cents per barrel in 1970 to about $3.00 per barrel by October 1973 and then to $7.00 per barrel by January 1974. In addition, as a result of the participation agreements between the producing countries and the oil companies, the governments earn additional income from the sale of their newly acquired oil. Its amount, of course, depends on the percent of government ownership and the price they charge for their oil. Agreements had been concluded, as recently as late 1972, under which producing countries acquired a 25 percent participation in the oil-producing operations and were also committed to sell most of their participation oil to the oil companies at agreed-upon prices; now producing countries are demanding that these arrangements be changed in their favor. Only a few arrangements have yet been concluded, but most of the producing countries will probably insist on at least the equivalent of 60 percent participation and a price for the sale of their oil corresponding to about 93 percent of the posted price—both changes most likely to be imposed with retroactive effect as of January 1, 1974. On such a basis, the government income from the total oil-producing operations in key countries would average about $9.25 per barrel.[1]

Meanwhile, the oil income of the Middle East producing countries has increased from $4 billion in 1970 to $9 billion in 1972, and to a presently estimated $60 billion in 1974. The oil revenues of all OPEC countries are increasing from $15 billion in 1972 to nearly $100 billion in 1974. Allowing for all their own foreign exchange requirements, OPEC producing countries will still have available surplus revenues on the order of $60 billion this year alone. And there remains a clear and present danger that under conditions as they exist now, the supply of oil from individual producing countries or a group of them to individual importing countries or a group of them might—as in October 1973—at a time unknown, again be curtailed or completely cut off for a variety of economic, political, strategic, or other reasons.

The quick pace at which the producing countries have effected this radical shift in the balance of power is perhaps the most dangerous aspect of the current situation. Whatever the merits of their case (of which more later), the world faces frightening repercussions on account of the suddenness with which oil costs of importing countries and oil revenues of producing countries have been inflated. There just has been no time for mature consideration by the societies that have to deal with this new exercise of oil and financial power, be they recipients or dependents, producers or consumers.

The security of international oil supply operations is further affected by regional conflicts in the producing areas of the Middle East—in particular the still unresolved issues posed by the Israeli-Arab confrontation. There are other potentially dangerous and divisive possibilities, as reflected in Iran's policy of establishing herself as the major strategic power in the Persian Gulf and the Indian Ocean. This could, in due course, aggravate what is already a latent conflict between Iran and some

1. Incidentally, Saudi Arabia has implied that in its judgment the present high level of posted prices would have a disruptive effect on the international payments accounts and should, accordingly, be reduced somewhat. While it might be difficult to obtain the support of OPEC for a cutback of posted prices, Saudi Arabia could easily achieve a similar result by reducing the price at which it sells its own oil to a level equal to the tax-paid cost of the companies' equity crude plus a per-barrel profit comparable to what the producing governments have said the companies are entitled to earn. Such a price would be some $3.00 per barrel less than 93 percent of posted prices.

of the Arab countries—not only Iraq, where the hostilities are acute, but perhaps even Saudi Arabia. There are also disputes between Iraq and Kuwait, unresolved boundary issues between Saudi Arabia and Abu Dhabi, and internal conflicts such as the Kurdish problem in Iraq. Further problems are posed by inherently unstable governments in many of these areas and by uncertain and unpredictable rules for the succession to power.

Moreover, within the Persian Gulf area there are varying economic strategic relationships between some of the producing countries and Western powers on the one hand, and the Soviet Union and even Communist China on the other. Moscow is deeply involved in Middle East affairs and with the strategic and national policies of some countries, particularly Iraq and Syria. As the producing countries increasingly assert their oil and money power, they are also likely to become increasingly involved as hostage or pawn in any major power struggle.

How can the nations of the world handle this new situation? What is the role of the international oil companies? Above all, how can the producing and importing nations avoid a confrontation or simply a series of reciprocal actions that must tend more and more toward economic chaos and grave political danger? Is there a way to reconcile the various national interests and to achieve constructive overall cooperation?

II

The first key fact that must now be recognized is that the position of the international oil companies has changed completely over the past few years. Up to about 1969 the major concession-holding companies still could determine levels of production, investments, exports and prices. Moreover, they still possessed substantial bargaining leverage in their negotiations with producing countries, largely by virtue of the surplus producing capacity that obtained in the Middle East, and even in the United States, into the latter sixties.

All this has now gone. The producing countries have taken over from the companies the power to set production levels, to designate or embargo export destinations, to direct investments and to set prices. The oil-producing affiliates of the international oil companies have become completely subservient to the directives issued by the oil-producing countries. Nothing perhaps reflects the present state of affairs more dramatically than the fact that American- and Dutch-owned oil companies had no choice last fall but to become the instruments for carrying out the embargo on oil shipments to their own home countries.

Thus, the companies no longer possess any real leverage. About the only role that is, in effect, left to them in established producing areas is that of a contractor providing technical services, getting in return some privileged access to oil—at costs and prices determined by producing governments. The extent of even this "privilege" and the time over which it will be available are subject to unilateral cancellation at any moment, as were all preceding arrangements.

At the same time that they have been deprived of effective control over their producing operations, the role of the international oil companies in consuming countries has come under increasing fire, fueled also by the recent sudden increase in company profits. During the emergency, consuming governments largely abdicated any effective role; the companies thus had to make far-ranging decisions as to allocation of supplies, pricing, treatment of nonintegrated companies, and many other issues. It was the companies that kept sufficient supplies moving to all countries; now, after the event, some of their decisions are being challenged by consuming governments. It is extremely doubtful whether the companies still possess the necessary flexibility to cope with another similar crisis.

If the role of the major international oil companies in established producing areas is diminished, it is nonetheless important to understand what their remaining position is. The technical services they can provide are extensive, and vital to continuing development of the producing countries' resources as well as to efficient producing operations. Moreover, none of the producing countries is prepared to handle alone the disposition of the huge volumes of production they control: the downstream facilities of the majors provide assured outlets for the mainstream of their production, while remaining quantities of crude can be sold directly or used to support refining and petrochemical production in their own countries or in joint ventures abroad.

Because of their size, scope, technical competence and financial strength, coupled with their important positions in the production and development of oil, gas, coal, shale, tar sands, and atomic resources in areas politically secure, the international oil companies are bound to play a major—if not the major—role in expanding dependable additional sources of energy supplies. Even though their foreign crude-oil resource base is subject to progressive erosion, the major internationals will accordingly continue to provide for the importing countries over the years ahead the most flexible sources of energy supply.

However, the international oil companies are no longer able to assure the continuity or price of regular supplies to oil-importing countries. And while they can hope to maintain continued preferred access to substantial production in support of their affiliates' crude requirements, even that is uncertain and contingent on the producing countries' self-interest in extending such offtake rights.

Downstream investment in refining, marketing, and transport thus tends to become extremely risky, because the viability of such investment is predicated on secure supplies. Meanwhile, as a logical part of their own development program, producing countries are using their control over crude availability to spur refining and petrochemical investment in their own countries and to acquire tanker fleets—all of which will in due course add to consuming countries' foreign exchange import costs and adversely affect the flexibility and security of their supplies.

In the circumstances, oil-importing countries can no longer expect the companies to fulfill their earlier most important role, as an effective intermediary between the interests of producing and consuming countries. Nor can the international oil companies function, as in the past, effectively to preclude direct dealings between importing and producing countries relating to oil supplies, prices, etc., which may easily lead to political confrontations. To the extent that the companies maintain their operations in producing countries, they in fact reflect the producing governments' economic, political, and strategic policies. To be able to hold on to whatever tenuous residual rights or preferences the producing countries might still be willing to extend, the companies will have no choice but to acquiesce in virtually any kind of conditions imposed or exacted.

All this points to a far greater involvement by consuming-country governments in oil industry operations than heretofore. One major objective will be greater "transparency" in oil company policies. Oil-importing countries cannot be in the dark with respect to negotiations in producing areas, when the decisions vitally affect the security and price of their essential oil supplies. They will want to know more about investment plans and policies in their own countries. And with transparency will inevitably come progressively more government interposition throughout internal oil economies.

But here, too, the international oil companies will have a continuing role to play. Producing countries will become increasingly involved downstream, as direct crude sellers and through investment. Consuming countries will become increasingly involved upstream, through various exploration and crude arrangements. Within this emerging fragmentation of world oil trade, the integrated facilities of the companies could provide an important, perhaps the major, core of efficient operations.

In sum, whatever arrangements on supply, financing, and pricing the oil companies may still be able to conclude formally with producing countries, in practice and underlying reality such arrangements cannot be ignored by the importing countries but are bound to be decisively affected by their policies. Moreover, with the vital concern the importing countries have not only for price but for availability of oil, it now appears inevitable that their governments will also in due course establish a comprehensive policy of surveillance and consultation — perhaps even some measure of control — with regard to oil company operations encompassing the whole range of oil activities vitally affecting their countries.

III

As the problems of oil have become matters that in many key respects can only be handled directly between governments, so their gravity has now become all too clear. Faced with the major "supply shock" of the October 1973 oil embargo and the overall cutback in Arab oil production, the immediate reaction of practically every importing country was to engage in a competitive scramble for oil supplies, coupled with offers to adapt its Middle East policy to Arab demands, and promises of all kinds of financial inducements. It was indeed a humiliating experience for historically independent and proud nations. What we were witnessing, in fact, was not only the fragmentation of the operations of the multinational oil companies, but also the polarization of the oil policies of the importing countries, with foreign petroleum ministers skillfully influencing individual importing countries through the device of handing out oil rewards and punishments.

Then, late in 1973, the advance in world oil prices dictated by OPEC countries was of such magnitude that practically every importing nation was suddenly confronted with major balance-of-trade problems of immediate and continuing effect. The cost of foreign oil supplies for all importing countries will exceed $100 billion in 1974, compared with some $20 billion in 1972. For developing countries alone, it will jump from $5 billion in 1973 to $15 billion in 1974 — and the $10-billion increase will exceed all the foreign aid that these countries received in the previous year. Meanwhile, as noted, the OPEC producing countries will accumulate, during 1974 alone, surplus holdings of foreign exchange not needed for their own import requirements of some $60 billion — or nearly two-thirds of the net book value of total U.S. private foreign investment.

Obviously, this surplus accumulation of funds will somehow be recycled into the world's monetary system initially, probably mainly into the short-term Eurodollar market. But this process will not necessarily result in the availability of loans to the various importing countries in accordance with their individual foreign exchange needs. The creditworthiness of the borrower will decide whether or not Eurodollar loans will be available; many of the developing countries and some developed countries will not qualify under this criterion. Foreign grants and soft loans — some of them probably never to be repaid — will have to be made available, and the Monetary Fund and the World Bank are addressing themselves to this problem. I doubt that anything like adequate amounts can be made available.

But the financial oil drainage is *not* only a short-term and passing issue. It will be with us for many, many years—if oil prices remain at present levels (or rise as is now occasionally threatened), and if the oil-producing countries themselves are not prepared to make favorable loan arrangements to needy countries in addition to whatever the developed countries are able and willing to do. To the extent that oil imports are financed by a continued recycling of surplus oil revenues via investments or loans on commercial terms, oil-importing countries will face pyramiding interest or individual charges on top of mounting direct oil import costs.

Equally if not more disturbing is the question whether or not the producing countries owning already large surplus funds will be willing to continue to maintain or to expand their production and accumulate financial holdings that might result, in part at least, in nothing but paper claims that could not be repaid. If the producing countries make direct foreign investments, the bulk of such investments will obviously be placed in the advanced developed countries, where it would appear to be safest and most profitable. That will leave the less-preferred developed countries and the developing countries out in the cold. Moreover, the scope for such investments owned directly by foreign producing governments is likely to be limited. Accordingly, oil-exporting countries with surplus revenues might well decide to reduce production—to conserve their liquid gold in the ground rather than increase potential paper claims above ground. Oil revenue surpluses could thus well conduce to oil supply shortage.

There are thus valid reasons to fear that even where present policies of producing countries provide for expanding oil production, circumstances might arise where, in what they consider to be their own self-interest or even for any political whim, the governments involved abruptly cut their level of oil exports. Kuwait, Libya, Abu Dhabi, Ecuador, and Venezuela have already announced restrictions in their production. Iran has threatened to do so if the importers object to price levels.

The financial dilemma for oil-importing countries is clear. In order to finance oil import costs, they will have to look to progressively expanded foreign investment by, or indebtedness to, producing countries. Without any amelioration in the cartel prices and payments terms, the alternative for importing countries would be rather severe reductions in oil imports and oil consumption. To cut back imports drastically, to levels that could be financed out of current income, would hardly be a viable solution. The resulting shortfall in total energy, and the economic consequences of declines in production, employment and trade, would further undercut the oil-importing countries' ability to finance even sharply reduced levels of oil supplies. The contraction of energy consumption and economic activity would thus become a cumulative spiral.

In sum, the short- to medium-term implications of the present situation are simply not bearable, either for the oil-importing countries — especially the nations already needy — or for the world economy as a whole. In the wake of this topsy-turvy winter, with the Arab oil embargo against the United States now lifted, the temptation is momentarily strong to suppose that the oil crisis has now genuinely eased. The major industrialized countries of the world once again look forward to economic growth, though at lower rates, with worldwide balance-of-payments deficits, and with a terrible economic and political problem of inflation, to which oil prices have made a substantial contribution. But the oil balance-of-payments burden is just starting and the transfer of funds to oil-producing countries just beginning. In any case, no significant *lasting* relief at all is in sight for the needy oil-importing countries. The fact is that the world economy — for the sake of everyone — cannot survive in a healthy or remotely healthy condition if cartel pricing and actual or threatened supply restraints of oil continue on the trends marked out by the new situation.

IV

As a first step, the insecurity of oil supply and the financial problems that have arisen clearly call for a wide-ranging coordinated program among all importing countries. This was the main reason why the American government called for a conference of the major oil-importing countries in February of this year. This cooperative effort falls into two basic parts: first, what must be done internally by the importing countries; and second, what a coordinated policy should be vis-à-vis producing countries. With the oil-producing countries already cooperating closely through OPEC, cooperation among the oil-importing countries is a simple necessity; properly understood and handled, it can be the only way to achieve constructive overall adjustments.

Among themselves, the importing countries must first establish and coordinate their research and development programs with regard to existing and new energy resources. Unnecessary and time-consuming duplication must be avoided, and research and development efforts should be concentrated on those resources where optimum results can be expected. The skills available for research and the engineering resources that would have to be employed, if not pooled, should at least be utilized in accordance with a program for maximum overall efficiency.

The oil-importing countries must also establish a concurrent and consistent program of energy conservation which would provide for far greater efficiency in the use of energy resources. Here too the research effort and the measures to be taken should be coordinated on an international basis.

Whatever the course of foreign oil prices, policies to conserve consumption and to spur the development of alternative energy sources will remain relevant for the future. Moreover, a high degree of government involvement is essential to the success of such efforts—including the probable necessity of government guarantees putting a floor under the selling price of alternative energy sources. For if—as we shall see later—there is a chance that foreign oil prices will fall, then private interests working on projects for tar sands, shale, gasification of coal and the like, will not be willing or able to continue their efforts. If a major effort to develop alternative energy resources is to be sustained, particularly in North America, the criterion cannot be orthodox economic soundness weighing the price of alternative energy against the actual (or predicted) price of foreign oil. Rather, the decisive criterion must be the price to which foreign oil could and would *rise* if the alternative energy supplies were not forthcoming. The public interest in avoiding dependence on foreign oil dictates public support and a substantial measure of price guarantees by individual countries, notably the United States but perhaps others as well, again acting in coordination.

Thirdly, the major importing countries must be able to agree on a problem that has so far eluded their efforts—that of adequate stockpiling and burden-sharing. On stockpiling, no importing nation should now have on hand perhaps less than a supply equal to six months of its imports. And there must be clear contingency plans for restrained consumption and for sharing, if oil supplies are again cut off or curtailed—whether for political or economic reasons. Remaining oil imports must be parceled out according to some formula based not on the previous percentage of imports from the sources cut off, but on the basis largely of need—so that those fortunate enough to possess substantial national energy resources would have the smallest, if any, claim on the oil still flowing. Beyond that, I do not believe it would be politically feasible to establish rules that would require countries able domestically just to cover their minimum requirements to export some of their domestic energy supplies to a less fortunate country.

Moreover, oil-importing countries must abstain from trying to resolve their balance-of-trade problems by unduly pushing their general exports to other oil-importing countries or by restricting their imports from them. Such policies would only aggravate the problems of these other countries. Competitive devaluation of currencies or inflation of export prices would be self-defeating, since the oil-producing countries clearly intend to adjust the level of oil prices in accordance with an index of currency values as well as the cost of manufactured goods and other commodities in world trade. The oil-importing countries may have to act in many other ways in order to avoid such dangerous repercussions as severe deflation and unemployment. To deal with the situation will require an unprecedented degree of self-restraint, prudent economic management and political sophistication and wisdom. Past experience suggests extreme skepticism that the countries will in fact consistently follow such policies. But if they do not, the consequences for all of them could become very serious indeed.

Bilateral transactions between oil-importing and producing countries or their respective companies will inevitably be of growing importance. But in concluding such deals the importing countries must abstain from trying to obtain unilateral advantages — by making arrangements for oil imports that would tend to preempt sources of supply through discriminatory practices, or by transactions designed to tie up for themselves an excessive part of the import capacity of the oil-producing country. They must also resist the temptation to offset their oil deficits by the competitive rearming of the various Middle East countries, a practice bound in the end to produce a military disaster for all.

So much for the minimum initial requirements for cooperation among the major oil-importing countries. A measure of common appreciation does now exist for most of these "headings of cooperation" by at least a large majority of the relevant importing countries, although they have yet to be fleshed out by practical working arrangements or adequate guidelines for national behavior.

The hardest questions remain. Even if cooperation is achieved in all these respects, can it serve to do more than shorten the period of extreme vulnerability and cushion the impact of continued one-sided decisions by the OPEC countries? Is consumer cooperation truly adequate if it does not address itself to the key questions of price and supply?

I believe the answer to both questions is in the negative. When the brewing crisis came to a head last fall, the initial reaction of many importing countries was to try unilaterally to take care of themselves for both economic and strategic reasons — through barter arrangements, major investment offers to various producing countries, even in some cases extravagant arms supply deals. This tendency was an understandable reaction in the first phase of the new crisis, and indeed a continuing degree of individual national initiatives is not only inevitable, but can be healthy in some respects, in providing an infusion of economic and political alternatives into the changing relationships between oil-importing and oil-producing countries.

Already, however, the limits of the individual approach are obvious.

Even for the most aggressive of the oil-importing nations, it has not worked effectively; they find themselves with very large obligations in return for very small increments of favorable treatment, or for nothing more concrete than a generalized promise for the future. Moreover, where there have been specific deals, these are as much subject to abrogation or revision as the basic arrangements themselves. "What have you done for me lately?" is not a question confined to the dialogue between politicians and voters.

Moreover, precipitate attempts by individual countries to go it alone can only obscure the nature of the problem, which is basically a common one that engages not only the interests of all the importing countries but the interests of the producers in a viable world economy and in their own regional and national political stability. The producers are bound not to see the problem in this light if one importing country after another posits this arrangement or that as its own selfish modus vivendi. And to defer attempts at resolution of the common payments problem while individual initiatives are being exhausted is bound to make eventual general agreement more difficult, because so many inconsistent cards will have been played.

Thus, it is my conviction that a constructive accommodation between the interests of producers and importers, enabling the latter to pay for and finance adequate oil imports, is possible only if the importing countries share a common appreciation of the need for a price adjustment as well as for the establishment of financial mechanisms to this end. Just as far-reaching cooperation among the producing countries has brought about the present situation, so a similar cooperation among the importing countries is now an essential prerequisite to a balanced solution. Only if the major importing nations act to coordinate their policy can they expect to be able to present the supply and financial problems they are facing in an effective manner — and to make clear the implications of these problems for the producers themselves. Moreover, only then could they impress upon at least the relevant producing countries what I believe are the two central elements in a satisfactory long-term arrangement — some downward adjustment in the level of foreign crude oil prices to all consumers, and specific relief, including long-term deferment of payments, for the neediest of the oil-importing countries.

V

If cooperation among oil-importing countries is essential to the development of constructive cooperation with producing countries, so too is a full and fair understanding by the importers of the case of the producing countries. Many of its key points were presented vividly in last

July's issue of *Foreign Affairs* by Jahangir Amuzegar of Iran; these points and others have since been developed in a series of public statements by various leaders of producing countries. Nonetheless it helps to go over the main elements that enter into the attitudes of the producers, and to explore the validity of their arguments, seeking to arrive at a clear picture of what their long-term interests are.

A major goal of producing countries is rapid and consistent progress in their economic development so that they can become economically viable and secure by the time their oil reserves peter out. In the meantime, the pace of their industrial progress depends largely on the size of their oil revenues, and the level of oil prices is of decisive importance for their present and future prosperity.

The producing countries also cite additional reasons to justify the huge price increases that they imposed in the course of 1973. The large increase in oil prices, they say, is warranted by the alternative cost that would have to be incurred if oil had to be replaced by other energy sources such as shale oil, oil from tar sands, etc. Even though there is currently still a surplus of potential oil supplies, oil reserves may well be exhausted in perhaps 20 to 30 years. But in a free competitive market, prices would not, *at this time,* reflect *future* shortages of supply and would thus provide no encouragement for the development of substitutes. Accordingly, the oil-producing countries say that high oil prices are now necessary so that research and development programs for new energy sources will be promptly initiated. Otherwise, with the long lead time required, energy would be in short supply when world oil production begins to decline.

Also, so they argue, high oil prices now will result in oil conservation and encourage the use of oil for the most essential and valuable purposes where it cannot be so easily replaced, such as for petrochemical production. The highest-value use, they maintain, should in practice be the basis for oil pricing.

The producing countries also assert that the high current oil prices redress the injustice of too low a level of prices in the past, when oil prices had fallen behind those of manufactured goods and food which the oil-producing countries had to import. Relatively low oil prices in the past have, they maintain, unduly enriched the developed countries at their expense. (Whatever the degree of validity of this argument for past periods, it should be noted that the increase in oil prices between 1970 and January 1974 has, according to a United Nations analysis, amounted to 480 percent and was extraordinarily larger than that of practically any other commodity. The share of petroleum in world imports of about $316 billion during 1970—the last year for which detailed statistics are available—amounted to about 7.7 percent; at January 1974 commodity prices, the value of 1970 imports would have increased to $618 billion, of which petroleum would have accounted for as much as 23 percent.)

Oil-producing countries are aware that high oil prices may harm the progress of other developing countries. But primary responsibility for economic assistance, so they postulate, rests on the rich developed countries. And even though oil-producing countries maintain that in development terms they are still poor, they have stated that they, too, will make a substantial contribution to support developing countries, and a number of them have indeed done so. In addition, they will endeavor to convince other raw-material–producing developing countries that they, too, could improve their economic position substantially if they would only follow the OPEC example.

The producing countries also complain that in the past they have been deprived of economic development based on their oil resources, such as refineries, petrochemical plants, tankers, and energy-intensive industries. Instead, enormous quantities of gas have been flared. Accordingly, it is a basic part of their development policy that investment in local petroleum-processing plants should be undertaken on a large scale within the oil-producing countries, and that they should participate far more in the whole operation of the transportation and exporting of oil.

Obviously, there is substantial merit in many of the points now so forcefully advanced by the oil-producing countries — and it is no effective answer to point out that Western initiative was largely responsible both for the discovery of oil and for the development of its manifold uses. The major oil-importing nations, in particular, must give heed to the legitimate grievances and aspirations of the oil producers.

On the other hand, the producing countries cannot continue to take the position that the economic situation of the major importing countries is no concern of theirs. It is one thing to adjust oil prices to the real or imagined wrongs of the past, another to carry that adjustment to the point of jeopardizing the future economic, political, and strategic viability of importing countries. For if this happens, the viability of the producing countries themselves must surely be affected over the years to come.

There is thus no alternative for the importing countries but to try to convince the producing countries that there must be responsible accommodation between the interests of importing and producing countries. In order to carry conviction, it is essential that there be basic unity among importing countries about the underlying assessments and their policy goals. In the light of the extremely sensitive relationship between consuming and producing countries, a contrary position of one or two major importing countries would tend to destroy the effectiveness of this approach. It would also further strengthen the producing countries in the sense of power that they believe they hold over importing countries, and would encourage them to conclude that they could effectively maintain their internal as well as external security in the face of evolving world chaos.

In actual fact, however, many producing countries, in spite of the extraordinary concentration of oil and money resources in their hands, are as yet quite fragile entities, without substantial strategic and military strength in world affairs. They have been able to assert themselves because of the disunity among, and unwillingness of, importing countries to take any firm position vis-à-vis the producing nations. Whatever the concern of producing countries and companies in the pivotal transition from surplus producing capacity to tightness of world oil supplies, the oil-importing countries were largely complaisant about the course of events. Now, unrestrained exercise of their oil and money power by producing countries presupposes that the importing countries will continue to acquiesce and remain passive, even if the world's economic and political stability is at stake. This cannot be a safe basis upon which the producing countries could proceed. If the worst is to be avoided, the producing countries must be made to recognize the danger of pursuing such a course.

There is also the danger that this concentration of oil and money resources would tempt the Soviet Union to make use of fundamentally weak and socially unstable producing countries — by proxy, so to speak — in order to undermine the economic and political stability of the non-Communist world. Soviet adventurism cannot be ignored, especially the application of Soviet power through controls over certain governments such as those of Iraq or Syria, as well as by internal threats through Soviet support of subversive opposition to governments. There exists, in practically every one of these countries, the potential for sudden revolutions by extreme elements.

All of these factors are clearly known to the various dynasties and national governments. Most of them must have inevitably reached the conclusion that their hold on power, which is sometimes tenuous, depends in the final analysis on a satisfactory relationship with the non-Communist world. We are all interested in the maintenance of a peaceful cohesion among Middle East countries. But they must recognize that if this cohesion is mainly used to enable them to enforce their will on the rest of the world through the use of oil and money power, they would not only undermine the position and strength of the importing countries but would also expose their governments and nations to extreme risks.

The oil-exporting countries must be aware that their own independence could not safely be assured if the United States and its allies were to be fatally weakened vis-à-vis the Soviet Union. It would not be in their self-interest to refuse to supply the vital oil needs of the world or to insist on an unmanageable level of prices, and risk the economic, political, and strategic consequences of such policies.

VI

So far I have been making the case for unprecedented cooperation among the oil-importing nations, and for much greater understanding by both producing and importing countries of each other's needs and of the common interests that affect both groups. If reason alone controlled human affairs, one might conclude that a satisfactory solution was possible from greater understanding alone.

Unfortunately, that is not the case. One must in the end come back to the harsh economics of the energy situation worldwide, and of the rapidly rising trends in oil consumption that have lain at the root of the present crisis. For it is these trends essentially — far outstripping the growth of indigenous energy sources — that have made the oil of the OPEC countries, especially in the Middle East, so vital to practically every nation of the world, and have thus given the OPEC countries the bargaining leverage to establish the present unilaterally controlled price and supply situation. With all the understanding and sympathy in the world, the producing countries cannot be expected not to use a bargaining position as strong as the present one of OPEC and its Middle East members. In last July's *Foreign Affairs,* Carroll Wilson argued that the United States would be placed in an intolerable state of dependence on Middle East oil if it did not develop other sources of energy to the maximum and at the same time curtail the rate of growth of its energy consumption from 4.5 percent to a suggested three percent. Essentially the same analysis must now be applied to the oil-importing nations as a whole, not for the sake of eliminating a critical degree of dependence on the Middle East — for that is simply not in the cards at least for the rest of this decade — but for the sake of containing thereafter the problems of oil supply and finance and of establishing now an acceptable degree of balance in the bargaining positions of producers and consumers of oil.

The starting point should be the period from 1968 through 1972, when energy consumption in the non-Communist world as a whole increased at 5.6 percent per year, and oil consumption by 7.5 percent per year. The result was that Middle East oil production went up by an average of 12.5 percent per year.

Now the prospect for the period from now until 1980 is for a substantial expansion in non-oil energy sources and in oil production within the major oil-consuming countries. Yet it remains as clear as it was a year ago that no drastic technological breakthrough is in sight at least in this time frame. We are still talking about natural gas, coal, hydroelectric power and nuclear fission as the primary alternatives to oil—and one need hardly add that even substantial increases in some of these are still fraught with difficulty.

In response to the new situation, it is already reasonable to postulate some conservation at the margin in response to higher energy costs. Given the dynamic energy needs of Japan, the developing countries, and to a lesser extent Western Europe, however, it is difficult to see that "conservation at the margin" will in itself produce a dramatic drop in the growth of energy needs. Supposing, for example, energy consumption grew at only 4.6 percent per year instead of the 5.6 percent of the 1968-72 period, the picture might look something like [Table I].

Obviously, this is a broad-brush projection. But it is enough, I believe, to demonstrate two fundamental conclusions: (1) that even *at current prices* this rate of oil imports could not be sustained by the oil-importing countries on a current payments basis; (2) that with production increases fairly well spread among the producing countries, none would be under any pressure to lower prices or to increase production further. (This is a modest conclusion; actually the pressure would be greater for production cutbacks than for increases. The oil simply might not be forthcoming.) In short, mere "conservation at the margin"—itself more than many governments are now asking of their people—will neither avoid economic calamity nor provide a balanced situation vis-à-vis the producers.

To get these essential results I believe we shall have to go considerably further. Again for illustrative purposes, let us see what the situation would be if the oil-importing countries could manage genuine austerity in their use of energy, cutting their growth rate to, say, 3.3 percent. (The reduced U.S. growth rate would have to be less than this; with all U.S. energy waste, it would still involve a major change in habits and ways. For Japan and the developing countries, the impact on production growth would be far more severe. In short, this kind of reduced rate of increase does deserve to be called austerity.) In such a case, using the same assumptions for non-oil sources and indigenous oil production, a revised table would look like [Table II].

This level of austerity would, I believe, be just adequate to permit the major industrialized nations to maintain viable economic and industrial operations, including continued growth but at a lower rate than might have been projected on the basis of previous oil prices and supply availability. Even then, most of the oil-importing countries would, at least until the latter part of this decade, be exposed to a very substantial and—in the case of some countries—nearly unmanageable financial burden. In short, while the deliberate initiation of such austerity would require an act of political will far exceeding what is actually happening in

TABLE I

ESTIMATED ENERGY CONSUMPTION WITH 4.6 PERCENT GROWTH

| | 1972 | 1975 | 1980 | 1972-1980 |
	(Millions of Barrels Daily Oil Equivalent)			(Average Annual Percentage Growth)
Primary Energy Demand	80	91	115	4.6
From Nonoil Sources	35	38	48	4.0
Oil Consumption	45	53	67	5.1
Indigenous Oil Production	18	19	27	5.2
Oil Imports	27	34	40	5.0
Needed from the Middle East	18	23	29	6.3

TABLE II

ESTIMATED ENERGY CONSUMPTION WITH 3.3 PERCENT GROWTH

	1972	1975	1980	1972-1980
	(Millions of Barrels Daily Oil Equivalent)			(Average Annual Percentage Growth)
Primary Energy Demand	80	87	104	3.3
Oil Consumption	45	49	56	2.7
Oil Imports	27	30	29	0.8
Needed from the Middle East	18	19	18	0.1

most importing countries, the choice will in the end be compelled by financial pressures. The longer it is put off the worse it will get.

Once undertaken, this austerity policy could in time achieve some trade balance between the producing and consuming countries. In particular, the huge annual accumulation of surplus funds by Middle East producing countries would start to decline about 1978 and would reach manageable proportions shortly thereafter. Put differently, the importing countries would in aggregate terms be able to pay for their oil by a steadily increased flow of goods and services to the producers. At the same time, however, since the ability of the importing countries to supply goods and services is concentrated in only a handful of them, the financial burden of oil imports would vary greatly, remaining very substantial for the less-industrialized developed countries and especially for the developing countries which are net consumers of oil. Thus, it would remain essential to have financial mechanisms and arrangements that would cushion this differential impact and make it bearable.

Turn now to the situation of the oil exporters. The second table suggests that their total exports would level off and then start to decline slightly by the end of the decade, as the importing countries managed to increase their non-oil sources of energy and as indigenous oil sources were tapped more fully (principally the North Sea and the North Slope in Alaska). The table also assumes that oil producers outside the Middle East will increase their total capacity somewhat, and will be motivated to produce at maximum attainable levels — since practically all of these nations need their oil revenues for immediate development purposes. Thus, the total demand on the Middle East would tend to decline by the end of the decade.

This is not to suggest for a moment that the Middle East oil producers would then be in difficulty. They would still be supplying more than 60 percent of the oil moving in world trade, and Middle East oil would remain vital to Japan, Western Europe, and the developing nations — in an austerity situation, any further cuts would reach the bone more rapidly than in the present somewhat "soft" situation. In short, the Middle East producing countries as a group would remain in a strong position.

At the same time, the production levels of individual countries in the Middle East would be placed seriously in question. Kuwait (like Libya in North Africa) is already pursuing policies designed to conserve its oil reserves and thus to stabilize output below previously attained levels of production. On the other hand, Iran and Iraq look to increase their production very substantially from present totals of roughly 8 million barrels a day to 12–13 million barrels per day. If these trends were to continue and if the need for Middle East oil were to level off at 18 million or so barrels per day, it is evident that the remaining suppliers — especially Saudi Arabia and Abu Dhabi which had previously benefited from oil revenues far in excess of their development needs—would then have to accept a drastic reduction in their levels of production, or alternatively to seek to increase their output by reducing their prices (and thus giving consumers an incentive to ease up on their austerity).

It is an open question, which of course cannot be analytically resolved, whether in the light of these circumstances the various Middle East producing countries would decide to "fight it out" among themselves by competing for exports through price reductions. They might seek to go in the opposite direction, to enter into a production and export control agreement under which they would rearrange their respective production and export levels. At the same time, they might try to increase their prices and tax takes so as to provide for the needs of those Middle East countries that would have to reduce some of their previously anticipated production. On a rational basis, the latter course might be chosen, since any price and tax reductions would tend to force others downward as well, so that the Middle East as a whole would obtain lower revenues for the same or a higher level of production than before the initial price and tax reductions.

In trying to assess what under such conditions the producing countries might actually decide to do, we must think not only or even mainly in economic terms, nor draw only on past experience with regard to the cohesiveness of private cartels in similar circumstances. At most, the economic facts of supply and demand frame the problem; it will still be decided by national governments in the producing countries, and their policies are likely to be governed by an extraordinary combination of political and strategic as well as economic factors.

On the basis of such a broad assessment, the short-term argument for controlling production and maintaining or further raising prices and tax takes must encounter a growing awareness of wider relevant considerations. For such a course—in effect responding to consumer austerity by higher producer prices—would surely leave the importing countries with even worse financial problems than are now in prospect. Even more heavily than now, the burden of paying for restrained but more expensive oil imports would fall upon lagging economies suffering from extremely serious financial problems. Even more than now, the producing countries would have to ask themselves whether they could expect to remain islands of prosperity in a worldwide depression, or of political stability when the will and ability of strategically powerful nations to support them had been eroded.

VII

To sum up, four elements are essential to move to a reasonable adjustment: far-reaching cooperation among the oil-importing nations, an understanding by the importing nations of the interests and aspirations of the producing countries, a clear-cut (and painful) program of energy austerity by the oil-importing countries, and a recognition by the producing countries that even in an austerity situation any attempt to hold prices high must result in worldwide dangers to which they could not be immune. Only with far-reaching consumer cooperation can it be expected that the producing countries will come to this necessary conclusion; at the same time cooperation without austerity will not do the job. Both are needed, and a large new dose of political will, not yet in sight, will be required to achieve them.

The key to a reasonable solution is time: to make the financial burdens on all oil-importing countries tolerable and to bridge the gap until the day not too far distant, when the producing countries, at least in the aggregate, will have reached the point where they can be paid in goods and services — and where they will have joined, for practical purposes, the ranks of the developed nations.

And the basis for such an adjustment, in turn, is the acceptance of a principle that, while the sovereignty and control of nations over their natural resources remains unquestioned, such control cannot and must not lead to the unrestrained exercise of power, but must be based on a mutual accommodation of interests or, as the United Nations Declaration on the Establishment of a New International Economic Order puts it, on an appreciation of "the reality of interdependence of all the members of the world community." Otherwise it will be destructive to all.

Such a principle is not, of course, confined to the case of oil. The April meeting of the United Nations General Assembly, and the United Nations reports prepared for it, have underlined the degree to which the rise in food and fertilizer prices over the past two years — created in these cases by market forces in combination with national domestic agricultural policies — have damaged the interests of the needy developing countries in particular. The United States especially has it in its power to adopt measures that would ease the actual cost of food supplies to this group of countries; one suggestion would be that the United States provide grain and other crucial food to needy countries on concessionary terms or through the application of PL 480 funds. A similar move might be undertaken by the major countries that export fertilizer. Now, as preparations are underway for a World Food Conference in the fall, such moves would be even more in order, based on the continued operation of market forces for most consumers but with measures to cushion the impact on needy countries.

Oil remains the biggest and most difficult case. Since 1970 the price and availability of oil moving in world trade have been determined progressively by the OPEC countries unilaterally, to the point where the present situation effectively is one of price imposed by a cartel. Completely free market prices for traded oil are not a practical alternative; in a free market the existence of large reserves and the very low cost of developing and producing such oil would mean a market price that would be very low indeed. Such a price would not be acceptable to producing countries — since it would not provide them with the budgetary and foreign exchange revenue badly needed for their economic development. Nor would it in fact serve the interests of importing countries as a whole — since it would lead to wasteful consumption of oil on the one hand, and on the other would provide no inducement to the major countries to push forward in good time with research and development on new and more costly energy resources which will be needed even more once readily available supplies of oil begin to stagnate or decline.

Accordingly, the price of oil moving in world trade is bound to be a kind of administered price, not necessarily negotiated directly between producing and importing countries but at least established in a way that would attempt to accommodate and reconcile the economic and financial interests of both groups. In addition, the specific plight of the needy oil-importing countries should be provided for, if not through a two-tier pricing system, then at least by long-term deferral of payments and easy credit terms for loans.

In sum, I believe that the world situation would now call for solemn undertakings that would assure the essential oil requirements of all the importing countries on terms and conditions that are economically and financially sustainable. This should be accompanied by measures to deal along the lines proposed with the cognate cases of food and fertilizer. At the same time, it is imperative that all the necessary provisions be made to safeguard the essential economic interests of the producing countries into a future when their position will inevitably become less strong than it is at present. Such a combination of actions would be an act of statesmanship in which the oil-producing countries and the oil-importing countries could and should join not only for the common good, but perhaps even more so in their most cogent self-interest.

Today, governments are watching an erosion of the world's oil supply and financial systems, comparable in its potential for economic and political disaster to the Great Depression of the 1930s, as if they were hypnotized into inaction. The time is late, the need for action overwhelming.

18

A Conference Between Oil-Producing and Consuming Countries

For one who was involved in the U.S. preparation for the Conference on International Economic Cooperation (CIEC) and who attended its early sessions, a reading of the following paper by Mr. Levy is startling. Each of the recommendations he made—as to size of the conference and the topics to be discussed—was largely disregarded, but, long before CIEC ended in 1977, the lessons from that experience were those laid out in advance by Mr. Levy.

The paper is still germane and could again be used to stimulate a common look by producers and importers at a general problem—the obtaining of oil in ways that meet their particular and common interests.

I. Introduction

The prerequisite for an effective dialogue and an accommodation of interests between oil-producing and oil-consuming countries is the coordination of oil policies among the consuming countries.

The world's oil-supply and oil-financing problems are not only posing major economic issues, but are also affected as much—if not even more so—by political and strategic considerations. Only if the major consuming countries act together, is there a chance that they might be able to influence the oil policies of the oil-producing countries. Based on the realization that the economic and political welfare of the OPEC countries depends on a continued, effective, and friendly relationship with the major importing countries, the effectiveness of the major importing countries, vis-à-vis OPEC, would be badly hurt if, in their negotiations, they were unable to bring to bear their combined political will and economic strength.

Notes written on January 9, 1975, for a projected agenda and consultation in advance of the Paris meeting of the Conference on International Economic Cooperation (CIEC).

II. Who Should Participate in the Conference

A. Consumer countries participation

1. Only a few major importing countries—how many and which ones?
   a. Any role for OECD?
   b. Any role for the Common Market?

2. Participation by oil-importing developing countries—how many and which ones?
   a. Any role for UNCTAD [United Nations Conference on Trade and Development] or other organizations of developing countries?

B. Producing countries participation

1. Only a few major producing countries—how many and which ones?

2. Any role for OPEC?

C. Recommendations

1. Preferred position: conference limited to some ten to twelve major importing and producing countries—say, the United States, United Kingdom, France, Germany, Japan, Saudi Arabia, Iran, Kuwait, Venezuela, and Indonesia

2. Fall-back position:
   a. In addition, three oil-importing developing countries as participants—say, India, one from Africa, and one from Latin America
   b. Observer status for OECD and/or Common Market, OPEC, UNCTAD

D. Justification

1. The chance for a successful accommodation of interests of the producing and consuming countries would be greatly enhanced if the conference could be limited to a few key countries on each side.

2. The pressure of some consuming and producing countries to include also oil-importing developing countries may, however, become overwhelming, and one country each from Latin America, Asia, and Africa might have to be added; but these developing countries will probably be induced by the expectation or promises of special oil deals with OPEC countries to support the latter position in all major issues.

3. To reduce pressures for further enlargement of the conference and perhaps also to assure more effective communication among all the interested countries, consideration may be given whether OECD, OPEC, and perhaps UNCTAD should be invited as observers.

III. Consuming Countries Cooperation on a Program of Limitation of Oil Imports

A. Introduction

In the dialogue with the producing countries, the consuming countries must be able to present to the producing countries an analysis of their future oil-import requirements—for, say, the next five to ten years.

Such an analysis depends of course to a considerable extent on future price developments; but for this purpose it would probably be advisable to assume that present prices, in constant 1974 dollars, will prevail over the next five to ten years. To show higher levels of imports at lower prices would, in any case, leave the probably misleading impression that importing countries would forego much of their conservation efforts and their domestic energy development program whenever the producers should decide to cut their prices.

The same set of figures should also provide the basis for the analysis of the financial effects of present oil prices on the world's economy.

For economic and strategic reasons, it is essential that the major importing countries reduce their oil imports to the lowest levels consonant with unimpeded economic and industrial progress through conservation and urgent development of energy resources. All major importing countries must share in such a program in a coordinated and equitable manner as a prerequisite for an effective cooperative effort among them to share supplies during an emergency and to assist each other in providing for the internal and external financial costs.

It should be noted, however, that in all foreseeable circumstances, the oil-importing countries—as a group—will remain dependent for at least the next ten years or so on very substantial levels of oil imports from OPEC countries—especially those of the Persian Gulf.

Also, while the United States can contain and even reduce—if not eliminate—its dependency on oil imports within the next ten years or so, most of the other major oil-importing countries will not be able, within that time framework, to develop their energy resource base to achieve an effective independence from imports.

Over the longer term, new oil and gas discoveries, atomic energy, and successful research in new sources of energy supply, such as solar energy, should reduce the oil-import requirements of many of the other countries; in any case, because of the finite size of oil and gas reserves, such new resources must be found and developed during the next fifteen to twenty years if the world's energy requirements are to be met.

B. A coordinated program of oil supply and conservation

1. The role of IEA and French cooperation
    a. During supply emergencies
    b. In the overall program of IEA

2. Target levels by countries or a group of countries for conservation, domestic supplies, and imports during the next five to ten years

3. Review of policy measures to achieve targets

4. Relationship of such measures to eligibility for "safety-net" financing by a new facility

C . A coordinated program for research and the development of additional and alternative energy resources

1. The role of the IEA and French cooperation

2. The problem of capital availability
    a. Capital requirements and financial coordination between governmental and private resources
    b. Review and coordination of measures that may be required to induce the necessary investment and to protect it against unforeseen price reductions of foreign oil

D . Oil import requirements of consuming countries and supply availability from producing countries

1. Review of global, regional, and country import demand over the next five to ten years

2. Availability of supplies from producing countries
    a. Availability by producing countries
    b. Exploration and production programs involved

3. Terms and conditions for assurance of supplies
    a. Producing countries' allocation of imports to be supplied from specific producing areas
    b. Prescription of crude versus product imports
    c. Enforced use of tanker fleets of producing countries
    d. Political conditions for supplies
    e. Possible effect of IEA burden-sharing program on the

political availability of supplies from various producing countries during an emergency

IV. Consuming Countries Cooperation on Economic and Financial Policies Related to the Problems Caused by the Oil Price Explosion

A. Introduction

The large advance in oil costs has led to an increase in the share of oil in world trade from some 5 percent to well over 20 percent within the course of eighteen months. Likewise, because of the limited economic absorptive capacity of many of the oil-producing countries, OPEC countries are currently accumulating surplus financial holdings at a rate of $60 to $75 billion. As a result, practically all the oil-importing countries of the world are incurring huge trade deficits, vis-à-vis OPEC.

To cope with this problem, it is imperative that the OECD countries coordinate their policies on trade, investment, internal and international financing, and domestic and foreign economic policy.

B . A coordinated program for economic relationships between OECD and OPEC countries

1. Optimizing trade with OPEC countries
   a. Support for OPEC economic development programs
   b. Coordination of trade policies vis-à-vis OPEC countries
   c. Coordination of sales of military hardware to OPEC countries

2. The problems posed by the OPEC buildup of export industries—especially refining, petrochemical, and tankers

C . A coordinated program for economic policies in OECD countries

1. A policy for counteracting the deflationary effect of higher oil prices

2. Encouragement of investments in export capacity for goods and services that could be used to repay OPEC loans

3. Enlargement of the world network of trade to reduce the financial strain of oil payments to OPEC

4. A policy of nondiscriminatory trade relationships among OECD countries

D . A coordinated program for financial policies by OECD countries

1. A policy for OPEC investments
   a. Guidelines for investment of OPEC funds in monetary in-struments — public or private
   b. Guidelines for OPEC portfolio or direct investments
   c. Guidelines for other OPEC investment

2. A policy for recycling of OPEC surplus funds among OECD countries   .
   a. Loans — private and public — among OECD countries
   b. Reinvestment of OPEC funds received by some OECD coun-tries in other OECD countries
   c. Reduce exports and increase imports of OECD countries with excess OPEC investment of funds
   d. The "Kissinger Safety-net"

3. A policy for financing of the oil-import costs of needy developing countries
   a. The relative financial contributions of OECD and OPEC countries
   b. The Witteveen fund
   c. The Kissinger trust fund
   d. The U.N. fund
   e. The Shah's proposal for an OECD-OPEC-LDC cooperative fund
   f. Direct bilateral and multilateral OPEC financial contribu-tions to LDC countries

4. A policy for a balanced distribution of OPEC surplus funds among OECD and LDC countries
   a. OPEC balanced investment with or without OECD guarantees
   b. Restrictions on the inflow of excessive OPEC funds by some OECD countries
   c. OPEC to share credit risk of oil-import financing jointly with OECD through a new international facility

V. An OECD Assessment of OPEC Oil Prices, Indexing of Oil Prices and of OPEC Held Assets

A. Introduction

It is most unlikely that OPEC prices will be reduced in a meaningful manner through economic reasoning or pressures in the immediate and median term. OPEC revenues become increasingly built into the budget and balance-of-payment requirements of many of the OPEC countries.

Even if OPEC prices were to be reduced substantially, it is unlikely that importing countries would give up either their conservation efforts or the development of alternate energy resources. Instead, they would tend to protect the economic viability of the new energy industries by subsidies, special price arrangement, import tariffs, quotas, or otherwise.

Any OPEC price reduction would thus be translated nearly directly into a corresponding decline of OPEC revenues. The only, and even then by no means certain, chance of inducing OPEC to reduce prices or, for that matter, not to increase them further, would be predicated on a firm and united approach by the OECD countries that would convincingly demonstrate to OPEC a clear and present danger for severe economic and political worldwide repercussions that would surely also jeopardize the stability of the OPEC countries, their governments, and dynasties. Such an approach might perhaps induce at least some OPEC countries to share in the financing risk for needy oil-importing countries perhaps in the form of either a part deferral of oil payments due them, or acceptance of restricted local currencies, or the grant of concessionary loans.

Such a reduction in OPEC financial claims would be most helpful and must obviously be explored in any consumer-producer countries' dialogue.

    1. Assessment of the economic, political, and perhaps even strategic consequences of OPEC prices at 1974 levels on OPEC investments, the balance-of-payment position of OECD and LDC's, and on world trade and finance for the period 1975–1980 and 1980–1985

B . A comparison of oil price development with those of other raw materials, manufactured goods, and the terms of trade of OPEC countries during the last ten to twenty-five years

C . The indexing of oil prices

    1. Possible methods of indexing

    2. Effect of indexing on balance of payments and surplus OPEC assets

    3. The economic and political effects of indexing

    4. Why indexing must presently be kept in abeyance

D . The protection of surplus OPEC financial assets

    1. Special means for protection of such assets

VI. Possible OPEC Suggestions for the Agenda and
Coordination of OECD's Response

Obviously, the oil-producing countries will add their list of demands to ours. They will certainly insist on complete sovereign control over their natural resources. Accordingly, they would claim that they are entitled to determine unilaterally the rate of development and exploration of their resources, its pricing, the level and direction of exports, and the terms and conditions under which they would take over foreign investments.

In particular, they would undoubtedly insist that the level of oil prices be indexed either in accordance with the rate of inflation of the industrialized countries or the development of prices for OPEC imports of food, industrial equipment, and military hardware.

They would probably also raise the problem of how to protect the terms of trade of LDC's with other raw material or agricultural export industries.

They would, moreover, claim freedom to make their own decisions for the investment of their surplus assets and would attempt to make arrangements to protect the purchasing power of such investments. They would argue that if they produce more oil than they would need to provide for their financial requirements in order to cover existing world oil demand, they would be entitled to receive special considerations.

These are only a few of the more obvious items that the producing countries may wish to raise during a dialogue between importing and producing countries. A coordinated response among the importing countries to such demands is obviously needed.

19

U.S. Energy Policy in a
World Context

In April 1977, at a meeting of the Council on Foreign Relations, Mr. Levy extended his argument for a more intensive commitment to a national and international energy policy. The essential points of his address were later restated (June 1977) in a memorandum to the White House in a further effort to stimulate attention and action on U.S. energy policy.

There could be no "Energy Fortress America," for the situations of allies and developing countries (and the USSR) put the obtaining of oil in a context of complex global relationships. The key role of Saudi Arabia, in view of the special relationship that exists between that kingdom and the United States, is but one factor that gives the United States a strong role in supply to Europe and to Japan. Mr. Levy restates his theme by emphasizing that even if greater efforts are made to reduce dependence on imports, toward the decade of the nineties rising volumetric demand will bring the world closer to the time when there may be physical limits to supply and the possibility of further sky-rocketing of prices. He warns further of an ever-greater competition among importing nations for whatever supply the oil-exporting countries determine is in their best interest to provide.

I. Introduction

In about three weeks time, the President will announce the outline for a new U.S. energy policy, dealing with all aspects of our current and future energy supply and demand position.

II. The Energy Setting for the Next Ten to Fifteen Years

In establishing its policy our Government must undoubtedly take into account that there can be no "Energy Fortress America." Any U.S. energy policy can only be viable within our given political, economic, financial and strategic framework if it is coordinated with the vital

Lecture delivered before the Council on Foreign Relations, Inc., April 1977.

interests and actions of the other member nations of the non-Communist world. I will, in short order, develop the arguments in support of this intimate interdependence. But let me perhaps first set the scene by giving you as succinctly as possible the world energy picture as it would now appear to evolve during the next ten to fifteen years. The statistics are drawn from the recent excellent report on the "World Energy Outlook" by the Organization for Economic Cooperation and Development.

A. The Prospects for Oil

We will concentrate our comments on the oil sector, as oil will remain the major basis of energy supply for the non-Communist world — certainly during the medium-term — and as the major international policy issues will arise in connection with the availability and payments for oil.

Accordingly, I am addressing myself to two questions:

First, is there going to be enough oil available to cover the essential needs through the 1980's and beyond the early Nineties; and

Second, what will be the cost of the oil and what are the balance of payment implications for many of the developed and most of the non-oil-producing developing countries?

If current policies governing supply expansion and conservation are continued, the oil import demand of OECD countries by 1985 would amount to 35 million barrels daily (as compared with 25 million barrels in 1974) and for oil-importing developing countries to some 4 million barrels per day, or about the same as in 1974. The combined total for the non-Communist world would thus reach 39 million barrels daily. By 1990, this total would have increased to 45 billion barrels. About 90 percent of the imports will originate in OPEC countries.

On the basis of optimistic assumptions for maximum conservation and a massive effort of developing all sources of energy, total oil imports in 1985 would still be 29 million barrels daily and 25 million barrels in 1990. As the underlying assumptions for arriving at these estimates have been set forth in the OECD Report, I will not repeat them here.

To achieve the supply expansion and the demand reduction implied in the optimistic OECD case would pose a most difficult task. Without burdening this presentation with further statistical details, let me just mention that it would presuppose an almost nine-fold increase in atomic energy production between 1974 and 1985 — which in terms of oil would be the equivalent of about nine and a half million barrels daily — an over 40 percent rise in world coal output — sufficient to replace by 1985 the equivalent of over six million barrels per day of oil — and an advance in U.S. oil production that would presuppose an annual discovery rate of over four billion barrels per year, or some 50 percent above any previously sustained level of discovery.

Accordingly, we will base our analysis on an intermediate case reflecting more or less the arithmetic average between the two cases; implying an oil import level of about 34 million barrels daily in 1985 and 35 million barrels per day by 1990. We should stress that even these figures still reflect a very optimistic assessment indeed of our future oil import dependence.

B. The Future Cost of Oil Imports

The cost of OECD oil imports in 1985 — with an inflation factor of seven and one-half percent per annum — would reach in then current dollars some 233 billion dollars and for oil-importing developing countries another 33 billion dollars, making for a combined total of nearly 270 billion dollars. For 1990, the corresponding oil import bill would amount to about 400 billion dollars.

III. Major Issues Implied in the Oil-Supply Picture

Let me now review some of the policy implications that are posed by the forecast just given. There is first and foremost a real question whether enough oil can be produced for the period beginning around the early Nineties.

A. Physical Limitations on Future Oil Production

Let us assume a future average discovery rate of some 15 billion barrels of new oil a year, a figure that is somewht higher than previous experience suggests. Given this optimistic assumption, the ratio of the world's current oil production to proven reserves would decline from some 33 years as of now to about 20 years by 1990 — with the ratio for OPEC countries declining from 40 years to 27 years. Less than one-half of 1990 production would be obtained from new discoveries, the balance would come from reserves known today.

Three major conclusions emerge. *First:* Towards the beginning of the Nineties, even ignoring any restrictions oil-producing countries may impose on their level of output for political or economic reasons, we may in fact be approaching a time when physical limitations will impinge on maintaining, and even more so, an increasing world oil production. This applies to most oil-producing nations, except perhaps Saudi Arabia and a few sheikdoms where almost half of the world's known oil reserves are located. Because of the long lead time from exploration to development, the supply availabilities through much of the Eighties are already largely determined; the only major opportunity for obtaining massive new supplies depends on continued free access to known Middle East reserves.

Second: We may soon be confronted by a severe competition among the oil-importing countries for access to oil supplies that may translate itself into policy and strategic as well as economic conflicts.

And *third:* When oil reserves begin to trend downward, towards a level where current production could no longer be sustained, oil prices would not only respond to inflationary factors, but the real price of oil would also rise and may sooner or later skyrocket.

As the national energy demand, the local energy supply and thus the oil import requirements of all the members of the non-Communist world are interdependent, the United States, as the single largest energy user and oil importer, plays a particularly significant role.

What the United States can achieve in the field of conservation is of worldwide relevance, not only because it would affect U.S. oil imports, but also because it could provide the technology and would set a pattern for progress in conservation elsewhere. The same observations hold true for U.S. research and development efforts in the field of energy supplies from all sources.

A coordinated energy research and development program including all the resources of the non-Communist world is absolutely essential. A future energy crisis can — if at all — only be avoided or mitigated if such a maximum program is carried out, and if we are lucky and skillful enough to discover in time very large new hydrocarbon resources, or are able to accomplish dramatic technological breakthroughs for new sources of energy.

In this connection, it should be stressed that a substantial expansion of atomic energy would appear to be absolutely essential for most of the OECD countries, which, unlike the U.S., do not possess large oil or coal reserves. A U.S. policy of going slow because of the still unresolved dangers of atomic proliferation and waste disposal would, if followed by other OECD countries, lead to an energy crunch which might otherwise have been avoided or at least postponed. And needless to say, if the non-U.S. OECD countries should proceed with their atomic development programs, as I believe they will and probably must, we would still be exposed to the dangers of proliferation and waste disposal, because the atomic threat knows no boundaries. Any U.S. policy of "atomic abstention" would not only tend to reduce or delay the chances of coping with atomic dangers, but would also affect our international influence and standing in this field.

B. Political and Economic Limitations on Future Oil Production

Long before limitations on the physical availability of oil would occur, producing countries might impose politically or economically motivated restrictions on the level of their oil production and exports. Here, too, the United States, as the leading power of the non-Communist world, is best placed to assure the unimpeded flow of oil in the world's trade.

It is the United States that has the capability to provide protection for the major oil-producing areas against external as well as internal threats; and the relevant producing countries know this full well, whether they strive openly for a so-called special relationship with the United States or take it tacitly for granted. Likewise, only the United States has the power potential to secure the availability of OPEC oil for world markets in case internal, regional, or other external forces threaten to interdict its free flow.

Also, oil exploration, production and exports rely in most of the major producing countries on the technical, managerial and marketing competence of American oil companies; and overall economic development is substantially dependent on a major input from the U.S. industrial and technical complex.

The United States thus possesses an indispensable—but not necessarily always effective—position of special influence and bargaining leverage. If the issue of restricting oil exports for political or economic reasons should ever become a threat to the welfare of oil-importing countries, the extraordinary position of Saudi Arabia in terms of the richness of its oil reserves and the abundance of its financial strength is—for better or worse—of particular relevance. The special relationship that has developed between the United States and Saudi Arabia provides an invaluable opportunity for exercising a moderating influence. This is equally relevant in convincing the Saudis that in the interest of a stable world, producing countries must adopt a responsible policy in their decisions on oil pricing.

This presupposes a willingness of the importing countries to provide sufficient inducements to producing countries to maintain production levels beyond their own economic and financial needs. This could, among others, also involve complex arrangements for the protection of OPEC's surplus financial reserves against erosion through inflation and also other kinds of understandings that would join the interests of the producing countries to those of the importing nations.

The creation of the International Energy Agency (IEA)—through the initiative of the U.S.—has eased considerably any threat of a future oil embargo by providing for the accumulation of strategic reserves and for automatic burden-sharing among the importing countries; in addition, the IEA also establishes the institutional framework for a broadly-based cooperation on all major energy problems among importing countries and for the reasonable resolution of issues that may arise between importing and producing countries.

Nevertheless, there remains still more than a nagging doubt whether the non-Communist world will be able to cover its future energy needs if all our intermediate efforts do not lead in time to major increases of energy supplies from known or yet unknown sources of energy.

IV. The Financial Dimensions of World Oil Imports

Let us now turn to the complex problems arising from the balance of payment burden that importing countries must incur for their oil purchases. As mentioned previously, the cost of oil imports of the non-Communist world would reach in current dollars some $270 billion in 1985 and $400 billion by 1990.

For the foreseeable future, the non-oil-producing, less-developed countries and also a number of the financially weaker developed countries face foreboding problems in covering their current account deficits. Only those few among the oil-importing countries that are financially strong or industrially advanced would be able to benefit directly from the deposits of financial surpluses by OPEC countries, their investments, or their imports of goods and services. Most of the others must rely for an improvement of their foreign exchange position on sustained economic progress or on financial credits and grants they might receive from financially strong countries or international institutions.

Much has been said about the past success of recycling, implying that it is a problem that would fade away in due course. In fact, each passing year during which we have somehow managed to cope makes the next one more difficult, as increasing debt levels in many countries are approaching the limits of their creditworthiness. Because of the apparent success of recycling during the last three years, the awareness of this threat to the world's financial system has been dimmed; but a great deal of attention is now again being given to it.

Let me refer to a recent warning by Arthur Burns, which he expressed before the Joint Economic Committee of Congress, where he stated that he had "communicated in strident tones" to leading bankers his concern about the risks of repayment of the $50 billion of loans that had been made by American banks to developing countries that are not oil producers.

Likewise, at a recent OECD meeting in Paris, the Chairman of the OECD Economic Policy Committee expressed a nagging worry about the accumulating current account deficits. He asserted that "assuming only moderate future oil price increases, the cumulative current account deficit of OECD countries between 1975–1980 could be estimated at $110 billion, and that of the non-oil poor countries at $160 billion."

Finally, Alan Greenspan, the former Chairman of President Ford's Council of Economic Advisors, stated last month before the Conference

Board that at present world price relationships, the non-OPEC countries must, as a group, borrow at least $40 billion each year, cumulatively, year after year, with no way of shunting the cumulative debt on somebody else. . . . He concluded that "cumulating year after year, $40 billion deficits will eventually create such a huge debt structure that most Western industrial nations, and ultimately the U.S. itself, will find it difficult to meet the interest and amortization charges on the loans. . . . Realistically, either the real price of oil must come down or world oil use must fall dramatically."

There is no easy way out of this dilemma. It would be self-defeating to try to cover the balance-of-payment deficits by solutions that would lead to an over-expansion of world liquidity and would result in continuous and potentially rampant inflation—even though the debtor nations could then repay their existing obligations with a fraction of the real value of the amounts originally received. Nevertheless, the temptation for at least some countries to mitigate their debt burden or to avoid default by passively accepting or even welcoming inflationary forces could prove to be dangerously attractive.

At the same time, however, oil prices would tend to rise with inflation; and the higher the rate of inflation, the greater the pressure on producing countries to restrict oil production rather than to accumulate financial reserves that might lose purchasing power through inflation. And with lower production, oil prices would increase even faster—thus triggering a downward slide of our economy at an ever increasing speed.

It is thus essential that the existing institutions such as the World Bank, the International Development Association, and the International Monetary Fund handle, where appropriate, the refinancing and new credit requirements of a large number of countries. This effort must be spearheaded and supplemented by agreements between the strong OECD and OPEC countries to supply the funds that are needed for the solution of the financial problems. What is required in many instances is a rescheduling of existing obligations, an abatement of interest rates, new soft loans and grants. In short, what we are really talking about are international arrangements for a sustained real transfer of wealth from the prosperous to the poorer countries, with its inevitable effect on the standard of living in the richer countries.

V. What About the Future?

In looking now to our energy future, we face indeed most difficult and perhaps even intractable problems. On the one hand, there is the danger of declining energy supplies that would obstruct progress toward an expanding and prosperous world economy; on the other hand, increasing

oil import costs might exceed the financial capability and the foreign exchange resources of many oil-importing countries. But only broadly
based economic progress would at least mitigate the balance of payment
problems that oil imports would pose for many of them.

It would be foolish to deny that the future is clouded, that the task we
have to undertake is very difficult, and the prospects for success at best
uncertain. It is indeed not pleasant to arrive at so pessimistic a prognosis.
But it would be wrong to interpret what we have said as an appraisal of
the future that is immutable and inevitable. Yet only by frankly assessing
the future problems that may confront us, and taking timely and decisive
actions, do we provide ourselves with the opportunity to reverse the
course of events and invalidate our earlier prognosis.

And with the immense stakes at issue, failure is not an acceptable
option. It is thus incumbent upon us to marshal all available forces of
human inventiveness and to accept the necessary economic sacrifices so
that a shortage of energy will not extinguish the light at the end of the
tunnel.

20

The Years That the
Locust Hath Eaten:
Oil Policy and OPEC
Development Prospects

Mr. Levy finds a widespread belief that the oil and payments crises have diminished in importance, the oil "surplus" and decline in the real price of oil contributing to this phenomenon. Demand falls.

Yet nothing has changed in the fundamentals of supply. We are still drawing down on oil reserves, and the prospect of the time when we shall confront a declining physical availability of oil draws closer. A clear signal of the advent of this period will be the resumption of higher and higher oil prices. In short, if the world is to have a successful transition from the years of oil as the preeminent commercial fuel, it must be accomplished within the next twenty to twenty-five years.

The author shifts his attention next to a phenomenon that ought to haunt importers as well as exporters of oil: the dawning realization of the producers that there may be no way by which they can continue to obtain huge revenues from other sources as oil is slowly displaced by alternative forms of energy. Nothing in the way of downstream investments in tankers, refining, marketing, or petrochemicals can earn them anything near the sums which oil has brought their countries. And, because oil revenues raised expectations which cannot now be postponed, much less denied, a crushing dilemma confronts most producing states: By what means can their present "welfare economics" be perpetuated?

The answer, obviously, is to prolong the oil era through joint discussions between the producers and the consumers. Unless these discussions begin, the desert beckons, or so the reader will conclude. But what crises will erupt as the inescapable facts of the plight of the producers become evident?

Reprinted with permission from *Foreign Affairs*, Winter 1978-79, pp. 287–305.

I

For the last five years the world has been trying to cope with a set of problems triggered by the sudden oil price explosion of late 1973: the availability of oil to cover future energy demand, the economic and financial upheaval attending the jump in oil prices, and the utilization of a flood of petrodollars by OPEC countries for their national development and other purposes. These three issues are intimately interrelated and interact on each other; they can thus be properly assessed only in conjunction with each other.

The relationship between oil supply and oil demand has always depended not only on trends in world oil discovery and consumption—including the impact of conservation and the progress made in developing additional energy sources—but on the price and production policies of major oil-producing countries, based in turn on calculations of their political and economic interests. The post-1974 upheaval in the economic and financial structures of the Western industrialized countries, and of the world as a whole, has been kept within controllable limits in part by an economic slowdown and the resourcefulness of Western public and private financial institutions—but certainly also because the principal OPEC countries were not then able or willing to cut production and to press their undoubted bargaining leverage to the utmost. Price advances by OPEC have not kept pace with the overall rate of inflation and the decline of the dollar since the fourfold price increases of 1974, and the real price of oil has dropped substantially. Meanwhile, the great bulk of the new oil money, or petrodollars, flowing to the OPEC countries has been soaked up, often through prodigious spending by these countries in the West. As a result, the shock to the industrialized economies has been cushioned, and the flow of petrodollars directly into the financial system—while itself enormously increased and the source of continuing major problems—has not turned out to be the nightmare many had feared in 1974.

The American public's sense of urgency has thus tended to dissipate—as the limited energy legislation just passed by Congress attests. At the same time, responsible officials throughout the world have clearly felt that neither the West nor the United States in particular has yet faced up to the long-term scope of the energy crisis, especially the oil situation. Are the factors that have operated in these past four years lasting or temporary? Have we not, in fact, paid a far steeper price, even in these years—in the form of a recession, unemployment and inflation—than we have lately been prepared to recognize? May we not be headed, within the next decade at most, for far more serious upheavals, in which the OPEC producing countries can—and may, if for no other reason than to protect their vital self-interest—completely reassess their present internal development policies, which, in turn, may drastically affect their policies on the supply and price of oil? And what should we do about the serious possibility of interlocking adverse developments?

II

Let us deal first with the energy-oil balance. The present situation is one of oil surplus, stagnating OPEC production and declining real prices for oil. What has brought this about? On the demand side, there has been a substantial slowdown in the use of oil since 1974, especially for industrial purposes, partly because of the slow rate of world economic development and partly because of the higher cost of oil. Whereas energy consumption in the major industrial countries increased more rapidly than Gross Domestic Product in the years preceding 1974, the ratio between the two rates of increase—or the "energy coefficient," as it has come to be called—fell substantially in the years following.

On the supply side, the earlier discoveries in Alaska and the North Sea have now come to fruition and are making a substantial contribution. To this have lately been added increases in Mexican production based on recent prolific discoveries. At the moment, therefore, the oil crisis appears to be invisible.

But what about the prospects for the future? Every estimate for future oil demand shows at least some quantitative increases in world oil requirements for some time to come. For instance, taking into account the most likely availability and full utilization of all non-oil-based energy resources, a conservative assessment would project non-communist world oil consumption as likely to advance from 51 million barrels daily in 1977 to 62 million barrels per day in 1985.

With domestic production of non-OPEC countries estimated for 1985 at 25 million barrels per day, including some 8 million barrels daily of non-OPEC developing countries—about twice their current output—required OPEC production would be 37 million barrels per day as against 32 million in 1977 (which includes OPEC's internal requirements). This assumes that there will be no call, in terms of net oil trade, on OPEC resources by the communist-bloc nations. Present OPEC productive capacity has been estimated at about 39 million barrels per day, of which Saudi Arabia would account for some 11 million.

The above figures would represent an increase in oil consumption of 2.5 percent per annum between 1977 and 1985—versus a rate of 7.5 percent between 1965 and 1973. This is predicated on an OECD economic growth rate of 3.6 percent per year from 1977 to 1985 — versus 4.7 percent from 1965 to 1973 — and an "energy coefficient" of 0.81 between 1977 and 1985, as compared with 1.13 between 1965 and 1973. This assessment points to a tight margin of oil availability in spite of what we believe are relatively moderate estimates of oil and energy demand. If OECD energy needs were to increase by only one-half of one percent per year more rapidly than our estimate, requirements by 1985 would be almost four million barrels a day higher — a precarious balance indeed between energy demand and available supply.

We might also refer to a much more pessimistic recent report of the International Energy Agency in Paris. Based on a "realistic assessment" of each IEA member country with energy policies as now in place, it assumes a 4.3 percent economic growth rate, 0.7 percent higher than the conservative assessment above. Taking account of the estimated energy balances for non-IEA countries, the IEA projects requirements from OPEC in 1985 at 42 to 48 million barrels per day, as compared with estimated available OPEC production of 36 to 38 million. This gap between supply and demand of 4 to 12 million barrels per day is, as the IEA points out, "a notional gap because in the long-term the market will see to it that supply and demand would reach equilibrium. This situation, however, would imply strong upward pressure on prices and adverse consequences for economic growth."

In cruder but all-too-plausible terms, consuming nations would be bidding against each other not only in terms of price, but also in terms of political actions. Some would have to accept a severe reduction in the supply of oil that would be available at prices they could afford to pay. All would suffer individually, and the strain on the cohesion of the key Western allied nations could be very grave indeed, not to mention the friction between rich and poor countries.

In each of these projections of future balance, the estimates of available future OPEC production — and of worldwide production generally — involve considerable uncertainties, especially for the post-1985 period. It takes time to discover, develop, and bring substantial quantities of new oil to markets. But may not the new discoveries now being emphasized — in China two years ago, more recently in Mexico and in the Arctic — confound those who argue that the world must expect oil to diminish steadily as a component of total energy supplies?

Conceivably, if the highest hopes of every prospecting organization in the world were to be realized, the discovery of new reserves might keep pace with levels of consumption that are increasing more slowly than in the past. But, neither history nor recent experience provides dependable assurance for any such hypothesis. Even at a conservative rate of estimated demand for oil, cumulative consumption from 1978 through

1990 would amount to nearly 300 billion barrels, or about one-half of the total existing proven reserves. The 1978 ratio of production to proven reserves is currently 32 years; the break-even rate of discovery to maintain this ratio must start at 18 billion barrels a year and rise steadily to some 23 billion barrels a year by 1985.

As against such needs, it has recently been estimated by EXXON, on the basis of geological assessments and probability analysis, that the finding rate during the next decade will fall within an average range of 12–18 billion barrels a year—more than in the past except during the initial boom period in the Middle East. Even if one takes a slightly higher estimate of the rate of discovery—say, 18–20 billion barrels of new proven reserves a year until 1985—the production-to-reserves ratio would decline from 32 years in 1978 to 25 years in 1985. The ratios would be higher than the average for Saudi Arabia and a very few more producing nations, but much less for most of the other oil countries, thus setting an effective physical limit on their level of output. There would then be little room, if any, for many of the producing countries to expand or even maintain their production on the basis of extant reserves.

The large new discoveries in Mexico and the potential elsewhere, such as in the Arctic and East Asia, will of course be most welcome and may ultimately stretch the lifespan of reserves by a number of years. But nothing now in sight changes the basic prognosis of declining physical availability of oil. This does not mean, of course, that reserves would actually run out by the dates that present arithmetic would suggest, for producing countries would tend to cut back production along the way in the face of impending declines in their reserves, while importing countries would be scrambling for other energy sources. The point is that the kind of pressures on production and pricing policies already predicted by the International Energy Agency for the 1985 time frame can only get worse thereafter as the implications of declining physical availability take hold.

Moreover, the new or enlarged producing areas will certainly not operate without regard to the supply/demand and physical availability factors that will be conditioning the policies of the present members of OPEC. On the contrary, it must be assumed that new production will be integrated sooner or later into the OPEC supply and pricing pattern as that pattern itself evolves. Not in the medium-term—nor even in the long-term—is new production likely to cause a meaningful break in oil prices for any sustained period that would substantially reduce the financial burden of the importing countries.

These are the facts of life in the world of oil; they are as well known in the sophisticated circles that guide present OPEC policies as they are in the consuming countries. In formulating an energy policy, we must thus assume that the period available to us for transition from an oil-based economy to one founded substantially on new energy resources will probably not exceed 20 to 25 years. The need to provide for the world's medium- and longer-term future is clear, but not the means of getting from here to there.

Coal will certainly make a substantially increased contribution, but only in the few countries with an extensive resource base. It is unlikely that within a relatively short time span, the environmental compromises would be reached and facilities could be put into place that would permit the production, internal transportation, exports, and utilization of large additional quantities of coal from the few richly endowed countries. Moreover, shale oil, tar sands and very heavy oils will become a significant factor only if there are technical breakthroughs, such as *in situ* production. The prospects for solar, wind and wave power, and for energy from biomass, must presently be evaluated as relatively marginal within the foreseeable future.

Atomic energy is the one technically and economically feasible source that could make a major contribution to supply, but its development is stymied by the problems of potential weapons proliferation, waste disposal, and political and public opposition. Whereas only two years ago it was predicted that by the year 1985 the member nations of the OECD would have in excess of 300,000 megawatts of nuclear capacity in operation, the Department of Energy, in its "1977 Annual Report to Congress," now assumes that by the mid-1980s there will be no more than about 200,000 megawatts of nuclear power on line. As far as the United States is concerned, the Department of Energy currently estimates that by the mid-1980s nuclear capacity will be slightly less than 100,000 megawatts or about one-half of the OECD figure. This compares with U.S. government targets for 1985, set only a few years earlier, of more than 200,000 megawatts. Further delays or cutbacks can only intensify the crunch.

III

Against this background and aggravated by the decline in the value of the dollar, we must expect that during 1979 OPEC prices will increase more or less in line with inflation and the fall of the dollar — perhaps by eight to ten percent for the year, possibly in installments. This would increase the cost of OPEC's oil exports by more than $12 billion in the coming year alone. If the Iranian oil industry has not resumed reasonably full-scale operations by the end of this year, the cost of oil will most probably advance much more steeply.

After 1979, assuming continued increases in demand, the rate of price increases — probably by the early to mid-1980s — might accelerate, not only to make up for past "losses," but also to reduce or eliminate the current account deficits of many OPEC countries, which in 1977 already had borrowed over $11 billion in the international market. Moreover, around the mid-1980s or early 1990s, when the specter of imminent oil shortages begins to haunt the world, the opportunities and pressures for large advances in the real price of oil are almost certain to become decisive from the standpoint of oil-balance factors alone.

We have already experienced the economic consequences of the 1974 oil price explosion; and since 1974, the progress of the world economy has become dangerously sensitive and vulnerable to the economic and political effects of any future sizable advances in the cost of oil. The impact of the 1974 price rise has not been uniform among nations, but has shifted over time among developing as well as developed countries, including the United States, and often unpredictably. Between the end of 1973 and early 1978, the total foreign debt of non-OPEC Third World countries, partly as a result of the high cost of their oil imports, has increased from an estimated $95 billion — of which $30 billion was owed to commercial banks — to $210 billion, of which $90 billion was obtained from private financial institutions. At present, the United States is struggling with a persistent, huge oil trade deficit, and with uncertainties affecting the dollar exchange rate, aggravated by potentially volatile dollar holdings abroad.

The pace of economic progress of a large number of countries has been sluggish and unemployment has remained high. Likewise, inflation is still rampant; at the same time, however, inflation is, to a significant extent, the reason that the international debt service burden remains, in general, within manageable limits as compared to inflated current export receipts of many of the debtor countries.

In this connection, it must be emphasized that even the halting recovery we have experienced since 1974 would have been virtually impossible had world oil prices increased between 1976 and 1978 with inflation and the fall of the dollar; instead, the cost of oil in real terms has declined by perhaps 20 to 25 percent during this period — mainly because of the restraint exercised by Saudi Arabia with the support of Iran and of a few other OPEC members. Only because of this substantial reduction have we been able up to now to avoid a serious and long-lasting recession and to handle effectively the enormous problem of financing world oil imports and the so-called recycling of petrodollars.

In short, the period of declining real prices for oil is coming to an end, and may, within the not too distant future, be followed by an accelerating increase in real prices, with the timing dependent on the oil supply/demand relationship. As far as the importing countries are concerned, the only leverage they have is related to the level of their oil requirements as compared with oil availability. The former depends on their rate of economic growth and the success of their oil conservation measures. They find themselves between the Scylla and Charybdis of a slow rate of development with the risk of a recession and political instability, or a policy of sustained growth entailing the danger of an early oil shortage accompanied by high oil prices. Either course might bring about economic and financial turmoil with ensuing political instability.

Thus it would be dangerous to base future policy on the illusion that the financial issues centering around the oil problem have been successfully resolved, or to assume that because there has been no real catastrophe in the past there might not be extremely dangerous situations facing us in the future. In spite of our past successes in making the necessary financial adjustments — assisted by slow economic growth, high unemployment and excessive inflation in most of the importing countries and wasteful expenditure of part of their revenues by producing countries — the problems have not faded away like the Cheshire Cat in *Alice in Wonderland,* with only a grin remaining until that, too, vanished.

IV

Up to this point, we have been giving a current assessment of the central "market" factors for at least the past five years. The picture that emerges is disturbing enough, but our disquiet is bound to be intensified if we turn to a serious examination of the internal economic situations of the major producing countries in OPEC. Now, with five years of experience to judge from, it is high time for us to take this element of the situation into much greater account than we have heretofore. For, in the last analysis, the availability of oil from OPEC countries will depend not only on their judgment of supply/demand factors and of the state of their proven oil reserves, but also on their economic policies and on overall political considerations.

In particular, we will now review the progress and prospects of the economic development program of OPEC countries; and, because of the extreme relevance of this assessment fo their future welfare, we will not dwell on other factors — such as inflationary pressures on their economy or political decisions related to say, Arab-Israeli developments — which might also affect their future oil production policy. Nor will we deal with the ever-present contingency of a political upheaval in any one of the major producing nations, or a protracted oil workers' strike, or a serious accident or sabotage that would put essential oil facilities out of operation for a long time. Any of these events could upset the world's oil supply/demand balance practically overnight with potentially very harmful consequences for the prosperity of virtually every one of the oil-importing nations.

We must expect that sooner or later many producing countries will seriously question the value of much of their development program in terms of its potential contribution to their economic progress, political stability, employment, budgetary receipts, and foreign exchange income. Many of them will painfully realize that their industrial efforts could not possibly begin to replace the government and foreign exchange revenues that they have become accustomed to receiving from their oil production, nor provide them with a prosperous non-oil-based economy.

When confronted with a sudden huge influx of oil money, most countries immediately set out to prepare a program on how to make the best possible use of their newfound riches. They began to formulate an economic development plan, build up an infrastructure, provide exchange for imports for current consumption, improve the welfare of their citizens and allocate more funds for military purposes. They also had to decide how much they wanted to retain for foreign investments and savings.

The challenge they face may perhaps most simply be described this way: during the relatively short period when they can count on a large flow of oil revenues, they have to develop an economy that can provide them with sufficient government revenues, foreign exchange income and employment for the period when the oil bonanza begins to peter out.

The preparation of a plan—and even more so its implementation—requires a great deal of time, and its feasibility and real value to the country depend on its ability to draw on the advice of competent experts. The magnitude of the problem OPEC has to cope with has been without precedent. Many of the countries are confronted with a very unfriendly environment for the creation of a modern economy: a hostile climate; lack of arable land, water, power and other resources; a high degree of illiteracy; a scarcity of managerial talent or experience; at best, a very small skilled labor force and, likewise, a shortage of available or socially adjusted unskilled labor. Inevitably, and in the best of circumstances, there was bound to be a lot of confusion, mismanagement, waste, lack of coordination within a country—and even more so within an area—and thus substantial duplication of effort.

Development programs were rapidly formulated, involving sometimes very costly projects of a prestige character but of dubious immediate value to the country, such as a huge atomic energy development program—apparently now being cut back—in one of the nations possessing enormous natural gas resources on which it could draw for a very long time. Coordination of industrial development, manpower needs, housing requirements, and water, power and transport availability was often—as one might expect during this chaotic period — by no means perfect.

The most immediate issue facing the producing countries in 1974 was to build up the port and transportation facilities in order to accommodate the vast increases in consumption and in imports for development purposes that were triggered by the oil bonanza. This has more or less been accomplished — albeit at a very high cost — resulting partly from the speed with which these projects were undertaken. There was some large overexpansion of port facilities and airports both because of lack of coordination and national prestige considerations. Certainly inexperience and other cost-increasing factors also contributed, but this was almost inevitable considering the amount of money available and the rate at which it was spent. At the same time, educational, training, and health facilities were ordered, frequently without regard to the staffing problems, level of possible utilization, or future cost of operation.

We do not intend to go into a country-by-country review of a specific project analysis. Much went right and much went wrong, and there is no point in presenting a catalogue of specific successes and failures. Many of the difficulties and dilemmas posed could not have easily — or sometimes even possibly — been avoided, given the unprecedented nature of the problem, and the political and social circumstances as they exist in the separate countries. These observations apply, of course, in varying degrees to the different OPEC nations.

Three fields of special interest to the producing countries are forward integration from crude-oil production into refining, producing at least commodity petrochemicals for export, and tanker transportation. Even though the investments are large, the value added is relatively small, and the employment provided is somewhat limited. In addition, there is a locational and transport disadvantage for exporting refined products in comparatively small tankers versus crude oil in supertankers. Just as the number of citizens directly and indirectly engaged in their country's oil operations is relatively small, the part of the population that would benefit directly from the oil bonanza as employees or as providers of equipment and services for the oil industry is relatively limited. And the creation of a specially privileged class of those connected with the industry would of course create other problems, such as setting wage or profit standards for other economic or agricultural activities that such undertakings could not possibly sustain.

Between 1973 and 1977, OPEC's growth in refining capacity has been less than the increase in domestic demand; and, excluding Venezuela, exports of refined products are only about 5 percent of crude exports. However, by 1985 another 3.5 million barrels per day of refining capacity has been scheduled for completion. Likewise, the buildup of large new petrochemical facilities is underway or contemplated. In addition, obvious fields for investment that are being pursued are energy-intensive industries such as aluminum and steel.

The main problem confronting OPEC here is, of course, the current surplus refining and petrochemical capacity in many of its markets, coupled with the need to overcome the construction, operating cost and transport disadvantage of OPEC's new facilities by below-market pricing of crude or feedstocks and by cheap financing. The OPEC tanker fleet — still relatively small — will undoubtedly increase substantially, but it faces the problem of a world surplus tanker capacity. At the moment it requires heavy subsidies. However, the desire of the producing countries to upgrade at least some of their crude oil themselves is perfectly obvious and understandable. As the Kuwaiti Oil Minister put it, "Investment should be considered not purely from the commercial point of view, but from that of the economic and social profitability for the nation, especially in the long run — and also as part of the social costs as a means of filling the technological gap and widening the industrial base." Accordingly, OPEC, as the world's major crude supplier, will somehow be able to export refined products and petrochemicals, and also to utilize its tanker fleet. But this can most likely be done only at some financial cost either to OPEC or to the importing countries or to both, and presupposes constructive cooperation between the two parties.

The problem of launching an effective economic development program has been immensely aggravated by the inevitable and huge pressures on the governments to improve the economic well-being of their citizens almost immediately after the dramatic increase in the flow of oil revenues. A policy of gradual change in accordance with the rate of economic progress would — in the light of the high expectations raised — be politically and socially very dangerous, if not impossible. But rapid movement toward a welfare state would in due course have equally destabilizing and harmful effects.

As the government owns all of the oil revenues, it is the public sector that would have to provide the financing, not only in the proper field of governmental activities — such as for the build-up of an infrastructure — but also for most of the development projects. These would then either be government-owned or in some form or fashion be made available, fully or in part, to private owners — usually on favorable terms and frequently only to a small select group. At the same time, the government has to engage in activities that would improve the welfare of its citizens at large. This would be achieved by direct or indirect transfer payments to its nationals — such as paying for their education, their health services, subsidization of housing, food or other necessities of life.

In some instances, in order to "spread the wealth," the government in fact made land available cheaply or without cost to its citizens, land which would either increase substantially in value or which the government would buy back at higher prices. In all these circumstances, it was inevitable that most of the countries would be plagued by rampant inflation, further increasing the cost of the government's welfare and development program.

There has also been an explosive increase in the employment — amounting in the millions — of foreign skilled and unskilled labor, needed in practically all phases of economic activity, which has not only brought social and political problems, but has also involved large remittances of several billions of dollars per year to the expatriates' home countries.

It should surprise nobody that, during this period of hectic chaos, there was a mass movement to the main cities from the outlying areas and villages; that agricultural production could not keep pace with increases in demand, and frequently even declined; that many traditional industries suffered; and that imports of all kinds of consumer goods expanded at explosive rates.

All this was accompanied by a building spree of unheard-of dimensions, frequently uncoordinated with available water, power, and sewage facilities and often providing luxury or high-rent accommodations. In many urban areas, there is still a huge shortage of housing for the poor — with the large original slum population swollen by the new inflow of people in search of the "good life" in the cities. Rental costs have often reached fantastic levels.

Equally, with billions of dollars spent on the establishment of educational and health facilities and on the buildup of a modern military force, the government must be prepared to maintain and operate them after their completion. And the annual operating and maintenance costs may well amount, for an indefinite future, to one-quarter to one-third of the initial construction cost. Already, some of the countries have to cope with budgetary and foreign exchange deficits.

The point at which individual oil-producing countries will be confronted by a decline in oil production and revenues differs, of course, among the various oil producers, depending on their level of production and the richness of their hydrocarbon resources. Saudi Arabia and a few other producers have sufficient reserves to give them ample time for slow adjustments to this post-oil period, and they can absorb a large amount of an at least partially inevitable waste of their financial endowment. Many others are not in such a fortunate position.

But all of them have to cope with the political and social problems that have been posed by this vast inflow of money: the feverish rate of development; the negative impact on agriculture and traditional industries; their increasing dependence on subsidies for imports, or for industries providing domestic substitutions; the unhealthy urbanization; the excesses of a building boom; the large influx of foreign labor; inflation; the lopsided distribution of wealth; and many other politically and socially destabilizing factors. They will all realize that rapid and forced development tends to weaken, if not destroy, established social and cultural values, and mostly without replacing them by new ones. Sooner or later there may be a wave of disappointment, frustration and resentment, most likely directed largely against the foreigner and the producing countries' national governments and their institutions. The present turmoil in Iran is indicative of what may lie ahead.

To sum up, since 1974 OPEC government revenues, which coincide with most if not all of its foreign exchange income, have amounted to some $550 billion. An estimated $400 billion may have been spent on goods, services, military expenditures, and so on. The value received on an OECD cost basis would appear not to have been more than perhaps some $200 to $300 billion.

For example, the capital projects of the oil-producing countries cost — for a number of reasons — around two to three times as much as competing facilities located in developed countries. They involve, as of 1976, an estimated "locational premium" for a project in Arabia as against the Texas Gulf Coast ranging from 2.1 times for industrial construction to 2.8 times for military establishments; the ratios for electrical power generation, housing and hospital construction costs are estimated in the same range. These figures take into account factors related to ensuring comparable performance, as well as transportation costs, delays due to bottlenecks, extra service fees, expenditures for housing, sewage, and procurement of expensive foreign labor and management. Many enterprises are also burdened with a substantial additional accommodation or, if you will, "under the table charge," which may vary roughly between 5 and 20 percent of the amount of the contract, depending on the "political" situation and the nature of the project. Likewise, the operating costs for such projects — because of locational disadvantages, lack of supporting services, foreign labor, etc. — are substantially higher than those incurred in OECD countries.

However, even after the oil age has passed, many of the OPEC countries will still have to depend on substantial government revenues and foreign exchange income. This poses another problem inherent in the character of the large rent on crude oil that the countries are able to command as a result of the OPEC pricing policy. For each one billion dollars received by OPEC for its crude oil exports, perhaps $900 million accrue to the country as government revenue, and are obtained, moreover, in the form of free foreign exchange.

In contrast, for a usual industrial development project with an output of one billion dollars, the government tax authorities—provided that an effective tax system is in place—might collect in direct taxes on the industry no more than $50 million. The foreign exchange income to the country depends on its receipts from exports which, in turn, are contingent on its competitiveness in world markets, and its cost for foreign raw materials, semi-finished products, and part of the expense of any foreign labor that might be needed. However, as we have mentioned, quite a number of projects—because of the high level of construction and operating costs, and the expenses of transportation to more distant markets—are most likely noncompetitive in world economic terms and might be unable to operate profitably, once a continued flow of oil money or a below-market-price supply of energy or feedstocks is no longer available to subsidize operations. Under such conditions export revenues could, at best, be only a small fraction of that obtained previously from oil exports.

At the same time, the operation and maintenance of ports, transportation, health and educational facilities, the upkeep of a modern military force, and the support of a welfare economy in quite a number of these countries will become an ever-increasing budgetary drain on a prospectively much lower level of government revenues.

According to a recent survey of the London-based Economist Intelligence Unit, of all the Persian Gulf countries, only Iran, Iraq, Oman, Bahrein and Dubai might potentially be able to build up credible non-oil-based economies—and, except perhaps for the last two, only if there is a massive shift in their development philosophy and policy.

The odds at this time are that when the oil revenues begin to peter out, a number of the OPEC countries will find themselves not too much better off than before—like Spain, after it had been inundated by gold and silver from its Latin American empire in the late sixteenth and early seventeenth centuries. As the Controller General of Venezuela pointed out in December 1975, "In many countries, being rich is a consequence of the efforts and work of the people. When you make something you can manage it. The creation of wealth and its management are part of the process. We have never had such a process. The wealth came out of the earth. We have a consequence without a cause."

It should be noted that not only oil-rich developing countries, but also those few developed nations that have been suddenly endowed with an oil or gas El Dorado—such as the U.K., Norway and Holland—might be easily tempted to dissipate their oil revenues. In this vein, the head of the Dutch Central Bank has described the economic effects of his country's income from natural gas as "a curse in disguise."

What does all this imply for future OPEC oil exports and prices? Confronted sometime in the future with declining oil production and

revenues, producing countries will realize that the rate at which they exploit their oil resources and the allocation of their oil earnings will
become increasingly critical — as, for example, among welfare, development of agriculture and internal industries, production for exports, and
foreign investments. Many of them will question whether they can really
establish a self-sustaining non-oil-based economy and inevitably consider
the alternative of slowing down their development program, as well as
possibly "welfare" expenditures and military purchases. This would
enable them to stretch their oil reserves by producing less, and to sustain
the future viability of their economy as much as feasible through an increased flow of revenues from foreign investments. Kuwait has in fact
been doing this by putting a ceiling on its production and establishing a
"Fund for Future Generations" derived from 10 percent of all its government receipts. The present unstated policy of providing adequate production for the world's needs at manageable prices would then be replaced by one of lower production at higher prices.

In such a situation the importing countries — at least during the adjustment period — would have no choice but to continue essential oil imports
at high prices, rather than curb their receipts drastically with a sudden
crippling effect on their countries' economies. The continuous stringency
of oil supplies and their high cost would be bound to cause most serious
economic and political problems for developed as well as developing
countries. Moreover, for the industrialized nations — which have greatly
benefited from the vast expenditures on development projects and
military equipment by OPEC countries — a reduction in the purchase of
goods and services and an increase in the funds allocated to foreign investments would be very harmful; during a period of sluggish economic
growth and high unemployment, it would further impede their chances
for recovery.

In addition, the outflow of interest and dividends on much higher
OPEC foreign investments in importing countries could, within a
number of years, approach and even exceed the inflow of new OPEC
funds. The early relief for the balance of payments of oil-importing
countries would thus become increasingly less.

For many OPEC countries, such a change in current development
policy might not be possible without economic and political upheavals.
And for some of the poorest non-OPEC LDCs — which in 1977 provided
Middle Eastern oil countries with a labor force of some 2.5 to 3 million
foreign workers, transmitting nearly $5.5 billion to their homelands — a
severe reduction in emigrant remittances coupled with the higher cost of
oil imports and a general slowdown of economic growth would be a
devastating blow.

A change such as indicated here in OPEC's oil production, development and foreign investment policy, would obviously take place gradually and also would not apply with equal force to all of the OPEC countries. The damage to their own economic systems and political stability, and the effect on the prospects of importing countries and their cooperative relationships with each other and with the OPEC nations, makes it imperative for them to proceed with caution and concern for the future well-being of all parties concerned.

In spite of the huge inflow of oil money, only 3 or 4 years after the start of the oil bonanza, some OPEC countries have already incurred an increasing foreign exchange deficit on their current account and are unable to balance their internal budgets. This will inevitably force them to take a hard look at the level and effectiveness of their expenditures for development and possibly for military purposes, and also to calculate the potential optimum level of their oil revenues. They might well decide that they cannot afford to ignore their more urgent interests even though it would detrimentally affect the prosperity of their Western customers— and would, of course, also be harmful to them.

V

It is not easy to formulate, in light of all these factors, a rational policy for the industrial democracies that would also take account of the legitimate vital interests of the OPEC countries.

An energy policy for importing countries must be based on realistic assumptions somewhat weighted on the prudent side. The price for being too optimistic about the availability of oil supply, and thus facing a serious shortage at an early period, would be economically and politically destabilizing. The cost of being too pessimistic, on the other hand, would at its worst involve the misdirection of some resources, or a loss of interest on capital spent earlier than necessary. It would thus be much better to pay the smaller additional expense of doing too much too early than risk the enormous cost of doing too little too late.

What seems clear is that we have not as yet succeeded in establishing an effective energy policy for the oil-importing countries to cope with the supply and economic-financial problems with which they are likely to be confronted, nor have we succeeded in making a constructive contribution to what presently appears to be, at least in part, an ineffective development effort of the oil-producing nations. What is needed is a common major endeavor, that would include the oil-importing and exporting countries, to engage in a critical evaluation of what went wrong and why, and then attempt to formulate a constructive national and international policy and an agreement on its subsequent implementation.

Oil is a finite resource whose depletion is in sight. In spite of temporary current surpluses, it is vital that a maximum effort be made to provide as early as possible for its gradual replacement. The consuming countries, with the United States in the lead, must thus set as their most important goals the further improvement of the energy-GDP ratio, establishment of optimum conditions for the expansion of traditional sources, and the development of large dependable new energy supplies. Taking for granted a relatively high and increasing energy cost at least during a transition, there is, I believe, a reasonable prospect that in due course we will be able to bring production costs down, or perhaps, stabilize them. Such a development may be achievable through concentration on conventional atomic, breeder and — perhaps later — fusion energy. This whole effort should involve a more effective coordination than has yet materialized with the Europeans, Japanese, and others.

The question must also be asked whether it is really in the interest of the oil-importing countries to put undue emphasis on the availability of ample supplies of oil at low prices, as this would inevitably, within a relatively narrow time span, be followed by shortages of oil with a price explosion. Any freeze of current oil prices, or even more so their reduction, would particularly affect all endeavors to develop non-OPEC-based energy resources, be they oil- or non-oil-based, as such efforts will be very costly.

We have a wider national and international interest in an energy price that is high enough to encourage the optimum development of new traditional as well as nontraditional energy resources — even though this could and does in fact represent very serious financial and balance-of-payments burdens, as well as a troublesome impediment to economic growth worldwide.

We also need to rethink our policies toward the developing OPEC countries. Up to now we have mostly accepted without question, even when wasteful, their desire for rapid development and large military expenditures. After all, this has been of great economic benefit to the developed world and has enabled it to cope with the petrodollar problem. But the balance of factors is moving in the direction of change, based on the declining physical availability of oil and an incipient realization on the part of producing countries that they need to revamp their development programs, the awareness that they might have to stretch their oil resources and revenues, and that they could in the post-oil future become substantially dependent on revenues obtained from their foreign investments. None of this is, of course, absolutely certain to happen, but no responsible nation can afford not to plan for such a contingency.

What is needed, therefore, is a candid exchange of views with OPEC on the goals and practicability of their development programs, even though we may run the risk that they would interpret any advice or guidance we offer as another manifestation of neocolonialism. In particular, we must try to engage them in serious discussions as to which enterprises make sense, and must be willing to assist them constructively in developing as many industries offering the prospect of economic viability as they can handle, by providing them with technology, managerial talent and access to markets. Obviously, such an effort can only be pursued with any chance of success on the basis of a consensus among OECD countries and a coordination of their policies which, because of the intense competition among the developed nations for Middle Eastern business, might be very difficult indeed to achieve. But it is absolutely essential that selfish national interests not be allowed to undermine a common and balanced approach to any range of problems that confront us.

Any such policy would have its costs and would undoubtedly involve a substantial throttling back of OPEC programs. It would result in a slower but more sensible development program, which would ultimately be in everyone's interest. We cannot afford to ignore the fact that political unrest, labor strife, and social and cultural disintegration would be as threatening to the stability of OPEC nations as they would be to a secure and uninterrupted flow of OPEC's oil to importing countries.

There are undoubtedly very difficult times ahead. Up to now we have not fully evaluated our own and OPEC's vital concerns, nor have we resolved various conflicts of interest inherent in the issues we face. In any case it seems certain that we must adjust ourselves to a period of slower economic growth, which we hope will provide us with the time and opportunity to develop an energy base for the future without endangering in the meantime the non-Communist world's economic and political system.

We cannot much longer afford a situation in which the importing countries waste a substantial part of their energy while the producing countries waste a substantial part of their oil revenues. In the past we have too often been stymied in our efforts to cope with these problems by entrenched national or private interests on all sides. If we should ultimately fail, this period in our history could truly be characterized as "the years that the locust hath eaten."

Part 6

OIL – THE YEARS AHEAD

Introduction

It remains Mr. Levy's thesis that the continuing inability of the importing nations (virtually all of the OECD nations) to coordinate their efforts to obtain oil on manageable terms will eventually erode their relationships. Divisive actions to secure supply will corrode the importers' security, fragment their alliance, leave them vulnerable to further actions of oil producers, and open them to Soviet initiatives further destabilizing to the Middle East.

The reader will recall Mr. Levy's persistent concern that we have, as yet, no adequate process whereby the interests and roles of the international oil companies can become incorporated into the larger responsibilities and roles of government, despite the strategic dimension of oil. Because this concern permeates so much of the writing included in this volume, it must reflect many years of experience in attempting to deal with the ways in which the two parties act on each other. It must also reflect the fact that increasingly government has found it necessary – sometimes for good and sufficient reasons – to be involved. The relationship between companies and government – notably in the United States – has been happenstance, which may not be an adequate means for pursuing the overall national interest in dealing with such momentous matters as access to oil.

Consumers of imported oil are seemingly more interested in the current "surplus" in supply and further declines in oil prices as indicators of a longer-term trend than they are in the durability of current Saudi policy, a resumption of the Iraqi-Iranian war, the fate of the Iranian revolution or, indeed, in the fact that everywhere producers of oil are drawing down on their oil capital. We are still not finding enough additional reserves to delay the coming of the day when it will be clear enough to all that physical limits to oil supply are our lot.

In the concluding part, two of Mr. Levy's most compelling writings are included without comment, for none is needed for the reader who has traced through this volume the expanding strategic dimensions of oil. It may well be the case that just as we read in 1982 of the concepts about oil that moved Walter J. Levy to write for our benefit forty years ago, in the next century others will read again these last selections and ask how could the facts and ideas offered us in 1980 and 1981 not have compelled us to take the steps essential to our security and well-being? As Eugene V. Rostow has written about Mr. Levy and his arguments, the fact that governments have not done what seems sensible and necessary "is not a reflection on the persuasiveness of his arguments. Rather it identifies the outer boundary of reason in the affairs of man."

21

Oil and the
Decline of the West

I

The year 1979 was one of grievous setbacks for the future security of the oil supply of the Western world, its economic and financial prospects, its strategic capabilities, and its political stability.

To begin with, we were completely unprepared for the collapse of the Shah's regime in Iran, even though there were many early warning signals. And our government and business community share a substantial measure of responsibility for shortsighted policies which contributed to the destabilization of the Shah's regime.

What followed in terms of oil alone should now be a familiar story. During the course of 1979, the decline in Iranian oil production was more than made up by other producing countries. And taking account of a virtually unchanged world oil demand, importing countries were able to increase their oil stocks during the year by well over one million barrels a day, more than has been achieved during recent periods. Nevertheless, a temporary decline in world oil production led to apprehensions by importing countries and their oil companies that they might be unable to cover their future needs. Accordingly, importers tried to obtain added supplies and to increase stocks at almost any cost. This, in turn, resulted in panic buying at largely uncontrolled and escalating spot oil prices.

Obviously, the Organization of Petroleum Exporting Countries (OPEC) would not maintain its official quotations at a lower level if an increasing proportion of its oil was purchased on the spot market by importing countries or companies at much higher prices. In due course, OPEC increased its official prices to more than double their previous levels. Also, OPEC countries would naturally try to sell more and more of their oil directly or through intermediaries at the higher spot prices. This would mean that the established customers for OPEC oil could only obtain smaller quantities of the oil they had previously been able to acquire directly from the producing countries. Accordingly, more and more companies and countries were unable to purchase oil from their

Reprinted with permission from *Foreign Affairs*, Summer 1980, pp. 999–1015.

regular major oil company suppliers; instead, they were forced to turn to producing countries or trading companies to assure themselves of supplies, and they showed themselves willing to pay them practically any price that they asked for.

As early as February 1979 it was painfully clear that this state of affairs posed a massive danger for the world oil economy and that it required coordination and cooperation among importing countries and among their companies if this buying panic were to be stopped. As a minimum, the major importing countries would have had to establish a firm policy for themselves and their companies not to buy oil at above OPEC price levels; at the same time they had to be willing to establish an international and national allocation system that would assure all countries and companies an equitable share in the oil that was available at OPEC prices. Without such arrangements, higher spot prices would sooner or later be incorporated into higher official OPEC prices. This would be especially damaging because OPEC prices are not freely fluctuating market prices. Once raised, they are unlikely to come down again, because any future softness in prices would be countered by a cutback of OPEC production.

The governments of the major importing countries were, of course, aware of this problem. But either they did not really comprehend its importance or they lacked the will and leadership qualities to act. The relevant international institutions, such as the Organization for Economic Cooperation and Development (OECD) or the International Energy Agency (IEA), either felt that they did not have the constitutional power to deal with this issue, or that they would not have the support of their member governments. Industry generally opposed any course that might involve national or international official controls or interference.

While it is, of course, not certain whether any national or international arrangements, had they been made, would have succeeded, in actual fact nothing was even attempted to stem the tide of upward-spiralling prices. It would appear that most of the wounds of 1979 have been self-inflicted.

So we lived through 1979 with Iran in disarray, with the oil economy in turmoil (even though there was no overall sustained shortage), and with the Soviets invading Afghanistan. It was indeed a year illustrating the impotence of Western power and the failure of national and international leadership.

II

While 1979 has passed, the problems it created or aggravated are going to stay with us, probably for the indefinite future. Let us first review the medium term to 1985.

With a recession accompanied by a substantial retardation in world economic growth, and with continued conservation and sustained development of energy from all available non-OPEC sources including coal and nuclear energy, it now appears that world energy requirements *could* be met *if* OPEC production, after a decline during 1980 (as compared with 1979), would then increase again and reach about the 1979 level by 1985. This would require, in effect, that political and economic conditions in the major oil-producing areas, notably the Persian Gulf, be such as to lead to sustained and increased production to such levels. It would also require the adherence by the Western nations grouped in IEA to the oil import limitation targets for 1985 and intervening years, which in turn would require greatly increased conservation and further development of indigenous energy sources.

But this is only the statistical supply and demand part of the story, and even this much depends on the doubtful and difficult conditions just stated. Moreover, even under these conditions, the financial problems of recycling petrodollars and particularly meeting the needs of the less-developed countries (LDCs) are sure to take on a much more serious dimension than in the 1974–78 period. This is a conclusion universally shared today by those in positions of public or private responsibility, including members of the banking community who assessed the situation in the earlier period and believed that the private banking community could to a very great extent handle the problem. Today, however, there is solid agreement that the omens are far darker.

Specifically, at current OPEC prices and assuming future increases at even somewhat *less* than the anticipated rate of inflation (the most favorable possible assumption), OPEC countries might accumulate a surplus of about $115 billion during 1980 and of some $350 to $450 billion between 1980 and 1985. This would imply that the importing countries would suffer a corresponding balance-of-payments deficit during this period, which would have to be financed somehow by the recycling of the petrodollar surplus.

For the year 1980, the deficit of developed countries has been estimated at about $50 billion and that of less developed countries at nearly $70 billion. The foreign debt of LDCs might reach about $440 billion in 1981, compared with about $385 billion in 1980 and $150 billion in 1975. And with petrodollar surpluses continuing to accumulate, the financial and balance-of-payments position of oil-importing countries would deteriorate at an accelerating rate. It is most unlikely that our national and international financial system can cope with this problem without risking sustained recessions, a slow rate—if any—of economic growth, high rates of inflation, widespread unemployment, industrial and national bankruptcies, and political upheaval.

The debt problem could, of course, be solved if the values of the currencies in which the debts are incurred decline in their purchasing power to such an extent that the repayment of debts, when due, can be done at a fraction of their original value. All of this did in fact occur between 1974 and 1978, a period which has been portrayed by some as the "golden age" of petrodollar recycling.

But it seems now that the jig is up. The recycling "success" in the past was predicated on some confidence in the value of the currencies involved, on the willingness of oil-producing countries to spend ever-increasing amounts of petrodollars for national development and military purchases, and on their readiness to suffer substantial declines in the real price of oil and to accept between 1974 and 1978 the virtual disappearance of their annual petrodollar surplus.

Now the producing countries are trying to establish a policy under which oil prices will not only go up regularly in step with the rate of inflation, but also will increase on a regular basis at rates exceeding the rate of inflation by an additional amount depending on the increase in the Gross National Product (GNP) of the OECD. In short, they are seeking a regular advance in the real price of their oil. Many of them have also cut back their earlier economic development programs so that the former wild increases in annual import expenditures have recently been coming down substantially.

Furthermore, the producers are now placing even greater emphasis on increasing the value of their oil exports by adding refining, petrochemical and transport operations to their national programs. This would of course further add to the foreign-exchange burden of oil purchased by the importing countries and would thus increase the petrodollar surplus even more.

More important, perhaps, the question arises whether the producing countries would really be prepared to continue to produce oil at a rate that would continuously generate surplus petrodollars for them. As they are well aware, they would in effect be exchanging oil in the ground, whose value will certainly advance at least with inflation, for monetary assets whose value would tend to decline with inflation.

If, alternatively, they were to reduce their production, they would not only stretch the life of their oil reserves, but as real prices in tight oil markets are likely to increase, their revenues would go up. It is true that the world economy would suffer very badly by any resulting oil shortage, but the producing countries might argue that, at least to some extent, their loss from the world's depressed economic activity would be less than the erosion in the value of their surplus financial assets that they would suffer through inflation.

The minimum protection the producing countries could be expected to demand, if they were to continue to produce oil at levels needed by the importing countries, would be an indexation of their petrodollar accumulations in line with inflation. To take care of this problem, I have recently suggested that this might be done by making available to them inflation-indexed energy bonds that would be issued by an international agency. As any additional cost that could result from such indexation would have to be underwritten by the oil-importing countries, the financial burden on the latter might, obviously, increase.

III

Let us now turn to some of the other major problems that affect the security and availability of oil supplies.

The producing countries, having taken full control over their national oil operations, in fact do not recognize as binding supply or price arrangements even if freely concluded by them. Recently they have gone so far as to change agreed-upon prices retroactively. This, they argue, they are entitled to do under the doctrine of sovereign control by producing countries over their natural resources. Because the contracting party in the producing country is also a government-owned oil company, they contend that any change the government requests in the terms and conditions affecting crude oil production and sales would in fact constitute a sovereign act, so that the government oil company that had entered into a contract would be entitled to claim *force majeure* vis-à-vis its customers.

But undoubtedly, the increasing unilateral application of this doctrine is also related to the ease with which the host countries have been able to apply it, and to the lack of opposition by the affected private or public interested parties against unilateral expropriation or the cancellation of legal and contractual rights. Because of the fear of being arbitrarily cut off from supplies, Western nations and their companies now accept within a wide range practically any economic or political terms that a producing country may impose on them. This subservience, however, rather than safeguarding the remaining rights and position of the companies, in fact encourages the host countries to continue to proceed as they see fit. We have thus entered a period in international oil of near "lawlessness" in the relationship between producing countries, the oil companies and the importing countries.

The issues are not only supply and price stability. They also include exploration and development efforts that are now exclusively dependent on policies of producing countries, which obviously are not interested in creating any surplus of supplies that might endanger OPEC prices.

Moreover, especially since 1979, producing countries have cut back the oil they supply to the major international oil companies, frequently below the level of their direct requirements. The "Internationals," therefore, can no longer provide oil supplies to third parties as in the past. More and more of the oil is sold directly (or sometimes through trading companies) by producing to importing countries. As a matter of fact, the share of the Internationals in world oil trade has declined from 78 percent in 1974 to about 44 percent in 1979, and is declining even further.

At the same time, the terms imposed by producing countries for oil supplies include more and more political and other extraneous conditions, related, for instance, to the interest of the producing countries in the Palestinian problem, or in their nuclear capabilities or in the political postures of their government customers.

Thus, oil companies no longer perform an effective independent role as a buffer in the relationship between oil-producing and oil-importing countries. They have practically no bargaining leverage with regard to any decisions affecting their operations in producing countries. Moreover, any action by OPEC on supplies or prices that would lead to a higher cost of its oil would, as OPEC is fully aware, also tend to benefit the oil companies, as their own non-OPEC production would also become more valuable.

This is at best a messy situation all around, where the producing countries can have it nearly all their way, because there are no countervailing powers they have to consider. The only question they face is whether, because of their own interest in the economic and political well-being of their customers, it would be prudent for them to exercise self-restraint.

This interdependence is indeed a very weak reed to lean on. It is unlikely to become a controlling factor in the decision-making process of OPEC countries as long as the various importing countries and their oil companies, in the spirit of *sauve qui peut,* are willing to go to practically any length in order to secure their individual oil supplies.

IV

Ideally, one might perhaps have hoped that the major importing countries would have formulated an effective energy policy, and also established a coordinated approach to OPEC with regard to supply and financial problems caused by its actions. Instead, what has dominated international oil relations has been the fear of importing countries and their companies that OPEC may cut off their supplies, or impose even stiffer conditions at the slightest sign of resistance or of a common policy approach by the importing countries. The latter have acted as if they were in such a weak position that in order to obtain continued supplies they must act separately and try to gain favors by ingratiating themselves with OPEC countries by any means feasible.

This policy has been a failure. And the experience of 1979, previously described, has demonstrated how ineffectiveness resulting from fear and lack of common purpose has badly hurt the West, and in fact accelerated the disintegration and Balkanization of the world oil economy. Now again individual importing countries move in various directions, each one suspicious of the other, while pretending on the surface some desire for a unified approach.

The International Energy Agency (IEA), which was specifically established to deal with emergency supply situations, operates under terms of reference which do not allow it to deal with the actual situations as posed now or for that matter in 1979. And when its terms of reference did in fact permit it to intervene, the Agency apparently tried its utmost to avoid any actions, perhaps out of fear that OPEC might not like it.

Without going into details, it would appear that in order to cope with current problems where oil importers might be confronted by OPEC countries with extraneous or detrimental terms on supply or on pricing, the importing countries should agree among themselves on a common policy, backed up by an allocation scheme—as we had earlier suggested as the appropriate response to the problems of 1979.[1] Interestingly enough, Saudi Oil Minister [Ahmed] Zaki Yamani recently suggested that the developed and developing countries should jointly adopt a scheme for the equitable distribution of world energy consumption.

Under such a scheme, all the quantities available on regular terms should be shared equitably among the various countries. It would at least reduce the fears of some countries or companies of being left out of the supply stream unless they were prepared to make special deals on basically unreasonable terms—which, when once accepted, might set the pattern for all later OPEC transactions.

However, it is clear that as a result of recent developments affecting the international oil trade, it has now become much more difficult for importing countries and their oil companies to participate in an international oil allocation program. Any allocation scheme would require some redistribution of the flow of world oil; it is predicated on a substantial degree of flexibility in the world oil supply system that had previously been assured by the dominant role of the international oil companies in controlling and directing most of the movements of oil in world trade. As mentioned earlier, this role has now been greatly reduced.

Instead, restrictions on destinations in many recent OPEC export

1. See Walter J. Levy, "A Warning to the Oil-Importing Nations," *Fortune*, May 21, 1979, p. 48.

contracts and the proliferation of direct oil supply deals between the governments of importing countries and OPEC national oil companies might deprive the importers of the necessary flexibility for the diversions of oil shipments. Moreover, the importers might well fear that if they arrange any such diversion, the producing country might cancel their oil supply arrangements. And in those cases where the consuming country has obtained oil supplies only by granting the OPEC country special political or economic advantages, it would, in any case, most likely be reluctant to make such oil available for reallocation to other countries.

There is thus a clear and present danger that recent developments in the structure of world oil trade may have undermined the basis for the emergency reallocation system of the IEA and for a self-defense program of the importing countries as suggested here.

This is a matter for urgent consideration by the governments of the importing countries. They are now confronted with a challenge to their ability to try to cope as a group with major oil supply shortages or with a continued deterioration of the terms under which OPEC oil is made available to them.

The importing countries might well be unable to agree on a joint policy. But if they should fail to take a common stand on protecting their freedom to reallocate purchased oil among themselves, they would in fact endanger their capacity for an effective self-defense against a loss of vital oil supplies and hence seriously jeopardize their future economic, political and strategic viability.

V

We have discussed until now mainly the supply, financial and structural threats that are confronting world oil operations. The year 1979 also brought into the open the geopolitical and internal revolutionary dangers threatening oil-producing countries. The collapse of the Shah's regime and Soviet aggression in Afghanistan illustrate the vulnerability of practically every one of the producing countries. Moreover, the Iranian revolution has brought to power an extreme orthodox Muslim movement with grave anti-Western and xenophobic policies that might, if unchecked, spread far into the whole Muslim world.

All of this turmoil is accompanied by intraregional conflicts among the various countries, with continuously shifting alliances and hostilities. There are also the on-and-off relations between several of them and the Soviet Union, ranging from treaties of friendship and massive supplies of Soviet arms to complete elimination of Soviet influence.

There is also the perennial Arab-Israeli conflict, apparently eased by the Israeli-Egyptian peace treaty, but now ominously threatened by the possible failure of the Palestinian autonomy discussions. While a resolution of these issues will not solve the problem of oil relations between the importing countries and the Middle East, the lack of a solution – or even of visible progress – might at any time lead to a conflict which could jeopardize directly or indirectly the uninterrupted flow of oil, or its terms of trade. Needless to say, so long as this problem remains a festering sore the stability of the Sadat regime and of the peace treaty with Israel might also themselves be at stake.

Finally, we face the problem of the internal stability of most of the Middle East regimes. There is very little doubt about the antiquated nature of many of them, and the inadequacy of the existing governmental structures to cope with modern economic problems and cultural stresses to which the oil-producing countries and sheikdoms are now inevitably exposed. Rapid modernization backed by Western governments – in part, at least, because it helps to solve the petrodollar recycling problem – and supported by Western industry through the establishment of huge and sometimes excessive industrial and infrastructure projects is bound to have an explosive effect on Middle East societies.[2]

Nobody can predict when and how the governmental, social and cultural systems in the various countries will change so that they can cope effectively with the problems that confront them; but change they will, and, more likely than not, by convulsions or revolutions rather than through a process of gradual evolution. In the meantime, these countries remain exposed to the often destructive forces of rapid economic development; of foreign education; of huge unearned wealth coupled with immense corruption that enriches a small group of rulers, their relatives and hangers-on; of a massive influx of foreign labor which will do much of the work and may well become a restless and dissatisfied underclass. And waiting at the gates are, on the one hand, the forces of Muslim orthodoxy as manifested already in Iran and in the attack on the Mosque in Mecca; and on the other hand, the subversive forces of Marxism as they attempt to spread their philosophy throughout the area through the Soviet footholds in Afghanistan, Aden and the Horn of Africa.

There are, on all sides, many parties who benefit from the maintenance of the present situation. It is difficult to prepare an objective analysis of this problem, and even more so to have it accepted or even considered by the policymakers of the oil-producing and importing

2. See also Walter J. Levy, "The Years That the Locust Hath Eaten: Oil Policy and OPEC Development Prospects," *Foreign Affairs,* Winter 1978/79, pp. 287–305. [Chapter 20 in this book.]

countries—as the Iranian debacle so tragically and vividly demonstrated.

Minor or cosmetic reforms as they are now being planned in Iraq, Saudi Arabia, Kuwait and North Yemen are unlikely to stem this tide of internal and external instability and corrosion. Without going into details, the pervasive strength of all these forces is illustrated by the fact that 13 of the present Arab heads of state, or more than half of them, have reached power by forcibly removing their predecessors in one way or another; and in the past 15 years Arabs have fought Arabs in 12 fierce wars. This is the area on which, for better or for worse, we depend for stable oil supplies.

VI

Following the Soviet invasion of Afghanistan, President Carter announced that an attempt by any outside force to gain control of the Persian Gulf region would be regarded as an assault on the vital interests of the United States, and repelled by the use of any means necessary, including military force. This has now become the so-called Carter Doctrine.

It would appear that it was absolutely necessary to state clearly our overwhelming interest in Persian Gulf oil, on which we depend for over 30 percent of our oil imports, Western Europe for over 60 percent, and Japan for over 70 percent—and will continue to do so for many years to come. To have remained silent would certainly have been held against us by the producing countries and our Western allies—even though neither our allies nor the Persian Gulf countries have really given us their unqualified and open support once we spoke out.

But of course the Soviet threat to the area is of much longer standing: in Afghanistan the communist radicals seized power in April 1978; in the Arabian Peninsula the Soviets made earlier arrangements with communist South Yemen; and in the Horn of Africa the Soviets some time ago cooperated first with Somalia and then switched their support to Ethiopia.

To give some credibility to the Carter Doctrine, we have moved a substantial number of ships from the Sixth and Seventh Fleets into the area, denuding greatly our forces in the Mediterranean and in the Pacific. We are building up a Rapid Deployment Force and will provide in due course supporting services in terms of ships and airplanes through new supply stations in Kenya, Somalia and Oman—in addition to enlarging the base on Diego Garcia in the Indian Ocean.

With the countries in the area that are directly affected—such as Saudi Arabia, Kuwait, Iraq and Iran—our military relationship remains, however, somewhat tenuous and ambiguous. As a matter of fact, their official attitude toward the Soviet Union and the United States is more that of "a plague on both your houses." It is reflected in the Iraqi proposal for a charter for Arab neutrality in an East-West conflict, which has received support from many Arab countries.

There is also the Saudi opposition to the use of their oil production for increasing our woefully inadequate strategic stockpile, and the somewhat ambiguous statement by Crown Prince Fahd that if U.S. forces should ever invade Saudi Arabia to prevent an interruption of oil supplies, the most that can be done is to blow up the oilfields.

Furthermore, there are serious doubts as to how safely we can depend on those countries where we intend to establish supply stations, such as Somalia with its hostile attitude toward Ethiopia and Kenya, and Oman where everything hinges on the policy of the ruler, who has already played a very lonely game because of his support for the Camp David agreements. We know how these rulers come and go, or may change their minds. The disappointing experience with Pakistan when the Carter Administration tried to establish an effective cooperative relationship in early 1980 is indicative of the kind of problems U.S. efforts are facing nearly everywhere else.

Moreover, with the intraregional conflicts which have been rampant, and above all with the grave internal political instabilities of almost every country in the area, a political upheaval, or a foreign or locally inspired attack on regimes or oil facilities could occur at any time, even without Soviet overt or covert interference. In most instances, we will probably never know whether or not there was any Soviet direct or indirect involvement.

In actual practice, the Carter Doctrine may thus more likely than not involve us in an attempt to protect the status quo against internal upheavals or intraregional attacks. This would be a most difficult and probably impossible assignment for U.S. military forces.

Accordingly, the basis of cooperation with many of these countries, with their frequently wavering loyalties and alliances, and their often dubious or unclear motivations, may well prove to rest on feet of clay. In addition, our ability to project sufficient power into the area over distances of 6,000 miles or more against a nearby land-based superpower is limited. In any case, even if all should go well, it will take several years before the military buildup of our forces and the adequate preparation of new supply stations can be completed.

The one thing that seems to be certain is that if fighting in the Persian Gulf should erupt, the first targets that will be destroyed, either by foreign or local forces, are the vital oil facilities. Some 60 percent of Persian Gulf exports pass through three ports, with eight critical pump sites controlling the flow of oil. While the United States itself might be able to handle a sustained interruption in Gulf oil supplies through drastic belt tightening, this is emphatically not the case for Western Europe or Japan, and the very possibility of such an event is one of the major factors inhibiting the support of these nations for U.S. policy.

In short, it would appear that the Carter Doctrine, if it were ever to be tested, would of necessity mean that the United States would react against Soviet moves to control the Persian Gulf by military or other actions at times and places of its own choosing, but not necessarily in the Persian Gulf itself. The immediate importance of the Doctrine rests perhaps mainly in the assurance to the countries in the area that the United States is actively concerned about their fate, if the Soviets should ever attack them. Its real value is based on the hope that the Doctrine will be accepted as credible and prove to be a deterrent to the Soviet Union—and will thus never be tested.

But the Doctrine creates many more problems than those mentioned up to now. Not only are the Persian Gulf countries trying to keep any U.S. military effort at some distance, but it is also not at all certain how much support, if any, many of our NATO allies and Japan are prepared to give us—even though the loss of Persian Gulf oil would hit them much harder than us. Instead, some of them, especially the French, seem to prefer to work out for themselves and perhaps for Europe a new special political and economic relationship with the Persian Gulf oil producers. They try to obtain oil supply assurances on economic terms acceptable to them by agreeing to political and other conditions—such as on the Palestinian problem and on military and nuclear supplies—that would appeal to the producing countries.

At the same time they hope that the policy of détente can be maintained, and in due course include some understanding between Western countries and the U.S.S.R. on some kind of accommodation concerning the Persian Gulf area—even though the U.S.S.R., which is and probably will remain much less dependent on foreign oil than the Western countries, might well choose to have it all its own way.

In the light of all these factors, the effectiveness of the Carter Doctrine as a deterrent to the Soviet Union is at best uncertain. The people in the area already tend to look at it partly as a selfish attempt of the United States to protect its oil supplies, and partly as a means to keep conservative governments in power against internal or external regional opposition. And our allies, as mentioned, seem to be tempted to try to go their own way. In terms of achieving U.S. policy objectives, the Carter Doctrine might in the end prove to be as ineffective as was the Nixon Doctrine policy of the 1970s, which sought to establish regional security through a local national surrogate government such as Iran.

VII

The medium-term prospects for the security and availability of oil and for the economic and political stability and strategic security of the Western world are indeed disturbing. If we now consider the longer term outlook, the picture looks equally forbidding. Not only are all the economic and political problems to which we have already referred likely to remain with us; but in addition, even by the year 2000, the massive challenge of moving from a mostly oil-based energy economy worldwide to one that can largely draw on other more amply available energy resources will probably still remain largely unresolved.

A comprehensive and authoritative projection of the overall energy picture up to the year 2000 that is currently available is the Exxon publication, *World Energy Outlook,* released in early 1980. This study postulates a very high rate of expansion of energy production from non-oil sources during this period. Specifically, it forecasts a nearly 120 percent increase over 1980 in the non-communist world's use of coal; a more than quintupling of nuclear power; a more than doubling of hydro-power including solar, geothermal, etc.; and a buildup of synthetic fuel production from coal, tar sands, and oil shale, from virtually zero to 7 million barrels per day.

In addition, the Exxon projections reflect a highly successful effort in improving the efficiency of energy use. Between 1980 and 2000, the average annual growth of non-communist world Gross National Product, adjusted for inflation, is estimated at about 3.5 percent, while energy consumption is projected to grow at only 2.5 percent per annum. This reflects a substantially expanded conservation effort from the past. For example, according to Exxon statistics, between 1965 and 1973 energy use in the non-communist world grew more rapidly (5.5 percent per annum) than economic output (5.0 percent per annum).[3]

Even on such assumptions, however, the Exxon study concludes

3. In the case of the United States, the change is even more dramatic. For the period between 1978 and 1990, the economic growth rate in the United States is projected at about 2.5 to 3 percent per year, while the growth in total energy demand is projected at a rate of only 0.8 percent per year. This of course reflects the high consumption of energy in the United States and the resulting possibilities for a greater degree of conservation than is possible in other industrialized countries. In the same period, for example, energy demand in Europe is projected to rise by 2 percent annually and in Japan by 2.9 percent. For other nations than the United States, Canada, Europe and Japan, the projected growth in energy demand up to 1990 is 5.8 percent per year. The result, naturally, is a substantial progressive change in the percentages of total world energy demand by various countries and areas—with the United States dropping from 41 percent to 33 percent, and Europe from 27 percent to 26 percent, while the "other" countries increase their share from 19 percent to 28 percent. Exxon, *World Energy Outlook,* pp. 6–7, 26–31 (New York: Exxon Corp., 1980).

that there would remain in the year 2000 a demand for oil of 60 million barrels daily, which would be 15 percent above the 1978 demand level. Oil and gas combined would by the year 2000 contribute 86 million barrels daily oil equivalent, or 52 percent of total non-communist world energy demand as compared with 72 percent in 1978. Exxon also assumed that:

- The combined net oil exports from the Soviet Union, Eastern Europe, and the People's Republic of China to the rest of the world would remain roughly constant during the period, at 1.0 million barrels daily, with declines in availability from the Soviet Union offset by increasing amounts from China;

- total non-communist world oil production outside OPEC would increase by some 7 million barrels per day to 26 million barrels daily by the year 2000; and

- production (including natural gas liquids) still required from OPEC countries would, at 33 million barrels daily, be 10 percent above its 1978 level and amount to 55 percent of total non-communist world oil supply in the year 2000.

The average annual addition to oil reserves through new discoveries in the non-communist world, between 1980 and 2000, was projected by Exxon to range between 9 and 15 billion barrels. To assess the reserve-to-production ratio for the year 2000, let us use the figure of 12 billion barrels, the midpoint of this range. Accordingly, the reserve-to-production ratio would decline from 31 years in 1980 to roughly 20 years by the year 2000. For most of the producing countries, except for a few of the oil-rich countries, the reserve-to-production ratio by the year 2000 would be 10 years or less.

In the meantime, with a continued decline in the reserve-to-production ratio during the 20-year period, it is almost inevitable that real prices for oil would take off. The ensuing financial and economic problems could far exceed those which would be incurred between 1980 and 1985 and would — within the framework of our society and institutions — appear to be beyond our current capacity to cope. Moreover, many of the producing countries would certainly, for reasons of economic or political policy or because of physical limits set by productive capacity, reduce their production when their reserve-to-production ratio declines below a certain minimum. There is thus a "self-destruct" element in the relationship between the projected size of oil production and the economic and political consequences that it could entail.

VIII

The question thus arises: If indeed the problems can be kept manageable, what must the importing countries do to assure their future political, economic and strategic viability?

From all that has been said so far, it would appear that the oil importers would probably need 30 years or more to create an energy economy based overwhelmingly on sources other than oil—and even this goal might not be achievable if we wished to sustain a viable rate of economic progress. During the 30 years-plus when we must surely still very much rely on oil, a large part of that oil must be obtained from the oil-rich countries of the Persian Gulf. Even in the unlikely case that within the next 10 to 15 years massive new discoveries should be made, comparable to those of the Middle East, it would take perhaps some 10 additional years before they could be fully developed.

It is thus imperative—during the period when the importing countries must procure each year more than 25 million barrels a day from OPEC producers and some additional substantial quantities from non-OPEC sources such as Mexico—that the real price of oil be kept at a manageable level. This may well mean that for some time to come prices should not increase at a much higher rate than that of inflation. The underlying concept would have to be that oil must be conceived in terms of a "common heritage of mankind" that must serve both the welfare of the producing countries and that of the importing countries.

That might well be considered to be an unrealistic utopian fantasy, especially as it would have to be based on an accommodation between oil producers and oil importers where both parties take full account of each other's vital interests. Above all it presupposes that the United States, the Soviet Union and possibly China agree on common principles that would apply to their policies affecting the area, and thus would be willing to abstain from any actions that might interfere with the maintenance or establishment of peace and tranquility in the Middle East.

Specifically, it would require the conclusion of effective arrangements between oil-importing and producing countries on the size of needed oil exports, on a sustainable level of prices, on the planning and implementation of development programs for producing countries and on many other areas of concern to all the parties involved.

It would also imply that the threat of instability within producing countries and that of intraregional quarrels in the Middle East would be contained and neutralized. Within the Middle East, the Arab-Israeli conflict must be concluded, which in fact means that the autonomy issue and the Palestinian problem must be equitably resolved. But there are many other potentially explosive quarrels affecting the region—such as those centering around Lebanon; or the relationship between Iran, Iraq and other Arab countries; that of South versus North Yemen; the isolation of Egypt within the Arab world; the problems that are posed by the Libyan attitude towards its neighbors; and so on.

Within the various Middle East countries, the modernization of their political systems and of their economies must proceed without upsetting their traditional values. The new Orthodox Muslim movement, as it might be spreading from Iran, might otherwise engulf all those forces in the area that are seeking to achieve reasonable political and economic progress.

If all this were possible, we could probably solve the major problems that are related to the world's long-term dependence on Middle East oil. However, this kind of scenario does not reflect the world as it is now and is likely to be in the future; and we have not much reason to hope that the various producing countries, the importing countries, and the super-powers will ever agree on such a rational course of conduct—especially as the immediate dependence of the Soviet Union on Middle East oil is less than that of the United States and of most other Western nations.

Instead, we will probably be confronted by a series of major oil crises which might take any or all of several forms: fighting for control over oil resources among importing countries or between the superpowers; an economic-financial crisis in importing countries; regional conflicts affecting the oil-producing area; or internal revolutions or other upheavals in the Middle East. At best, it would appear that a series of future emergencies centering around oil will set back world progress for many, many years. And the world, as we know it now, will probably not be able to maintain its cohesion, nor be able to provide for the continued economic progress of its people against the onslaught of future oil shocks—with all that this might imply for the political stability of the West, its free institutions, and its internal and external security.

22

Oil: An Agenda
for the 1980s

I

A year ago, in reviewing the problems of oil supplies and Western security, I focused on the deplorable developments that had occurred during 1979, and emphasized the grave dangers involved if most of the oil-consuming nations remained dependent on oil from the Organization of Petroleum Exporting Countries and were unable to achieve effective international coordination of their energy policies. [See preceding paper.] It now appears appropriate to examine how circumstances have changed—or remained unchanged—during the intervening year and to suggest lines of action, for both the short- and medium-term, that should be pursued vigorously.

Events since the spring of 1980 continue to make apparent the inherent dangers for the non-communist world of dependence on insecure sources of oil supplies. Despite generally abundant oil availability, OPEC nations raised official crude oil prices from an average of $20 per barrel in September 1979 to $32 per barrel by August 1980. In the following month came yet another major oil supply disruption, this time the result of the outbreak of war between the two OPEC nations, Iraq and Iran. This war, which still continues, brought about a sudden reduction of approximately four million barrels daily (b/d) in available world oil supplies, and for a while threatened an upheaval of the same magnitude as followed the 1978–79 Iranian Revolution.

However, this time the major oil-consuming nations and their oil companies were in a considerably stronger position. Very substantial oil inventories had been accumulated in response to events of the previous year. Through the availability of these stocks, weak oil demand, and the prompt Saudi Arabian action of increasing its production to partially offset lost Iranian and Iraqi oil exports, the importing nations managed to avoid the disastrous spot-market competition which had done so much to cause the price explosion of 1979. Nevertheless, in December 1980, the OPEC nations imposed still further price increases, bringing the level of permitted "maximum" official sales prices up to $41 per barrel. And,

Reprinted with permission from *Foreign Affairs*, Summer 1981, pp. 1081–1101.

by January 1981, the average of official OPEC sales prices had risen to $35 per barrel.

The ensuing world oil glut and accompanying price weakness served to highlight the crucial role of Saudi Arabia within OPEC. The Saudi decision to increase its production from a "normal" level of 8.5 to 10.2 million b/d and to maintain its "marker" crude price at $32 per barrel represented a determined effort to persuade other OPEC nations to moderate their price increases. These Saudi actions helped the major oil-consuming countries to fare much better than might have been expected in the face of the Iraqi and Iranian supply reductions.

Meanwhile, the combination of three factors — economic recession in the industrialized nations, the progressive removal of price controls on oil produced in the United States, and the response of international oil markets in general to substantially higher oil prices — began to have a major impact on oil demand. Oil consumption dropped significantly in Western Europe, Japan and especially the United States — where the required level of oil imports declined to 6.5 million b/d in the first quarter of 1981 from 7.9 million b/d over the same period a year earlier. It began to appear that improved energy conservation together with the expansion of non-oil energy sources might lead to a situation where future requirements for OPEC oil would be very substantially lower than had been generally forecast prior to 1981.

At the same time, the position of OPEC countries was beginning to show signs of fundamental change. The Iranian Revolution had brought home to all of them the grave dangers of forced-draft economic development, with all its difficult political and social implications. Most of these nations also were concerned about the drastic impact of worldwide inflation on the value of investments they were continuing to make in the industrialized world. Thus, many OPEC nations increasingly emphasized the desirability of limiting output, so as to produce only the amounts of revenue needed for their national economic needs. Moreover, they increasingly realized that if in fact they limited production and exports, they could in many circumstances expect to see substantial price rises in the resulting tight oil market. And they might be able to cover their revenue needs even with lower levels of production.

In contrast, other OPEC members, Saudi Arabia in particular, demonstrated an acute awareness of the potential damage that would be inflicted on both major industrialized nations and less-developed countries by a policy of limiting output in order to raise real (inflation-discounted) oil prices. The Saudis also realized that such higher prices, by accelerating the pace of conservation and production of oil and non-oil energy substitutes outside OPEC countries, could seriously restrict current, and even more so future, levels of demand for OPEC oil. But, with the first group of OPEC countries strongly resisting the Saudi policy of price moderation, the Saudis have been unable to achieve their goal of a unified pricing structure for OPEC. The OPEC meeting at Geneva in May 1981 again failed to reach agreement, with both sides maintaining their price positions (stabilizing prices for the time being, possibly for the rest of 1981), the majority of the participants agreeing on a 10 percent reduction in output, but the Saudis adhering to their present production level of 10.2 million b/d. The continuing conflict within OPEC underscores how difficult and complex a task it remains for consuming nations to reach any meaningful accord with OPEC on long-term pricing and supply policies.

These latest developments, following the major structural changes of the international oil industry from the early 1970's, raise questions which must be addressed from a long-term perspective. In the following analysis, I will review the problems posed for the world oil economy during the 1980's — a period for which the strategic, economic and physical preconditions are, to a substantial degree, already apparent. The main thrust of this analysis will be directed toward the issues posed in achieving a balanced accommodation between the vital interests of oil importers and exporters, and the consequences that might ensue if such effort should unfortunately fail.

First we must consider the outlook for oil in the non-communist world. Do the circumstances of the present oil glut indicate that the world's oil importers will cease to be perilously dependent on OPEC oil exports?

Second, how can the oil-consuming nations better marshal their existing and potential energy resources in an effort to ease the extent and consequences of continued dependence on imported oil? This has to do not only with massive production and conservation efforts but with much more effective coordination of policies to deal with potential disruptions of oil supplies.

Third, assuming that the oil-importing countries are able to achieve comprehensive energy policies, how might such policies assist in moving toward an essential accommodation with the oil-exporting countries, and what are the realistic prospects for such an accommodation?

And finally, what actions are needed to contain and possibly deter contingencies which could disrupt the vital flow of oil from the OPEC countries, especially those in the Persian Gulf? In this regard, what must be considered are not only the dangers of Soviet actions, but also intraregional conflicts, political turbulence or changes of regime in individual producing countries, and the threats that might be posed by drastic changes in the oil policy of one or more producing countries.

II

The experience of the past 18 months is clearly reflected in the latest authoritative projections of world energy balances in the 1980s. Taking account both of the sharp decline of oil demand that has already taken place and of the continued stimulus of higher real oil prices on energy conservation and production of oil and non-oil energy resources outside OPEC, most forecasts now generally anticipate only slight, if any, expansion in non-communist world oil demand over the decade. In contrast, forecasts made as recently as the late 1970s, although projecting only a moderate rate of oil demand growth, nevertheless typically projected a substantial increase in the volume of oil required.

Thus, the latest comprehensive projection by Exxon concludes that oil demand in the non-communist world, excluding OPEC countries, will remain approximately unchanged at 50 million b/d through the decade, with the demand of OPEC countries themselves raising the overall total from 53 to 56 million b/d by 1990.[1]

These Exxon projections are predicated on only moderate real growth of the non-communist world's gross national product (GNP)—three percent per year versus five percent over the 1960s, but roughly comparable to the economically troubled 1970s—and on very substantial further improvements in the efficiency of energy utilization. (In the case of the United States, for instance, there would be a projected decline of energy required per thousand dollars of GNP from 5.9 barrels per day of oil equivalent in 1979 to 4.8 barrels by 1990—in terms of constant 1979 dollars.) On these assumptions, but taking account of substantial increases in consumption among the less developed countries, total non-communist world energy consumption would increase from 98 to 125 million b/d of oil equivalent (b/doe) over this period, or an average annual rate of growth of 2.2 percent.

Exxon anticipates massive development of non-oil energy resources between 1979 and 1990. Total non-oil energy supplies would increase from 45 to 69 million b/doe and their share in meeting non-communist world energy demand would increase from 46 percent in 1979 to 55 percent by 1990. For example:

- Gas supply would rise from 18 to 23 million b/doe despite the effects of sharply declining production from current sources of supply.

- Coal output would advance from 17 to 26 million b/doe even

---

1. Exxon, *World Energy Outlook* (New York: Exxon Corp., 1980).

excluding expanding volumes of coal used in the production of synthetic oil and gas.

- The combined contribution of nuclear, hydro, geothermal, solar, gasohol, and other miscellaneous sources of commercial energy would rise from 10 to just under 20 million b/doe, accounting for the largest part of the non-communist world's incremental energy supply.

Reflecting the increased incentives provided by higher real oil prices on efforts for exploration and development of new sources of oil supply, total oil production outside OPEC is forecast to advance from 21 million b/d in 1979 to 26 million in 1990. This increase would include a rapid commercial expansion of synthetic liquids production (from such sources as shale oil, tar sands and coal), which would rise from current fractional amounts to upwards of 2 million b/d. To meet the non-communist world's oil needs of 56 million b/d, the level of OPEC production required would still be 30 million b/d, less than the 32 million b/d OPEC produced in 1979 but 5 million b/d above the currently depressed OPEC production level of approximately 25 million b/d.

The Exxon projections also indicate that during the present decade annual non-communist world oil production will exceed new discoveries, and accordingly, the reserves-to-production ratio will decline from 29 years to about 24 years by 1990. This is predicated on the assumption that OPEC countries maintain their oil output at levels that accommodate the future needs of the oil-importing countries and do not restrict production in order to stretch the life of their reserves.

In sum, although it now appears that conservation and alternate energy supplies will combine to make oil demand a significantly smaller percentage of total energy use than it has been in the past two decades, the projections still indicate a major oil requirement and continued substantial dependence on OPEC oil. Even if the total oil demand should fall by 1990 substantially below that projected by Exxon, there is no realistic prospect that either the major industrialized countries or the less developed countries can become anywhere near self-sufficient or reliant on non-OPEC sources.

Moreover, as the current world oil surplus well illustrates, the world remains enormously dependent on the production policies followed by one key OPEC country, Saudi Arabia. However, the Saudi policy of maintaining its oil production well in excess of market requirements and at prices well below the general OPEC level provides no realistic basis for anticipating long-term oil market weakness. In an interview on U.S. television, Saudi Oil Minister [Ahmed Zaki] Yamani bluntly described the 1981 oil situation as a glut that "we engineered . . . in order to stabilize the price of oil." [He] also indicated that the Saudis could "live happily" by reducing their production from over 10 million b/d to as little as 6 million b/d if such a reduction were required to support a unified OPEC pricing policy.

If world oil demand should remain depressed and if surplus production should continue (reflecting either a continuation of current Saudi production policies or the effects of possible restoration of Iranian and Iraqi production, or both), real oil prices will tend to decline as long as such conditions prevail. However, it is extremely unlikely that the Saudis would continue their present policy if oil prices were to tumble below the current Saudi level. Moreover, protracted oil market weakness and declining real oil prices would inevitably retard energy conservation, slow the pace of development of non-OPEC energy resources and thereby detract from efforts by oil importers to decrease dependence on OPEC oil.

Up to now we have focused our review of prospects for world energy balances on the distribution of oil supply and demand for oil-importing countries as a whole, rather than for individual countries. There are, however, widely divergent degrees of dependence on imported oil as between the United States (37 percent of oil supply in 1980), Western Europe (81 percent) and Japan (virtually 100 percent). But all of us have become so interdependent in our political, economic and strategic exposure that there is no individual salvation for any one country. If the United States, for instance, were able to achieve a substantial degree of energy independence, it would of course be an extremely welcome development. However, the less fortunate circumstances of our allies would, nevertheless, still dangerously impinge upon us.

Moreover, even if oil-importing countries do their utmost to reduce their import dependency, and OPEC countries maintain levels of oil production as needed by oil importers and establish a pricing and development policy which (at least from their viewpoint) might be described as moderate, the potential financial effects on the overall well-being of the oil-importing world could still be grievous. For the poorer industrialized and less developed countries, it could be even crushing.

In addition to the continuing economic vulnerability of the importers, the events of the past 18 months have again underscored the variety and depth of the political and strategic problems which affect the Persian Gulf. These could, at practically any time and any place, interrupt oil production and thus supplies to importing countries—as they have now done three separate times in the past eight years. Contingencies could arise from the Soviet threat, regional fighting, internal upheavals, terrorism, the festering Arab-Israeli issue, or a sudden shift in the production and pricing policy of one or more OPEC countries. It is nearly certain that we will have to cope with one or even several of these contingencies in the years ahead.

The overriding conclusion is thus inevitable. Even in the short- to medium-term no firm reliance can safely be placed on the future availability of the required volumes of Middle East oil at manageable prices. If nothing else, the experience of the 1970s should have taught us this. In spite of the present world oil glut, the outlook for most of the 1980s still looks to be highly precarious and, accordingly, it would be extremely imprudent if oil importers were to base their planning for the future on current market conditions.

III

In facing the prospects of long-term dependence on imported oil and uncertain oil balances, the consumer nations must redouble their efforts toward instituting a comprehensive, coordinated energy policy. The consumer nations must deal with two types of problems which require close cooperation—improving their energy resources position and coping with oil supply contingencies. It would be the height of folly if efforts to cope with these problems were relaxed because of current easing of world oil balances. These issues should be confronted now in the calm of loose world oil balances rather than later in the storm of some future crisis.

Once in place, a coordinated policy is essential for an effective accommodation between importers and exporters. Except during the present phase of a supply glut, individual importing countries and their oil companies have in the past acquiesced in practically any demand by OPEC countries regarding the volume and price of oil supply and even certain political terms as well. They have been inclined to do so out of fear that refusal to submit to the stipulated terms and conditions might jeopardize their ongoing oil supply position. It is not surprising that oil producers have acquired an unrealistic sense of their own power. Unfortunately, they have thus acted as if they could afford to ignore the real degree of interdependence between the political, economic and strategic welfare of the importing and producing countries.

During the 1970s, the essential failure of oil importers to achieve effective cooperation among themselves can be traced, to a considerable extent, to the major shortcomings of U.S. energy policy and the consequent inability of the United States to provide world leadership. After the 1973–74 oil price shock, artificially low oil prices and a rapid buildup of oil imports made it extremely difficult for the United States to assume a constructive role vis-à-vis the rest of the oil-importing world in the coordination of international energy policy initiatives. However, as a result of decontrol of oil prices, sharply declining oil imports, and a revived commitment to building the Strategic Petroleum Reserve, the United States is now in a much stronger position to induce, if not insist on, cooperation among consumer nations.

A comprehensive resources policy on the part of consumer nations must deal with a number of complex issues. Concerted endeavors are vital on the following fronts:

- An optimum energy conservation effort must be pursued through the operation of the price mechanism, tax incentives and other suitable measures. It should be noted, however, that there are obvious limits to how far conservation can successfully be carried before the cost of achieving additional energy savings would exceed the benefits to be derived. Equally, economic vulnerability to any future supply shortfall would increase as conservation progresses because there would be that much less "conservation fat" left.

- A sustained program for oil and gas exploration and development must be put into place, supported by the necessary price and tax incentives. Wherever possible, the creation of a surge productive capacity that would only be available during supply emergencies should be encouraged. In addition, technological and financial assistance for oil projects of LDCs should be extended.

- A policy to replace oil and gas by coal, wherever feasible, should be pursued through investment, tax and other incentives. But if this should prove to be insufficient, direct government involvement may be required; mere market forces may not in all instances be effective, as in the case where electric utilities are able automatically to pass on higher oil costs to their customers. Additionally, an internationally coordinated research effort should be undertaken to cope with the environmental hazards of expanded coal use such as air pollution, acid rain, and the problems that might be posed by the possible "greenhouse effect" (i.e., a warming of the earth's atmosphere with a potentially dangerous rise in the level of ocean waters bringing possible detrimental consequences for coastal areas and also for agriculture).

- The production of synthetic oil and gas should be established and expanded as a matter of highest priority. In addition to a multinational cooperative effort on synthetic fuels research, joint efforts may also be necessary for the commercial development of new productive facilities because of the concentration of coal, shale oil, tar sands, and very heavy crude oil in relatively few countries. In this respect, curtailment of the operations of the newly-created U.S. Synthetic Fuels Corporation may well prove to be counter-productive. Because of unresolved technological problems, the huge financial cost involved, and the long-deferred and uncertain payout from investment, it is highly questionable whether private industry will launch as massive an effort in this field as is required without substantial government support.

- International cooperation in nuclear research and development is essential, with the problems of waste disposal, nuclear proliferation and plant safety deserving particular attention. In light of the uncertain nature of future energy balances, a large contribution of nuclear energy would be most helpful, if not essential, especially for the many oil-importing countries with a small or virtually non-existent national energy resource base. Accordingly, the development of atomic energy should only be curtailed if the reasons for doing so, after the most exhaustive inquiry, are overwhelming. And even then, international efforts to curtail nuclear energy would probably fail, not only because the Soviet Union would be unlikely to subscribe to such an effort, but also because many energy-starved countries might not agree.

- Finally, a major research effort on a coordinated international basis is warranted for the development of energy from so-called exotic sources (e.g., solar, wind and tidal water power) despite the very limited early contribution to energy supplies that can be expected. There is always the chance of a technological breakthrough that could change future prospects.

In addition to establishing a mutually cooperative and progressive energy resources policy, consumer nations must move to develop more effective means of coping with oil supply disruptions. The absence of effective oil importer coordination greatly contributed to the 1973–74 and 1979 oil price explosions. A responsible policy for energy coordination among oil importers must reflect the underlying likelihood of future supply emergencies.

First, the major importing countries should continue to pursue aggressive stockpiling of substantial oil reserves that would be available for use during future crises. The management of oil stocks must be made subject to a joint or coordinated policy as agreed upon by the relevant oil-importing countries. Past experience has demonstrated that the actions of individual nations or companies can easily run counter to the common good. For instance, the special interests of countries or companies in assuring their future supply availability, or in benefitting from an appreciation of the value of their oil stocks as a result of crisis, might induce them to add to rather than withdraw from their reserves during an emergency. Such a course of actions would increase the severity of the crisis and contribute to the upward pressure on prices, as occurred during the Iranian upheaval in 1979.

Second, the oil-importing countries and their companies must agree not to purchase oil at above OPEC official sales prices during a crisis period or at least be penalized if they should do so. This is necessary because importing countries and their companies are tempted to purchase oil at excessive spot-market prices during periods of actual or even feared future supply shortages. Such transactions do not increase total oil supplies but only serve to redistribute such supplies among importers, forcing countries that are thereby deprived of imports into the spot market at ever-escalating prices. In due course, such higher prices tend to establish a new official level of prices as established by OPEC. All of this has occurred in the past and will continue to do so if there is no policy in place for pre-crisis and crisis cooperation.

Third, there is a need for a policy of equitable sharing of oil supplies among the various importing countries during periods of actual shortages. As presently constituted, the International Energy Agency's oil sharing mechanism is only triggered by a seven percent shortfall. This is clearly inadequate inasmuch as an oil price explosion can occur well before the trigger-level is reached. The terms of reference for the IEA should thus be revised to permit an earlier response to an oil supply crisis. An effective policy for the international sharing of supplies would also tend to reduce the pressure on importing countries and oil companies to obtain their requirements on the spot market at whatever cost.

Since the dismal 1979 experience, which pointed up the need for further oil-importer coordination, the IEA Secretariat has been endeavoring to obtain approval from member countries for more responsive crisis management policies. Unfortunately, some of the important IEA countries have continued to resist such changes. It would be most unfortunate for all concerned if such disagreements could not be resolved before the world is confronted by a new supply emergency.

IV

In addition to the energy problems facing oil-importing countries, there are also massive difficulties that confront oil exporters. Oil importers can ignore these only at their own peril. Cooperation, however, can provide a basis for an effective reconciliation of their diverse interest.

To assess the main lines of action for potential importer-exporter accommodation, I will draw upon the underlying assumptions, pricing proposals and policy suggestions contained in the thoughtful report prepared by OPEC's Long-Term Strategy Committee. This committee of OPEC specialists (under the chairmanship of Saudi Oil Minister Yamani since its inception in 1978) presented its recommendations at a special conference of OPEC ministers in May 1980. Although it has become increasingly uncertain whether these specific proposals will be implemented ([the chairman] himself now indicates that some of the committee's proposals may be inappropriate because of changed oil market conditions), the Strategy Report still provides an excellent basis for consideration of issues which must be addressed in order for oil importers and exporters to reach a realistic understanding.[2]

In its outlook for future world oil balances, the Strategy Report cited the growing reluctance of producing countries to produce oil at rates higher than needed for internal development. Fundamentally, this reflects OPEC's preference, if completely uninhibited, to produce only as much oil as needed for its local demand plus a level of exports that would provide for its revenue requirements. Producing countries would, obviously, be very much interested in extending the life of their reserves and the time span during which they could count on substantial oil revenues. With the nagging doubts about the success of efforts to build up viable national economies (not primarily dependent on oil revenues) and concerns about the many economic and social problems that rapid and forced industrial development pose, many OPEC officials would consider a lower rate of oil production and economic development as more responsive to their national welfare and interest. The maintenance by OPEC of higher levels of output than their national economies require thus imposes distinct obligations on the oil-importing world which it cannot afford to ignore—provided that importing countries, in turn, are able to secure adequate supplies of OPEC oil at prices they can afford to pay.

Steps by oil importers to assist OPEC in achieving its long-term objectives for industrialization must cover a wide range of issues. Oil-importing countries must not consider OPEC purchases mainly as a means for recouping as fast as possible their petrodollar outlays. While it might be difficult to discourage some OPEC countries from engaging in

2. Although the text of this report has not been officially released, its key recommendations have been widely summarized both in trade and general publications. My specific point of reference is the summary contained in a special supplement to *Platts's Oilgram*, May 6, 1980. It is noteworthy that the May 1981 Geneva meeting of OPEC directed the Committee to conduct a "further review of OPEC's long-term strategy and present a report to the conference as soon as possible." *New York Times*, May 27, 1981, p. D13.

uneconomic or otherwise unsound projects, it should at least be tried, especially where the ultimate futility of such expenditures is only too obvious. However, as long as importing countries and companies compete among themselves for lucrative OPEC contracts without any coordination, each one would feel that if it did not get the order, some competing firm would. Similar considerations should apply to the sales of military equipment which can either not effectively be used by the oil-exporting country, or which might lead to overmilitarization, and provoke adventurism and regional conflict. Such self-restraint by Western suppliers can obviously not be achieved easily – if at all – especially as individual OPEC countries may be determined to proceed with certain industrial or military purchases. But a coordinated effort to establish a rational approach to this problem must at least be attempted.

Importing countries must also be prepared to accept the output of new OPEC industrial facilities without discrimination. Admittedly, this might present problems when such output would replace production from existing facilities within the oil-importing world, or when, as is frequently the case, such output is subsidized by non-commercial local supply of energy or feedstock for, say, petrochemical production, and/or financed by non-commercial loans. In the latter type of situation, depending on the circumstances, the imposition of some countervailing duties may have to be considered. Nevertheless, to reach a mutual accommodation of long-term economic interests for both sides, constructive and determined efforts must be made to deal with these issues.

Oil exporters must also be provided non-discriminatory access to investment opportunities for their surplus funds within importer countries. This would lead to an increase of OPEC ownership in the importers' domestic means of production, including equity interest in corporations, real estate and so on. Where exclusions from such ownership are necessary for security or other essential national interests, they must be applied only on a non-discriminatory basis. Moreover, consideration might also be given by appropriate international institutions to make available to producing countries non-transferable, no- or low-interest bearing bonds that are indexed against inflation.[3]

A closely related area requiring exporter-importer cooperation is the establishment of effective mechanisms to provide financing for oil-related deficits of the weaker oil-importing countries. Private financial institutions which up to now have handled a substantial part of this transfer may over a period of time not be able to continue at the levels

---

3. For further details, see my "Recycling Surplus Petrodollars via Internationally Insured Indexed Energy Bonds," *Middle East Economic Survey*, 7 April 1980 (Supplement), pp. 1–7, and *The Institutional Investor*, July 1980, pp. 77–82.

that would be required. Also, there may be a need for arranging for a lender of last resort to supplement, or perhaps even to replace, a sizable part of the private recycling flows.

In dealing with the oil-related financial problems of the less developed oil importing nations, the OPEC strategy document proposed that an international aid progam be set up to provide LDCs with financial assistance through loans or grants for balance-of-payments and development purposes. To accomplish this objective, OPEC suggested that a new international organization be established jointly by OPEC and industrialized countries to provide financial aid and technical expertise for the development of the LDCs' energy resources.[4]

OPEC countries with large financial accumulations must be brought increasingly into the international financial support network. Since their own prospects for economic development depend on the solvency of their oil customers, it is obviously very much in their own interests that OPEC countries increasingly cooperate with the financially strong oil-importing countries and international financial institutions. In this way a financing and transfer program could be established that would extend over a number of years, rather than operate on an uncoordinated short-term or ad hoc basis. The implementation of such a financial assistance program, however, would pose many negotiating problems such as that of respective OPEC-OECD financial contributions. In this connection, it should be also noted that the World Bank last year proposed to set up an energy affiliate, to be jointly financed by OPEC, the OECD and the Bank. This effort, it was hoped, would lead to a doubling of energy production by the oil-importing LDCs from the current 7.8 million b/d oil equivalent to over 15 million b/d by 1990, resulting in gross foreign exchange savings at present prices of about $90 billion. It is to be regretted that the United States recently announced that it will neither support the creation of such an organization nor participate in it; I hope this decision will be reconsidered.

The pivotal issue of oil pricing must also be directly confronted as part of the framework for eventual exporter-importer accommodation. OPEC's Strategy Report suggested that oil prices should increase in line with the impact of inflation on international trade and with changes in certain currencies. There also would be a gradual rise in real oil prices—related to the real growth of GNP in OECD countries.[5]

4. According to the strategy paper, OPEC's contribution would be based on the cost to LDCs of future oil-price increases, put at $3.4 billion per year and that of the industrialized countries would be related to the rate of inflation of goods exported by them to the LDCs, estimated by OPEC at $9.3 billion annually.
5. According to OPEC's tentative estimates, the inflation adjustment might be six to nine percent a year, and if the GNP of OECD countries were to advance on the average by three

The Strategy Report's pricing position, however, does not answer the key question of what oil price level would provide a reasonable and acceptable base for future escalation under a long-term pricing formula. During the period between 1978 and May 1980, when the OPEC committee prepared its strategy document, crude oil prices rose from about $13 per barrel to some $30 per barrel—a rate of increase far in excess of the committee's own pricing policy proposal. Moreover, OPEC itself stated that "oil prices should in the long-term approximate the cost level of alternative energy supply" and, as [Saudi Oil Minister] Yamani explained, this ultimate level should be attained "gradually, not all at once."

Present OPEC prices have even as of now substantially reached the estimated cost of some alternative supplies.[6] Moreover, any realistic approach to oil pricing must provide for a decline as well as for an increase of the real and also the nominal price of OPEC oil when circumstances warrant it. At this time, there is clearly no valid reason for an advance in the real price of OPEC oil. Rather—in line with the Report's own stated policy goals—real oil prices should decline, as it will take many years before substantial quantities of alternative energy can become available. This issue is a proper subject for review by OPEC countries and the importing nations.

In dealing with the problems posed by oil shortages, the OPEC strategy document made a number of recommendations. For the financially weak less-developed oil-importing nations, the Report advocated, as a general policy, preferential treatment for the security of oil supplies on the basis of an internal agreement among all OPEC members.[7] The Report also suggested that some price restraint may be called for during shortages because the "bulk of crude and demand for petroleum products is influenced more by the policies of producing and consuming governments than by a free market equilibrium." Once a shortage is over, it considered the possibility of two options—either freezing prices in real terms until the floor price catches up or, alternatively, establishing a new floor price and moving from there.

This suggestion for price restraint during future supply disruptions, if

percent per annum, this would result in an average floor price increase of some 10 percent a year. In nominal terms, prices would thus double every seven years. If this kind of adjustment had been applied between 1974 and 1980, OPEC prices would have risen from $10.84 to $24.26 per barrel. In fact, prices now are some 50 percent above this level, largely because during the 1979 oil supply crisis, spot prices increased widely, followed by a substantial jump in OPEC prices.

6. For example, one major oil company recently stated that shale oil and intermediate Btu gas from coal appear to be competitive with oil at current prices.

7. As LDC oil demand (as also OPEC's own domestic requirements) is expanding much more rapidly than that of the industrialized world, the satisfaction of LDC consumption would require an ever-increasing proportion of total oil availabilities.

it could be implemented, is most constructive. What OPEC countries need for this purpose is the ability to draw on a substantial reserve productive capacity for dampening price increases during a period of oil shortage. Such a reserve could also provide for an unexpected surge in demand so as to make certain that it can be covered without discontinuities. Experience has shown that a mere supply/demand balance is not enough to eliminate upward pressure on prices. With a very uncertain future, maximum availability of oil should at least exceed world demand by several million b/d; otherwise the markets will get nervous. As asserted by the Report, "all the risks in supply forecasts are on the downside." Accordingly, the industrialized countries would require an OPEC assurance of secure oil supplies at manageable prices. Only then will it be possible to establish the confidence of importers in future oil availability.

Finally, how then to establish workable arrangements for future oil exporter/importer dialogues? The OPEC paper recommended starting with informal talks on selected issues with experts from a few countries on each side, to be followed, if successful, by formal OPEC-OECD discussions. This would appear to represent a realistic approach that should be acceptable to the importing countries. It is especially welcome that the strategy paper does not insist that oil discussions must also include all the outstanding issues between the industrialized world and the LDCs.

In practice, initial discussions should include those countries in the two groupings that would in fact have substantial capability to carry out the decisions reached, and would also possess sufficient influence to ensure that such decisions would be implemented by at least most of the other relevant members of their group. This might involve, as lead nations, Saudi Arabia, Kuwait, Venezuela, and, perhaps, Iraq on the side of OPEC; and the United States, Great Britain, Germany, France, Japan, and possibly Italy on the side of OECD.

V

Despite efforts to reach a balanced accommodation with the oil exporters and despite efforts to cope more effectively with oil supply disruptions, the oil-importing countries may nevertheless be confronted by contingencies that could endanger at any time the oil fields and transport routes to the importing countries. Even with Iraqi and Iranian production cut back to a very low level as a result of the war between the two countries, perhaps as much as 15 million b/d or about two-thirds of OPEC's current export would potentially be at risk. The threat to Persian Gulf oil supplies can come, as we have already noted, not only from

Soviet overt or covert operations, but also from the Arab-Israeli conflict, intraregional disputes, internal upheavals or revolutions in major producing countries, and terrorist attacks on oil facilities.

Indeed, the ultimate political, economic and strategic destiny of the importing countries is held hostage in the Persian Gulf, particularly in Saudi Arabia. U.S. Secretary of State Alexander Haig has warned that a potential disruption of access to Persian Gulf oil "would constitute a grave threat to the vital national interest. That must be dealt with; and that does not exclude the use of force if that is necessary."

To keep the threats to oil supply under some measure of control, the diplomatic and economic policies of the major importing countries must be carefully balanced and coordinated. It will not be easy to reconcile the diverse interests and positions of the various members of the Western alliance, including Japan, but the underlying common concern in assuring secure access to Persian Gulf oil on manageable terms is overwhelming. What is at issue is the survival of NATO and the whole alliance as an effective and cohesive world power group. Because the stakes are of such magnitude, it should be possible to reach an agreement on a coordinated policy aimed at containing potential threats to the continued availability of Persian Gulf oil.

Such a coordinated policy should include not only the necessary measures for continuing close consultation, but contingent agreement on a limited direct or indirect military contribution by U.S. allies. But the major responsibility for any potential response by force by oil-importing nations falls on the United States because no other Western power can match U.S. military resources. Moreover, no other Western country has the means to check Russia, which would certainly be sorely tempted to interfere in any confrontation affecting oil-importing and producing countries. It is self-evident that a struggle over oil might easily trigger hostilities between the two superpowers. But if the United States is prepared, as it must be, to intercede against a Soviet move into the oil-producing areas of the Persian Gulf, it must equally be prepared to respond to a non-Soviet event, or one not traceable to the Soviets, which threatens the essential flow of oil.

There are many problems which stand in the way of gaining effective regional support for U.S. efforts to defend the Persian Gulf. Even though the Saudis and other producing countries must be aware that they would need protection against hostile Soviet moves, they somehow hope not to be drawn into any East-West conflict. Nearly all of the Persian Gulf nations desire to keep our military power at best at an "over the horizon" distance, and to be at their call only when they have become directly involved. They thus ignore that when help finally arrives it may be too late to save them. They apparently fear that a U.S. military presence in their countries would threaten their internal and external security rather than enhance it.

The likelihood that Saudi Arabia or other relevant Middle East countries will give the United States substantial military-related facilities is remote. Such Western facilities, as Prince Saud, the Saudi Foreign Minister, has put it, would be like "lightning rods" that would provoke the Soviets to ask for the same rights. In the meantime, the United States is confronted by the hostility of Iran, Syria, Libya and others in the general area. Colonel Maummar Qaddafi, the Chief of State of Libya, only recently advocated an escalation of pan-Arab activity in order to launch a strategic counteroffensive against U.S. imperialism in the Middle East.

Under these conditions, the military potential of the United States in the area must necessarily depend on rapid deployment forces and limited base or supply facilities in Oman, Bahrain, Somalia, Kenya and the Indian Ocean island of Diego Garcia. Even a limited military presence in the area could well have the character of a tripwire.

In countries where our supply facilities are located, we would apparently be prepared to strengthen their internal security forces. In many instances, the entrance fee for obtaining access to facilities would involve supplying military hardware to the country concerned. While this can provide only very limited, if any, capabilities for these countries to resist Soviet incursion, it might well strengthen their position against internal opposition—but it might also tempt them to engage in military adventures against their neighbors to settle old debts. As a matter of fact, the United States may have to contend with a host of problems in those nations where it has been able to obtain facility or supply rights. These problems could affect not only the security and dependability of U.S. tenure, but draw the United States into these nations' internal and external problems—with many potentially difficult and unpredictable consequences.

The recently formed Gulf Cooperation Council may improve some aspects of Persian Gulf security, but it certainly lacks the ability to cope with Soviet incursions. The Council (whose members are Saudi Arabia, Kuwait, Qatar, the United Arab Emirates, Bahrain and Oman) aims to promote economic harmonization, and perhaps very gradual political security. Apparently, as indicated by the UAE Minister of Petroleum, the group also plans to improve and coordinate the land, sea and air defense of oil fields and terminals. However, many of the member states of the Gulf Cooperation Council lack critical elements of the necessary political, military, educational and human assets. None of them possesses more than a symbolic navy and small land and air forces — which even in the case of Saudi Arabia depend on massive foreign assistance.

In case of a terrorist attack or of regional fighting that would endanger oil installations, an effective joint oil defense and a rapid repair capacity for oil facilities, if and when implemented, could prove to be invaluable. There remain, however, some nagging doubts about the staying power and operating capability of regional organizations. Past experience has not been too comforting in the light of national jealousies and fears.

It is noteworthy that the new organization does not include Iraq. While one of the reasons for this omission might be Iraq's war with Iran, there probably is also a substantial amount of distrust and fear about potential Iraqi ambitions for hegemony over Gulf Arab states.

Meanwhile, the Iraq-Iran War continues to pose a wide array of problems which could severely endanger the security of oil supply. The longer the war lasts, and the more remote the chances for a settlement that restores Iranian sovereignty to the thalweg line of the Shatt al-Arab [River], the more likely is the risk of the disintegration of Iran. Iran is threatened by separatist efforts by its large Arab, Kurdish, Azerbaijani and Baluchi minorities and by conflicts between moderates and radicals in the political as well as religious arena.

Clearly, the disintegration of Iran would be a disaster both for the region and for Western interests. It could involve a danger of confrontation with the Soviet Union, a breakdown of the country into various ethnic units, or a takeover by a radical faction, such as the communist Tudeh Party. Any Iraqi takeover of or control over the oil-producing Arab-populated area of Khuzistan would not only strengthen the Iraqi goal of hegemony over Persian Gulf countries, but would also leave the remaining parts of Iran without oil production. They would in fact become international basket cases that would be up for grabs by the Soviet Union or by other neighbors. A takeover of the government by the Tudeh Party would put the western shore of the Persian Gulf under communist control.

If, on the other hand, Iraq should be unable to achieve the main objectives that caused it to enter the war, its government might be in jeopardy, with an extremely uncertain outcome for its own political future. In any case, as of now, Iran is trying its best to unseat the present Iraqi government by inciting its Shi'a majority against the ruling Sunni minority.

If the war should continue indefinitely into the future, the possibility cannot be excluded that Iranian and Iraqi oil facilities would again become targets for attack. Worse still, as a desperate and last gesture, the country threatened with defeat might also try to destroy other oil facilities in the region or attempt to sabotage the flow of oil through the Strait of Hormuz.

In the light of these contingencies, what can or should be done? There are at this stage of the game very few options available. But the deep concern of the United States and its allies about the possible consequences of the war must be made clear to all parties concerned, and especially to the Soviet Union. In particular, we should state that we would not acquiesce in any spreading of the war to other areas; nor would we recognize a takeover of the Iranian government by the minority Soviet-inspired or perhaps even Soviet-directed Tudeh Party.

We must, of course, be prepared to face Soviet opposition to such a policy. This is a risk we may have to take, because the consequences of doing nothing might even be worse. The basis for any actions that may have to be taken would be the actual or implied prohibition against aggression under international law or under the U.N. Charter.

The present situation concerning Iran and Iraq illustrates the dangers that may arise either from a regional war or from an internal insurrection. The most obvious justification for Western intervention in either case would be a request for assistance by an involved party.[8] In the case of an insurrection, it would be easiest if the existing government were to ask for help. But even without such a request, intervention would most likely be considered if the revolutionaries receive military or other support from outside hostile forces such as the Soviet Union or any of its proxies. Such outside support would tend to transform the internal struggle into an external one.

If the revolutionaries do not receive any open foreign help, and the threatened government has not been able to ask for Western support, we would still have to consider how best to protect our vital interests if revolutionaries, once in power, cut off essential oil exports. If we are prepared to act in the event of an internal upheaval which jeopardizes our security and is supported by some Soviet assistance, we might equally not be able to afford to remain passive if a link to the Soviets is not self-evident. The basis for action would be the inherent right of every nation of self-preservation.

In addition, there remains the possibility of a nonviolent event that drastically reduces the supply of oil from the Persian Gulf. Even a peaceful change of government or an abrupt shift in the oil policy of major producers could disastrously interfere with the flow of oil if this were to result in a sudden substantial cutback in oil exports or a massive price

8. See my "Joining in Other People's Wars," *The Economist,* March 7, 1981, p. 12.

increase that importers are just not able to pay. As [Oil Minister] Yamani put it,

> Saudi Arabia . . . alone is in a position to inflict very severe damage on the world economy as a whole or a selected group of nations. . . . If the Saudis simply cut production to the level needed to meet their own development plans there would be a depression in the United States in which the rate of unemployment would at least double, the price of oil would double again and the inflation rate would rise.

It should be stressed, however, that as of now major producing countries in general and Saudi Arabia in particular have not been pursuing policies that would confront the importing countries with such stark issues. Saudi Arabia especially has, wherever possible, followed a course of moderation and has exercised its influence to temper the policies of the more radical oil-exporting countries. There is reason to hope that this moderation will continue inasmuch as oil-producing countries must be aware that an unlimited capacity to destroy cannot be safely used without also incurring the risk of being destroyed. Over the past eight years the major oil-importing nations have accepted very great increases in the price of oil; they have responded fully to the economic and financial demands of OPEC nations and are now well along on policies of conservation and alternate energy production that are enabling the OPEC nations to limit their production and to stretch out the period in which their oil resources will be of enormous importance for the long-term development of the OPEC nations. What [the oil-importing nations] cannot accept is any abrupt change of policy, by one or more major OPEC countries, that would have the effect of reducing production or increasing prices beyond bearable limits.

Clearly, forceful intervention can only be the absolutely last recourse after everything possible to achieve a peaceful settlement has failed, and force should only be used when the most vital interests of the importing countries are in jeopardy. From a realistic point of view, for any military intervention to be acceptable or, at least, to be tolerated by the international community, the case for self-preservation must be obvious and self-evident. Such a response must not give the appearance of being merely the brutal or frivolous application of overwhelming power. It is also important that any intervention quickly succeed, not only to retain public support, but to ensure the effective protection of the jeopardized oil resource.

Obviously, any decision on foreign intervention must take account of all military possibilities, especially since such intervention could trigger a preemptive strike on oil facilities by any one of the warring parties or others. Moreover, it is quite possible that during the 1980s there might be a cluster of small nuclear powers in the volatile Middle East–Indian Ocean area, including perhaps Israel, Iraq, Pakistan and India. Contingency planning must certainly address itself to all of these risks. We must also entertain no illusions about the difficulties of maintaining the flow of oil production and exports in war-torn areas in the face of a possible hostile population, or so to speak, of producing oil while sitting on bayonets.

The issues posed here are as serious in their implications for world peace and stability as are those involved in the ultimate nuclear responsibility of the United States for the defense of the Free World. But it is important that everybody concerned be on notice that under extreme conditions, and after all possibilities to resolve a crisis peacefully have been exhausted, the application of power cannot be excluded. No nation can be expected to accept its demise without counteractions.

Whether or not a military response could effectively reestablish access to oil is in many instances by no means certain. However, the willingness, if necessary, to make use of one's deterrent capabilities is the major guarantee, or at least hope, that these capabilities will not have to be tested. The awareness that there exists a risk of a serious confrontation is an essential if unspoken element in establishing bargaining limits between oil exporters and importers.

VI

In this article I have tried to face up frankly to issues that are sometimes put to one side, or discussed only in the internal policy councils of the major nations concerned. I do so in the belief that an honest presentation of positions that would be virtually inevitable in the event of crisis can help to mitigate the chances of any such crisis arising. The importance to the world economy of assured supplies of oil at bearable prices is so great—so essentially unique—that I believe it best to discuss the issues now, at a time when a supply emergency may not appear imminent.

But the main thrust of the article is on the constructive possibilities of the present decade. The world *does* remain heavily dependent on OPEC oil and especially on oil from the Persian Gulf. For at least the next ten years that dependence will persist even if the importing nations continue—as they must—to take massive action to conserve energy and use it more efficiently and to expand the production of oil outside OPEC and the production of non-oil energy sources. What has happened to oil prices in the last decade should be ample incentive to maintain and increase these efforts.

Given such policies, and the other actions outlined in this article, however, the way could be open for a realistic long-term accommodation between the interests of oil-producing countries and those of all oil-importing countries. Both in terms of world economic progress and world peace, such a goal is worthy of the greatest possible effort by all concerned.

POSTSCRIPT

There can be no concluding chapter to this volume; all of the issues presented in these selected papers will be with us for many years to come. Moreover, Walter J. Levy is thinking and writing about them, continuing to elucidate those which he considers to hold risks for all and to lay out the opportunities yet to be seized.

In doing so he will continue to impress upon us his special quality of being able to comprehend the "universe" of oil. It is a faculty he has had from the time he began to consider the strategic dimensions of oil. Howard W. Page, a legendary figure in international oil and for many years an indispensable guide to the Standard Oil Company (N.J.) — now Exxon — and to governments in the Middle East and elsewhere, recalls the early years of the ECA experience and the broad yet detailed range of questions Mr. Levy asked. He was "quick to grasp facts and fit them together into a whole picture," Mr. Page recalls. Over many years, "we did not always agree on the tactics of solutions but we were almost always agreed on the basic problem and on the general direction the solution should take." One is not wrong, then, in singling out for mention that capacity of Mr. Levy's to comprehend the "universe of oil" — and his talent for describing it to others.

In this volume, then, we have seen in his writings the encompassing of an extraordinary period in the relations between states and the crucial role of oil as a key determinant of their actions. From the early discussions of oil in the World War II strategies of Germany and Japan and in the immediate postwar recovery, the reader has been drawn deeply into the years in which oil acquired its largest strategic dimensions. These were also the years that witnessed the peak of Western oil power. In a remarkably brief period, much of the control over international oil trade passed from the industrial importing states to the governments of the oil-exporting states. By the early seventies very large escalations in price, actions mainly by Middle East producers to withhold supply to achieve political objectives, limitations on destinations, and the supply of petrodollars to importers for development projects or weapons had intruded into the previous commercial terms for oil — a casualty of the pervasive involvement of governments.

Government intervention was scarcely limited to the oil exporters; the oil-importing states became inextricably involved in the obtaining of supply. With the oil states determined to maximize their return on the sale of a depleting resource, the oil users were equally determined to pursue every avenue to obtain assured access to whatever volumes were placed in international trade.

From this complex interweaving of energy, financial, political, and defense interests, Mr. Levy has written of the particular dangers to free world alliances that intensive competition for oil supply generates. His hopes for coordination of policies and practices remain unmet, but his search for the ways and means to accomplish it continues.

We are at the beginning of the next energy transformation, when there will be, increasingly, alternatives to oil and the extraordinary role the fuel has played in world economic and social transformations. One is tempted too easily to consider this prospect as already arrived, and thus the perplexing and sometimes even dangerous considerations affecting oil seem no longer to be of such concern.

But note carefully the observations of Mr. Levy in these papers: The time is now when most producers of oil must anticipate the eventual conclusion of the petroleum era and the exhaustion of their reserves. For others, the oil era will close with very substantial reserves still left in the ground. For most of them, their political, social, and economic expectations will still be unmet with no substitute for the role that oil has played for them in their revenues. How will these producers attempt to manage? What assistance can the industrial world be to them in that most critical of periods? Will supply be severely curtailed—while the importing nations still require it? Can we, together, discover the means whereby the oil era can be prolonged to our mutual advantage and time obtained for exporters to adjust and for the importers to find the alternative energy sources? Or will we seek special advantages and privileged access and risk increasing competition for a vital requirement?

Over these forty years Mr. Levy has insisted that those of us who tend to focus on some narrow aspect of oil are in danger of looking through the wrong end of a telescope. In doing so, we miss the true dimensions of international oil that, in its totality, must be one of the most exciting and engrossing subjects of our time. He proves it.

ABBREVIATIONS

ARAMCO	Arabian American Oil Company
bbl.	barrel
b/d	barrels per day, barrels daily
CIEC	Conference on International Economic Cooperation
ECA	Economic Cooperation Administration
EEC	European Economic Community
ELF-ERAP	ELF-Entreprise de Rechérches et d'Activities Pétrolières
ENI	Ente Nazionale Idrocarburi (Italian National Oil Company)
f.o.b.	free on board
GNP	gross national product
IEA	International Energy Agency
IPC	Iraq Petroleum Company
LDC	less developed countries
LNG	liquefied natural gas
mmb	million barrels
mmb/d	million barrels per day
NATO	North Atlantic Treaty Organization
OAPEC	Organization of Arab Petroleum Exporting Countries
OECD	Organization for Economic Cooperation and Development
OEEC	Organization for European Economic Cooperation
OPEC	Organization of Petroleum Exporting Countries
UN	United Nations
UNCTAD	United Nations Conference on Trade and Development

INDEX

Other Titles of Interest from Westview Press

† Available in paperback and hardcover.

DATE DUE

JAN 31 1984			
MAY 16 1984			

Oil Strategy and Politics, 1941–1981

OIL STRATEGY AND POLITICS, 1941-1981

Walter J. Levy

edited by Melvin A. Conant

Westview Press / Boulder, Colorado

Published in 1982 in the United States of America by
  Westview Press, Inc.
  5500 Central Avenue
  Boulder, Colorado 80301
  Frederick A. Praeger, President and Publisher

Library of Congress Cataloging in Publication Data
Levy, Walter J.
  Oil strategy and politics, 1941–1981.
  Includes index.
  1. Petroleum industry and trade—Addresses, essays, lectures. 2. Petroleum industry and trade—Political aspects—Addresses, essays, lectures. I. Conant, Melvin A. II. Title.
HD9560.5.L46   333.8'232   82-1963
ISBN 0-86531-403-9   AACR2

Printed and bound in the United States of America

gue for directly. For one thing, to try to establish it, I would have to say something pretty definite about what the suspicion amounts to. I would have to explain what a philosophical theory or doctrine is supposed to be. And to explain why such a thing could never satisfy us, I would have to say what it would be for a philosophical theory to satisfy us. That would mean identifying and describing what we seek or aspire to in philosophy. And that is just my problem. That is what this book is about.

There is a further reason for not trying to prove that no satisfactory philosophical theory is possible in this area. If it could be established at all, it would presumably be something of a philosophical theory or doctrine in its own right. It would therefore imply that if it is true it could never satisfy us; if it did satisfy us, it could not be true. I do not try to prove or even to argue for such a bold antitheoretical thesis, even in the restricted area I have chosen. I simply try to draw attention to the very special character of a philosophical theory or doctrine of the kind we seek and to identify some of the ideas we rely on in taking it for granted that such a thing is possible.

I do hope that in my efforts in that direction I say only what is true, even if it is too much to expect it to be found satisfying. For many readers, I know, my efforts will seem too negative, too noncommittal—in a word, too untheoretical. I am familiar with that reaction, and I try not to be defensive in the face of it. I think much more careful work is needed right back at the beginnings of the philosophical questions that grip us—at the earliest fundamentals, as it were—before we can be sure that we know what we are doing. Only then can we try to do it in the right way. My worry is rather that I do not get deeply enough even into those fundamentals. I certainly do not get as far as offering answers of my own to philosophical questions about reality. But I hope my reasons for finding puzzling the very idea of a philosophical theory of reality prove to be philosophically rewarding.

My interest in the question does not come from a wish to put an end to the search for intellectually satisfying philosophical theories, or even to discourage it or limit its range. Quite the contrary. I believe that the urge to achieve the kind of view of ourselves and the world that is embodied in the philosophical quest for reality arises from something deeper in human nature than any abstract argument against it is ever likely to reach. It is present in all our best efforts to understand ourselves and will probably always be with us. I think it is idle to try either to discourage or to encourage philosophical theorizing about the human condition. The point is to understand what it is and what it aspires to.

The only seed of doubt I would be pleased to sow is the suspicion that perhaps the goal is not fully reachable, that the kind of understanding of ourselves and the world that is embodied in that quest is not really available to us. Not because of ignorance, difficulty, or limited capacities—all of which are familiar enough—but because of the very nature of the task. That is at least a possibility I would like to keep alive. Finding something like that to be so, or even having reason to suspect that it might be, could in itself amount to an illuminating form of self-understanding—perhaps the best we can hope for.

Any movement either towards or away from that conclusion can be based only on a detailed scrutiny of specific applications of what I am calling the quest for reality. There is no settling the matter *a priori* and once and for all. Sixty years ago, metaphysical theorizing was declared meaningless on the sweeping grounds that its results were neither true by virtue of meaning alone nor confirmable or disconfirmable in experience. But metaphysical theorizing of the proscribed kind was involved in reaching that very conclusion. It proved to be essential to philosophy then just as it is today, in what in some quarters are still proudly thought to be enlightened scientific times.

Nowadays one is more likely to find philosophical questions dismissed out of hand on the even more sweeping grounds that we are led to ask them only because we have come to think in certain ways—certain "contingent" ways of thinking, which, if things had been different, we might never have come to adopt at all. The implication is that if we simply abandon those old ways of thinking, the problems, or their urgency, will vanish. But that form of criticism as it stands is absurd. What it says about philosophical problems is true of all intellectual problems. Without some particular ways of thinking, we could never try to understand anything. It is a "contingent" fact, which could have been otherwise, that we now have such a thing as a quantum theory of matter, for example, or the theory of natural selection or number theory. But the "contingency" of those ways of thinking does not mean that any problems that arise within them are unreal or not worth a serious person's attention, or that if we cannot solve the problems we can simply abandon the ways of thinking that give rise to them. If philosophy is to be dismissed for the "contingency" of its problems or its ways of thinking, it must be shown how and why those ways of thinking and the problems they generate are somehow confused or idle or unintelligible or otherwise illegitimate. And the only way to show that in a convincing and illuminating way is to examine particular philosophical issues carefully, to identify and understand their special character, and to trace them convincingly to their sources.

In my own efforts in that direction here, I do not aspire to completeness. I identify a number of issues that are central to the project I consider, but I explore some of them only far enough to sharpen the questions on which the success of the enterprise can be seen to depend, without trying to settle the matter. The conditions of success that I concentrate on more fully raise what seem to me the most interesting and most fruitful issues to explore. On those important questions, I do carry the investigation far enough to argue for definite conclusions.

A great deal has been written on the topics I discuss, especially in recent years, and as regards coverage of that material, I do not claim or aspire to completeness either. Much of it is devoted to attacking or defending one or another philosophical theory of the nature of colour. My interest is more in the metaphysical project which such theories are meant to advance. The issues I concentrate on are crucial to the success of such theories, but I do not always pursue them by taking up in detail this or that person's theory, and certainly not by trying to cover them all. Beyond those works explicitly discussed or mentioned in the text, I have added a bibliography of some of the writings I have found most interesting and helpful. It is meant only as a guide. I am sure there are many I have forgotten or have lost track of which are as important and useful as some of those that are there.

I first thought of a book along roughly these lines when I was invited to give the John Locke Lectures in the University of Oxford in 1987. I am extremely grateful to the Faculty of Literae Humaniores, and especially the Sub-Faculty of Philosophy, for that great honour. It was a thrill to give the lectures, and the response of that shrewd and apparently enthusiastic audience encouraged me to press on. During that year in Oxford, I was a visiting fellow at New College for Michaelmas term and at All Souls College for the other two terms, and I am happy to thank both colleges for their invitations and their generous support and hospitality. I also received a Humanities Research Fellowship from the University of California, Berkeley that year.

Many years have passed since then, and I have given a great many talks in a great many other places about the questions I started from. It is my impression that if there were many who agreed or were sympathetic with what I was arguing on those occasions, they tended to remain silent. I was nonetheless strangely encouraged by the opposition. Each of those talks and discussions has had good effects on my thinking, but by now they can no longer be separately identified or traced to their sources. I can only thank all those who contributed.

I was fortunate in being invited for longer visits to a number of universities and so could enjoy the greater benefits of sustained discussion over several days or weeks. I am indebted to many different individuals and institutions for those opportunities. I would like to thank the philosophers at the University of Buenos Aires for inviting me to give the Tanner Lectures there in 1988, and for the accompanying seminars by their invited commentators. I was the Nelson Visitor at the University of Michigan for a week of seminars and fruitful discussions in 1989. I spent 1991–92 as a visiting fellow in the Law, Philosophy, and Social Theory Program at New York University and participated in its excellent weekly colloquium, as well as in many more informal conversations. I am extremely grateful to the directors of the program and to the Law School, for their generous support, and to Ronald Dworkin and Thomas Nagel for the rich stimulation they provided. I also held a fellowship that year from the National Endowment for the Humanities.

I gave a series of lectures and discussions on these questions at the University of New Mexico in 1994 and at the University of Saskatchewan in 1997. In 1997, I also gave six José Gaos Lectures on the reality of colour at the Instituto de Investigaciones Filosóficas at the Universidad Nacional Autónoma de México. I am grateful to the Instituto for inviting me, and for much more over the years. For the first half of 1997 I was Visiting Professor at the University of California at Los Angeles, where I learned a great deal—and had a good time—in a seminar on earlier versions of some of these chapters with a group of incredulous, resourceful, and apparently indefatigable graduate students. I am indebted to them for their resistance.

As always, I have learned more than I am sure it seems from seminars and discussions with graduate students at Berkeley, who have patiently heard and criticized my thoughts on the colours of things and on a lot of other things for about as long as they should have had to. Soon after I had given the lectures in Oxford, Thompson Clarke and I gave a seminar together in Berkeley, which, as usual, closed off one line I had thought promising and eventually set me off in a completely new direction. I have given seminars on the reality of colour to at least two different generations of graduate students (with a little overlap) and have kept closely related questions about the intentionality of thought and perception at the centre of seminars on other topics in recent years. A more-or-less final version of most of this text was held up to searching criticism by a large group of perceptive graduate students and faculty members in a seminar in Berkeley in the spring of 1998.

Donald Davidson's sympathetic reading of what was a complete version of the manuscript a few years ago provided just the encouragement I needed at the time. In regular meetings with me for several months, Matthew Henken and Michael Idinopulos gave an earlier version of the